Writing on Ice

Writing on Ice

The Ethnographic Notebooks of Vilhjalmur Stefansson

Edited and introduced by
Gísli Pálsson

Dartmouth College
Published by University Press of New England
Hanover and London

Dartmouth College
Published by University Press of New England, Hanover, NH 03755

Printed in the United States of America
5 4 3 2 1

CIP data appear at the end of the book.

Publication of this book has been supported generously by The Gladys Krieble Delmas Foundation, the Stefansson Arctic Institute, Akureyri, Iceland, Dartmouth College Library, Office of the Rector of the University of Iceland, and the Research Fund of the University of Iceland.

For my parents, Bára Sigurðardóttir and Páll Gíslason

Contents

Illustrations

Figures

The following illustrations appear between pages 140 and 141

Maps and plates appear between pages 196 and 197

Preface

This book presents selections of the ethnographic notebooks and expedition photographs and drawings of Vilhjalmur Stefansson. It has a somewhat long history, although its final concept and structure only materialized during the last three years or so. As a student of anthropology at the University of Iceland about three decades ago, I came across some of the writings of Stefansson, mostly Icelandic translations of his popular works. Stefansson was a household name in Iceland, closely associated with the Icelandic community in North America in which he grew up. Indeed, many of his publications on the Inuit were made readily available in Icelandic. Stefansson spent years among the Inuit, learning their language and recording their ways of living. His life and work was, therefore, of obvious anthropological interest, although he may have been primarily seen by his contemporaries as an adventurous explorer. My interest in Stefansson, however, also has another dimension. During my sabbatical leave at the University of Iowa in the spring of 1987, I became interested in the Icelandic immigrant communities in North Dakota and Winnipeg in which Stefansson grew up. The following summer, I visited some of these communities, exploring how they had changed, and how they had adapted to complex multicultural contexts of natives and immigrants. Somehow, I thought, Stefansson's life and career were rooted in these communities, in particular the relationships between Icelanders and Indians.

My stay in Iowa City and my interest in Stefansson's ethnography and the North American Icelandic community brought me into contact with June Helm, Professor of Anthropology at the University of Iowa, an expert on indigenous North American communities. Helm, I learned, had visited some of the communities where Stefansson worked early on. More importantly, it was during a conversation with her that I learned that Stefansson was reported to have a son, Alex, with an Inuit woman who accompanied him during one of his expeditions. Helm had met Alex and was able to provide important background information. I was puzzled by Alex's existence, since none of the writings on Stefansson that I had explored mentioned him. My intention was to locate Alex and hear his version, or his family's, of the Stefansson story. Because of other commitments, however, it took about ten years to get back on the track, and by then I had learned that Alex had raised six children, and that he himself had died in 1966, four years after his father died.

In the meantime, I came across important documents on Stefansson and his relations with the Inuit, thanks largely to Philip Cronenwett, Director of the Special Collections of the Dartmouth College Library to which Stefansson and his widow, Evelyn Stefansson Nef, donated much of his personal papers and library. Cronenwett sparked my interest in Stefansson's field diaries, which are part of the Stefansson collection at Dartmouth College. The idea of editing Stefansson's diaries for publication seemed daunting at the beginning, but the more I thought about it the more appealing it became. Not only did the diaries provide an important avenue to my earlier and almost aborted project on Stefansson's background and ethnography, but theoretical developments in anthropology also helped to refocus my interests. In particular, the growing interest in the context and practice of ethnographic fieldwork, the relations between guests and "natives," and the ways in which ethnographies are constructed, made the diaries highly appealing for a case study.

I worked on the diaries on and off for about three years, along with a series of other academic commitments. While the work on the diaries was often tedious and tiring, it also offered exciting discovery with frequent unexpected turns. And, in July 2000, just as I had completed the manuscript and sent it off to the publisher, I embarked on a two-week field trip to the Northwest Territories in Canada, along with filmmaker Hákon Már Oddsson. While the main aim of the trip was to collect material for a documentary on Stefansson's Inuit family, it allowed me to further explore some of the issues addressed in my introduction for this book. On my return to Reykjavik, I made important last-minute changes to the manuscript, largely based on my interviews in Inuvik with four of Stefansson's grandchildren, Frank, Georgina, Rosie, and Shirley, all of whom kindly provided essential facts and observations about Stefansson's relations with his Inuit wife, Fannie Pannigabluk, and their son, Alex.

Many people have been of assistance in one way or another in the preparation of this volume and I thank them all. Philip Cronenwett and his staff at Dartmouth located many of the unpublished sources that I use in exploring Stefansson's work and made copies of letters and images readily available to me. Without Cronenwett's generous support, encouragement, and professional advice, this volume would not have been possible. Níels Einarsson, Director of the Stefansson Arctic Institute in Akureyri, Iceland, along with his colleague Jón Haukur Ingimundarson, also provided important encouragement and advice. Their institute funded the massive job of reading and typing the diaries, while the library at the University of Iceland provided the necessary equipment for reading the microfilms. June Helm of the University of Iowa continued to provide information important for my project, including critical information on visual material on Stefansson available in Canadian archives. Tina Sangris, at the Prince of Wales Northern Heritage Centre in Yellowknife, Canada, helped to locate important images relating to Stefansson. The staff at the Aurora Research Centre in Inuvik provided essential support in preparing my field trip to Inuvik and arranging my stay. Mark Nuttall of Aberdeen kindly commented on the draft for the introduction. I have also benefitted from discussions with several other anthropologists, including Anne Brydon, Don Kulick (Stockholm), and Gerald Sullivan (Wellington, New Zealand).

My biggest debt goes to my research assistants Kristín Erla Harðardóttir, Baldur A. Sigurvinsson, Ásdís Jónsdóttir, Óðinn Gunnar Óðinsson, and Jónas Gunnar Allansson (all post-graduate students at the Institute of Anthropology at the University of Iceland). Not only did they provide invaluable assistance in reading the microfilm edition of Stefansson's diaries and rendering them in electronic form, they also offered important observations and insights on Stefansson and his work. Reading the microfilms was a massive and arduous job, and there were times when we were all about to give up, given the difficulties of Stefansson's handwriting and the condition and the scale of the documents. I am also grateful to Nelson Graburn, Department of Anthropology, University of California at Berkeley, who kindly translated many of the Inuit words in the glossary and made several modifications and corrections. Finally, I am indebted to my daughter, Rósa Signý, who helped in editing the manuscript.

Parts of the introductory text in this volume appeared in my article "The Intimate Arctic: An Early Anthropologist's Diary in the Strict Sense of the Term" (*Ethnos,* 4 1998). That publication drew upon a paper originally presented as a Keynote Address at the twenty-eighth Arctic Workshop at the Institute for Alpine and Arctic Research (INSTAAR) at the University of Colorado, Boulder, on 12 March 1998. I thank Astrid Ogilvie, one of the organizers of that workshop, for pushing me to give that talk. Parts of the introduction were also presented, under the title "Arcticality: Observation and Rhetoric in the Writings of V. Stefansson," at the twelfth Inuit Studies

Conference, "Inuit Communities, the Northern Environment and Global Processes," at Aberdeen University, 23–26 August 2000. Most of the visual material used in the book is borrowed from five sources: the Special Collections of the Dartmouth College Library, the Northwest Territories Archives in Yellowknife, the National Archives of Canada in Ottawa, Robert S. Peabody Museum of Archaeology in Andover, Massachusetts, and the National Museum of Iceland. I greatly appreciate the permission to reproduce these images.

A sabbatical leave at the Department of Anthropology, University of California at Berkeley in the spring of 2001 allowed me to make final changes to the manuscript and correct the proofs. I am grateful to the staff, in particular Paul Rabinow and Laura Nader, for their hospitality. I would also like to thank especially Philip M. Pochoda and M. Ellen Wicklum at the University Press of New England for their interest in my project and their kind, thoughtful, and efficient cooperation throughout the production process.

This publication has been made possible thanks to generous financial support from the Gladys Krieble Delmas Foundation (thanks to David H. Stam, trustee), the Stefansson Arctic Institute, the Office of the Rector of the University of Iceland (Rector Páll Skúlason), the Research Fund of the University of Iceland, and the Special Collections of the Dartmouth College Library.

Berkeley, California G. P.
April 2001

PART I

HISTORICAL BACKGROUND

INTRODUCTION

Between 1906 and 1918, anthropologist and explorer Vilhjalmur Stefansson (1879–1962) went on three expeditions into the Alaskan and Canadian Arctic, each of which lasted between sixteen months and five years. He published some twenty-four books and more than four hundred articles on his travels and observations, including his autobiography.[1] There is also a voluminous literature on his life and work.[2] Stefansson was an ambitious and successful explorer, and he soon became a public figure in North America and Europe, well known for his description of the "Blond Eskimo" (Copper Inuit), his discovery of new lands in the Arctic (including the islands of Brock, Borden, Mackenzie King, and Meighen), his approach to travel and exploration, and his theories of health and diet. His fame was partly fueled by a series of controversies, involving, among others, dogmatic missionaries and envious competitors in the race for public recognition and media attention.

Stefansson's successes in exploration, however, as Collins points out, "have tended to obscure the fact that he was primarily an anthropologist," although some anthropological works have referred to his writings, and he continues to be cited in ethnographic and historical works on indigenous peoples of the North American Arctic, particularly Iñupiaq ("North Alaskan Eskimo").[3] Even Stefansson's ethnographic collaborators, including Diamond Jenness, tended to undermine his anthropological contributions. This volume seeks to redress the balance, drawing attention to Stefansson's anthropology, his practice as a participant observer, and his description of Inuit society and culture. Part I provides an introduction to Stefansson's fieldwork, his diaries, and their significance. Part II presents extracts from the diaries of his two ethnographic expeditions, the first and the second. Little of value on either Inuit society or native-white relations can be found in the diaries from the third expedition, and for that reason I did not include them in the present volume.

Stefansson was born in the Canadian Icelandic community at Arnes, Manitoba. His parents, Ingibjörg and Jóhann, along with 250 other colonists recruited by the Canadian government in 1877, left from north Iceland to settle near Winnipeg in "New Iceland," as the settlement came to be called. Originally, they had planned to emigrate to Brazil, to escape the depressing economic context of Iceland, but opted in favor of North America. In 1881, Stefansson's parents and their four children moved from New Iceland to Pembina County in North Dakota, where many of the Manitoba Icelanders had resettled. As a child, Stefansson was educated in the Icelandic tradition. Later on he attended primary school, where he learned to speak English. Stefansson attended university from the age of eighteen, first at the University of North Dakota and later at the University of Iowa, where he graduated in theology in 1903. He developed an interest in comparative religion and anthropology, and, for some time, he seems to have been torn between the priesthood and anthropology. In the end, he decided in favor of anthropology, "with the mental reservation that it was to be a humanistic anthropology."[4] Having been offered a scholarship by the Harvard Divinity School, he moved to Boston. It was there that he developed the arctic interests that set the stage for his career. Most of his working life, however, he lived in the Arctic, New York City, and Hanover, New Hampshire.

Stefansson kept extensive diaries during his expeditions. These are potentially of central importance for understanding not only his relationship with the Inuit and his descriptive ethnographic work but also for understanding the changing human and environmental dimensions of the Arctic at a critical period at the beginning of the twentieth century. This introduction begins by discussing the background and agendas of Stefansson's three expeditions. Each expedition, as we will see, has its own profile and characteristics. I then discuss the field diaries of Stefansson and other early twentieth-century ethnographers, in particular those of Malinowski (published in 1967), and their significance for the discipline of anthropology. Anthropological field diaries, I argue, represent an important source of ethnographic information. Finally, I provide a commentary on certain aspects of Stefansson's writings and career, focusing on his relations with his hosts and their representation (or lack thereof) in both his diaries and publications.

While Stefansson was a perceptive ethnographer and explorer, he was silent in both his publications and his diaries about important aspects pertaining to his fieldwork, including the ethnographic contributions of his Inuit companions. I suggest that the narrative trope summed up in the concept of

FIGURE 1. Stefansson, his mother Ingibjörg, brother Jóhannes, and sister Rósa. Photo: Edward D. Bland. *(Courtesy of the National Museum of Iceland; MMS 27067.)*

flowing with the "friendly Arctic," frequently employed by Stefansson to emphasize mutual involvement and collaboration of informant and ethnographer, contradicts his silence on his own relationship with some of the Inuit. If Stefansson "went native," "living their life," as we are lead to believe by his own account, why do neither his diaries nor his publications mention the fact that he was living with a native woman named Fannie Pannigabluk? I attempt to situate Stefansson's writings in the context of the dynamics of the team of explorers, the standards of anthropological practice among his contemporaries, the power relations of early twentieth-century expeditions, and the North-American Icelandic community in which he grew up. His fascination with the "Blond Eskimo" and their potential Norse background, I suggest, was partly driven by the existence of Alex, his son with Pannigabluk, who was born during the second expedition. Stefansson's observations and rhetoric were the products of both his time and his own life, firmly rooted in the unfolding of his expeditions and career and the ideology of early twentieth-century anthropology and exploration.

Attempts to find out "what really happened" in history are often plagued with uncertainty. Apart from the problem of translation, of rendering the "foreign" world of the past in terms understandable to modern readers, there is the lack of direct evidence—the impossibility of revisiting the site, so to speak. Unfortunately, one cannot participate in lives that have already been lived, including the lives of early anthropologists and explorers. Historiography, however, is not pure fiction, nor is an anthropology of the past an impossibility. As Baxter remarks, while "it is difficult, often impossible, to observe at all, let alone as a participant observer . . . it seems sensible to use the published observation of those who have participated"; written texts may allow anthropologists, he argues, to follow Evans-Pritchard (one of the pioneers of British social anthropology) who insisted on "putting 'flesh and blood' into our analyses."[5] To some extent, indeed, the voices of earlier generations can be recovered, from letters, diaries, various kinds of published material, and the memories of people who witnessed the events of the past. In the case of Stefansson, a variety of important and informative material is available, including his diaries, letters and publications, and the oral history of his Inuit descendants.

STEFANSSON'S EXPEDITIONS

The Anglo-American Polar Expedition (1906–1907)

After receiving his first academic degree in religious studies from the University of Iowa in 1903, Stefansson became affiliated with the Anthropology Department and the Peabody Museum at Harvard University. He planned an anthropological field trip to Africa at the suggestion of his teacher, F. W. Putnam: "Putnam pointed out that nobody connected with our department has as yet made much of a study of Africa. What would I think of that field?"[1] In 1906, Stefansson planned to join a British Museum expedition destined for Central East Africa. In the end, however, he chose the Arctic. During the summers of 1904 and 1905, he voyaged to Iceland to study the relationship between health and diet. In 1905, he became a teaching fellow at Harvard, "looked upon as the Anthropology Department's authority on the polar regions."[2] Partly as a result of his early article on the history of the Norse colony in Greenland Stefansson was invited to participate in an expedition to the Arctic, the impressively named "Anglo-American Polar Expedition" (see maps, plates 1 and 2, following page 198).[3] That expedition was led by the Danish naval adventurer Ejnar Mikkelsen and the American geologist de Koven Leffingwell.

The main purpose of the expedition was to look for undiscovered lands in the Arctic, north of Alaska. Mikkelsen and Leffingwell, however, were forced to add an ethnographic dimension to the expedition; they had difficulties in funding their enterprise and one backer requested that a qualified "ethnologist" accompany the group to study any natives who might be encountered on the way. Stefansson's role was to study native groups along the Mackenzie River and to collect artifacts for the Peabody and Royal Ontario Museums. Because of funding problems and his reluctance to travel by ship on the *Duchess of Bedford* along with the rest of the team, Stefansson was to travel by rail from Winnipeg to Edmonton, and, from there, on to

Athabaska Landing and Herschel Island to join his mates. In April 1906, he began both his journey across Canada and his lifelong career as anthropologist and explorer.

The Mikkelsen-Leffingwell expedition, from Stefansson's point of view, was both a failure and success: the *Duchess of Bedford* failed to arrive at Herschel Island as was planned to provide him with supplies. On the other hand, this forced Stefansson to live as best he could and to adapt to the reality of the Arctic. He decided to remain true to his ethnographic task and study indigenous groups by living with them, sharing their food, staying in their camps, and learning their language. In 1906, the "southern" supplies on which the Inuit had become dependent (mainly foodstuffs from white whalers) failed to arrive, and, as a result, the Inuit had to revert to their traditional hunting practices. Diubaldo points out that Stefansson felt this provided an exciting opportunity to observe the Inuit almost in their "natural" state and, moreover, "living with them was much better from an ethnological point of view than merely living amongst them, as other white men had done."[4]

In August 1907, Stefansson severed his ties with the Mikkelsen-Leffingwell expedition and began his journey back home. He was not too impressed with the results of his scientific mission. During his fieldwork, however, he became committed to the ethnographic study of Inuit culture. At Herschel Island, he met Captain "Charlie" Klengenberg, who told him an exciting story, claiming to have encountered and stayed with native tribes who apparently had never seen a white man and yet looked like white men in some respects. This mysterious story was supported by a small collection of knives and other implements made of native copper. While the story seemed almost too romantic to be true, it provided a glimmer of success, which drove Stefansson to organize a second expedition to the Arctic. He confided to Putnam, his mentor at Harvard, that he had evidence of truly primitive Eskimos in Prince Albert Island.

Stefansson's first expedition was relatively short and his ethnography, mainly among the Inuit of the Mackenzie Delta, was somewhat limited, although it provided interesting sketches of early fieldwork, Inuit society, and relations between "natives" and "whites." During this expedition, other scientists and explorers employed Stefansson in a secondary role as an anthropologist and assistant, and perhaps partly for that reason his ethnographic diary entries were rather brief. Nevertheless, he provided interesting observations on Inuit society and relations between Inuit, Indians, and whites as the expedition moved on. Stefansson's works on the Mackenzie Delta Inuit seem to have been underestimated; he observed and recorded the end of a way of life described by the late nineteenth-century explorer Émile Petitot. In the early days of the expedition, he tended to focus on the logistics of the expedition, but, later on, his discussion of indigenous languages and customs grew "thicker" and more detailed. Unlike many of his contemporary anthropologists, he was keen to observe both tradition and change; an interesting early paper focused on the trade jargon of Herschel Island.[5]

The Arctic clearly appealed to Stefansson, despite the difficulties it posed for Western travelers. Part of its charm lay in its exotic property rights and communitarian ethic. Stefansson comments in his diaries:

> To continue the moralizing of yesterday—my experience with Husky communism is likely to make me a convert (at least, a mild sort of one) to the general doctrines of communism. The system is certainly admirably adopted to the conditions here. The seemingly very strong objection [. . .]—that some are lazy and will become parasites—seems to have little force in the actual life of the H[usky]. Some [. . .] are more energetic than others, and accomplish more, but all try and all do something. The fact that one works harder than another worries neither of them, nor the community in general. Of course, a complete communism might not work so well as this modified one.[6]

Such enthusiasm was not unique to Stefansson. But while many of the early armchair anthropologists and evolutionists—including Morgan, Marx, and Engels[7]—had fabricated ethnography and history by postulating a utopian primitive society without class divisions and private property, Stefansson had found it alive and well. During the second expedition, however, he observed that communism seemed to be "disappearing fast."[8]

The Stefansson-Anderson Expedition (1908–1912)

Stefansson was determined to return to the Arctic for a second expedition, this time as the commander of an expedition of his own. His main ambition was to locate and observe the mysterious Blond Eskimo he had heard about during the first expedition and he felt confident that he would be able to face the difficulties involved. His experience of the first expedition and the sensational stories he had heard about Eskimos who had never seen a white man helped to provide the necessary connections and financial support. His popularized articles based on the first expedition also outlined a new approach to arctic travel and exploration which appealed to potential sponsors, a strategy also taken advantage of by other explorers, including Robert E. Peary.[9] Stefansson argued that the costs of an expedition could be significantly reduced if one was prepared to live as the Inuit did. These articles caught the attention of the leading personnel of the American Museum of Natural History, including Clark Wissler, Curator in the Anthropology Department. After a series of negotiations, Stefansson was offered a contract. A former fellow student at the University of Iowa, the zoologist Rudolph M. Anderson, was appointed to join Stefansson. Anderson, who at the time was working for a military academy, was trained in biology and his scientific background and credibility helped in providing funding for the expedition.

The stated purpose of the expedition was threefold. In a commissioning letter to Stefansson, the American Museum specified: "The intent of this commission . . . is to provide you with the means of pursuing fieldwork in anthropology; of providing Mr. Anderson with the means of pursuing fieldwork in zoology, and with the design to secure to the American Museum of Natural History valuable collections in the branches of science above mentioned."[10] An (apparently) somewhat earlier statement from the American Museum describes the uniqueness of the Stefansson-Anderson Expedition in the following terms:

> The present expedition . . . differs essentially from ordinary Arctic ventures in this, that where it is usual to take along with the party everything that the party is expected to need during its stay in the field, in this case there will be taken neither food, clothing nor house materials, and *there will be complete dependence on local resources.* Seeing the object of the expedition is [*sic*] chiefly ethnological, it is in a sense desirable that this should be so; for *the only way in which one can become familiar with the real life of a primitive people is to live with them in their houses, and as they do,* rather than to live near them in one's own "civilized" way [italics added].

Stefansson and Anderson left from Toronto in April 1908, reaching Fort McPherson by early July. This time the two of them spent four years in the Arctic, sometimes working separately on different trails. Stefansson and Anderson appear to have been generally on good terms during the expedition. Nevertheless, there was some tension between them. Unlike Stefansson, Anderson did not try or pretend to live the Inuit way; Stefansson, Hunt remarks, "was unable to interest Anderson in the Eskimo language. Anderson's energies were directed to biology and zoology, and he saw no compelling reason to take up arduous language studies."[11] Soon after the two of them arrived in the Arctic, Anderson made cynical remarks about Stefansson in a letter to his sister.

> One point of disagreement is that he considers any attention to cleanliness, hygiene and camp sanitation as "military fads." If you have read his articles . . . , you may have noticed that there is only one really great Arctic and Eskimo authority—who has learned more in one year than all previous explorers combined.[12]

The project turned out to be more costly and time consuming than expected. Stefansson probably knew all along that an ambitious project of this kind needed more time than the contract with the American Museum specified. Understandably, he was eager to pass on information about his successes, in the hope that necessary funding would be maintained. In a letter to Wissler at the American Museum he proudly announced the "discovery" of non-Eskimo Eskimos:

> West of the Coppermine we found over 200 people who had never seen a white man, whose ancestors had never seen one, who knew of no past relations with people to the west, and whose territory was supposed by geographers to be definitely known to be uninhabited (so labelled on official charts of the Canadian Government). . . .
>
> The general appearance was non-Eskimo—a sort of "portly" appearance. . . . It is hard to be specific in this matter, but the general impression is definite. My Eskimo companion was impressed no less than I. He said, "These are not Eskimos, they are just like fo'cas'le men"—he has worked many years "before the mast" as a whaler.[13]

Wissler, however, had doubts at this point about the scientific merits of the results. Although he would publish extracts from Stefansson's diaries a few years later, at this stage neither he nor anyone else knew how valuable Stefansson's ethnography might be.[14] In the middle of the expedition, the American Museum withdrew its support. That decision may have been partly informed by a discouraging note from Anderson, who wished to return from the field and join his future wife, emphasizing a conflict of scholarly interest between the anthropologist and the zoologist:

> Collecting work on the move is difficult and usually unfruitful, and, at best, only skims the ground superficially. While this method of exploration may

> demonstrate that a white man can live where an Indian or Eskimo can and perhaps endure as much, the corollary seems to be that they are aborigines not able to accomplish much more than a bare living, and a white man cannot be expected to do much scientific work under similar conditions.[15]

The news about the withdrawal of the Museum's support came too late and Stefansson and Anderson stayed on in the Arctic. Anderson may have been right to some extent in his note on the "superficiality" of Stefansson's approach and methodology. As Burch points out, Stefansson confused the identity of some Inuit groups.[16] Nevertheless, Anderson's critique seems to have been overdriven, motivated by personal concerns.

Ironically, one of the strengths of Stefansson's ethnography from the second expedition may be credited to his intimate relationship with Fannie Pannigabluk, an Inuit widow originally from Alaska, a relationship that Stefansson would not mention in his accounts to his colleagues at the American Museum. Stefansson hired Pannigabluk as a seamstress, and later she became both his key informant and his wife, in Inuit terms. They had one child, Alex, who was born in 1910. Stefansson makes no reference in the diaries to intimate relations with Pannigabluk (or anyone else, for that matter), and his son is never mentioned. As we will see, however, the letters of some of his friends and collaborators provide important information on the paternity issue. Also, significant church records were found from the All Saints Church in Aklavik, the Northwest Territories. The records, which are currently kept in Inuvik, state that on 15 August 1915 Reverend C. E. Whittaker baptized forty-five-year-old "wife of V. Stefansson" and their five-year-old son (Alex) Alik Alahuk (Pannigabluk's former husband was named Alahuk). Alex's children suggest that Stefansson and his family lived for a while at their cabin Nunaluk ("old ground"), built by Pannigabluk, on Nunaluk Spit on the Arctic coast near Herschel Island (see plate 5). Nowadays, the cabin is known in the region as "Stefansson's cabin."

During the second expedition, Stefansson occupied a leading position, in charge of both logistics and research. Here he appears in the role of a more independent and alert observer than during the first expedition, keen to note minute details important for understanding social life in the Arctic. And in this case, the diaries are massive, with vocabularies, dictionaries, grammatical notes, personal names, descriptions of events, ethnographic observations, and drawings. Much of the text focuses on daily activities related to the organization of camps, the collection and storing of food, interaction with Stefansson's companions (including Inuit), and travels across a complex and changing landscape. There are particularly rich entries on the behavior of animals and hunting expeditions that Stefansson seems to have taken pride in. Stefansson appears to have made a distinction between his "scientific" tasks and his role as ethnographer, his "Eskimo stuff," although the differentiation is neither explicit nor consistent.[17] The former typically involved collecting one kind or another of specimens, describing travel routes, examining archaeological remains, and measuring people's heads, a frequently mentioned activity, and these details seem to have been partly recorded in separate journals. The ethnographic observations included in the diaries focus on a range of issues. To mention a few, he includes lengthy discussions of shamanism, religion, folklore, kinship, clothing, food, language, cleanliness, tattoo, as well as concepts of time, labor, and wages.

Sometimes Stefansson made no entries for a few days, at other times he filled many pages of observations on particular issues or the events of the day. During the first days among the Copper Inuit, Stefansson's notekeeping is unusually detailed, with several pages on the first encounter itself, as if he was driven by an ethnographic compulsion. Stefansson describes his encounter and that of his Inuit companions with the Copper Inuit in the following terms:

> Started . . . on trail of people leading towards Victoria Island. . . . At about 4:30, some eight miles from our camp came upon a village. . . . From roof of one house saw . . . three men, . . . sealing evidently. Headed for nearest. . . . Getting near first man B[illy] and I halted team while T[annaumirk] went ahead to try not to frighten him by all approaching. The man sat on his snow seat bent forward as if watching for seal, occasionally raising his eyes only . . . to T[annaumirk]. When T[annaumirk] got within some paces man suddenly stood up, seized an iron snowknife that lay on the snow beside him, and poised himself as to receive an attack or to be ready to spring forward. This scared T[annaumirk] and he went no nearer, but started to talk. The other never smiled or paid attention for some time repeating monotonously (about twenty times a minute, as often as one breathes) ha-ha-ha-ha, etc. Evidently he at first understood nothing of what T[annaumirk] said, but he soon began to. Then he began talking and T[annaumirk] did not understand. T[annaumirk], however, knew . . . a Victoria Island phrase; *alianaituaraluit* (they are good) which he then used, and showed by lifting his coat he had no knife. After about five minutes of parley [the man] laid down the knife and soon after began an examination of T[annaumirk]'s clothing, which seemed to satisfy him we were harmless. . . . He then told T[annaumirk] to tell B[illy] and me to follow a little way behind while he went along a line of sealers to tell that we were *alianaituaraluit*.[18]

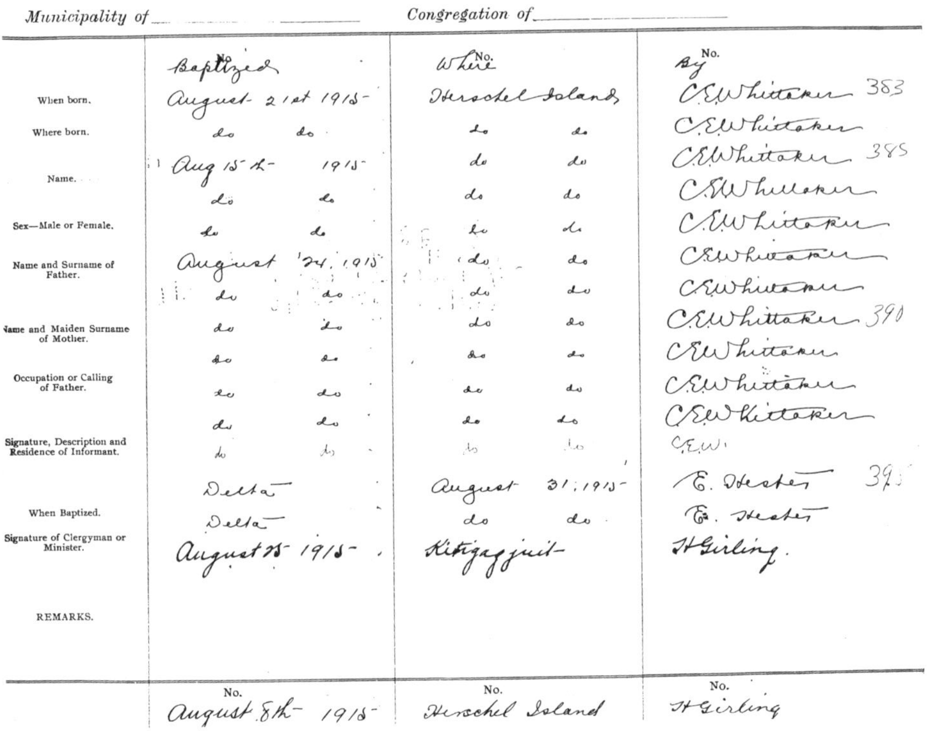
Municipality of ______ *Congregation of* ______

When born. Where born. Name. Sex—Male or Female. Name and Surname of Father. Name and Maiden Surname of Mother. Occupation or Calling of Father. Signature, Description and Residence of Informant. When Baptized. Signature of Clergyman or Minister. REMARKS.

Baptized No.	Where No.	By No.
August 21st 1915	Herschel Island	C.E.Whittaker 383
do do	do do	C.E.Whittaker
Aug 15th 1915	do do	C.E.Whittaker 385
do do	do do	C.E.Whittaker
do do	do do	C.E.Whittaker
August 24, 1915	do do	C.E.Whittaker
do do	do do	C.E.Whittaker
do do	do do	C.E.Whittaker 390
do do	do do	C.E.Whittaker
do do	do do	C.E.Whittaker
do do	do do	C.E.Whittaker
do do	do do	C.E.W.
Delta	August 31, 1915	E. Hester 39[illegible]
Delta	do do	E. Hester
August 15 1915	Kitigaaryuit	H Girling
August 8th 1915	Herschel Island	H Girling

FIGURE 2. Church records from Herschel Island about the baptism of Pannigabluk and Alex Stefansson, August 15, 1915. Photo: the author. *(Courtesy of the Anglican Church of Ascension, Inuvik, Canada.)*

Stefansson's enthusiasm at this point is understandable. For one thing, the whole expedition was justified by the attempt to establish whether the rumors he had heard during the first expedition about the existence of "blond" Eskimo were true. Moreover, anthropologists have for a long time been fascinated with "discoveries" of tribes previously unknown to the West, with people reported not to have seen a "white man," and Stefansson was no exception.[19] Not only were such lost or freshly discovered tribes seen as evidence of earlier modes of existence, of "disappearing worlds" ready to be mapped and recorded before the final onslaught of modernity, the first encounter with such extreme isolates in the cultural mosaic of humanity also inevitably presented a "translation" problem, a classic theme in Western thought, witnessed by the biblical theme of the Tower of Babel. If two groups of people failed to share a common language, and language was the key to culture, how could they possibly communicate across their cultural boundaries? And how might "we" be confident that our translations were truthful or correct? Anthropologists, indeed, have presented them-

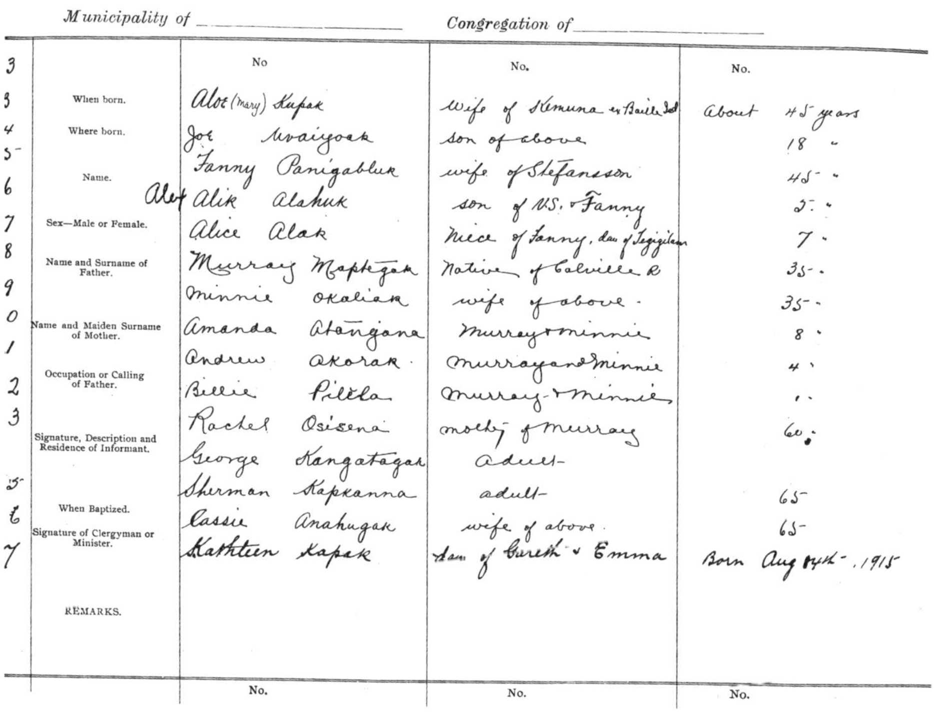

Municipality of ______________ *Congregation of* ______________

When born.
Where born.
Name.
Sex—Male or Female.
Name and Surname of Father.
Name and Maiden Surname of Mother.
Occupation or Calling of Father.
Signature, Description and Residence of Informant.
When Baptized.
Signature of Clergyman or Minister.
REMARKS.

	No	No.	No.
3			
3	Alot (mary) Kupak	Wife of Ikmuna ex Baillie Isd	About 45 years
4	Joe Nvaiyoak	son of above	18 "
5	Fanny Panigabluk	wife of Stefansson	45 "
6	Alof Alik Alahuk	son of V.S. & Fanny	5 "
7	Alice Alak	Niece of Fanny, dau of Tegigilan	7 "
8	Murray Maptegak	Native of Colville R	35 "
9	Minnie Okaliak	wife of above	35 "
0	Amanda Atangana	Murray & Minnie	8 "
1	Andrew Akorak	Murray and Minnie	4 "
2	Billie Pilkla	Murray & Minnie	1 "
3	Rachel Osisena	mother of Murray	60 "
	George Kangatagak	adult	
5	Sherman Kapkanna	adult	65
6	Cassie Anahugak	wife of above	65
7	Kathleen Kapak	dau of Gareth & Emma	Born Aug 14th, 1915

No. No. No.

selves as expert in the "art of translation."[20] Given such a metaphor, the role of the anthropologist is to go behind the baffling chaos of cultural artifacts, to discover order in the foreign, and to transfer implicit meaning from one discourse to another. Anthropologists, in sum, are presented as semiotic tour guides, escorting alien "readers" in rough semiotic space. While such fascination sounds increasingly ethnocentric and archaic to anthropologists in an age of deconstruction and globalization, at the time of Stefansson's fieldwork and long after it easily caught the attention of both the academic community and the general public.[21]

When Stefansson returned to Seattle and New York in the fall of 1912, his story about the Blond Eskimos (the Haneragmiut, Kanghiryuarmiut, and Nuwukpagmiut) caused quite a stir. The media reported that Stefansson had discovered the descendants of the Norse colonists who had settled Greenland from Iceland a thousand years earlier. The disappearance of that colony had remained a mystery and Stefansson's original reputation as an Arctic scholar was, indeed, launched by his account of the case; later he would argue that the Inuit had assimilated the Norse.[22] Stefansson complained that the newspapers had twisted his words and exaggerated his statements. Nevertheless, he seems to have seriously entertained such speculations from early on. In a letter to Wissler, Stefansson drew attention to both the philological similarities of Icelandic and the Inuit dialect in question and the physical appearance already mentioned: "These are two points that suggest, as far as they go, the possibility of some connection with the 3,000 lost Greenland colonists."[23] While critics accused Stefansson of vulgar sensationalism, others saw his statements about the Norse Inuit as a valuable hypothesis to explore.

Interestingly, Stefansson's speculations about the Norse ancestry of the Copper Eskimo may have been partly triggered by his own involvement with the Inuit. A few months before he sent his letter to Wissler, Alex—the son of Stefansson and Pannigabluk—was born. Perhaps the physical presence of that Icelandic Inuit, his own child, helps to explain Stefansson's enthusiasm about the medieval Norse connection. For the rest of his career, his mixed identity as scientist and showman was a repeated point of attack.[24] However distorted and unpleasant these debates may have been for him, they established his fame, which turned out to be important for his career, for the funding of yet another arctic expedition.

The Canadian Arctic Expedition (1913–1918)

The third expedition was an extensive one, spanning five years, which is longer than most anthropological expeditions either at the time or ever since. Here, however, Stefansson's role as geographic explorer and adventurer takes precedence for a variety of reasons, some of which have to do with the geopolitics of the time and the constraints of funding large-scale expeditions, involving teams of men and expensive equipment. It took long and complex negotiations with a host of people and institutions to secure the necessary financial support, including the American Museum of Natural History (his previous sponsor), the National Geographic Society, and the Canadian government. In the process, Stefansson had to sacrifice some of his ethnographic goals. As Diubaldo points out:

> This new arctic foray was not, in reality, an extension of the 1908–1912 expedition, for the simple fact that the emphasis and direction of the venture had now shifted to geographic exploration. Archaeological and ethnological study of the Eskimo in and around Coronation Gulf—the purpose for which Stefansson had started organizing the expedition—had slipped to a secondary place.[25]

Nevertheless, there was an important ethnographic element. Two anthropologists were hired for the expedition, Henri Beuchat, who had worked with Marcel Mauss on *Seasonal Variations of the Eskimo* and Diamond Jenness, who later became a leading expert on Inuit society.[26] A last-minute Memorandum for Instructions specified their roles as follows:

> The anthropological work shall consist of ethnological work and archaeological research. So far as practicable, the work shall be divided between the two anthropologists (equally), one being given the eastern and one a western territory. When circumstances force them to work in the same area, Dr. Beuchat shall study religion, festivals, folklore, social organization, text and linguistics, and Dr. Jenness shall study physical characteristics, hunting, fishing and technology in general.[27]

During much of the third expedition, then, Stefansson himself was experimenting with navigation and travel routes and the mapping of particular regions of the Arctic while Jenness worked on Inuit ethnography. Much of Stefansson's diary entries focus on weather, hunting, travel across ice, inventories of food and equipment, logistics, the daily activities of his team, and his observations of his men. In this case, as a result, Stefansson's diaries are more limited and less informative anthropologically speaking than one might think. There is relatively little of value on either Inuit society or Inuit-white relations. In fact, the diaries can hardly be described as "ethnographic," although anthropological observations are scattered here and there. Jenness's diaries, *Arctic Odyssey,* are far richer in ethnographic content than those of Stefansson, although they, too, leave out much of the information on interpersonal relations that one might expect to see. This is partly because all the diaries of the third expedition were considered as belonging to the expedition, not as private documents.

For these reasons, the present volume excludes the diaries of the third expedition. Stefansson's extensive published narrative of the expedition, *The Friendly Arctic,* reads more like a travel account than an ethnographic monograph. While he remains fascinated by the Inuit—particularly the Copper Inuit with whom he, again, spent some time—most of the volume deals with geographical issues, the politics of exploration, and the logistics, mental attitude, and technology necessitated by traveling on ice and in extreme cold. The Inuit, in a way, have been removed from the center stage, and the Arctic, however "friendly," remains a natural space to be explored, conquered, and domesticated by Western "civilization." Stefansson concludes his account with a grand modernist vision:

> I shall offer here my opinion that the most valuable result of the expedition will be not any of its concrete achievements but rather the general change in the trend of the world's thought which should follow from a broad consideration of all that was done and of how it was all done. . . . This expedition has contributed materially towards making easy what once was difficult. . . . It is human nature to undervalue whatever lands are distant and to consider disagreeable whatever is different. But we have brought the North a good deal closer. . . . To the members of our expedition the glamorous and heroic Polar Regions are gone and in their place is a friendly but commonplace country. To the reader the same will be true in proportion as he succeeds in seeing . . . that it is the mental attitude of the southerner that makes the North hostile. It is chiefly our unwillingness to change our minds which prevents the North from changing into a country to be used and lived in just like the rest of the world.[28]

The third expedition was plagued by conflicts between the members of the Stefansson's team right from the start. Several of his men questioned his integrity and leadership, and the tension between Stefansson and Anderson, already brewing in the second expedition, became difficult to control. Accounts of the expedition are also colored by an accident—the result, some would say, of a logistic mistake[29]—in which eleven of Stefansson's men lost their lives when their ship, the *Karluk,* became locked in ice, broke, and sank in November 1913. One of them was Beuchat. He froze to death when he tried along with three other men to reach land on his own. Mauss wrote on the tragic fate of his brilliant student and collaborator: "In the wreckage, all the notes that Beuchat had begun to take were lost along with many studies he had brought with him to finish during the long Arctic winter."[30]

At one point, when the ice was closing in on *Karluk,* Stefansson tried to get Beuchat and Jenness ashore so they could carry on with their ethnographic work, but the ice proved too thin. Later on, Stefansson managed to get a hunting party ashore. In the meantime, however, the *Karluk* and her crew were carried off to sea by a fierce storm. Most of the crew were rescued, but Stefansson would only know this months later. As Stefansson awaited news about the fate of *Karluk* and her crew, he wrote: "*No ships in sight*. This looks bad for me—there must have been some misfortune for the ocean is all open here."[31] The following day, when he finally receives the news of the ship, he commented:

> Crossed river F about a mile south of camp [. . .] I came upon a *footprint of a heeled boot*. This was one of the gladdest sights of my life—it showed white men had been there not many days before, for the tracks were nearly fresh

> [. . .] At the cape itself I found no traces, but ca. mile or more east along the coast I got to the top of a hill from which I saw the tips of two masts. I could hardly believe my eyes—somehow it seemed unnatural to find a ship in Banks Island. . . . I ran a half mile for fear they might start off at any moment [. . .] The ship was the *Mary Sachs* [. . .] Crawford now came out [. . .] and finally saw me when I was 15 yards or so off. Then his eyes stuck out like pegs. [. . .] *News:* The *Karluk* was crushed in January near Wrangell Island [. . .] Before she was crushed MacKay, Murray and a sailor [Morris] had left to land on Wrangell [Beuchat was there too, but for some reason is not mentioned]. [Captain] Bartlett and all others got safely ashore on Wrangell. Bartlett [. . .] was so "all in" that he did not come on deck for a week. [. . .] He had been a few days on Wrangell but saw no traces of MacKay's party. [. . .] Everything but food and notebooks lost. [. . .] So end all the hopes and dreams that centered around the *Karluk.*

Reading his mail the same day, Stefansson comments: "My mail [. . .] is most satisfactory. [. . .] My book [My Life with the Eskimo] has been very favourably, and in some cases enthusiastically, reviewed both in America and England, though the sales were interfered with, unfortunately; news of the *Karluk*'s drifting off coming out at the same time as the book."

FIGURE 3. Scientific staff of the Canadian Arctic Expedition at Nome, Alaska, July 13, 1913, prior to sailing of the *Karluk*. *(Courtesy of the National Archives of Canada, Ottawa. Neg. no. PA-74063.)*

FIGURE 4. Arctic chocolate wrapping paper. *(Courtesy of Dartmouth College Library, Stefansson's diary.)*

While Stefansson's attention during the third expedition was often directed away from ethnography, preoccupied with geographical exploration and growing problems of logistics and leadership, the expedition proved important for the development of the anthropology of the Arctic, thanks largely to Jenness who, with the death of Beuchat, became the chief ethnographer of the expedition. Saladin d'Anglure suggests that on the North American side of the Arctic, two scientific expeditions had an impact on anthropology, one of them being Stefansson's Canadian Arctic Expedition and the other one Rasmussen's Fifth Thule Expedition between 1921 and 1924.[32]

Stefansson finally returned from the Arctic in the spring of 1918. The expedition's geographical accomplishments—the discovery of the world's last major landmasses—were seen as a stunning success. In the following years and decades, Stefansson would draw upon his arctic experience and his reputation as an explorer, lecturing and writing about the Inuit, geopolitics, health, and a series of other issues. His career as an essayist and public speaker on arctic issues was far from peaceful; repeatedly he was involved in controversies with both anthropological colleagues (including Jenness), fellow explorers (Anderson, above all), and politicians, in Canada as well as the United States. He is reported, however, to have captured his audience with skilful rhetoric and rich visual material, in particular his hand-colored lantern slides. Some of this visual material is included here, in Part II, to give the reader a sense of the ways in which Stefansson saw and represented the Arctic to the larger world. Photographs, of course, are not only an important source of ethnographic information, they also shed light on the ethnographer and his or her project; thus, Sullivan shows how Margaret Mead and Gregory Bateson used photographs as rhetorical devices to present a particular image of Highland Bali, exploiting the capacity of visual material "to simultaneously illuminate and obscure, to simultaneously draw in and stand apart."[33] Woodward provides an interesting analysis of Stefansson's choice of ethnographic images and photographs, drawing attention to his focus on the "friendly" Arctic.[34] Most of the expedition photographs in the present volume were presumably taken by Stefansson himself, by George H. Wilkins, the "official" photographer of the third expedition, or by Diamond Jenness.

REFLECTIONS OF FIELDWORK

Around the time when Stefansson was completing his extensive arctic fieldwork, another anthropologist who later became regarded as the pioneer of the ethnographic method known as participant observation, Bronislaw Malinowski, embarked on his trip to the Trobriand Islands in the South Pacific. With the publication of the diaries of Malinowski, *A Diary in the Strict Sense of the Term,* anthropologists became sensitized to the dilemmas of fieldwork and the making of ethnographic texts.[1] Not only did Malinowski elaborate on his shortcomings, his text revealed all the prejudices anthropologists tended to associate with ethnocentric missionaries; Malinowski, it seemed, disliked his informants (some of whom he called "niggers"). As a result of the publication of the diaries, a lively discussion has taken place in recent decades on the fieldwork encounter and its representation in anthropological accounts.[2]

Interestingly, excerpts from Stefansson's diaries were published almost immediately after Stefansson's return from the second expedition, more than half a century earlier than those of Malinowski.[3] The anthropological community does not, however, seem to have responded to them. Stefansson's style, as we will see, was different from that of Malinowski and so was his audience. Moreover, Stefansson's diaries were edited by one of his colleagues, Wissler, who discarded precisely the kind of material that sparked the debate on Malinowski's diaries.

In his introduction to the second edition of Malinowski's diaries, more than two decades after the original publication, Firth provides interesting reflections on the reception of the volume.[4] His contribution to the publication, he says, drew adverse comment from his friends and colleagues who argued that the revelations of the diaries damaged Malinowski's reputation. The first reviews were indeed mixed. Some reviewers found the diaries tedious and boring and saw no point in publishing them. Others, however, found them fascinating and informative reading, illustrating the inevitable dilemmas and frustrations of fieldwork. As time went by, however, Malinowski seemed to emerge as a sympathetic and humane figure, as someone heroically admitting his weaknesses in the face of boredom, anxiety, and loneliness. Unexpectedly, Malinowski's diaries acquired an established place in anthropology, almost as a classic. Even Firth was taken by surprise:

> In this second Introduction to the *Diary* I would modify one judgement in the first Introduction. Though this book is undoubtedly lacking "in its purely ethnographic sense" I would no longer rank it as "no more than a footnote to anthropological history." The concept of ethnography has altered and widened, and the book has accordingly moved over to a more central place in the literature of anthropological reflection. It is . . . a highly significant contribution to the understanding of the position and role of a fieldworker as a conscious participator in a dynamic social situation.[5]

The discussion following the publication of Malinowski's diaries has often been referred to, after a well-known collection of critical essays originally presented at a seminar in Santa Fe, as the "writing-culture debate."[6] While the "road from Santa Fe" has been a rough and noisy one, evoking at times the image of the Tower of Babel, this debate has, no doubt, had a powerful impact on both ethnographic practice and interpretations of earlier texts.[7] Not only has it raised important questions concerning the exoticism of anthropological accounts and the authenticity of field reports, it has also drawn attention to a series of related issues concerning the subjectivity and presence of the anthropologist and his or her relations with local informants, the moral dilemmas of fieldwork, and what may be called the social relations of ethnographic production.[8]

One result of the writing-culture debate has been a growing interest in the field diaries of anthropologists. Thus, Boas's journals and letters from his field trip among the Inuit have recently been published: *Franz Boas Among the Inuit of Baffin Island 1883–1884*. That publication is interesting if only for the fact that it seems to have been during this "initiation trip," or *Erstlingsreise* as Boas called it, that Boas's theoretical views shifted quite dramatically from environmental determinism to historical (or cultural) particularism, from the idea that human institutions are rather mechanically adapted to the material environment in which they are embedded to the notion that each culture obeys rules of its own, modifying the environment in the process.[9] Boas's diaries also have implications for students of Stefansson's work; not only did both scholars work among the Inuit, the former provided a kind of model for the latter. For Stefansson, Boas, *the* contemporary spokesperson for ethnographic relativism, was "a somewhat intransigent theorist who was nevertheless the leading Eskimo authority of the day."[10]

Another recent publication in the same genre is *An American Anthropologist in Melanesia: A. B. Lewis and the Joseph N. Field South Pacific Expedition, 1909–1913*.[11] While Lewis's extensive collection of artifacts from Melanesia is well established, his ethnographic contribution has been relatively unknown. Much of Lewis's text is relatively impersonal in style, although he never intended the diaries for publication. Welsch's extensive commentary helps to situate Lewis's diaries in the context of anthropology and exploration, at a time when intensive ethnographic fieldwork was beginning to replace what Welsch calls "name expeditions," large-scale expeditions that combined ethnography and specimen collection for natural history museums.[12] Finally, the diaries of Jenness from the Canadian Arctic Expedition, were recently published, edited by Jenness's son.[13] These are obviously important for the understanding of Stefansson's work. Interestingly, as we will see, they provide some information on the presence of Stefansson's Inuit wife.

Given this background, the publication of Stefansson's field diaries is a timely venture. Obviously, however, the publication of private documents such as fieldwork diaries can raise important ethical questions. Malinowski's widow, Valetta Malinowska, justified her decision to publish her husband's field diaries, about two decades after he died, in the following manner:

> I know that some people will think that a diary is of a basically private nature and that it should not be published; and those who hold this point of view will probably be severely critical of my decision to publish my husband's diaries. But after seriously weighing the matter, I reached the conclusion that it is of greater importance to give to the present and future students and readers of Malinowski's anthopological writings this direct insight into his inner personality, and his way of living and thinking during the period of his most important work in the field, rather than to leave these brief diaries shut away in an archive.[14]

Firth suggests that while he agreed "somewhat unwillingly," at the request of Malinowski's widow, to contribute an introduction to Malinowski's diaries, he did not think the general public had any right in getting access to them. In fact, he thought the publication represented an "invasion of privacy."[15] If it had not been for the enthusiasm of Malinowski's widow, the diaries would never have appeared. In a sense, however, the discipline needed them, at a time of decolonization, self-doubt, and identity crisis. Coy may be right that "if Malinowski's diary had not been revealed by a public-spirited second wife we should almost have had to have invented it."[16]

As to the ethics of publishing Stefansson's diaries, it is important to keep in mind that parts of the diaries were made available to the public, with Stefansson's approval, already in 1914. Secondly, the entire diaries have been available to the public, in Stefansson's handwriting, on microfilm since 1971.[17] Finally, now with the principal players long gone, Stefansson's text seems unlikely to harm anyone. The events described occurred almost a century ago, and almost forty years have passed since the author died. More importantly, perhaps, exposing the diaries may significantly contribute to the understanding of Inuit society and the relations between Inuit and their guests (missionaries, anthropologists, government agents, whalers, and the like) at the beginning of the twentieth century, a decisive period on the arctic frontier. Inevitably, the contracts that come to prevail in the encounters between ethnographers and their hosts, and the themes that emerge from such contracts, are shaped by established relations of power. There maybe some truth in Appadurai's remark that "until there are as many persons from Papua New Guinea studying Philadelphia as vice versa, the appearance of dialogue conceals the reality of monologue."[18] Ethnographic diaries may allow one to identify and amplify idigenous voices, voices often submerged in contemporary scholarly publications. Such amplification of the Inuit voices in Stefansson's diaries may help to heal some of the wounds inflicted by the racist colonial regime of which anthropology, somewhat reluctantly, was part from early on.[19] Censorship and silencing will certainly not help in that respect.

THE EXPEDITION DIARIES AND THE PRESENT EDITION

Stefansson's field diaries consist of hundreds of handwritten pages contained in nineteen books. Stefansson wrote his observations and accounts every day or two, sometimes in different parts of his journals, discontinuing the chronological order. Part of the text is in telegraph-style, in particular notes on weather, landscape, and daily routine. In between are lengthy observations of social life, occasionally elegant essays, well written and nicely structured. Scattered in the text are numerous images, maps, drawings of tattoos, clothes, and tools, some of which are reproduced for the first time in this volume, and some of which were drawn by Stefansson's Inuit informants.

Stefansson's handwriting and writing style vary from one time to another, depending on his moods, the flux of the expedition, and the context. Sometimes he is handicapped by the frozen ink in his pen. Thus, he provides a "lesson on fountain pens," an important concern for writers in "ice parties." "The moral is: in cold weather never . . . fill your pen, and keep it point-end up while it freezes."[1] He is also bothered by the occasional lack of light (lamp or oil) in the evening, when he is most likely to take notes, and the shortage of paper, "paper famine."[2] The latter concern is evident when he comments on the excitement he experiences during the first days among the Copper Inuit, anxious to give priority to his ethnographic task:

> *Brief entries* only will hereafter be made of other things than ethnological information, geology or geography and other things that concern the purpose of our trip to the Arctic, for I am becoming worried about the capacity of my two notebooks, especially if we should stay all next winter, as I at present feel inclined to do. Hunting, mishaps without serious consequences, . . . short or long mileage, etc. will be left to take care of themselves largely.[3]

Generally the entries are written in English. Sometimes, however, Stefansson reproduces sayings or statements in the Inuit language used by his companions. Occasionally he also switches from English to Icelandic, the language he grew up with in Manitoba and North Dakota. By using Icelandic, he was sometimes looking for a spontaneous translation of Inuit terms. At times, on the other hand, he was effectively "locking" his diary, preventing his travel companions (and possibly many of his academic colleagues in the West) from reading sensitive information. This is indicated by the fact that he even Icelandicized personal names. Thus, he writes:

> *Skrælingi minn segir að gángari lögreglusveinn, sé nú giftur skrælingjakonu þeirri er Unalína nefnist, og verið hefur frylla lángs nokkurs, frysta st´yrimanns á hvalfángara skipinu 'bogahaus.' Mun það satt vera, og mun fitharaldur einnig hafa fryllu tekið.*[4]
>
> [My native says that the policeman "Walker" (*gángari;* from *ganga,* "to walk") is now married to a native woman named Unalin, formerly the concubine of a certain Long, a mate on the whaling ship *Bowhead.* This is true, and Fitzgerald *(Fitharaldur)* also has taken a concubine.]

The Old Icelandic term used by Stefansson in this context, *skrælingi,* is a loaded one, much like Malinowski's reference to "nigger."[5] In Stefansson's time, it had gained the meaning of "uncivilised" or "barbarian." Stefansson, however, seems to use the term where he would use "native" in English, short perhaps of a more faithful translation.

Stefansson may also have "edited" his diaries with later readers and their purposes in mind. Sometimes part of a page is missing (occasionally, however, the missing pieces were used for memos or drafting letters), some words have been made unintelligible, and at least once a drawing has been glued on two pages, apparently on top of some text.[6] It is also possible that some pages (even journals) are missing from the collection. This is not an unlikely possibility, keeping in mind Stefansson's concern with what kinds of issues might be properly mentioned in his biography and what should be left out. Stefansson's biographer D. M. LeBourdais wrote a long manuscript on Stefansson, but withdrew it from publication because he and Stefansson "had disagreed on one or two rather minor points."[7] The major disagreement, it seems, concerned references to Stefansson's health: "We argued all day without coming to an agreement. 'Such things are never mentioned in biographies,' he insisted." As it turned out, LeBourdais published a shorter book than planned about Stefansson, apparently with Stefansson's approval.[8] Stefansson's friend Richard Finnie commented that Stefansson's reticence about sickness was understandable; "it was unromantic and out of harmony with the picture of a hardy explorer and hunter on the march."[9] Interestingly, in his preface to Mirsky's account of the history of arctic exploration, Stefansson reflects on the difficulties involved in getting and stating "the facts." Stefansson credits the author for writing a history,

> not for the aggrandizement of a nation or the ennobling of youth but rather to get at and state the facts. Her messages, when any, are those of the characters themselves. Those messages may conflict, for *the explorers contradict each other and sometimes themselves.*[10]

Every diary, of course, is a personal construction of events, not a straightforward presentation of facts, and Stefansson's companions are likely to provide somewhat different accounts of the events collectively encountered by them. Jenness, Stefansson's companion during the third expedition, comments upon Stefansson's account in both the diaries and *The Friendly Arctic:*

> This book based largely on Stefansson's personal diary . . . does not tell the whole story, much of which lies buried in the diaries of other men. In front of me as I write, indeed, is the initial volume of my own diary, recording many scenes and events that have no place in Stefansson's history.[11]

Jenness does not elaborate on the differences between the two diaries, his own and that of Stefansson. Elsewhere, however, he severely took Stefansson to task, challenging his ethnography and his conclusions and his claims about flowing with the Arctic.[12]

A few times Stefansson's diaries offer some reflection on themselves and the kind and amount of information they provide. Once Stefansson wrote a separate entry marked "This diary," commenting on the act of writing, the significance of his observations and how others might read and use his notes:

> Somehow I find it difficult to keep in mind the possibility that this record may sometime be worked out by someone other than myself and that entries sufficient for my purpose may not be of much significance to another.[13]

The same entry continues, indicating that he is worried about having too much data to be able to tell a meaningful story: "I must evidently get home soon to make a beginning of letting known my results—else I shall be submerged in accumulated mass. . . ." Almost a year later, Stefansson expresses a concern with having had too little data due to temporary shortage of paper: "*Have abundant paper now* and promise of more, so shall when time allows make fuller diary entries . . . and include many things I have been habitually omitting."[14] Also he writes:

> *A review:* The entries for the past month or two do not perhaps give a picture of the daily routine—that is not needed for me, for it cannot be forgotten. The present paragraph is written for others: My own constant effort has been acquiring a knowledge of the language—rather its nature than of its vocabulary, for I have decided that a pretentious dictionary is not worth attempting. My ear is continually giving me new ideas . . . and my alphabet is therefore even yet a very unstable thing.[15]

Malinowski was concerned with similar issues in his diaries. One important difference exists, however. Stefansson's diaries are not particularly personal in the "strict" Malinowskian sense, although, as I will argue, the reader is sometimes able to at least guess between the lines. Stefansson's attitude toward descriptions of intimacy contrasts with that of Malinowski. Malinowski, with his Catholic background, was more to the point, elaborating in his private journals on his bad moments, his frustrations, and his prejudices, while the Protestant Stefansson suppressed his moods and relations and "cleaned" even his diaries. There is little about the author's emotional states, the frustrations of fieldwork, and the details of his involvement with his companions. At one point, near the end of the second expedition, Stefansson makes a direct reference to his emotions:

> One reason for keeping one's emotions out of this journal is that anyone with imagination can guess what they are. They need only set before them a dreamer thrown among the harshest realities of our earth, one who longs for sympathy placed among people not unsympathetic but as incapable of seeing the things he sees as we are of seeing ultra-violet light.[16]

There are some important exceptions, however, about Stefansson's quietness about himself. Thus, he writes: "For the first time in [the] Arctic I have caught epidemic cold."[17] The same year, on his birthday, he remarks:

> This is my thirtieth. It is in some ways more satisfactory than the last, for a year ago Billy and I were on our vain inland chase after polar bear near Beechey Point, without fire in −35° weather. But then that birthday had the advantage

> of being only the 29th: between the two there lie too few and too small accomplishments, too many miscarried plans and imperfectly accomplished purposes.[18]

Once Stefansson professes that he wishes he were in a warmer climate and that he might never return to the North—if, that is, he made it back home:

> *A confession:* Lest sometime in a warmer clime the less agreeable memories of the north may blend with the pleasanter into a uniform agreeable haze—lest I come to believe I "enjoyed every day of the year" up here—I will set down now the fact that I don't enjoy today and that I sincerely wish myself in a warmer, more civilized land. Every few minutes I subconsciously make and renew various resolutions (which I shall doubtless break if the opportunity offers) of never going north again if I ever get south from this venture.[19]

Lonely and critically short of food, he comments: "I feel more blue than ever in my three years up here."[20]

In the months preceding Stefansson's "homegoing trip," at the end of the second expedition, his diary entries on Inuit language and ethnography are particularly rich. Also, near the end of the expedition he is unusually honest about himself and his arctic blues, as if he was anticipating culture-shock on his return home after a few years away. It is worthwhile to quote Stefansson at some length:

> *Psychological:* I seem to be a different person nowadays from what I have been for four years. There is an insatiable hunger for other men's ideas. . . . I can't go to sleep for six or eight hours evenings (after camping) for the desire to read or to write—letters to friends. Hence we are in camp about 24 hours each time we stop. Nothing is really lost by this, as my work is all behind me. . . . The fact that my work is behind me obsesses me too at times—I feel as if I were going to a court-martial for cowardice. Of course I must get out sometime to record my results and find out what others are thinking and doing, before I proceed with the work up here.[21]
>
> *Hardships:* Someone about two years ago sent Dr. Anderson a Sunday paper clipping giving a page of our "hardships" and the writer's reflections thereon. . . . In itself the experience of starvation is not nearly so trying as one might infer. . . . Our real hardships up here are subjective—mental. On the present homegoing trip, with my work ended but not finished, with unappraised achievements behind and unknown conditions ahead, I am in a mental con-

dition more trying than any physical hardship of the four years has been. . . . [T]he wisest man I know—George Foot Moore at Harvard—said to us once . . . "Pessimism and despair are luxuries of the upper classes—the poor and hungry have no time for such things." I have tried this out and found it so.[22]

Introspective: I can appreciate now the feelings of men who after being long under a monotonous ship's routine at sea long to get into port to go on an unrestrained drunk. . . . The antipodal extremes we seek vary somewhat with our inherited and acquired tastes, but in general the one who has been busy seeks rest, the one who has suffered nervous strain wants freedom from worry, one who has starved dreams of banquets, or at least of food, and I who have for four years been moving slowly, plodding from place to place, hunger for swift motion without effort, for rushing from place to place on extra-fare trains and five-day liners. More than all, I who have so long associated with people who believe in witchcraft, dream of being with men who doubt the nebular hypothesis. After the tent on the silent barrens I want Broadway by arc light and the Strand at five o'clock; after the igloo I want the Century Club and the Criterion; after the *kajigi* monologues on the forefathers' wisdom I want scientific conventions [. . .].[23]

When preparing for the trip back home, Stefansson sent a couple of telegrams to his sponsors, one of which was addressed to the Geological Survey in Ottawa: "All well; coming via Seattle. Shall I cable details?"

As already mentioned, selections from Stefansson's diaries from the first and second expedition have been published before. The editor, Wissler, however, only reproduces a fraction of the text. Moreover, his selection is highly biased, focusing on "stories" of the past (oral tradition) and "material culture" (hunting techniques, tools, clothing) rather than the living reality of the Arctic here and now. As a result, Wissler's editing tends to systematically leave out much material that many modern readers are likely to be interested in, including information on the making of ethnography and the relations between whites on the one hand and Inuit and Indians on the other. Often, too, he drops information that Stefansson was likely to consider as being sensitive, including entries written in Icelandic. Wissler makes clear, however, that while Stefansson had some suggestions regarding editorial policy, he was not responsible for the selection:

The editor wishes to state that at Mr. Stefansson's suggestion he selected from the journals of the expeditions such passages as in judgement contained useful anthropological data not fully presented in the author's book, *My Life*

> *with the Eskimo*. The author's absence on another expedition made it impractical to submit the selections for his approval, so that he is neither responsible for the choice of data nor the arrangement.[24]

A number of times, Wissler makes deliberate changes to Stefansson's text, changing the spelling or word order, and, occasionally, replacing words and altering style.

This volume presents selections from the complete, original diaries from Stefansson's ethnographic expeditions, all of which are kept in the Special Collection of the Dartmouth College Library in Hanover. In selecting from the diaries, I have generally been more truthful to the original text than Wissler. Not only have anthropological interests in field diaries changed substantially since the time of Stefansson's fieldwork, the sensibilities of the average contemporary reader are rather different from those of Stefansson, Wissler, and their contemporaries. What counts as "useful anthropological data" is not the same as before. Nevertheless, it has been necessary to leave out most of the original text. My editorial procedure was as follows: In the first stage, I instructed my assistants who read the entire diaries and rendered most of them in electronic form to focus on ethnography, personal experience, and relations with Inuit and Indians. Also, they were asked to leave out detailed and repetitive information, for instance on weather, landscape, logistic details, and physical measurements, although some of this has been reproduced in order to give the reader the flavor of the original. Occasionally, my assistants were unable to read Stefansson's handwriting, and some segments of the text were left out for that reason. Stefansson, one may note, seems at times to have had some difficulties in reading his own handwriting: "As for my diary for the summer [1910], it was written in my small pocket notebook in so microscopic a hand that it is difficult to read without a magnifying glass."[25] Having reproduced most of the ethnographic diaries in electronic form, we arranged the entries in chronological order. In the final stage of editing, I made further cuts to the text, keeping in mind the necessity of containing the text in a single volume of moderate size. The sheer volume of Stefansson's text made extensive cuts necessary; what is published here represents only approximately 15 percent of the entire text. Deleted text and my insertions (translations from Icelandic, questions, and rewording) are indicated with brackets: [ ].

No doubt, some researchers may be interested in issues that are not covered by the present edition, for instance details of censuses, measurements, geography, archaeology, and environmental history. For them the complete handwritten diaries are available on microfilm. I also refer the reader who may be interested in greater details to the informative biographies already available on Stefansson, some of which discuss the progression of Stefansson's ethnographic expeditions in detail.[26]

Sometimes I have reproduced Wissler's insertions into Stefansson's text (in particular, names of persons and places). Generally, I have also followed Wissler in avoiding phonetic symbols in references to Inuit words to make the diaries more readable. Stefansson's spelling of English is somewhat idiosyncratic ("enough" and "thought," for instance, are spelled as "enuf" and "thot") and I have usually erased such peculiarities to make the text more accessible. On the other hand, I have usually retained Stefansson's rather archaic Icelandic as it provides interesting information about his use of the dialect of the North-American Icelandic community. These extracts are also provided in English translation.

The spelling of Inuit terms and of the names of persons, places, and ethnic groups was often inconsistent in Stefansson's diaries. Linguistic and ethnographic mistakes were inevitable in the early stages of his fieldwork (he later mastered some of the relevant indigenous languages), and Inuit names, pronunciation, and terminology varied from place to place. Stefansson, having no dictionary of Inuit terms and few written sources to go by, constructed his own dictionary with the aid of special characters and phonetic symbols. In this edition of the diaries, Stefansson's spelling of Inuit terms is standardized where it has been possible to do so without compromising the flavor of the original, and many of the special characters (including û, í, é, á, ú, and ó) used by him have been eliminated, for simplicity's sake.

Anthropological field diaries are not only written in several ways, with different kinds of audience and agendas in mind, similarly there are many ways of editing them for publication. For instance, Welsch's work on Lewis's diaries from Melanesia includes practically everything in the original, omitting only occasional paragraphs on unrelated topics.[27] In addition, Welsch provides extensive editorial notes on the text. Müller-Wille likewise incorporates most of Boas's original text on the Inuit, excluding only sections written in shorthand, adding a few editorial notes here and there.[28] Malinowska, Malinowski's widow, who prepared her husband's diaries for publication, only omitted "a few extremely intimate observations," and in this case the reader is generally only offered a few explanatory notes on the text.[29] Jenness's son, who edited his father's diaries, includes most of the original and adds much explanatory notes, keeping, however, his anthropological commentary to a minimum.[30]

RELATIONS WITH THE INUIT: "AN ESKIMO TO THE SKIN"

The ethnographic diaries and some of the publications of Stefansson demonstrate that he was a serious fieldworker, participating in the lives of the Inuit he visited, studying their language, living their way of life, and probing their way of thinking. He comments with reference to his first expedition: "I was gradually broken in to native ways; by the middle of October, I had thrown away my nearly outworn woolen suit and was fur clad from head to heel, an Eskimo to the skin."[1] In his account of the second expedition, he offers the following description of the method that later became known as participant observation:

> They took me into their houses and treated me hospitably and courteously, but exactly as if I were one of them. They gave me clothes to wear and food to eat, I helped them in their work and joined in their games, until they finally forgot that I was not one of them, and began to live their lives before my eyes as if I were not there. This gave me a rare opportunity to know them as they are.[2]

Stefansson was fond of noting that when he arrived among the Copper Inuit he already spoke Inuktitut. As Burch points out, "he was . . . in a unique position—possibly in the history of ethnography—of being able to speak the language of the people he was going to study before they had ever seen a Euroamerican."[3]

The notion of the "friendly Arctic" summed up Stefansson's approach to the Arctic. Stefansson argued that arctic explorers often made the mistake of literally bringing their environment with them (food, clothes, and methods of transport). It would be far more productive and viable in the long run, he argued, to adopt Inuit practices and flow with the arctic environment.[4]

Pointing out that the Inuit saw no need to wage war with the environment in which they lived, he challenged the orthodox, literary notion of the Arctic as necessarily "barren, dismal and desolate."[5] Some of Stefansson's diary entries, however, qualify his claims about the friendly Arctic. After days of nauseating starvation, he comments:

> *My work* up here, I have been fond of asserting, entails few hardships. But just now it is pretty hard work, and has often been so these three years. To be five or six miles from camp every morning at daybreak and about that far from home at the last daylight, to carry home heavy loads over rocky ground when successful and still heavier loads of disappointment when unsuccessful—this makes a monotonous and a trying life. The continual nervous strain of a hand-to-mouth existence, where there is not even the shelter of a poorhouse in case of failure, has a telling and cumulative effect. Without in the least relinquishing my hopes of many more years of arctic work, I continually feel more strongly the desire to be so well equipped in the future that I shall have at least a year's supply of food somewhere awaiting me to tide me over a season of failure. Just *knowing* of such a reserve . . . would lessen by half the strain of the winter. This is a hard country for a hungry man.[6]

Stefansson was, largely, a relativist in both his diary entries and his publications, following Boas and his cultural anthropology, although the two seem to have disagreed on some minor ethnographic points. In an exchange of letters in 1938, he argued that the word *Eskimo* was a derogatory term used by Algonquins, suggesting that the native term *Inuit* be adopted.[7] Stefansson was an enthusiastic practician of the "scientific" art of measuring people's heads and the diaries, indeed, repeatedly refer to his measurements.[8] Such a practice was compulsive routine for physical anthropologists working in the Arctic at the time and some, including Danish scholars working in Greenland, seem to have continued it into the late 1960s. Unlike, however, many of his contemporaries, Stefansson does not seem to have been preoccupied with eugenics and racial purity.[9] In fact, despite his own term "native" or "barbarian" (the Icelandic *skrælingi*), he was eager to combat the ethnocentric preconceptions of missionaries and some of his fellow explorers.[10]

Stefansson's comments upon his interaction with his Inuit hosts and companions are usually brief and objective in style. Most often they focus on fairly pragmatic matters such as camping and cooking, the division of labor in the camp, and the organization of hunting. Many of the entries in the diaries elaborate on storytelling and the role of informants.

FIGURE 5. Fannie Pannigabluk in Aklavik around 1940. *(Courtesy of Saich/NWT Archives, Yellowknife, Canada, N-1990-003-0201.)*

Sometimes Stefansson refers to one kind of contract or another with the Inuit, usually for the purpose of eliciting stories. On one occasion he writes about annoying one of his informants with too much "cross-examining": "If I get him tired (as I have once or twice done) he becomes careless in his answers and unreliable saying 'yes' to anything or pretending he understands my question when he does not."[11] A similar remark appears elsewhere:

> The natives soon get tired of monotonous questioning, especially if a difficult point comes up—of course they don't appreciate that anything of importance can be involved. Their answers become careless and almost misleading—they try to make me think I understand things which I don't understand (e.g. by declaring verbs to be synonymous which are really not so (this to get me to quit asking questions).[12]

Often there are signs of mild disagreement and difference in opinion. A few times Stefansson challenges the folk wisdom of his hosts:

> My own opinion is that neither Eskimo nor Indians have a reasoned and reasonable theory of the movement of caribou, nor one based on sufficient (more than one-sided) observation. Neither seems to account rationally for the whereabouts of caribou when they do not actually see them.[13]

Sometimes Stefansson comments on tension resulting from differences in the understanding of location and logistics: "When I suggested we might be too far west of this river, [the Indian]. . . smiled superiously and said the people of the country understood such things better than strangers."[14] At one point, Stefansson mentions having quarreled somewhat angrily with one of his Inuit companions, who said he "would leave now that I was going to start treating him as a captain does a white sailor, he was no dog to be starved."[15] "I was forced to remind him," Stefansson adds, "that by white man's law a servant hired for a year who quit work without good cause before his time was up, forfeited his wage"; often the natives, it seems, would not cooperate when he wanted to take head measurements or to photograph. Once Stefansson states:

> wife and daughter refuse . . . to let me measure their heads. W. . . . says he has often tried but never been able to get a photograph of the daughter and took the mother when she did not know what was being done.[16]

These extracts from the diaries clearly demonstrate a conflictual and sometimes asymmetrical relationship between Stefansson and the Inuit that does not quite resonate with the egalitarian and sympathetic image he presented of himself in many of his publications. More revealing, perhaps, is Stefansson's treatment of his intimate relationship with one of his Inuit informants, the seamstress Fannie Pannigabluk.

STEFANSSON'S INUIT FAMILY

In the summer of 1987, during a conversation with June Helm, Professor of Anthropology at the University of Iowa, I learned that Stefansson was reported to have a son, Alex, with an Inuit woman who accompanied him during the second expedition. I later found out that the woman was named Fannie Pannigabluk and that she had died in Aklavik from tuberculosis in 1941. Alex died of heart attack in 1966, four years after his father. He and his wife Mabel Okpik, I also learned, raised six children—Rosie (b. 1933), Shirley (b. 1936), Alexander (b. 1939), Frank (b. 1941), Willy (b. 1943), and Georgina (b. 1947)—all of whom live in the Canadian Arctic. During a field trip in July 2000 to Inuvik, in the Northwest Territories in Canada, I interviewed four of the children of Alex and Mabel. This gave me an opportunity to explore Inuit accounts of Stefansson's relationships with Pannigabluk and their son and his silence about his Inuit family.

Pannigabluk and her son Alex lived in their camps in the Mackenzie Delta and on the Arctic coast. In the winter, they would subsist by hunting in the Delta, but during the summers they moved to the coast, as most people did, escaping from heat and persistent mosquitos. Pannigabluk was a fairly independent woman, a skillful seamstress and hunter. As Stefansson did not return after the third expedition, however, she was partly dependent on her brothers for support. In his youth, her son Alex was registered as "white," which caused troubles at times with some of the Inuit, but later on when his health deteriorated and he needed the particular privileges offered to natives he changed to Inuit-status. Alex's marriage to Mabel was arranged by their families, in the Inuit custom. They established a household in the Delta and in the town of Aklavik, where Pannigabluk would live with them until she died. Apart from raising their six children, they took care of ten orphans from time to time. All of their children live in the town of Inuvik, except Shirley who lives in Sachs Harbor on Banks Island. They have had a variety of jobs, including housework, hunting and fishing,

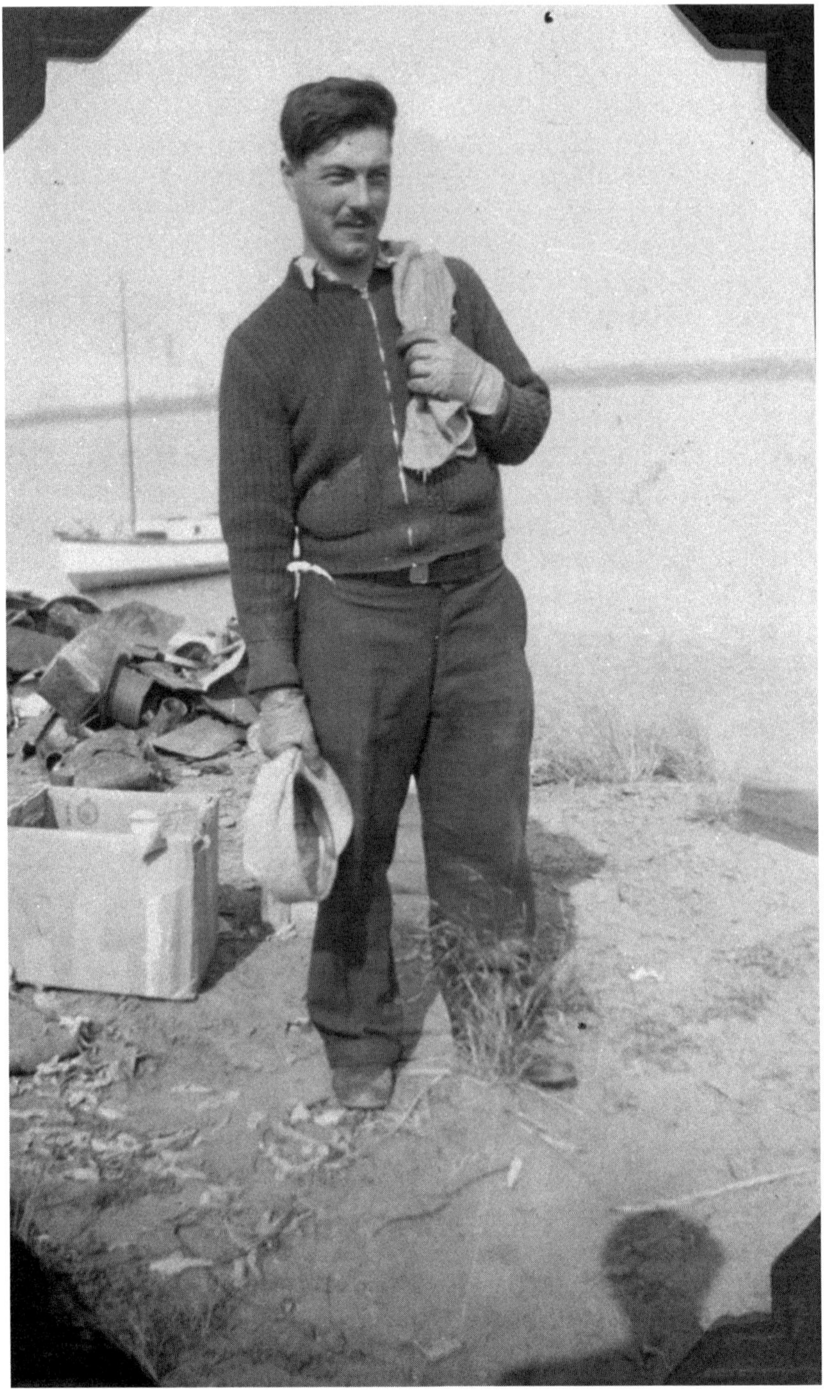

FIGURE 6. Alex Stefansson. Photo: Herbert Schwartz. *(Courtesy of the Wood/NWT Archives, Yellowknife, Canada, N88-041-0706.)*

teaching, and nursing. They are bilingual, which is not that common in the region nowadays, as Inuvialuktun is increasingly losing ground.

While the existence of Stefansson's son was apparently common knowledge in the Arctic, Alex's paternity had been a delicate and restrained issue outside the Arctic, which only surfaced a few times in the media and scholarly publications. Stefansson never publicly acknowledged either his son or his intimate, conjugal relationship with Pannigabluk. The silence about Alex and Pannigabluk and the latter's role in Stefansson's fieldwork invite a number of interesting questions regarding exploration, the fieldwork encounter, gender relations, and the making of ethnographies.

Stefansson's earlier works are not very informative on his relationships with his hosts and companions, including Pannigabluk and their son Alex. There is no mention at all of Alex in *My Life with the Eskimo,* published right after the second expedition, nor, indeed, in Stefansson's autobiography.[1] While there are many references to Pannigabluk in his earlier work, these references are typically brief and indifferent. Stefansson, for

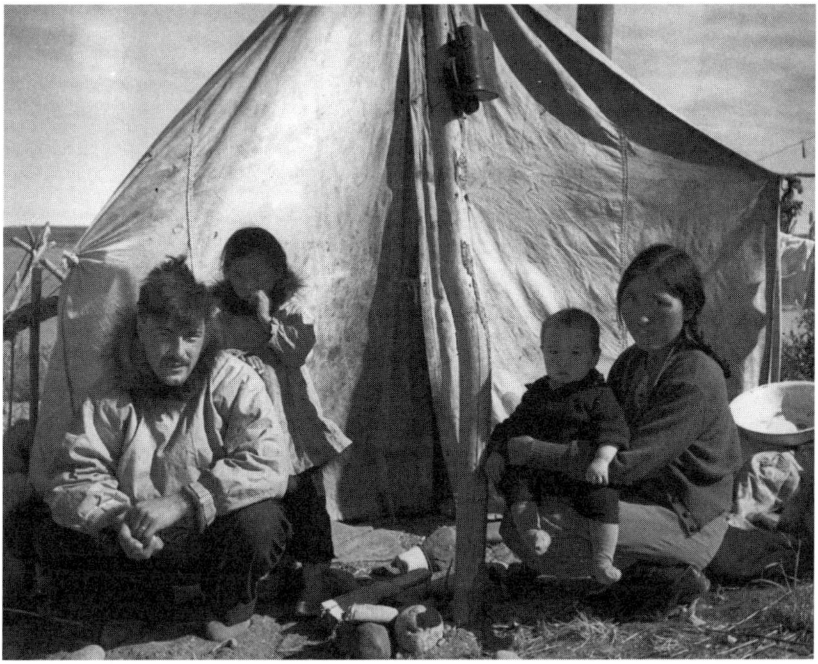

FIGURE 7. Alex Stefansson, his wife Mabel Okpik, and two of their children, 1939. Photo: Richard Finnie. *(Courtesy of the Finnie/NWT Archives, Yellowknife, Canada, N79-063-0062.)*

instance, has this to say about their encounter in the autumn of 1909, in the early stage of his second expedition:

> I took with me my favorite companion, Natkusiak, and an elderly country-woman of his named Pannigabluk, whose husband had died the year before and who had been taken on with our party as a seamstress.[2]

Stefansson notes that Pannigabluk was "talkative by nature" and that she "did not care very much where she went," but otherwise she is simply referred to as being "in charge" of his camps while he and his men were away.[3] On of the photographs in Stefansson's account of the expedition shows a woman leading the expedition team marching "across barren ground." That woman is probably Pannigabluk, but she is not named in the text.

Stefansson's autobiography, completed a few days before his death, is equally distancing and uninformative about his relationships with his Inuit companions:

> I boarded the *Karluk* with Natkusiak and a widowed Eskimo woman, Pannigabluk, who came from Natkusiak's part of Alaska. She was an excellent seamstress, something no party wintering on the arctic coast can afford to be without.[4]

In one case, Stefansson refers to Pannigabluk as being "persuaded," along with two Inuit men, to accompany him.[5]

Stefansson's Inuit descendants apparently saw no reason for suppressing evidence of their relationship to the explorer. Interestingly, one of Alex's children, Georgina Stefansson, wrote a personal note, "My Grandfather, Dr. Vilhjalmur Stefansson," in the magazine *North,* describing Stefansson's career and accomplishments.[6] Georgina, then in grade five in Federal School, wrote the following with the help of her teacher:

> As the grand-daughter of Dr. Vilhjalmur Stefansson, I am naturally very proud of him. Therefore I would like to tell you about him. . . .
>
> When he grew up and finished his education, . . . he decided to explore and to learn everything possible about the north, and the people of the north. . . .
>
> He married an Eskimo girl, Fannie Puniovaluk, who also helped him in his work. They had only one child, my father, who now lives at Aklavik, where he owns a freighter and hunts and traps in his spare time. . . .

> Although I have never met [my grandfather]. . . I have always been proud of him, and I feel that I do know him because of the stories my dad has told me about him.

Other Inuit accounts also suggest that Pannigabluk and Stefansson were married. Pete Suvaliq describes the encounter of his Inuit father with Stefansson and his team in 1914:

> All their clothing was made of cloth, even their boots. One of them was a scientist who was measuring adults' heads. . . . Stefansson wanted to learn to hunt from my father. . . . Stefansson knew how to speak the Iñupiaq language for *he had an Iñupiaq wife. His wife's name was Paniugluk.*[7]

June Helm, my original source on Stefansson's son, personally knew Alex as well as his wife Mabel and three of their children, Frank, Georgina, and Shirley. Alex had been the guide of her former husband, the late R. S. "Scottie" MacNeish, on his two archaeological expeditions on the Firth River in the summers of 1954 and 1955. According to Helm, who after these expeditions became a leading expert on sub-arctic native North American populations, Alex told her that his father had not married until after Alex's mother had died, the implication being that Stefansson was observing a moral commitment.[8]

While few references to Stefansson's relationships with Pannigabluk and Alex appear in printed works, there was a lot of gossip, usually generated and driven by the heat of personal rivalry. Kenneth Chipman, a young topographer during Stefansson's third expedition, eagerly commented upon the paternity issue in one of his personal letters from the Arctic:

> I don't know or haven't heard of a man in this country, white or native, who doubts that the kid is Stefansson's although he himself refuses to recognize openly the woman and child and to make provisions for them . . . people up here would accept the whole thing as a matter of course and pay no attention, but his failure to recognize them and make provisions (which is the usual thing and common among whalers and others) is arousing . . . comment.[9]

In his biography of Stefansson, Hunt briefly comments on Stefansson's relationships with Alex and Pannigabluk, in connection to the gossip about Stefansson. However, much of what the author himself has to say about the matter is both relegated to a footnote and unnecessarily favorable toward Stefansson:

> Apparently, Stefansson offered to take mother and child "outside" and support them, but Pannigabluk preferred to remain in the Arctic. It is hard to imagine that he neglected to do so, for he was invariably generous to Eskimos even where he had no obligations to them.[10]

Hunt adds that "Pannigabluk's family took pride in their relationship to Stefansson," pointing out that her granddaughter's note in the *North* "makes it clear that, despite gossip among whites, the Eskimos were satisfied. Had it been otherwise, Pannigabluk had ample occasion to complain, but she did not."

Alex may have been the source for the story about Stefansson's offer to take Pannigabluk and Alex "outside." According to Helm, Alex claimed that his father ("Vilhjalmur" in Alex's words) offered to take him and his mother with him when leaving the field, adding that his mother did not agree to that.[11] Alex also stated that if they didn't go out with him Vilhjalmur said that he would sever all relations with the child and the mother. Alex's children emphasize, however, that Stefansson only offered to take the child outside, not Pannigabluk. In their account, Stefansson and Pannigabluk physically struggled over the custody of the child until Stefansson gave in. Pannigabluk, who at this point, late in her fifties, had been married twice, would not accept losing her only child, her chief source of security, protection, and livelihood later on. Apparently, Stefansson had prepared his son for a trip to Vancouver and later to the east coast of the United States, where he would grow up in the world of whites.

Counter provides a moving and perceptive account of the silence around other Inuit descendants of Western explorers, including those of Peary, and the attempts by some of their white descendants to suppress the evidence on their Inuit kin.[12] Stefansson's silence about his descendants seems to have been partly motivated by similar concerns. In his case, however, he had no white descendants. Some of the white fathers of Inuit children in the Arctic freely accepted responsibility for their offspring, including some of Stefansson's contemporaries, notably Charlie Klengenberg. And some of them stayed in the Arctic, living with their Inuit family. Stefansson's position is probably somewhat different, however. From early on he seems to have been committed to return from the Arctic as a famous explorer and anthropologist; indeed, the dairies would support such a conclusion. And in those days, marriage to an Inuit would have permanently blocked access to fame and power.

Late in his life, Stefansson married a young woman, Evelyn Baird (now Stefansson Nef). According to her, Stefansson would not elaborate on the existence of his son, but when pressed he told her that he refused to recognize Alex both because his lawyers advised him to do so and because he was not the only member of the expedition who had sex with Pannigabluk. Stefansson suggested, according to his widow, that Anderson, one of Stefansson's closest collaborators during the second expedition, also had a relationship with Pannigabluk.[13] That story, however, should be taken with a grain of salt. The claim about the sexual relationship between Anderson and Pannigabluk may have served to justify Stefansson's rejection of his Inuit family. Anderson also participated in the third expedition, during which and after the relations between Stefansson and Anderson became increasingly tense and hostile. Judging from Stefansson's diaries, however, the relationship between him and Anderson was fairly smooth during the second expedition. He repeatedly speaks of "friendship" and "generosity," although he always uses the formal title "Dr. A." or "Dr. Anderson."[14]

After he left the Arctic, Stefansson apparently dated several white women. Rosie Stefansson offers the following story, told by her grandfather's relatives in the Icelandic community in Victoria on Vancouver Island:

> There was a woman that he used to go out with before Evelyn [Stefansson Nef]. I forget what was her name, but he used to make a mistake and call her "Pann." And she'd get really upset. He'd make the mistake, you know, he'd say "Pann!" And, you know, "Can I have this Pann?" And she'd get really upset.

That relationship did not last long.

Apparently, the only written evidence available indicating Stefansson's recognition of his responsibility for Alex is a letter from one of Stefansson's friends, Richard Finnie, a writer, photographer, and filmmaker:

> According to a story I heard many years ago, there was at least one occasion when Stef, albeit non-verbally, seemed to take responsibility for Alex. In the middle of a conversation with some white men at Herschel Island, Stef was approached by Pannigabluk, who said, "Missionary going to baptize Alex; give me five dollars." Without comment, Stef fished out a bill from his pocket and Pannigabluk marched off with it.[15]

As we have seen, Alex and Pannigabluk were baptized by Whittaker at Herschel Island in August 1915, in the middle of Stefansson's third expedition. The day before Alex and Pannigabluk were baptized, Stefansson wrote in his diary: "Started for Herschel after half an hour at Baillie [Island]." The following day he has this to say: "Writing—chiefly personal. Expect to [. . .] get my mail tomorrow." Whittaker seems to have been persistent in his battle with paganism, and some time after he baptized Alex and Pannigabluk, he publicly criticized Stefansson for neglecting his wife and child. Stefansson, one may note, has this observation about Whittaker and his view of baptism, in a diary entry from 12 January 1912:

> *Baptism* was explained by Mr. W. as making a man's head and its surroundings shine so it could be seen in the dark like the light of a window. Ilavinirk saw one baptised man [. . .] last summer, but the halo did not show because it was not dark, but he has no doubt it can be seen now that it is winter with dark nights. [. . .] Anaktak's mother Kajak refused to accept the faith. Mr. Whittaker then told them that they should test her with fire—if it burnt her she was to take the faith, if not she would have some ground for her pretensions to know more than other people as to what should be or should not be believed.

Whatever Stefansson's reasons for silencing the issue of Alex's paternity, Pannigabluk, too, seems to have been quiet about it. According to her granddaughter Rosie, Pannigabluk, herself "a strong woman," asked her family "never to tell" about the connection with Stefansson.[16] Pannigabluk, of course, was well aware of Stefansson's diary and perhaps she forbade him to write about Alex and their relationship, which would partly explain Stefansson's silence. Alex, however, kept the Stefansson name, and so do his children.

Soon after Stefansson's death, on 26 August 1962, the issue of his "Eskimo family" surfaced again, this time in the letters of friends and publishers. About five months later, Stefansson's biographer D. M. LeBourdais wrote a long and illuminating letter, inquiring about the matter. LeBourdais says that a publisher he was negotiating with (A. Wang) suggested certain changes to the manuscript. It is worth citing the publisher at some length.

> We are convinced that it is wrong to omit any reference to Stefansson's wife and son. . . . these facts are an important part of Stefansson's story, and it is bound to be mentioned in articles, reviews, and other books. What we think the galleys call for is the addition by LeBourdais of a description of that situation. . . . This more than anything would make the book worth buying. The facts will probably be discussed soon, and the apparent conspiracy to keep

> these facts from being well known cannot last. LeBourdais is in a particularly strong position to do us all a favor by setting forth the facts clearly and simply. Many people ignorant of the whole story think Stefansson contemptible in his apparent neglect of wife and son.[17]

"Unfortunately," LeBourdais comments, "this is a subject Stef never discussed with me."

LeBourdais added, citing Noice's work, that Pannigabluk and her five-year-old son were with Stefansson aboard the *Polar Bear* in 1915 and again on Melville Island in 1916.[18] He speculates that the fact that Stefansson makes no mention of Pannigabluk in *The Friendly Arctic* "might suggest that she was present in a private capacity and not a member of the expedition, as was the case during the previous expedition." This seems a reasonable conclusion. While Jenness's diaries make no references to Stefansson's wife, Pannigabluk is frequently mentioned. Thus, on 27 April 1914, Jenness writes that "Pannigavlu and her son went to the *Polar Bear* to obtain a tent and are expected back tomorrow," and, again on 27 May the same year, that "Pannigabluk had carried off a number of things from Martin's Point, a trunk of Stefansson's among them."[19] There are few references to Pannigabluk in Stefansson's own diary from the third expedition. Nevertheless, her name occurs. Thus, on 20 September 1915, Stefansson writes that "People moved into house except Seymor's family and Pannigabluk," and the following day he adds that "Seymor and Pannigabluk moved into the house." Nagy concludes from her oral history, partly based on tape recordings in Holman in the 1960s or early 1970s, that although she is not mentioned by Stefansson "as part of his . . . Canadian Arctic Expedition, it seems Pannigabluk was also there" since she is in the narrative of one of the informants.[20]

Stefansson's grandchildren suggest that when Stefansson left the Arctic after the second expedition (in 1912) he told his wife that he would return. However, Pannigabluk did not hear from him until the third expedition was in full course. According to the grandchildren, she went along with her son Alex to see Stefansson at Herschel Island. Finding him with his crew, she seized the tie around his neck and scolded him in front of his company for failing to stick to his word. The scene was reportedly witnessed by the local police, which attempted to intervene, but Stefansson told them that this was his sole responsibility. Following this incident, Stefansson and Pannigabluk lived together for some time. Pannigabluk spoke no English, but Alex quickly became bilingual, fluent in both English and Inuvialuktun. Stefansson seems to have taught him to read and write, an important asset for Alex later on when dealing with Western whalers and merchants.

Interestingly, one of the hand-colored images that Stefansson is reported to have shown during his many talks on the Arctic exhibits Pannigabluk and Alex (see plate 16). The relevant caption in the files in the Stefansson collection refers to "Copper Inuit woman and child outside by a skin doorway," with no indication of their relationship to Stefansson. The caption for the same photograph in black-and-white reads: "Pannigabluk, forewoman of those employed to make clothes for the ice party, and her little boy Eric." The photograph was reportedly taken on 18 March 1914, during Stefansson's third expedition, a few days after Alex's fourth birthday. Stefansson, one should add, is unlikely to be responsible for the errors in either of the captions; it is improbable that Stefansson tried to deliberately mislead his audience about the names and ethnicity of his Inuit family, although he would not otherwise dwell on their identity. Nevertheless, the confusion in names and identities is a little odd, given that Stefansson seems to have included the images in his arctic shows. Unfortunately, Stefansson's diaries from the third expedition begin on 22 March 1914, four days after the photograph was reportedly taken. The image just mentioned was probably taken by Wilkins, the chief photographer of the third expedition. Wilkins writes in his diaries:

> Pannigabluk and her child came in to see us. She is the Eskimo woman who travelled with V.S. for some time during his wanderings in the Arctic. [. . .] When looking down on the child from the side there is a striking resemblance to V.S. to be seen. Dr. Anderson seems indignant that V.S. had spoken so much about keeping the white men from intermingling with the Eskimo while he himself had a child up here. There was a report in one of the American papers to that effect before we left Victoria. The little boy is very bright looking and has rather pleasant features although his mother is particularly plain.[21]

Richard Finnie, Stefansson's friend, responded to LeBourdais's queries about Stefansson's family by saying that since Stefansson himself chose not to talk about the matter, "I should be disinclined as an old friend, now that he is dead, to try to make something out of it to satisfy a publisher's notion that it would help sell books."[22] A decade later, however, Richard Finnie notes in a letter to Erika S. Parmi, the Stefansson Collection librarian at Dartmouth College:

> I met Alex Stefansson at Herschel in 1930 and again in the Mackenzie Delta in 1939, when I visited with and photographed him and his family. . . .

The fact of Alex's existence and identity has been well known to northerners and northern travelers for many years . . . I once spoke of him to Stef, but he seemed not to hear. . . .

I don't want to offend or embarrass . . . anyone . . . , but now—with the principals dead—it is a matter of history. If I don't deal with it, someone else is bound to and perhaps with an attitude less charitable than mine. I should like to speculate on why Stef chose to blot it out.[23]

Richard Finnie also wrote a letter to Edward M. Weyer, a friend and Arctic scholar, with similar queries about missing facts. Weyer responded with a long letter.

The only time I can recall Alex's name being brought up when Stef was present was when you were showing him your album of photographs recently brought back from the Arctic. My recollection is that you pointed to a picture and said, "there's Alex," and Stef just went on to the next page.[24]

Somewhat apologetic, Weyer adds:

Eskimos would not have [the]. . . problem . . . within their own culture [of hiding the identity of the father of an adopted child]; and I hope Alex didn't. As you know, it is less important who a child's parents are than whose name-soul he is given, which in large measure determines who he is. Eskimos name their children after departed persons whose memory is so esteemed that they want the same qualities of personality to be "reborn" in another individual.

Richard Finnie responded a few days later, apparently with a refreshed memory:

The only time I remember actually speaking of Alex to Stef was . . . in the summer of 1931 [1930?]. . . I said, "While at Herschel Island I met Alex." (I doubt that I said "your son," because I knew that the subject was touchy and didn't want to risk offending him.) Stef's response was that there were people he didn't remember in the Mackenzie Delta area, and he immediately spoke of something else. . . .

If Stef did not really recognize Alex as his son, he could hardly have studied photographs of him in adulthood, for Alex bore a striking resemblance to Stef as a young man and was the only half-breed Eskimo I ever saw with a cleft chin.[25]

Despite his original reluctance to discuss Stefansson's son, Finnie later published a paper outlining "Stefansson's mystery." "Why," Finnie asks, "did he never publicly recognize or repudiate an Arctic family he was widely alleged to have founded?"[26]

Helm, just as Finnie, was struck by the striking similarity of Alex and Stefansson.

> Not long after the arctic sojourn with . . . the Stefansson family [Alex, Mabel Okpik, and their children], I went to an anthropology meeting [in Philadelphia] . . . , a featured speaker was Stefansson. As he stepped out on the stage, I saw Alex's [physical] proportions.[27]

THE INTIMATE ARCTIC: THE DIARIES

Given the comments of some of Stefansson's friends and companions on the matter of the Eskimo family, it is pertinent to take a look at his diaries. Pannigabluk is mentioned frequently in the diaries, often simply as "Pan." At first her name appears only sporadically. Her name (spelled as "Pungua-bluk") is first mentioned on 22 July in 1908. On 29 March the following year, Stefansson remarks that "the widow Pannigabluk" is, according to a letter from Anderson, "also" at Flaxman Island, Alaska. Her presence is noted a few days later, in connection with cephalic measurements:

> Pannigabluk, widow, Father Kuraluk, mother Port Clarence—widow 184–141–142–140 No lober [100+].[1]

From then on Pannigabluk's name appears regularly, indicating that she is a fairly permanent member of the camps of Stefansson and his men, until the end of 1911. As already mentioned, Stefansson's publications typically refer to Pannigabluk in connection with the everyday tasks of looking after camps, cooking, seaming tents, and making clothes. Such statements also appear in the diaries; "Pannigabluk made herself the finest boots I have seen," Stefansson once notes.[2]

Judging from the diaries, however, Pannigabluk had a much more important role than the publications indicate as one of Stefansson's key informants. Sometimes, it seems, Pannigabluk divided her time between her roles as informant and seamstress:

> Rewriting text of 'Man who married a goose' . . . trouble to verify text from Pannigabluk who is burdened with other work and easily gets tired anyway . . . Pannigabluk yesterday finished sewing a caribou skin tent cover and now working on boots.[3]

At one point, Stefansson suggests that Pannigabluk is more efficient than he himself in eliciting ethnographic information from the people they meet.[4] Pannigabluk frequently comments upon events that occur along the way and upon the people Stefansson and his companions run into. She elaborates on the names of Inuit people and native groups, the interpretation of dreams, seances, shamanism, hunting methods, polyandry, the raising of children, beliefs about animals, and numerous other issues. Stefansson, however, much like most if not all contemporary ethnographers, seems to maintain a private-public distinction, unable to think of Pannigabluk as a full collaborator in the making of ethnography. At times the diary indicates that in Stefansson's view Pannigabluk is a little too talkative, a point, as we have seen, underlined in some of his publications.

Although Stefansson makes no reference in the diaries to intimate relations with Pannigabluk, between the probable time of Alex's conception and the day of delivery there are a few significant entries involving Pannigabluk. There are no direct statements about Stefansson's relations with Pannigabluk, but some of these entries might be interpreted as evidence for intimate relations, indicating Stefansson's concerns for the pregnant Pannigabluk, for her well-being, and for the future of their child. These entries are generally presented here in the order in which they occur. According to Alex's children, Alex was born on 10 March 1910.

On 19 June 1909, around the time of Alex's conception, there is an entry about Pannigabluk's account of her brother and her mother. A few days later Stefansson writes:

> Pannigabluk could not sleep and wanted to go off duck hunting at 1: A.M. I had just been out to stop a dog fight when she told me so. I suggested her cooking instead. . . . Meanwhile I hunted but got no game [. . .] Woke Anderson and B[illy] at 4: A.M They had slept only four hours and P[annigabluk] and I nothing.[5]

Significantly, given the complicated relations between them later on, at this point Anderson and Stefansson were in the same camp. In the following months, Pannigabluk is mentioned more often than anyone else. Thus, there is an entry about Pannigabluk's body: "Pannigabluk plucks out, whenever they appear, any hairs from her armpit. Looks as if there would be quite a growth there if not plucked."[6] A few days later the diary records:

> Pannigabluk tells me Mary . . . is now a "bad woman." "In what way?" "She scolds all the time. Most women who live with white men get in the habit of scolding, contradicting and quarreling."[7]

Elsewhere the diaries refer to "race-blending," listing the names of people living with a person of a different racial background.[8] Reading some of these diary entries, one gets the impression of Pannigabluk as a strong, capable, and independent woman. Perhaps her statement about the "habit of scolding" testifies to her awareness of the danger of becoming too close to Stefansson, the potential threat to her autonomy posed by a stable relationship with one of the white men.

Once Stefansson includes a long comment ("Immaculate conceptions") about fatherless children:

> Pannigabluk says Eskimo women frequently have children that have no father—sometimes they die at or before birth, sometimes they live. When they live they do not differ noticably from people that have fathers. Some women are afraid of these fatherless children and kill them at birth. . . . Pannigabluk herself has had a fatherless birth—an abortion at Oliktok last spring when she was on her way west with Billy and Anderson. The fetus was about three inches long. She had never had connection with a man since the death of her first (only) husband—a full year previous the abortion.[9]

Again, Anderson is around, although he often travelled independently of Stefansson and Pannigabluk, looking for zoological specimens.

On 1 November Stefansson notes a "change of plans": "Pannigabluk announced this morning she would like to stay here to protect our meat and skins—and to avoid the trip to the coast, doubtless, for she is no great traveller. The offer was quickly accepted. I had thought of asking it but had refrained as I thought she would consider it a too lonesome job." About a month later, on returning to Pannigabluk who is alone in her camp, Stefansson comments: "found Pannigabluk all well up and cooking over a cheerful open fire in a cozy house . . . really a rather pleasant homecoming."[10] In his biography, Hunt notes the event, emphasizing that the hungry and weary travelers "staggered into camp," but he fails to notice its significance as a potential commentary on Stefansson's intimate relationship with Pannigabluk.[11] When Pannigabluk is about six months pregnant, Stefansson notes: "Pannigabluk sick ~~severe~~ stomach. Cannot travel."[12] Pannigabluk is sick for several days, but so is also at least one other person in the camp. On 23 December, we learn: "Have made no entry for a week because of no lamp at night. Today I am first in the house during the light hours—except Saturday, when my diary was in Pannigabluk's camp and I at home."

When Alex was six days old, Stefansson wrote a long entry focusing on Pannigabluk, entitled "Eskimos way of thinking": "When hungry . . . and impatient for me to come back, Pannigabluk said she used to have seances. . . ."[13] At the time of Alex's birth, Stefansson and Pannigabluk were not in the same camp and apparently Pannigabluk wanted him to stay with her. The entry, however, continues somewhat surprisingly on an entirely different note, with doubts about Pannigabluk's credibility and ethnographic accuracy. It seems that her failure to exactly forecast the success of hunting expeditions motivated one of the Inuit companions, Havinuk, to comment about her character: "Know now what sort of a woman Pannigabluk is, and will not believe her in anything she says. If she had spirits she would [have] told the truth, for spirits know everything and never lie." Perhaps in noting this Stefansson is distancing himself from Pannigabluk under the emotional strain of fatherhood. These remain simply speculations, however.

In the months following Alex's birth, Pannigabluk is frequently mentioned, particularly in connection with domestic issues. There is a long and interesting entry on "certain remarks and deeds of Pannigabluk's" that focuses on cleanliness, including the relativity of definitions of "clean" and "dirty" food utensils:

> On my telling Pannigabluk one day that certain water was dirty she said that was no matter, she was just going to wash the teapot inside with it. I am considered a sort of renegade because I insist on the teapots and my own cup remaining unwashed. I have often heard my natives tell strangers that with many good qualities I have the failing, differing thus from most white men, of caring little for cleanliness in my food utensils. That I prefer manifestly dirty dishes to apparently clean ones in an Eskimo house, is considered a curious eccentricity; some seem to think it is "put on."[14]

Moreover, Stefansson's diaries make several references to various issues relating to children and reproduction, including the health of unborn children, the practice of naming, native beliefs about name-souls, and taboos relating to menstruation. Often Pannigabluk is the source:

> Pannigabluk tells that among the western Eskimos . . . a woman who wishes her (unborn) child to be healthy and strong should eat the cartilage between the bones of the knee joint of caribou.[15]

Once Pannigabluk criticizes the beliefs of particular Inuit groups about children's upbringing:

> [They] believe that if a child "before he gets understanding" (before seven or eight years) is continuously forbidden to do things it wants to do, continually told "don't do that," "stop your noise" etc., [his]. . . ears become like dog's ears.[16]

It seems reasonable to assume that these entries reflect, albeit indirectly, Pannigabluk's and Stefansson's concerns with the welfare of a particular infant, their son Alex. As we have seen, Stefansson's relationships with Pannigabluk and his son are not entirely submerged in his diaries. The discussion in some of the entries quoted above, concerning pregnancy, children's health, upbringing, fatherless children, and Inuit women who live with white men, does seem to have a personal twist. Also, the presence of the body and bodily experience, largely absent elsewhere in both Stefansson's publications and the diaries (except in the occasional reference to sickness), is hardly a coincidence.

RACE, GENDER, AND ETHNICITY

The empty spaces in Stefansson's ethnography, imagery, and writings—in particular his relative silence on Pannigabluk, her role as key informant, and her relationship with the author—raise interesting questions about ethnographic representation. I suggest that Stefansson's silence in this respect be considered within the context of the history of arctic explorations. To draw upon Pratt's analysis of the "mystique of reciprocity" in imperial travel writings, the mystique seems to break down when Stefansson faces a real case of reciprocity, involving his relationship with Pannigabluk and his son.[1] At the same time, Stefansson's silence about the ethnographic role of Pannigabluk reflects a more general private-public distinction, a distinction characteristic of the gendered view of early twentieth-century science.[2] The arctic regions were seen as the last empty spaces in the colonization of the globe, the final frontier of "Man." Arctic explorers not only embodied the epitome of manliness, they turned the poles into theaters of male rivalry.[3] The poles offered the ultimate opportunity for white, Western, masculine inscription.

Such a bias, Bloom points out, structured the texts produced by arctic explorers in that the "complexity of the relation between master and servant in the pursuit of science . . . was consistently written out of the script."[4] One of Stefansson's key informants, Natkusiak (also known as Billy Banksland), was Stefansson's travelling companion on Victoria Island in 1911 when the two contacted the Kanghiryuarmiut of Prince Albert Sound. "Natkusiak's children and grandchildren obviously take great pride in their ancestor's accomplishments," as Condon points out, "feeling also that he perhaps has never received the recognition due him as an Inuit explorer."[5] Stefansson's grandchildren make a similar point about Pannigabluk's role for Stefansson's fieldwork and ethnography. As Rosie put it, "and *he* got all the credit!"[6] Georgina Stefansson explains:

> He didn't want to give anybody credit for surviving up here. Helping him survive. Because in his books he always acted like he's the hero. . . . It says: I went there, killed a whole bunch of caribou, and my seamstress and cook cleaned and sewed and everything, our clothes. Like it was never, he never talked about it as a mutual agreement. . . . Like, they . . . I don't know. . . . They mutually agreed to live together and survive together. And all of the sudden she wasn't included in the survival. . . . Like, they were fellow travelers instead of being people that did a lot of the trapping and hunting.

It seems necessary, then, to qualify Stefansson's individualistic account of his engagement with the "friendly" Arctic. As Georgina Stefansson put it:

> We were always told, I guess, by our dad, and all the people up here, that my grandfather wouldn't have survived if he wasn't with her. . . . Because he didn't know how to hunt and trap. Or fish or anything.

Rosie Stefansson similarly explains, with reference to a debate between Pannigabluk and Stefansson on traveling on sled in dangerous places:

> He was going, he went all by himself. And she tried to tell him that, you know, that was not the right time or that it wasn't good to go there, on account of a certain time of the year, and . . . he wouldn't listen. So he got somebody else to go with him. But when they came back the next year he was just about dead. She had to nurse him back to health. That's what she told us. She said: After that he sure don't think he's smart. That's what she talked to us like that. Your grandfather thought he was so smart he could live without me or anything. He could've died if it wasn't for me. So if you learn how to live white-man way how are you gonna live on the land. You could starve to death. And you don't know where to look for things. . . . He thought he was smart and he took off alone, cause she didn't want to go with him on account of the dangers of the, you know, you could get stranded somewhere.

The American explorer Peary and Stefansson were probably the most visible early twentieth-century explorers. Peary was an ambitious explorer who claimed in 1909 to have discovered the North Pole, although his claim was challenged by another American explorer, Frederick Cook. Much of what Bloom has to say about Peary's attitude to exploration and the Arctic applies to Stefansson as well. Both Peary and Stefansson, Bloom suggests, "anchored the authority of their discourse under the banner of science and progress."[7] And in this discourse, women were, by definition, removed from the scientific enterprise, muted in Ardener's sense.[8] The early Stefansson, then, was very much a man of his time.

Stefansson and Peary, however, exhibit important differences in personality and context. Peary made it clear, for instance, that he had an Inuit "mistress," at times employing pornographic language and imagery.[9] In his autobiography, published in 1898, Peary refers to the "embarrassing position" of "being left alone and unprotected, with five buxom and oleaginous ladies, of a race of naive children of nature, who are hampered by no feelings of false modesty or bashfulness in expressing their tender feelings."[10] Stefansson's publications and diaries have little if anything of this sort. Also, while Peary had no ethnographic ambitions, Stefansson thought of himself as both anthropologist and explorer. As a Canadian immigrant, Stefansson may generally have been overplaying the desire to fit the British hegemony.[11]

No doubt the roots of Stefansson's silence about his intimate relationship with Pannigabluk are partly to be found in the Icelandic community in Canada and North Dakota in which he grew up. To some extent, the cultural baggage of late-medieval Iceland informed the North-American Icelandic community's concept of the exotic, and, by extension, Stefansson's ideas of the native groups of North America. Early Icelanders often contrasted their social world with those of distant "others" across the sea, engaging in their own bizarre form of othering and cross-cultural comparison. Indeed, some of the medieval sagas suggest a form of folk Orientalism, largely based on foreign accounts imported through the gateway of Byzantium: an Orientalism informed by classical Latin heritage and the hegemony of the Greek empire. Oriental stories reached early Iceland through a long network of Nordic travellers, Viking raiders, and merchants, by way of Russia or the Mediterranean. While partly based on travels and observations, such accounts were heavily reliant on the texts of classical geographers and encyclopedic works. Eventually, they found their way into Icelandic texts. None of this, of course, is unique to the world view of early Icelanders, for similar ideas captured the imagination of other Europeans. There were some sporadic direct contacts, however, with alien groups close at home. Some of the Icelandic sagas, indeed, including *Eiríks saga,* refer to indigenous peoples on the western shores of the North Atlantic. We know that Norse settlers from Iceland and Norway stayed for extended periods in neighboring Greenland and North America. Viking settlements have been discovered in several places in both Greenland and L'Anse aux Meadows in northern Newfoundland, and a good deal of archaeological scholarship has attempted to explain why these settlements did not survive. In the days of

FIGURE 8. Stefansson, hunting in winter. Canadian Arctic Expedition. *(Courtesy of Dartmouth College Library, MMS CAE/SAP 010 9A/10A.)*

early Norse exploration across the North Atlantic more than thousand years ago, the Icelandic concept of *skrælingi* ("native," "barbarian")—a term several times used by Stefansson in his diaries in relation to the Inuit—referred to an inhabitant of Greenland (Eskimo or Inuit). Although in Old Icelandic or Old Norse ("Danish Tongue," as it used to be called) the concept of *skrælingi* was obviously not a neutral one, first-hand accounts by early Icelanders of their western neighbors were far less fantastic and ethnocentric than their saga accounts of the Orient.[12]

The limited experiences of "real" others, and the monolithic Icelandic cultural background, were unlikely to engender serious interest among Icelanders in comparative cultural or social anthropology. In North America, however, social life presented the immigrant Icelandic community with new experiences and pressing questions. In his autobiography, Stefansson described his encounter with members of the Sioux tribe, "the very tribe that the Icelandic community so greatly feared": "I cannot recall another time in my life when I made such a quick and thorough readjustment of long-held ideas."[13] Perhaps such encounters sparked Stefansson's interest in exploration and ethnographic description. Also, they may have informed his lasting negative impression of Indians compared to his rather generous impression of the Inuit. For Stefansson, some aboriginal peoples seem to have been more equal than others. He comments as follows upon his experience from the first expedition:

> One thing I noticed about the Eskimos in particular was their graceful, free-swinging walk. This was in direct contrast to the jerky, almost furtive movements of the forest Indians. I distinctively began to feel that the Eskimos were a superior race.[14]

Later on, when reflecting in his diaries on the relationship between social and ecological change in the Arctic, Stefansson indicates that the Indians, in contrast to the Inuit, are just as afraid of the "friendly" Arctic as Westerners:

> At present the caribou has in winter a wide zone of safety between the Indians who dare not face the barren ground and the Eskimo who prefer the sea coast. But the Eskimo fear the woodless barrens about as much as a fish fears water.[15]

For Stefansson, the mobile Inuit hunters seemed more heroic and appealing than the more settled and agrarian Indians.

While Stefansson usually provided the personal names of his Inuit companions, he tended to refer to others with the generic phrase "the Indian." This practice may both reflect Inuit stereotypes and those of the North American Icelandic community. The attitude of the Icelandic community towards aboriginal peoples, however, was both complex and contradictory. There was racism as well as admiration.[16] Brydon's analysis of public documents from Manitoba indicates that Icelandic settlers colonized the property of a Saulteaux-Cree hunter-farmer, John Ramsey, refusing to pay any compensation.[17] Ramsey claimed his rights in a written declaration in 1879, without any success.

The general Victorian view of sex and marriage among North American Icelanders may also have informed Stefansson's writings and his silence on his Inuit family. While he was a committed atheist and ignored the fervent religious sectarianism of the North American Icelandic community, he seems to have subscribed to its puritanical attitudes to sex. Apparently, whether at home or in the field, he was reluctant to talk about sexual matters.

Stefansson's life and career seem to have been frequent topics of discussion among the North American Icelandic community. While he was a public hero, both here and in Iceland, he was also the target of critique and cynicism. A poem, "White Eskimo," written by one of the leading Icelandic-Canadian poets, Guttormur J. Guttormsson, has the following lines:

> *Eftir Vilhjálms utanför til Eskimóa*
> *Hvítu fólki fór að snjóa.*[18]
>
> [With Vilhjálmur's trip to the Eskimo
> white people it began to snow.]

The poet seems to catch on to Stefansson's dual role as the father of an Inuit child and the inventor of "Blond Eskimo." The pun was effective; Stefansson was said to leave behind him a trail of whites, real or imaginary. In one of the narratives of the North American Icelandic community, Pannigabluk is reported to have appeared on the coast every spring for a few years, when the ships started to arrive, "waiting" in case Stefansson would return to his Inuit family. Interestingly, Pannigabluk's grandchildren tell a similar story. Whether true or not, the existence of the Icelandic narrative indicates that the Icelandic community was well aware of Alex's existence and, perhaps, less judgmental about the Inuit connection than Stefansson's silence might lead one to believe. When Guttormsson was introduced to Stefansson at a Canadian-Icelandic gathering in 1958, Stefansson turned away saying that he "knew none of the young poets." According to Bessason, who witnessed the occasion, "sparks would fly between the two men."[19]

The so-called "crisis in representation" has been partly driven by conflicting accounts of sexual behavior, by Freeman's challenge to Mead's ethnography of Samoans and the responses of his critics.[20] While Malinowski and some other anthropologists have produced detailed descriptions of the "sexual life of savages," and such descriptions have sometimes generated much heat and demanded public attention, ethnographers have rarely elaborated on their own sexual involvement in the field.[21] One reason is that sexual relations "refuse to stay objective and tidy; they bring real pain, joy and suffering to what is generally presented as an academic exercise."[22] Some Inuit accounts, including that of Stefansson's granddaughter, suggest that Stefansson and Pannigabluk were "husband and wife," "married" in Iñupiaq terms.[23] Given Iñupiaq practice and custom, the relationship of Stefansson and Pannigabluk must translate as "marriage." As Burch points out, a conjugal family was created "when a man and woman took up residence together and had sexual relations. That was all there was to it; Eskimos are among the few people in the world who did not recognize a marriage with some kind of ceremony."[24] As we have seen, however, the

FIGURE 9. Postcard: Stefansson among Icelanders in North Dakota, probably Edinburgh. Photo: N.N. *(Courtesy of the National Museum of Iceland; MMS 44552.)*

Stefanssons were not just husband and wife in the broad definition of Inuit custom; such an understanding was underlined in the records of the Anglican mission from 1915.

Stefansson's diaries sometimes discuss the sexual behavior of the Inuit. Thus, he compares attitudes and practices relating to "illicit" relations among Alaskan, Mackenzie, and Copper Inuit:

> Alaskan Eskimo generally . . . believe that if a woman has difficult labor it is because she has had sexual relations with someone and failed to tell about it. For that reason a woman in labor will rehearse all her relations with men from her youth up, but especially any that have occurred during pregnancy. This custom was unknown at the Mackenzie . . . till after the ships began bringing western women. In general, among the Mackenzie Eskimo there was about the same subterfuge and secrecy about "illicit" sexual relations that there is among Europeans. . . . Alaskan Eskimo considered it a duty of both parties to tell at once; otherwise serious misfortunes would follow. "Illicit" sexual relations were seldom, if ever, kept secret among them. Among the Copper Eskimo there is a semblance of secrecy in some cases. . . .[25]

Once during his stay among the Copper Eskimo, Stefansson notes: "Have seen no sign of the 'sexual hospitality' which Mackenzie Eskimo have told me was part of ordinary courtesy to a guest."[26] The practice of "wife exchange" is mentioned a few times, once involving the parents of one of his key informants:

> This is seldom more than one night at a time, and seldom except upon the two families meeting after a protracted separation. After another separation this may be repeated. This practice seems to be seldom indulged in except by close friends, partners, sort of blood brothers.[27]

Stefansson seems to be referring to the practice of "co-marriage," which is often misleadingly called "wife trading" in both popular and scientific writings. In Iñupiaq society, a man and a woman who engaged in sexual intercourse were considered married for the rest of their lives, even if they never had intercourse again.[28] This kind of marriage was different from that of residential spouses, but it was marriage nevertheless. Significantly, the children that any of the four ever had were considered siblings. The chance of observing such marriage during fieldwork might not have been that great, but the Inuit may have realized that such stories captured the imagination of white explorers.

A satisfactory explanation for Stefansson's reluctance to discuss his marriage with Pannigabluk or their son Alex should, perhaps, take into account the relations of Pannigabluk with Stefansson's collaborator Rudolph Anderson. It is clear from the diaries that Pannigabluk occasionally accompanied Anderson, who sometimes followed a trail different from that of the expedition leader, and stayed in Anderson's camps rather than Stefansson's. One of Stefansson's last diary entries about Pannigabluk also refers to Anderson. The last words are strangely abrupt:

> Dr. Anderson started for Baillie Islands at ca. 9: A.M—took two sleds, thirteen dogs, but very little meat as we fear hunger before he comes back in case I keep sick. Dr. Anderson took Palaiyak, Tannaumirk and Pannigabluk—the last to leave us permanently.[29]

The entry continues with some words, but the author has scribbled over them, apparently to make sure they are not readable.

Significantly, perhaps, Stefansson was unwell at this time. A few days prior to their separation he remarks:

> For the last two days . . . I have had a headache of varying severity and with symptoms which I take to be those of some kidney trouble—apparently chiefly the right kidney. Dr. Anderson had rubbed me energetically several times, applying counter irritant (capsoline) of which we have little left having

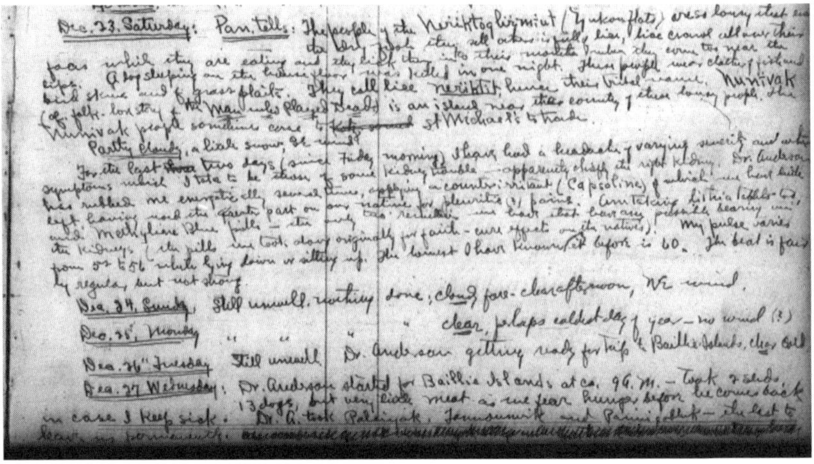

FIGURE 10. The diary entry about Pannigabluk leaving Stefansson "permanently." The diaries, December 27, 1911. *(Courtesy of Dartmouth College Library.)*

> used the greater part on our natives. . . . My pulse varies from 57 to 56 while lying down and sitting up. The lowest I have known before is 60. The beat is fairly regular but not strong.[30]

In *My Life with the Eskimo,* Stefansson refers to the split between himself and Pannigabluk, saying that she "had made up her mind to sever her connection with our party."[31] Perhaps Anderson and Stefansson were never sure which of them was the father of Alex, until Alex turned out to be the spitting image of Stefansson. As the leader of an expedition, Stefansson said, he was *chosen* to be the father.[32] There is no evidence, however, to my knowledge, of any contemporary rumor in the Arctic implicating Anderson as a father or husband, nor are there any personal letters to that effect. Moreover, Alex's children think the story about Anderson being Alex's father rather "funny."

Before starting his journey back to "civilization," after the second expedition, Stefansson settled his accounts with some of his key informants, including Pannigabluk. The settlements are described in the following manner:

> *Settlement with natives:* We owe Ilavinirk $\$600^{00}$. He asks me to take 400^{00} of this to New York and send him up $\$200^{00}$ worth of goods in 1913 and $\$200^{00}$ in 1914. In 1913 he wants 1000 35 cal. Winchester cartridges (for box magazine heavy rifle) 1000 30–30 cal. cartridge, [. . .] some cod lines, three or four aluminum pots, [a] shot gun, two [. . .] primus stoves, large (10 × 16 or so) wall tent, silk or linen, 100 yds. fairly heavy drilling or light duck, some kahki, 50 lbs. Golden Gate (or similar) English breakfast tea, and such small articles as I know they would like, up to value of $\$200^{00}$. I am to arrange for credit with Cottle for $\$200^{00}$ to be used by Ilavinirk. We owe Tannaumirk $\$200^{00}$: Dr. Anderson will give him some things and charge them, and I will try to get credit with Cottle for the balance. We owe Pannigabluk about $\$250^{00}$, but she is drawing a monthly allowance from the "Rosie H." for which we pay in fox skins at ca. $\$5^{00}$ for skin: Anderson will get her account whenever she shall leave Baillie for the Mackenzie and I am to try arrange credit for her with Cottle.[33]

Perhaps Stefansson's reference to the "monthly allowance" for Pannigabluk implicitly assumed responsibility for her and Alex.

We will probably never know the exact dynamics of the Anderson-Pannigabluk-Stefansson triangle, if there was a triangle at all. They may, however, partly explain Stefansson's silence about both Alex and Pannigabluk.

Also, they may help to account for the fierce controversy between Anderson and Stefansson later on.[34] Anderson not only joined forces with ethnocentric missionaries in their critique of Stefansson's approach to life in the Arctic and his respect for the wisdom of "illiterates" and "primitives," he also became one of Stefansson's most brutal critics. Decades after his collaboration with Stefansson ended, he would elaborate on Stefansson's communist inclinations, with all the implications such statements might have during the witch-hunts of the McCarthy era.[35] In 1950, Stefansson was called to a hearing at the Attorney General's office in Concord, New Hampshire, concerning knowledge of communist activities. His major scholarly ambition, the editing of the *Encyclopedia Arctica,* a massive twenty-volume work that began in 1946, had to be aborted due to Cold War accusations of communist inclinations. Stefansson was a controversial figure and his style of leadership as well as his cultural relativism, emphasizing the necessity and the charm of flowing with the rhythms and demands of the "friendly Arctic," annoyed many of his fellow travelers and competitors, including Anderson. Sexual competition and jealousy may have amplified such personal conflict.

While Stefansson was publically accused of communist inclinations and activity, his son Alex would emphasize his heroic battle against Russian expansionism. Here, Rosie Stefansson reflects upon her father's account:

> He said: You had a white man grandfather. White man grandfather! Yeah. He left when I was nine years old. . . . He was an explorer, and then he explained to me that . . . the Russians were right across the ocean and they were trying to take over and then there was different countries fighting over each other's country. And then the Queen wanted to claim this area and my grandfather was one of them. That's the way he explained it to me . . . He'd tell us: He had to, that was his job. So he said; What if your grandfather wasn't doing this Rosie? We would have been Russians maybe. Maybe we would have been claimed by somebody else, but he was here to claim this land and that is what we should be thankful for. . . . That's the way it is for white people.

Despite his important ethnographic contributions, Stefansson's texts, I have argued, no less than those of Malinowski and most of their contemporaries, are rather weak on the context of fieldwork and the making of ethnography. Stefansson has little to say about his relations with Pannigabluk and her ethnographic contribution, although, clearly, she was not just "around." Pannigabluk was presented as primarily a domestic worker, with no formal recognition of her role as either spouse, partner, or key informant. Her role is reduced to that of a talkative seamstress. The diaries, however, hint at Stefansson's intimate relationships with Pannigabluk. The frequency and timing of Stefansson's entries on pregnancy, children's health, upbringing, fatherless children, and Inuit women who live with white men is unlikely to be a coincidence. Some of the entries give an impression of Pannigabluk as a rather strong woman, suspicious, perhaps, that too much closeness might lead to degradation of self and character.

I have tried to account for Stefansson's reticence to admit and seriously address his intimate relationships in the field. The larger social context—the relations of race, ethnicity, and gender—characteristic of the expanding West at the beginning of the twentieth century is the most important factors. Generally, Stefansson presents himself, in both his diaries and his publications, in terms of the heroic image of a masculine hunter and explorer, engaged in dangerous excursions into the wild domain of natives and animals, extending the realm of rationality, science, and Western civilization into that of "Nature." For him and many of his contemporaries, fieldwork and geographical explorations were, above all, exercises for testing and strengthening the sensibilities of manhood against all kinds of odds.

Accounts of such gallant journeys inevitably placed the natives, particularly women, in the back seat, whatever their real contributions as spouses, partners, friends, key informants, or fellow fieldworkers and explorers. Gudeman and Rivera underline the need for expanding the community of ethnographic modellers.[36] For them, to engage in fieldwork is to participate in a continuous conversation that allows no boundaries in either time or space, extending from the distant past to the present and from the local community to the larger world. Marcus develops a similar argument, suggesting that the anthropological trope of complicity should replace the currently popular trope of rapport:

> The basic condition . . . for . . . complicity . . . is an awareness of existential doubleness on the part of *both* anthropologist and subject; this derives from having a sense of being *here* where major transformations are under way that are tied to things happening simultaneously *elsewhere*, but not having a certainty or authoritative representation of what those connections are.[37]

"Complicity," Marcus goes on, "rests in the acknowledged fascination between anthropologist and informant regarding the outside 'world' that the anthropologist is specifically materializing through the travels and trajectory of her multi-sited agenda."[38] It seems important to explore the

FIGURE 11. R. E. Peary, V. Stefansson, and A. W. Greely at the Explorers Club in New York. *(Courtesy of Dartmouth College Library; 2-3-86.)*

potential of such approaches, to move from the genre of the ethnographic autobiography and the monograph to the notion of fieldwork as a cooperative enterprise involving several sites and the mutual collaboration of anthropologists and their hosts.[39] It would be silly to force modern methodological standards upon Stefansson's approach and viewpoints. The point is not to establish *that* he failed to conform to our standards, which seems rather obvious, but rather to explore the differences between the two contexts and why they matter for the production of anthropological knowledge.

Most anthropologists nowadays would argue that it is important to be explicit about the effects of one's presence, on the scene as well as in ethnographic texts. Awareness of the so-called "observer's paradox" (to borrow an ethnolinguistic term) is seen as a condition for good, authentic ethnography; we know pretty well that while we arrive on the scene to record things as they are, our mere presence unavoidably shapes the course of events and, therefore, their representation; this, indeed, was one of the lessons of Malinowski's diaries. As a result, anthropologists generally feel compelled to situate their accounts and to reflect on the texts they write as well as their relations with their hosts and their readers. Recently, the theoretical and ethnographic gaze has been increasingly directed at intimate encounters and erotic involvement in the field and their suppression in ethnographic accounts.[40] The prevailing taboo on discussing intimate relations in fieldwork, it is argued, prevents understanding and elaboration of an important aspect of the ethnographic method.[41] "Leaving something unsaid," Seizer argues, "is . . . an effective means of prohibiting its entrance into discourse, much as the taboo on talking about sex in the field has done until now."[42] As Markowitz and Ashkenazi point out, the standard patriarchal model of fieldwork is dead. This model, they argue, may well have done the discipline an extreme disservice:

> It dissociated women, blacks, gays—anyone not of the power-controlling mainstream—from themselves, forced them into an inauthentic mold, and thereby reduced points of view. This had a direct effect on the reliability claims of anthropology. . . . It caused fieldworkers to prevaricate about the real process of data collection, affecting the validity of the research to an unknown degree.[43]

No doubt, much of the ethnographer's private experience in the field, including that of sexual relations, will always end "off record," no matter how reflective and self-absorbed anthropologists become, if only because too much and too "thick" description may violate relations of trust and the ethics of fieldwork—and the patience of the reader. Yet, intimate experiences may shed important light on the fieldwork encounter, gender relations, and culture context. The point is not to indulge in voyerism or to naively insist upon exposure but rather to ask how and to what extent anthropological practice might benefit (and lose) from intimate relations and their ethnographic description.

By now, a whole decade has passed since the conception of the "writing-culture" perspective. During this time, anthropologists have fiercely debated a series of "postmodernist" issues regarding ethnographic theory and practice, including the nature and role of textual accounts, participant-observation, and cultural representation, all of which are fundamental for a discipline traditionally focused on othering and cultural translation. Interestingly, Stefansson comments in his diaries about the ethnographic importance of the literary skills that allow the anthropologist to turn routine and everyday experience into fascinating but credible accounts:

> I . . . have often found on belated reference to my diary that *I have told to many men on many occasions . . . facts and feelings which seem to have been absent at the time of an "adventure" but which have by some mental process attached themselves to it later* and have become vivid as the real facts, or have now overshadowed them and even obliterated the facts. Where my contemporaneous record of an event is meager, *these adventitious elements are bound to remain undetected and become for me and anyone who believes me, as if they had happened.*[44]

As a result of the writing-culture debate, anthropologists now feel much less constrained than before by etiquette about how to write and what to write about.[45] No single standard dictates how people do anthropology; indeed, to the extent that the "writing-culture debate" started with the work of Clifford and Marcus, there are *many* roads from Santa Fe.[46]

ARCTICALITY

In recent years, historians and cultural critics have dissected the ideology and rhetoric of early explorations.[1] Some have examined the ways in which arctic environments and their inhabitants have been represented in text and imagery.[2] Anthropology, too, as we have seen, has been subjected to an internal critical reflection. Inuit ethnography, indeed, has its own clichés and theoretical assumptions, the famous work of Mauss and Beuchat on the seasonal variations of Inuit life being one example. Mauss's and Beauchat's analysis hinges on the simple ecological observation that the Inuit as well as the animals they hunt disperse and concentrate according to season:

> In summary, summer opens up an almost unlimited area for hunting and fishing, while winter narrowly restricts this area. This alternation provides the rhythm of concentration and dispersion for the morphological organization of Eskimo society. The population congregates or scatters like the game. The movement that animates Eskimo society is synchronised with that of the surrounding life.[3]

During the summer, the Inuit are isolated and fragmented. According to Mauss and Beuchat, "there is no religion," since the myths that "fill the consciousness of the Eskimo during the winter appear to be forgotten during the summer."[4] "Life," they add, "is that of the layman." During the winter, on the other hand, when the population congregates, there is a "genuine community of ideas": "By its existence and constant activity, the group becomes more aware of itself and assumes a more prominent place in the consciousness of individuals."[5] The contrast between summer and winter, then, parallels that between individual and society. In the individual mode, during the summer, the Inuit are "lost children, as it were," providing for themselves as individuals.[6] The isolated hunters or fishers keep their kill to themselves without having to consider anyone else. During the winter, on the other hand, individuals become social beings, subject to strict rules concerning the distribution of food. Food is collectively shared within a settlement rather than being limited to the individual or nuclear family. This suggests that the Inuit are perennially split between the individual and the collective. In winter, there is a lot of society in the individual; in summer, much less. For Mauss and Beuchat, the seasonal "morphology" of Inuit identity is not just an ecological necessity. The change of season provides an opportunity for the Inuit to respond to a "natural need":

> seasonal factors merely mark the most opportune occasions in the year for these two phases to occur. After the long revelries of the collective life which fill the winter, each Eskimo needs to live a more individual life; after long months of communal living filled with feasts and religious ceremonies, an Eskimo needs a profane existence.[7]

The work of Mauss and Beuchat, as Ellen points out, remains an "enduring paradox" in the sense that the observations and analyses that it contains have been interpreted in very different ways, exemplifying both cultural and materialist determinism.[8] Whichever stance one takes, the somewhat perceptive generalizations of Mauss and Beuchat were overtheorized simplifications, lacking the kind of realist grounding that Stefansson's ethnography provided.[9] Stefansson did indeed suggest that the Inuit regarded at least parts of the winter as vacation or "dancing time," an indigenous notion that Mauss and Beuchat may have drawn upon.[10] Given the length of Stefansson's stay in the Arctic, however, he was able to observe both regional and seasonal variations, how the Inuit continually adapted to the environment and the ways in which it was represented in Inuit discourse. In a letter from the field to the anthropologist R. R. Marrett, he challenged armchair anthropology in a cynical mood, commenting upon an issue of ethnographic interpretation:

> In point of actual fact you are probably more likely than I to be right, but that is because . . . the facts of archaeology, paleontology, and the rest, are really more open to you than to me who converse with Eskimo hunters while you sit in clubs and convention halls or walk in the field with learned men of your own and other sciences.[11]

This is not to say that Stefansson's approach was devoid of preconceptions, ideology, fiction, and rhetoric. On the contrary. At one point, early in the second expedition, Stefansson wrote in his diary: "the people we have seen so far are disappointingly sophisticated."[12] He did not elaborate on the sense in which the Inuit were sophisticated or why they disappointed him (he added, however, that they "did not seem to have much use for 'civilized' food"), but clearly, as every ethnographer would expect, he had his own preconceptions in the early stages of fieldwork. Be that as it may, his works often had a strong rhetorical line. Woodward shows how Stefansson's photographs reflect his "obsession" with the Eskimo snow house and the technological brilliance involved in making it. "It is probably fair," she suggests, "to lay at the great explorer's feet some responsibility for the continuing stereotype that Eskimos live in igloos."[13] Stefansson, as Woodward points out, "developed and promulgated a view of Eskimo people which remains the prevailing popular image of Eskimos throughout much of our world today."[14] He notes in his diary that "the Eskimo are the only Americans, north or south, who have ever employed the dome principle of architecture."[15]

Stefansson had several agendas—personal, ethnographic, and political—and their relationships were sometimes more conflictual than complentary. Thus, while he seems generally to have subscribed to the cultural relativism of Boas, he sometimes advocated a strong version of geographical determinism, even with a tinge of racism. For instance, he argued, partly drawing upon the work of S. Columb GilFillan, that nations that lay in the higher latitudes bordering the arctic seas would be the home of future empires as this was according to available evidence and sensible extrapolation *the* "path of supremacy."[16] Stefansson first outlined this argument in a brief article published in the *New York Times* in 1920. A few months later, GilFillan developed a similar argument in an article entitled "The Coldward Course of Progress." Stefansson reproduced GilFillan's graphic demonstration of the correlation between progress and mean annual temperature at the front of his book *The Northward Course of Empire.* Stefansson concludes his book with the following words:

> While we recognize that the general modern tendency toward city life . . . will inhibit somewhat the development of the northern frontier, we still feel that . . . other compensating factors will operate to such an extent that the North will soon come into its own and will be developed as rapidly as the West by our perhaps harder and more adventurous progenitors. . . . It is great good fortune that we still have our frontier land in which pioneers may struggle and build, where they may dream their dreams of empire, and eventually write upon pages now blank the story of those realized dreams.

Stefansson suggests, in the preface to his book, that his thesis on the North is "a corollary . . . implied" in the treatise *Civilization and Climate* of his "friend" Ellsworth Huntington. He seems, however, to modify a long-standing ethnocentric trend from Hyppocrates to Huntington that associated civilization with *lower* latitudes and temperate climates. Note, on the other hand, Stefansson's reference to "pages now blank" at the frontier, which does not seem to allow much room for the Inuit.

Arnold provides a useful account of the invention and history of the category of the "tropics," another extreme zone in Western discourse; tropicality, he argues, emerged as one manifestation of Orientalism, providing a contrast to the apparent normality of temperate regions.[17] The zoning of the world became "a Western way of defining something culturally alien, as well as environmentally distinctive, from Europe . . . and other parts of the temperate zone. . . . Tropicality was the experience of northern whites moving into an alien world—alien in climate, vegetation, people and disease."[18] With Stefansson's works, the Arctic Zone was similarly established, if not invented, as a fertile but somewhat slippery discursive space, as a rel-

FIGURE 12. Dartmouth College students build a snow house under the direction of Stefansson. 1960s. Lantern slide no. 229. *(Courtesy of Dartmouth College Library, Stef Mss 226.)*

FIGURE 13. Stefansson dragging a seal. The image was reproduced on the front cover of *The Friendly Arctic.* Canadian Arctic Expedition, 1914. Lantern slide no. 62. *(Courtesy of Dartmouth College Library, Stef Mss 226.)*

atively demarcated and monotonous site useful for the exploration of particular themes in contrast to the temperate Euroamerican world. The notion of arcticality implicit in his work made the Arctic both the home of howling, exotic wilderness (the source of "strange" knowledge and ancient wisdom) and a semi-domestic space (a "friendly" domain). Mixing ethnography and geopolitics in his own fashion, Stefansson both emphasized the lessons the Arctic invited for "us" (Western readers at home) and the future opportunities it provided out there for "civilizing" missions and the expansion of empire—in particular mining and international travel by airlines and submarines. Stefansson's rhetoric of arcticality, it seems, represented a peculiar combination of Boasian possibilism (the notion that culture modifies the environment), the vulgar environmental determinism of Huntington, and Western dreams of frontiers and empire.

I have dwelt upon some of Stefansson's omissions, silences, rhetoric, and biases because it is important to examine his anthropological practice critically. It is necessary, however, to situate his life and work in the age in which he operated. And his shortcomings should not distract from his many accomplishments. In many ways, Stefansson was ahead of his time. Indeed, he made quite an impression on the twentieth century. One of his greatest scholarly contribution is his two volume work on the voyages of Martin Frobisher (1576–1577), based on a variety of written accounts, in which he tried to analyze some of the earlier accounts of the Inuit.[19] As an explorer, he was highly successful, discovering and mapping, along with his Inuit and Western companions, some of the last remaining unexplored land on earth. His contribution to Inuit ethnography and anthropological field methods should not be overlooked, however. Along with some others, he pioneered the standard model of participant observation. Malinowski has often been credited with singlehandedly "inventing" the fieldwork method of modern anthropology. This is a gross simplification. Not only was Malinowski's fieldwork highly conventional in many respects—he traveled around a fair bit and spent more time with missionaries and other "whites" in the field than we are often lead to believe—by the time he arrived in Papua for his major fieldwork, as Welsch remarks, "the 'ethnographic method' had been born, if not accepted by the discipline as a fieldwork standard."[20] Stefansson, A. B. Lewis, and several others helped to set that new standard.

Stefansson's approach to ethnography, perhaps, may be characterized as both archaic and hyper-modern. It is archaic partly in its radical separation of the local and the global, the primitive and the modern. Stefansson notes in his diary:

> Unfortunately, the sixteen years of Herschel Island whaling that preceded the writer's first visit to the Mackenzie Delta had made it difficult to determine for that locality what ideas were local there or of ancient introduction, what ones were borrowed recently from the Alaskan Eskimo, whom the whalers brought with them, and what had been absorbed from the white men directly. Nevertheless a comparison will be attempted on the basis of what seems to be local and primitive in the Mackenzie district.[21]

Stefansson's emphasis on continual travel is also rather old-fashioned. He traveled twenty thousand miles by sled and dog team, moving from one camp to another, often, however, along the trail of the Inuit. While such excessive movement is not the preferred model nowadays, it clearly has many advantages over the traditional functionalist doctrine that favors an extended stay in a single location. Not only does the nomadic approach prove particularly useful among the Inuit and other seasonally transhuman populations, it allows the fieldworker to understand regional and international connections that would otherwise be missed. Interestingly, Stefansson's approach to his Inuit fieldwork may resonate with recent emphases on interconnections and multi-sited fieldwork, "studying through," as Shore and Wright put it, rather than "up" or "down" the social scale, "studying the localization of global processes."[22]

In recent decades, an extensive ethnography has emerged that documents Inuit and Indian society in the current age of the "snowmobile generations," relations with the colonial past, and the problems posed by the future.[23] In one way or another, much of this rapidly growing body of literature draws upon and critically engages with Stefansson's work on the Arctic. Burch concludes, summing up the relevance of Stefansson's work for contemporary anthropology, that given his knowledge of Inuit languages and the ethnographic challenge, in the case of the Copper Inuit, of working with people who had never seen a Euroamerican, Stefansson's work "must be regarded as a disappointment":

> His results, while informative and important, were far below what one has a right to expect, given his training and the extraordinary opportunities he had [among the Copper Inuit as well as in the Mackenzie Delta and Northern Alaska]. Stefansson was just too interested in being an explorer and an iconoclast . . . and not interested enough in being an ethnographer, to put together a systematic ethnographic account of what he learned. One subject he *did* treat with insight and attention, however, was Inuit religion. We may still read with profit what he had to say on that topic.[24]

Mark Nuttall suggests that Stefansson offers perceptive observations on Inuit kin relations, naming practices, and name spirits—particularly in the Coronation Gulf area.[25] Interestingly, Nuttall argues that while he may make no mention of his son Alex in his writings, Stefansson's understanding of name spirit inheritance is significant and highly personal, demonstrating either his ethnographic skills or his own experience of having to understand the importance of the name in Inuit society.

If Stefansson's anthropological publications are disappointing, we may ask, is it because his ethnography, the very material from which he had to work, was negligible, dull, or devoid of insight? Or is it because he never really "wrote up" the material at his disposal, however rich, preoccupied as he was with fame, publicity, and exploration? Or is his ethnography somehow submerged? Only by attending to Stefansson's field diaries are we able to firmly answer these questions. For exploring the similarities and differences in the two kinds of text, the diaries allow a systematic comparison of Stefansson's field experiences (to the extent that they are recorded and represented in the text) and Stefansson's publications. I suggest that the ethnography of the diaries of the first two expeditions rescue Stefansson the anthropologist from the showmanship of early twentieth-century exploration. During these expeditions, his ambitions were truly scientific and he managed to identify and record a variety of interesting and useful "facts" on Inuit society, although later on these ambitions would be pushed to the margin for a variety of reasons. Stefansson thought of himself in the Arctic as "a spectator with no material interests at stake," admitting (and regretting), however, that he "had a part in bringing . . . change about."[26] More than anyone else, perhaps, Vilhjalmur Stefansson both mapped and defined the Arctic in Western discourse, paving the way for authentic accounts of Inuit society, more informed and less ethnocentric than those previously available.

PART II

STEFANSSON'S ETHNOGRAPHIC DIARIES

THE ANGLO-AMERICAN POLAR EXPEDITION (1906–1907)

1906

MAY 18 *Alberta Hotel, Edmonton.* In starting out to join the Anglo-American Polar Expedition at Fort McPherson or Herschel Island, I left Boston [. . .] via Albany, Buffalo and Hamilton for Toronto [. . .] to complete arrangements with the U. of Toronto for selling them one quarter of the Ethnological collection.

I arrived in Toronto 10:45 A.M. Monday, April 30 and stayed then with Mr. and Mrs. Smith, 17 Triller Avenue until 1:45 P.M. the following day, when I started for Winnipeg by the Grand Trunk to North Berg and the C.P.R. then to Winnipeg. [. . .]

I remained at the Empire Hotel, Winnipeg, from noon Thursday May 3 to 2:30 P.M. Friday May 4 when I went by the G.N. to Grand Forks. Meantime I had seen Commissioner C. C. Chipman, who received me with real hospitality rather than mere courtesy. [. . .]

Saturday I [. . .] drove to see mother near Merl P.O. at Salberg's. [. . .] In G.F. Sunday morning, saw Rose, and Mary in evening. Serious talk with Mary. Splendid girl made wretched by religion. Hope she gets over it. Saw Rose again Monday. [. . .] Walked home with Mary.

Sister Inga was [. . .] delegate to lodge convention. Promised sending her \$100.^{00} (mailed her \$50 from Edmonton: intend sending B. Pálsson \$50 to be paid her by Sveinn Brynjolfson). [. . .]

Went to Winnipeg [. . .] Tuesday; found Dr. Howe, gone—had intended meeting him then. Stayed with Dysart at 135 Kennedy Avenue while in city—Dysart's guest. McKinglet also there [. . .]. Promised writing Dysart some time—also Steve Brynjolfson, Cap't McLean.

Conferenced with Dr. Björnsson and Sv Brynjolfson in regard to Bjossi. They will see him through. [. . .]

Left Winnipeg Friday morning May 11, at 8: A.M. over C.N.B. with Anderson—arrived Edmonton—Alberta Hotel—Sat. evening 10:15 P.M. (train said to be about on time).

Find H.B. less pleasant but not so cordial as in Winnipeg. Learn water is low in Athabasca—that means trouble. Received telegram saying our ship leaves Victoria Saturday, May 19, expecting to be at McPherson August 14 to pick us up. Interview in "Edmonton Daily Bulletin" yesterday—fair.

JUNE 6 Athabasca Landing. Left Edmonton Friday, June 1. Had accident at Rat Creek and had to turn back to Alberta Hotel for lunch. Left rear wheel [. . .] broken. Left hotel again at 1:15 P.M. Dinner at Lewis' stopping place; slept at French Widow's, Lily Lake. Breakfast then, lunch at Egge's, Dinner lodging, breakfast at Whitteys. Interesting people—especially Mrs. and eldest girl. Lunch at Billy Smith's, arrived Landing ca. 2 P.M. Sunday June 3.

Learnt boat would not sail before Thursday or Friday, June 7 or 8. Hotel fair, cooking not poor, Rate 1^{00} [. . .].

JUNE 8 Left Landing 1:30 P.M. [. . .] Passed "Liquor Boundary" [. . .]. Have sailed total about 25 miles since starting till 5 P.M. (miles counted by river curves). [. . .] Passed mouth of Lac la Biche River at 6:30—40 min. from Landing. Thick timber still.

7:30. Both shores show traces of fire 2–3 years ago. Birch (a few) on right bank.

8. Calling river settlement—left bank. [. . .] Small settlement Indian tents. [. . .]

JUNE 9 [. . .] About 4 P.M.—reached village at Pelican Portage. Some houses and a free trade's store. Also H.B. store. Burning gas well—dug by gov't some years ago.

Missionary—trades one quarter of mile farther down river. A house on opposite bank.

Some Indians camped near gas well—*could speak no English—Crees*.

JUNE 10 Lying at Pelican Portage today waiting for higher water [. . .]

The missionary trade—Robinson was said to have been deposed for trading for fur clothing, etc. sent west to the "heathen." He is said to differ from the typical missionary in this regard chiefly in having been caught. His wife, who lives at the Landing in a miserable shack, is the sister of a bishop Young. [. . .]

JUNE 11 Our cook taken sick yesterday forenoon: is still sick. [. . .]

Walked ca. 2 m. west yesterday. [. . .] Road leads west 90 miles to two Wabis Kaw lakes [. . .], 90 children there, many Indians said to be around there—live on fowl in summer—don't fish much. [. . .]

Had severe twitches [in tooth filled in Edmonton] last night. [. . .]

JUNE 12 Started at 4:45 and soon began scraping the bottom and stones, this evidently caused leak for at 5:45 we tied to the left shore again for repairs. Country here getting more open—what trees there are are same sort as before. [. . .]

JUNE 13 [. . .] After supper the sky pilot walked south some distance, found a skunk and killed it. He had never seen a skunk before and approached too near. He threw all his clothes into the river, but still the smell lingers on him and in his cabin.

JUNE 14 Still tied up. Raining steadily—too heavy for tracking, so it means another day's delay—probably. Rained most of night. Mosquitoes bad last night, but most of us slept well under nets. Those who had none suffered. [. . .]

Passing the time by playing chess with Benham, an English member of the *oil drillers' crew*. Win about 2 out of 3 games, or rather less. His playing is improving rapidly. [. . .]

JUNE 15 [. . .] Stewart has told several stories involving points of grammar, but the passengers don't seem as keen on those as on some other kinds of humor. A man had said to him "the *norther* you go the lighter it gets"; Lee, who is really witty himself, laughed at it, as did others and then repeated "the *lighter* it gets," thinking that's where the joke lay. [. . .]

JUNE 16 [. . .] After lunch several canoes went down to landing where goods stored 1½ miles south of the island: some to island. Anderson, Stewart, Pritchett, Lee and I walked to landing. Captain passed us on the way with Indian woman [. . .] from Pelican Rapids. Took her to tent farthest north. [. . .] Built bonfire and sat around it for some time.

JUNE 17 Clear weather—some clouds occasionally. No service proposed by the missionary—thanks. [. . .] No mosquitoes last night. Some sand flies this evening. Men who went to island in forenoon reported us news of Jim Wood and barger.

JUNE 18 Clear forenoon: slight showers afternoon. Five scows passed down river about 1:30; then 3 scows and Shott and two others [. . .] about 2:30. All these (Shott's) scows left Tuesday following our departure (on Friday) and had been delayed 2 days by breathing hole in one of scows. Shott said some Indians who came by trail to House River from McMurray reported Jim Wood started up river from there Saturday—due here: next Thursday. This news depressed even Mr. Anderson who remarked we should be at Smith by now.

The evening squaw who had been in Phillip's room returned with Phillip and Captain to her quarters on boat. Said where she was going to on island—one she had lived with before—wouldn't have anything to do with her any more. She will probably go back with steamers to Prudence where we picked her up first. She came back *following the two men at quite a distance—Indian fashion I suppose*. She stays in her room all day—sewing I believe (moccasins someone said)—and eats with the cooks and waiter.

JUNE 19 [. . .] Last night very cold—some say it froze. Strong wind from north today. Rear end of steamer broke loose (rope untied), but 10–12 of us swung it back. [. . .]

Afternoon: Went out hunting alone. [. . .] In evening we were told we would go down to "Steamboat Landing" in morning. An Indian reports Jim Wood due tomorrow evening.

JUNE 20 Awoke at 6:15 and found boat had been moving some time. Did not get up. Tied up at 6:45 about 2 miles above island—East bank. Walked down to bank opp. island with Stewart, Lee took him over in canoe; I returned to boat with Pritchard and Matthews—just home at 10: A.M. [. . .]

Later: About 9: P.M. Daly, the engineer, told me the cook's (Bray) pulse was getting slower and weaker, and asked what I thought about it. He had had severe vomiting for several hours before noon and till 3 o'clock, but was now quiet. I thought it might be [. . .] poisoning [. . .] , and told Daly so. About this time Bray had been telling the woman missionary that he felt better and would be stronger in the morning (strange they so often say that). A few minutes later he died so quietly they didn't know for some minutes he was dead. Died about 9:30, I think, though I didn't look at my watch.

Shortly before this a messenger arrived saying Jim Wood was at the island. After ten o'clock he came himself, with some men.

JUNE 21 10:30 Seems we shall probably start tomorrow. We are all getting our out-mail ready. I am mailing several [. . .] letters and post-cards—clumsily sealed letters with some wax given by P.M. at Landing. [. . .]

3:45 P.M. At 2:45 rough coffin of Herbert Bray the cook carried up bank to his grave. The [. . .] cooks were eating at the time, and only half the passengers stood around while the service was read by Winch the missionary—church of England service. Most of them put on their hats while the earth was shoveled in and ⅔ of them had staggered away before the grave was full. Death, apparently, does not impress them much. Stewart cut in tree near by: "Herbert Bray, died June 8, 1906." I finished the cutting—"1906" [. . .] . This we did before the service. Both of us took pictures. [. . .]

In the evening a scow finally came for us: considerable delay followed and it was dark (for it was cloudy) when Mr. S. and I pitched his tent at the Eddy ¼ mile below island, on E. bank. [. . .]

It is said we shall get away Monday morning. Shott expects to be away some time. Saturday he appears energetic—for this country. [. . .]

JUNE 22 [. . .] Indian girl from House River returned with steamer. [. . .]

Later. Went hunting after supper. [. . .]

JUNE 24 [. . .] Mosquitoes not troublesome yet, though a few are in the tent evenings and we put up the nets. [. . .] Several parties went out both sides of the river after moose. Late in afternoon one returned reporting having [. . .] broken leg of one. Several went out on its trail, but had no success. Another hunter later returned reporting he had killed a large bull moose.

Spent some of day playing chess and part afternoon with Mr. S. who read aloud from Hall's funny book of arctic trail.

No "divine" services.

JUNE 25 9 A.M. At breakfast we found 9 men had been sent out to get the bull moose killed yesterday. They will probably be gone all day, for they will report the moose "very far off" and will spend considerable time cooking a meal of it before starting back.

Tom Taylor our "assistant cook" or dishwasher and woodchopper, is said by Mr. Anderson to be half negro. He looks it—especially the nose—but others say father Scotch.

Heard (later) Tom Taylor's mother a negro captured in Minnesota massacre—father Sioux or [?]. Believe this time story. [. . .]

Moose hunters returned soon after we camped, some fellows—Lee etc—got pieces to roast over fire. [. . .]

JUNE 27 [. . .] We now have 12 scows and 2 york boats. The crew are between 70–80 and 18 passengers—of them 2 women, one child—Mrs. Mercredi, Miss Wilgress—Hay River missionary. [. . .]

Landed just above Boiler Rapids about 12. After dinner I walked down along West bank, took a time exposure of the upper (or middle) Boiler and a snaps-shot of one of Shott's boats shooting lower boiler. Picture should show bowman sighting channel with stick above his head. [. . .]

Besides their chanting, the Indians [. . .] are fond of shouting on all occasions almost, and of [. . .] playing practical jokes. At meals they fight for the utensils and the food, thus often spilling it and usually grabbing so much that the last get nothing. [. . .]

At 5:43 took picture of men eating—wasn't as good a scene as some-guess they saw me and the camera. [. . .]

JUNE 29 [. . .] At 9:00 Mr. Phillips, steam—boat inspector, arrived in canoe with 2 half-breeds [. . .]. Had left Landing Monday at 4 P.M. Brought no mail because Woods thought he would not overtake us. [. . .]

JULY 3 [. . .] Passed McKay at 7: but I was not up to see, for I did not realize we would get there so soon. Perhaps a dozen houses, whitewashed, looks pretty, it is said, at distance [. . .]

JULY 4 [. . .] It appears that yesterday, because the wind was from the lake, the river was very high. This scared out some Indians camped here—some of which we met last evening going up in their canoes. [. . .]

We tied up—anchored—shortly after 9: and soon after I went ashore to take pictures of the *Catholic and Anglican* missions [. . .] .

4:30 P.M. A HB official in charge of McKay has just been telling me it isn't over 8 years since [. . .] *buffalo were killed* near McKay and that all the old men there have killed lots of them, in their time. The elk [. . .] *have all gone,* but the *moose are more plentiful* than formerly—perhaps driven by settlement. [. . .]

JULY 11 [. . .] In leaving Smith's Landing at 7:35 Saturday evening, July 7, I left this book behind and have therefore made no entries in it up to the time of leaving Ft. Smith.

I made the walk over in an even four hours arriving at 11:35 at Mr. Pritchard's mosquito net, on top of the hill, where I slept after going down to the boat [. . .]. The first half of the walk the mosquitoes were thick, especially about two wet places ca. 5 m. from the landing. It was probably such places Mr. Kelly had in mind when he declared himself unwilling to walk to the fort for $25. [. . .]

JULY 10 I had an interesting talk [. . .] 3 brothers at the Catholic mission. [. . .] One brother was French: one brother German, and one Irish—O'-Connor has been in "the country" 26 years and gave interesting information in regard to various things [. . .] . The German brother spoke German only—talked with him half an hour. He said he was too busy learning French to put any time on Chipewyan. [. . .]

The missions were first to introduce gardening into the north and they now grow "everything but corn and tomatoes" at most missions south of, and including, Grand Hope. The Indians are especially fond of potatoes, but few of them will take the necessary trouble to cultivate them. Corn has not been tried at H.S. [. . .]

Captain told at supper [. . .] too good a story to be missed. Last year, on arriving at Simpson Mr. A. had 2 sacks full of "washing." He took [them] to a woman, giving her a bar of brown soap, and telling her to hang [the washing] 3–4 days over the fire before doing the washing, for soap wasted too quickly if not dry when used. [. . .]

JULY 13 [. . .] At Resolution where we landed at a little before midnight July 12, there were camped some *100 Indians* to whom treaty had been paid. They get $\$\ 5^{00}$ per head, and 100 sacks (100 lb.) flour were distributed yesterday. Mr. Laird of Mr. Convoy's party, came aboard: the rest stayed at Resolution.

Mr. Harry Jones, who had been on the Jackson-Armsworth expedition [. . .] , went with us to Hay River. He has a Slavey wife, and from her and from association with others he has obtained much valuable information: most of what he told me is noted on the last few pages of this book. He also has a large number of good photos, which he sells at $\$1^{00}$ the dog.

Mr. Laird says they paid about 150 dog ribs at Resolution—there are others farther north who do not take treaty. The rest of the 700 were about half-and-half Chipewyan [. . .] . At Hay River 300–500 Slaveys, more than half the Slavey tribe paid at Vermillion. Gov't gives Indians *3 days' rations* at treaty time: they also supply rations to the destitute through the missions.

Mr. Laird says there will be about 250 more payments this year under treaty 8 than last. Most of this increase is accounted for by *excess of births over deaths*—for there are only some 4–6 families that are new to the treaty payments this year.

JULY 14 [. . .] The two mission churches. Landed at Hay River some time after midnight. [. . .] Mr. Marsh made me a present of a *willow net* made by the same woman who made the one Mr. A. gave me in Edmonton (sent the Peabody). A new church with a tin roof and new residence are being built. [. . .]

JULY 15 After waiting an hour this morning near the end of Beaver Lake, we proceded, and reached Providence at 5:45. Here sister Ward, Montreal got off, and also the other sister, who comes to stay. Sister Ward, who is on an inspection tour, goes back with this boat. I took several photos—as did Mr. S. In the sister's garden most of the strawberries were gone, for we were too late for them, but the raspberries were ripe. A maple planted in 1868 shows in the picture—perhaps 6 inches indian 2 ft. up. In the school are *37 girls, 29 boys,* from "all over"—[. . .] *They can be told from the Slaveys* and others by the low nose and other features.

These are 12 "brothers" and "sisters" (how many of each I don't know) conducting the school, etc.—and they do it in the usual excellent style.

A field of Barley, of which Mr. S. took a picture, was all headed out and seemed about to begin ripening. The crop is usually a success. [. . .]

JULY 17 Left Simpson 5 A.M. [. . .]

9:35: Our first glimpse of the *Rockies.*

2:20 P.M. 3 Indians came out from two prosperous looking houses at the E. shore. They came to get doors, for their house which we had brought from Simpson—for they were building one of them. [. . .]

8:10 Passed old Fort Wrigley—it is said that on account of bad water and swampy ground most of Indians here *died—about 20 left.* [. . .]

Perhaps about 5 o'clock a range of mountains—lower than those on west appeared on the East. In general the mountains remind of those of Iceland—a little green on top, with steep sides. [. . .]

JULY 21 We were told [. . .], that the location of Old Wrigley had been so unhealthful that over *200 Indians were reduced to 20 inside* of six years—mostly consumption [. . .] . Epidemics of *enteric fever* go up and down the river frequently—at Good Hope we were told there was a good deal of it now. Norman is a rather pleasant place, with fair buildings and both English and Roman missions. [. . .] All the English church Indians had been forced to go inland hunting and most of the others were gone also. Those from Bear Lake normally come in to trade, but Dan McAllum, a hunter who has been up there some years, is beginning to trade for the company, and some of Hyslop and Magle's Indians did not come in at all this year—thus cheating them out of last year's *"debt."* [. . .] The trader here for Hyslop and Magle (Hyslop has an Indian wife) is a son of the Mr. Fraser who drove with us from Edmont to the Landing. [. . .]

JULY 22 We attended seminar by Bishop Reeve and Rev. Whittaker in the evening. There were mottos on the wall—the work of [. . .] Macdonald, now retired, who *reduced the language to writing*.

Mr. and Mrs. Whittaker had with them a little half-Eskimo girl about the age of their own daughter—say 6—whom they were taking to the school at Hay River. They are going on a year's outing [. . .] and are coming back to Herschel next summer. [. . .]

After the White service, one for Indians (conducted by their local preacher?), [. . .] there was considerable booze-fighting. [. . .]

JULY 23 Boat left ca. 2 A.M. with three outgoing policemen [. . .] Anderson somewhat boozed—bade me affectionate farewell.

Firth unapproachable for booze all day—slept in barracks—and Stewart delayed. *Some Indians here from Yukon side*—this will simplify his trip.

JULY 24 Stewart got started in afternoon and I walked with him ca. 7 miles to first hills—last few miles in rain. Returned same evening. Indian agreed to carry loads to Pierre house for $\$17^{50}$ for 50 lbs. [. . .]

JULY 25 A *trapper* from the Yukon arrived last night in an improvised canoe with two dogs—having lost 2 dogs a day up river (did not come back from rabbit hunt). He had starved for two dogs and was very weak. He reports the country in the mountains full of *moose and caribou, but no fur* [. . .].

JULY 24 Nothing has been happening. Mr. Firth has been rather inert from booze. [. . .] "Nothing could be done" to start until the Indians had been outfitted for the summer (fall) hunt. By now most of them are gone and the boat will be loaded after midnight tonight for Sunday is an uncommon nuisance here—worse than ordinary. The rest of the loading will be done tomorrow, and we shall probably be off by tomorrow night Monday. [. . .]

AUGUST 2 We left McPherson the evening of July 30–the exact hours and distances I shall copy later from Const. Walker. That evening we traveled reasonably though the current is slow, and little rowing done. *Roxy* (who has Mrs. and adopted girl and boy (nephew) along) is captain of the york boat and whale boat. He is an able [?] man, but the crew of three Indians seem not much good. They are exceedingly slow in obeying any command. Besides these, there are along Annie (wife of police interpreter, Herschel) and a little girl—seems adopted daughter. [. . .]

The journey is interesting [. . .] . Roxy and his boy of 13 are fine, the wife and girl of 14 seem all right. It is said R. is hurrying to the island to "seal" *her to a whaler*. This is probably true, for they look upon it as most parents would a wealthy marriage—it is marriage to them. (Later: not true.).

AUGUST 2 8 P.M. [. . .] We met a Husky family (see photo) shortly before the mouth of the Husky River (2:30)—man, wife, 2 children–prosperous looking [. . .] . Mrs. Roxy visited in the boat while the men talked between boats. [. . .]

AUGUST 3 [. . .] At 4:55 we pulled ashore, got some firewood and had supper. Apparently Walker thinks we are rushing the travel—he said today it would be a long time till they again went from the mouth of the Peel to the ocean without camping. Roxy is a good fellow, but the slowness of the north is upon everyone else. [. . .] The three Indians and Walker seem to regard it quite a hardship to sleep aboard, though they all seem to sleep very well. The night preceding the second August: after being up with Roxy all night, I cooked breakfast but could not get Walker or one of the Indians up to eat it. I went to bed at 9:00 A.M. and they were still sleeping but up before 12, when I woke up. This morning I woke up Sullivan to cook at 5: He could not wake half the crowd for breakfast, and 2–3 of them were just getting up when I awoke at 12. Still they grumble about the hardships.

Camped ca. 8 P.M. ca. 15 m. from sea.

AUGUST 4 [. . .] After caching most of stuff [. . .] we sailed leaving 2 Indians and Walker: Meantime I and Roxy's boy went hunting. [. . .]

AUGUST 5 [. . .] On the hill on shore opposite—for this "point" is an island these last few years—was a buried tent for a woman who died last winter.

There are said to be numerous household goods there—at the grave photographed there seemed none. It is said everything is buried [. . .] though some cases are well known to whites where inferior guns, etc, have been substituted for the good articles of the deceased.

In the early morning Harry Waugh took Roxy's kayak to see to nets. When he called breakfast (for he had got up to cook) the kayak was gone. It was blowing a stiff breeze and the boat was a good two miles off. Roxy seemed not a bit annoyed, and after breakfast he and Waugh went after it. [. . .]

AUGUST 6 Still camped at Shingle Point, where Roxy will live this winter and where we now have his property and family. The wind is heavy from NW:—too heavy to venture.

Yesterday a few minutes after landing we saw an iceberg. This rejoiced Roxy, for he said we would have a *still channel* along shore if the ice came in. When I went hunting I could see the bergs like a vast fleet winter sail. [. . .]

AUGUST 7 [. . .] In taking our camp I tried to get our friend with the whiskers in the picture, but he was "afraid." Roxy says most Huskies afraid—think it hurts them. [. . .]

The Husky houses may, some time later, be occupied [. . .] .

AUGUST 8 We left Shingle Point at ca. 5 P.M., yesterday, tacked about 2 miles, then tacked about 3, and finally rowed about 5 to King Point. Here I took photo of Amundsen's winter house, family of [. . .] "Dolphin" of Huskies [. . .] his wife seems half white. All the rest are their children [. . .] Husky capt's wife seems at least half white—features largely "white" almost that of Scandinavian immigrants. Mrs. Stein was first with Norwegian man before this one took her. [. . .]

After our landing ca. 2 A.M. we had tea with Husky cap't and family [. . .]. We had tea and coffee made on a *"pressure" kerosene stove,* and three kinds of meat—whale lean, skin and dried seal—all of which I tasted and liked about as well as the dried fish. There was also molasses. Everything seemed clean. The *way of eating meat* generally seems to be this. One takes a piece in the right hand, and a sharp knife in left, cuts of a small piece, either drops knife or holds it with last two fingers, while with thumb and other two he dips it into a pot of grease well above the finger nails, then thrusts the piece into his mouth [. . .] and pulls then the fingers out with a smack.

Each *cup and saucer* is kept in its own napkin, and wiped clean after each meal and wrapped in it. Each person has his own napkin and cup, though they lend both freely, if there are not cups to go around. [. . .]

A few feet from shore was the sunk schooner "*Bonanza*" San Fransisco [. . .] There is talk that she was sunk intentionally, being old. The story is she got crushed by the ice. She has been partly dismantled, though there is valuable stuff on her yet. [. . .]

AUGUST 9 Arrived Herschel ca. 12:30 A.M. [. . .]

Kagmalit. Fast hunters and most civilized Eskimos here. He only one who would carry mail to Yukon.

Uniglu—best hunter on Island. Good friend of Jimmy. Woman probably all right—2 or 3 children—boy old enough to hunt.

Maniksa, wife, girl of 16, girl good hunter and good girl—wife always talking—wants to be boss of tent. One who brought me on board. [. . .]

AUGUST 10 We landed at Herschel Island about 12:30 A.M. Some people were up, others got up, and the mail was distributed. [. . .]

The police invited me to meals and sleeping quarters: accepted: but next day Amundsen asked me to take meals with him, which I did till he left. They seemed a little fearful of another year in the ice and so lived chiefly on fish, etc.

At the officers meals there was a Dr. Wight (or Wright), Camb. Eng. Univ. and Harvard Medic (1898?). He was just completing a year as whaler—probably came to get cured of drink. [. . .]

Some years ago one mate shot another [. . .]—one of the plainest of a dozen murders all of which have gone unpunished. [. . .] Other captains—such as Newth of the Jeanette—are worst in their dealings with native women. One of the typical stories is that last winter a woman came to missionary Whittaker telling Newth had enticed her 11 yr. daughter out to the ship. Missionary went out, heard her screams in the cabin and found her there with her pants, etc. off. Newth said they had been wet and he made her take them off to dry them because he was afraid she might get cold and she cried because she didn't want to have them dried. This story is said to have held before Major Howard as J.P. and he is said to have written a letter to Newth exonerating him. Newth's wives are said to range usually from 11 to 15—usually 5 in number.

[In Icelandic:] *Gángari segir pað sé ómögulegt að gera við pessu vegna þess að hann segist hafa vistað pær sem bústyru [. . .] og að pær séu ekkert annað. Sagt er að bæði hann og [. . .] Haraldur hafi hjákonur og sem á einu með sjómönnunum um frylllíf þeirra* [. . .]

[Walker says that nothing can be done about this as he says he hired them as housemaids . . . and they are nothing else. It is said that both he and

Harald have concubines and that they are no different from sailors in that respect.]

AUGUST 11 At about 9:30 A.M. today Cap't Amundsen [. . .] started on his fourth attempt to get out. He and his crew seem a splendid set of men—8 counting the captain. They have given a good deal of provisions away, incl. about 2800 lbs. of flour to the whalers. [. . .]

The schooner "Olga" Cap't Klengenberg (Jorgensen) arrived yesterday [. . .] . The crew had been mutinous (the story goes)—one man (the engineer—they have gasoline) was shot in bed by the capt. who says he went in to disarm him after he had shot twice at the captain previously. He pulled a gun again, and the cap't shot him. [. . .] Another man [. . .] made three attempts to burn the ship, was placed in irons (was very sick at the time) and died, 2 went down through ice, so only 7 came back where 11 went. The trouble between capt and engineer is said to have risen from the fact that the engineer had made a whiskey still against the capt's orders and proceeded to use flour, potatoes etc. to make whiskey. [. . .]

They report plenty natives—"the cleanest they ever saw"—at Mints Inlet. They used copper [. . .] . Most of snow knives, etc. copper. Copper ice picks.

Saw about 250 natives, all told on Prince Albert. These said there were more. [. . .]

AUGUST 20 *Herschel* [. . .] Yesterday Cap't *Klengenberg* left for his home at Pt. Barrow with his wife and six children [. . .] in a small boat. He has invited me to stay the winter with him at Barrow. [. . .]

The *ula-hula* which the natives hold every night seems purely for amusement. There are usually 2–3 drums and all the crowd sings, the dancers excepted. They do have them for seal killing, curing disease of any kind, or for any good thing: also for evil [. . .]

AUGUST 28

[. . .]
tsila = outside
koonie = wife (jargon) [nuliesa]
nagosok = good
tautuk = see
[. . .]
o-bloomy = today
[. . .]

kingmuk = dog
kina atka = what's his name. [. . .]
tjuna pishunktu = what do you want?
ilhut = you
tusaryuk = understand
tusaryuk ilhut = Do you understand me?
[. . .]

AUGUST 29 Started about 9: A.M.—5 boats—Iaki, Kokatu, Iaki's son-in-law, and two others. It was a beautiful, warm day, but the breeze was dead ahead. We finally arrived at a good boat harbor [. . .] I was a little seasick—as were about ½ the natives—all Nunatama. [. . .]

SEPTEMBER 1 August 30 we went to Shingle Point, anchoring inside the first nose of the sand pit. [. . .] Roxy arrived home a half-hour ahead of us, having been bound on the coast several days. [. . .] Yesterday I made a bargain with Roxy to keep me till the freeze-up and then take me to Mr. H's camp, Husky Lake. [. . .] While camped here the Huskies are making a centreboard for Mr. H's boat and are doing a good job; as usual. I have been taking a few head-measurements of Minotones we have with us. [. . .]

SEPTEMBER 3 [. . .] The provisions I got from H. to give Roxy are: 50 lbs. (good) flour, 2 lbs. coffee, six plugs tobacco [. . .] . Soon our diet will doubtless be fish straight.

I notice the Nunatama we had with us (at Herschel I didn't know just who was Nunatama) have all given up pulling their hair, though the custom, they say, was no less universal among them than the Kagmalit. The Nunatama seem to have been entirely an inland people and they furnish one of the interesting problems of the region.

All the older men have labret holes, and most of them wear at least one. Those who wear two seem seldom, if ever, to wear two, even when they own pairs [. . .] . Most of them are of various stone, from gray to green, which they say they find in the mountains themselves. Many wear labrets used by their grandfathers, so it seems that a man's labret (or at least all of them) are not buried with him. I asked Kokatu about this, but could not make him understand fully though he told me both they were buried and were not buried—probably means that either the customs vary, or else they bury some of a man's labrets, and keep others.

Roxy tells me among the Kagmalit sometimes you bury labrets, sometimes son keeps them. When his own father died he had six labrets (3 prs.).

Roxy put one pair in grave alongside body: kept two pairs for himself. They have no scruples against selling these heirlooms, though they put a high price on them. Roxy says so far as he knows these customs are the same for the Nunatama. The labrets are always taken out of the lips before burial, whether they are to be buried or not.

Roxy says that nowadays, supposing a man has two rifles—one good, one poor they put poor rifle in grave and keep good rifle. He thinks perhaps this was different long time ago and then they put both rifles in grave.

Harrison's Huskies seem to be very kind and thoughtful in every way, when we left the tent, they would tie the door if we forgot to; they put special wrappings around my trunk because they saw papers in it. When flour is scarce, or tea, they will go without and give it you. If they see you chopping wood they come and offer to do it. They are really very cleanly. In taking cranial mesasurements I watched for lice but saw none nor have I caught any sleeping 2 nights with Iaki [. . .] . They wash every morning, and Saturday night last I found Mr. Kokatu taking a bath. Many of the women are good looking even at first sight, and all of them improve with acquaintance. Many of the men are about six feet, all are strong and active. [. . .] They can make almost anything—last Saturday they made a centre-board for our boat out of poor boards, and did it beautifully. Most of them have a brace and set of bits.

Some of their tastes are not cleanly to a white man's notion though most of them have their parallels in civilization. Roxy's cache, for instance, smells strongly already of decaying fish, while there are ship's ice houses less than ¼ of a mile away where all could be frozen. They roast their fish—stuck vertically near the fire on sticks run through their mouths—without removing the insides, which you merely leave behind in the dish when eating. They allow dogs to lick the plates after meals (so does Mr. Harrison) and dip their fingers deep in the seal oil and suck them off with a smack. But all these things you get used to.

None of them seem lazy, though there is doubtless a difference, especially in some working faster than others, for all of them are always working, one may say. Even at this time of year when their kerosene lanterns are lit at 9 P.M. they work by lamplight, especially the women. Daytimes, if the weather is not bad, the men are outdoors all the time and the women much of it. They spread blankets, skin, etc. to sit on and build a windbreak, lighting a fire if wood is plenty (as it usually is on this coast). [. . .]

In "things" there seems to be no communism beyond what would be expected in a camp of white men, but usually 2–3 families are in a sort of partnership. [. . .]

At mealtime they show a striking difference from Itkilliks (Indians) who hang around unbidden with longing eyes, even if they have just had a meal, while a Husky in our tent will get up when food is brought [. . .] They expect us to eat separately in H's camp [. . .] they think we prefer eating alone. [. . .]

Like all Huskies, the Nunatama sleep naked. They are fond of blankets—especially 4 point—though they use floor also. [. . .]

The summer waterproof boot is of seal, with a "shoepac" sole, the winterboot is of deer—the sole of the brow, the leg of the deer's legs. The hair of the sole is always in, the leg may be either. [. . .]

Roxy says "big seal" is "all the same" to eat as small seal—the skin is a little thick and is used to sole boots, while the other goes for uppers.

The tattooing of the Nunatama and Kagmalit differs little so far as I can see, both depend on taste of individual within certain limits. [. . .]

It is done by drawing a thread under the skin—charcoal, or occasionally stove coal smoke (soot) or lampblack.

I have never seen a child struck or punished by Huskies, and a dog seldom. Both are well behaved—especially the children, who always jump to do what they are told. It is said old people are occationally left behind to die on journeys—usually at their own request—but I have seen nothing like this. Iaki's old parents are with him. His mother is especially decrepit and whines with a bad head continually, but he humors her in every way. If he sees her trying to do anything that is difficult for her—as getting out of the boat—he runs to her and helps her; he lifts her very tenderly ashore where everyone else jumps. Among Indians she might be helped by some other woman [. . .], but not probably by her own son or any other man. The old people—we had two such couples—eat with their children but have their own tuperk—a very small one to sleep in. How it will be in winter I don't know. [. . .]

Both with H.'s Nunatama and with Roxy the men eat separately. Roxy's boy (ca. 14) eats with him, and so does another boy from Herschel Island whom Roxy brought down last time (about same age). The Nunatama children all ate with the women, what year the dividing line is, I don't know—probably when they begin hunting.

Our camp here consists of two tents set with doors opposite. One is Roxy, his wife, Mamline (Neviluk) ca. 14, a woman Roxy brought from Herschel, and her boy of 14 and Roxy's boy. The other is Whiskers, his wife and daughter (15). She smokes, Neviluk does not—probably sign of being past puberty—so Walker says.

Roxy was born at Kupik, other side Rullen Island ca. 55 miles. Alualuk, and another Husky, live there now. Speak a little English. They had implements of copper from Coppermine. [. . .]

Roxy says he is so used to Nunatama language now he hardly knows what words are Nunatama—has to stop to think [. . .] .

SEPTEMBER 4 At 8 A.M. Whiskers awoke our tent by telling Roxy there were 5 boats passing, coming from Herschel. [. . .]

These women (5 they are) have one strip of tatoo ca ½ inch wide on chin—some a little narrower. One is split slightly at the top, as if by a failure of having the tatoo lines of the band quite touch. All the men over ca. 30 years have labret holes, but none wear them: one younger (ca. 25) has them, one of almost 30 has none. Two boys ca. 14 and 12 have none. One of the men has his feet gone up to knee. Is cheerful and active—does all his own work apparently. He would not allow his head to be measured. Neither would 3 children—there are 16 in the party—no one old, for even the gray-haired woman seems not old.

I suppose their meal with Roxy and his partner is typical of such welcomes to travelers. The men went into the partner's tent, the women and children into Roxy's. Then they had some raw fish—they prefer it a little "high," Roxy says, so they had it out of the cache. Each man takes a fish, cuts off the fins, ca. 2 inches off the tail in front of the tail fin; and then eats with his knife the fish having the consistency of a fresh one ⅔ cooked. A dish of seal blubber was also on: of this each man takes a hunk; cutting off it a small piece for each mouthful of fish—as it were buttering his bread practically—he puts the blubber in his mouth immediately after the fish and chews them together. [. . .] Each cup (as I may have elsewhere described) is handed the guest in its own napkin. When through drinking he folds it after wiping the cup and saucer "clean" with it. They usually drink from the saucer to cool the tea. In folding, the saucer is placed on the centre of the napkin and the corners brought in as they just touch in the middle of the saucer bottom. The cup is placed right side up upon the corners of the napkin and the sides of the napkin brought up and stuffed into the cup. The napkin which is big and usually of some white stuff (seldom thick) fills the cup and makes of the whole a ball which may be rolled about without coming apart. This is a convenient thing in moving camp, or even in the crowded houses.

The eyes of all these people are dark brown (as coffee made weak so you can barely see bottom of cup before milk is added). A few of them have a slight tendency to widening of the nostrils (negro [. . .] fashion) but most of them not. Their teeth seem good, though some (especially women's) look yellow and are worn down in front. [. . .]

At about 3 P.M. another omiruk arrived with Nunas bound for the delta. I got measurements of six. One of these was not a Nunatama—a woman from the west somewhere (I got her people's name as Akwamiuk). She had olive complexion, and is the prettiest Husky I have seen—an Italian face of the best oval type. One man refused to be measured, and all but one child ran off, and he began crying. They left ca. 6 P.M. for the Sandspit [. . .] .

SEPTEMBER 5 [. . .] The fish catching continues good. Roxy's small nets get about 100 fish for hour at night, and ca. 25 pr. hr. in the daytime. We are hoping for westerly winds to bring the muddy water from Kay Point way down here in which case Roxy says the day fishing will be as good as at night. But he is in no hurry to catch fish, saying there will be so many by and by that he can get all he wants for himself and dogs in a few days. The fish apparently mistake the narrow bay behind the point for a river; and come up it in great numbers, but soon go back.

Roxy tells me the name Kagmalit was given them by the Pt. Barrow and Nunatama. They always referred to themselves (if not as "Innuit") as "the people of Kupik," or the people of "Kittegari." [. . .]

It was in his father's time but before his own that Kupik people first saw tea, sugar and flour, though they had pipes and leaf tobacco—[. . .] it was leaf tobacco I infer for their mistaking tea leaves thrown away after meals at the fort for tobacco and took it home, dried it and tried to smoke but were surprized to find the smoke "no taste like tobacco." Roxy says that when he was about 12, he and Oalyuak [. . .] who was a year older stole some tea from Nillian Smith (Indian) at McPherson thinking it was smoking tobacco. They threw it away when they found out it was not [. . .].

Certain peculiarities of Roxy's English make me think his people make no clear distinction between "f" and "p," though they have both sounds. His dog "Fanny" he calls "Panny" [. . .] Berries he calls "ferries" [. . .].

SEPTEMBER 8 [. . .] Both yesterday and today I went for a seven-hour walk for game—yesterday with a rifle and saw plenty ducks and three flocks [. . .] today with a shotgun and saw only a few ducks for certain [. . .].

Roxy says his (foster) daughter is named Neviluk because "my mother die this one come up." He says names of dead are seldom given to a child born the next week though it may be, but usually 1, 2, or 3 years after death. When I asked him why he sometimes calls her "mama" he said: "she got name all same my mamma (mother)."

SEPTEMBER 9 [. . .] Roxy and Anderson say that both Nunatama and Kagmalits used to pull out the beard when it came, but Kagmalits never did this. Sometimes this was not done. From people I have seen I am inclined to think the upper lip often escaped this process, I have heard of heavily bearded Nuna, though this may be an effect of white contact. [. . .]

Today there is a newmarried couple in our village—Oblutok's daughter and Ijiktjak, the young man staying the winter with Stein. The affair went this way: Day before yesterday he asked first the father, then the mother [. . .] . Both were willing; then he asked the girl and she said "no." Yesterday he asked her again and she said: "Don't know" and today she said "yes" on the third appeal. So far as I can learn the parents said not a word to her one way or the other. This is all from Roxy's account. He has seen wedding ceremonies at the fort and tells me nothing of the sort takes place among his people. The order followed in this case is the regular order (though I see nothing to prevent a previous informal understanding between the young people). If anyone of the three asked says no, the affair goes no farther, though the question may be asked another time with better success. When all three are once agreed, the couple sleeps together the night following the day on which the agreement was reached—in the house of the girl's parents, Roxy says this is because "little girl fraid, boy no fraid." In this case Ijiktjak has no home anyway. [. . .]

Iaki's wife	
Nunatama.	
18.5	18.5)12).6 [79
14.6	1295
11.8	1650
13.6	______ 1665
13.7	79-
lobe	
nose no. 1 [. . .] .	

The doctor has seen several cases of severe labor among Eskimo women, but [. . .] all children were half breeds, one, whose father was a negro, was in labor 3 days.

Eskimo Mr. Firth says that in the (his) old days there used to be 2 or 4 times as many Huskies as now. In the early days before he came, they frequently fought the Indians; each was afraid of the other, but the Huskies won the last battle, which was fought half way down the Peel from McPherson. As a result the Company, to secure peace, had to pay blood money [. . .] , for the Huskies. Even then they mingled little at trading time. Both before and after this the Huskies frequently were killed in endless vendettas among themselves, this and disease decreased their number rapidly. [. . .]

Marriage: closely consanguine [. . .] . Man who marries must live with her family (father, elder brother, or who ever is head of it) for 12 months mostly doing menial (often women's) work. Nowadays marriages often are performed after the twelvemonth; in rare cases either man or woman's family terminates arrangement. At end of year man takes wife to his own family. [. . .]

All men have a totem or medicine and some women have: they are always beast or bird. The totem is "selected" [. . .] about the time he goes hunting. The Enko or medicine man [. . .] can cause and cure diseases. [. . .] Medicine man chants in curing diseases. Can cure or cause sickness at distances by [. . .] drumming, chanting, waving arms etc. [. . .]

No regular midwives, but women occasionally attend each other; difficulties of birth are always greater if child has a white father. [. . .]

"Long ago" there lived a man whose wife and children were always complaining of the cold in winter. So he set a snare for the sun where he goes down, and finally caught him, but then it grew so hot they could not approach near enough to release the snare. Finally the long-nosed moose volunteered to help them, and got close enough [. . .] , but in doing so he burned his teeth. [. . .]

Eskimo. An Eskimo woman must not leave her house or tent a "week" after the birth of a child. The Indian who told me this said the Indians have no such custom. I saw (July 21) the face (in the doorway of a tent) of a woman who had had a child the evening before. She was grinning [. . .] , but never came out of the tent. [. . .]

Eskimo. One of them called William Husky* [. . .] . He is considered by the Eskimo as expatriated—one of the Indians. He camps on top of the hill at McPherson, while the Eskimo never do so. The relations of the two peoples seem entirely friendly, and he is not really looked down on—merely is a foreigner.

(*Later: Mr. Firth says this a mistake. Man is Indian, called "Husky" because he picked up unusually many H. words when a boy). [. . .]

SEPTEMBER 10 This morning (12:30 P.M. rather) a boat arrived bringing the Major [. . .] , Annie and Pong [. . .] . Though Major is on his way to the fort, apparently for all winter—[in Icelandic] *mögulegt samkomulag hafi ikki verið hið besta að eyunni* [possibly there was not much agreement on the island]. He is trying to hire Roxy to take him to the fort, so as to take the boat back again. Then Roxy is to bring the boat back to the fort in the spring.

In eating raw fish today (only slightly high, I could barely smell it in the tent) Anderson (Kotzebue) had to go out and throw up what he had eaten, at which the other five (some K. some N.) who were eating in our tent laughed very much. When he came back he told me that his people never eat raw fish unless it is well rotten. The K. and N. prefer it a little rotten, but are fond of it in all stages from fresh from the net to a cheesy consistency. His people bury fish in the ground to rot it. Here that would not do, it would freeze. He says that although he has tried repeatedly these several years he has been in the country to eat raw fish with the K. and N., he always has to vomit what he had eaten. If he eats more after vomiting he has to vomit that also. [. . .]

The new-married people behave today as if nothing had happened unusual. The girl does her mother's work as before, and the boy helps as usual. Neither is the object of any particular attention from the rest of the people—no joking etc. In fact, it seems to be a more ordinary and less worrying process than among us. The girl is 15 years, the boy 20.

One of the rather admirable qualities of the Husky came out today when Major H. was asking Roxy (as I happenend to hear from where I was reading in another tent) when I would pay him for my keep—apparently intimating that I might not pay at all. Roxy said he didn't know and changed the subject immediately [. . .] .

The good humor of all these people is wonderful. Even when sick they joke. [. . .] Some have what might be called solemn or austere faces [. . .] but even they laugh at almost everything anyone says. When they are wet and cold they joke about it—though they seem to feel the discomfort about as whites do—and when there is nothing to eat they joke about that. When they have been fooled in a trade (as into buying Capt. McKennes' bad flour at double prices) that is a joke, also when an Indian (Paul) shot Roxy's dog [. . .] . When Paul brought him a dog to pay for the one killed he was surprised [. . .] .

This evening I have been to Jimmy's tent for tea and a piece of bread and molasses. When one of the women—we have 12 tents now—has cooked bread and made tea, the word is soon to spread around and everybody goes taking his cup, and napkin. [. . .] If a man comes late and finds the tea all gone he often goes to the women's tent and joins them in about the same fashion that one would sit down at another table in a hotel if he finds his usual seat filled. [. . .]

The kindness of these people is such that I cannot see how anyone who knows them can wish more for anything than that he [. . .] could repay their kindness fully. [. . .]

SEPTEMBER 11 [. . .] Roxy traded his watch Sunday for a tent and some other things. He, his wife, and I sleep in this new tent which he has put on the N. side of the old one; the new-married couple will share the old tent with the children later on. [. . .]

Yesterday a child was born in a Nunatama tent. Roxy tells me that women sometimes die at childbirth; that doctors—man or woman—are (among Kag.) often secured to be with the woman—sometimes they hold her head, sometimes her hand. The child, he says, is never touched until completely delivered. The Nunatama used to have the custom of confining the woman to her tent for a certain period [. . .] he says his people never did this, that she goes out as soon as she feels able. The Nunatama have discontinued this custom, he says.

He tells me the Nunatama build snowhouses outside their tents in winter—but I shall doubtless see this later on. His people always have wood in their permanent houses. [. . .]

Anderson tells me that his "place man, and Nunatama Kagm: all the same" give their children the names of people who have recently died—irrespective of sex. Supposing he died, and a girl was born soon after, she would be called "Anderson." If 2–3 people die she will get their names. He never heard of more than three, and does not know how many a person might have, supposing many people die—thinks that would be "just as you like."

He says "long time ago" Nunatama women used to go outside tent, perhaps make small tent, when childbirth approached. Now they don't, and, as far as he knows, his people never did.

When a man dies among his people or Nuna, some people don't dare to stay in the tent with the dead man; some do, and these fix him for burial. They wrap him in skins or cloth or put him in a box, and then place on elevated platform. He says he helped put up the Nunatama platform grave I photographed in the Sandspit in August—that contained the body of a woman who died ca. 100 miles up the Delta and whom A. brought down in his whaleboat. He says "some people are afraid" to use clothes, etc., that belonged to the deceased, but he has worn such clothes, and many (both his and Nuna) now do. [. . .]

SEPTEMBER 15 1 P.M. I agreed yesterday to go help Stein get his house from King Point, and today we are under way in the Penelope. We hoisted sail at 11:30 but our NE breeze is so slight that we have covered less than two miles so far. There are on board Anderson, his brother and Oblutok who are going to the island and Stein, Roxy and myself for King Pt.

SEPTEMBER 17 [. . .] On the way, just east of Sabine Point, Roxy pointed out the village site where he lived some years ago as a boy. At this place he said there were twelve whaling boats always ready to put out, and he remembers the whale killing. His father at one time was the first to spear one. Just beyond King Point was a village that supported six whaling canoes; beyond, at Stokes Pt., was another, the size of which he didn't know. [. . .] It seems to have been the fashion to indicate the size of a village by telling how many whaling boats they had. [. . .]

Various men whom I have asked tell me they prefer boiled fish to rotten raw fish. It seems chiefly a matter of convenience to eat it raw, though it may be that the preference for boiled is a taste acquired since the whites came. [. . .]

SEPTEMBER 18 Last night about sundown a ship was reported coming from the west, and great excitement prevailed until it was found it was only a whaleboat magnified by the fog. [. . .]

Last week arrivals from Herschel [. . .] reported that most of the Huskies there suffered from coughs and colds. The last 3–4 days, Roxy and his wife have been severely affected, as is Mrs. Oblutok. It seems that when they have a cold they dress less than usual. [. . .] Yesterday Roxy kept poking a straw up his nose to make himself sneeze—this he apparently considered a good medicine for his cold. He tells there is more sickness in summer than in winter among his people, and thought the fall season is very bad for colds, etc.

Yesterday Anderson suffered from toothache. I am told there was toothache before the whites came just as now.

Two of the young Kagmalit with the present party are without the pulled haircut, one close cropped and the other cut on a level with his ear lobes. Oyanginna, who looks fifty has grey hairs and tends to baldness in front.

Roxy [. . .] says colds and other sicknesses were less common before white men came—attributes this to tea, flour, etc. Before, they drank only water or "soup" of deer meat, seal, and occasionally fish.

SEPTEMBER 19 [. . .] I asked Roxy this morning concerning certain scars on his breast. He said they had been made when he was sick inside under the spot where the scars are. He said this was not done by a doctor, but by anybody. "I just said: 'Here, you come out this place' and somebody come out." His wife and others whom I have seen have similar scars. He is just now thinking of having his head cut to relieve a headache that goes with the cold he has had some time. He says "By and by blood come, headache all right."

Naipaktuna, a Kagm., whose measure I took today, objected to having his picture taken. He is a young man—say 20—and speaks good English. He told me that now he was sick, and if the picture was taken while he was sick it might hurt him and make him worse; if it were taken when he was well he guessed it would not hurt much, and if he saw me some other time when he was well he would speak to me and tell me I might take it.

Happy Jack whom I measured yesterday (Nuna) told me by-and-by I might get his picture, today he came and wanted to know how much I would pay him and said I couldn't have it unless I paid for it. I was anxious for his picture. His cheeks are the highest looking I have seen—they project forward almost as far as the tip of his nose and so his nose comes out of a sort of hollow in his face.

On seeing more of the Kagmalit I found that tall men are much rarer among them than among the Nunatarmiut, while their women are all rather small. Many of those who are here now, seem to have weak eyes, and one woman is blind in one eye. All the young men have labret holes, and only two are without the pulled hair cut. One woman has a chin tattoo of three bands one-third of an inch wide each, separated by two spaces one-eighth of an inch wide. The bands are a trifle wider on the chin than at the lip. The woman's dress shows conspicuously the V-cut both before and behind. [. . .]

Happy Jack, who is a Point Barrow man, is married to a Kagmalit woman, the one [. . .] being blind in one eye.

SEPTEMBER 20 [. . .] Roxy's nephew, young Roxy, was quite sick. Stein tells me his wife (who, as almost all women here, has been a kept woman) contracted gonorrhea last winter from a "Portagee," and that he is suffering from it now. S. says gonorrhea is often fatal to the Huskies (cf. Jones statement regarding gonorrhea among Mackenzie Indians) though Roxy himself is said to have had it and still looks strong.

Roxy says that before Fort McPherson was established musk-ox skins were always thrown away and foxskins only occasionally used [. . .] for clothes for children under ten years of age. The musk-ox robes were too heavy to carry. When he first remembers, his people gave as many as forty foxskins for a small knife. Their tents were then usually made of mooseskins, although that animal is almost never killed now by people living at Kupik.

When he was a small boy deer were usually killed in the following way:

They were found in a position where they could be cornered against a lake or river, the men went out and cautiously made a semicircle about them. If there were too few men to completely invest the deer, scarecrows were employed alternately with the men. When all was ready the men began to howl like wolves. Sometimes the deer dashed into the water at once. Sometimes they ran toward the men, but were turned back by them and the scarecrows and finally took to the water. Then they were dispatched by spearmen in kayaks. He remembers as many as two hundred deer killed in one day. Sometimes the people considered enough had been killed and let the rest escape.

Roxy explains "Umialik" as man who has an umiak, and says that at Kupik, and among Kagmalit generally a man who owns a umiak is so called. Ilialuk is a name applied to a man who has neither umiak nor kayak, and who has no parents, even if he has children living.

Roxy says earrings, such as his wife wears now, long pendants of dentalia about one and a half inches long (two lengths, plus beads), were always made by his people, and who found dentalia on Husky Lake, also occasionally bought them from Nunatama.

Roxy says that he long ago gave up the use of skin underwear, prefers woolen or cotton.

SEPTEMBER 22 [. . .] All together it was my hardest day at sea.

This morning, on the believe of the police that the Narwhal would soon return from her whaling cruise, we decided to wait till Monday morning at the longest. But before noon the Narwhal appeared. Capt. Leavitt told me very little additional about my ship. He said Mikkelsen was aboard and asked him to be towed through the ice—ca. 30 miles. This Leavitt was unable to do. [. . .]

[In Icelandic:] *Skrælingi minn segir að gángari lögreglusveinn, sé nú giftur skrælingjakonu þeirri er Unalína nefnist, og verið hefur frylla lángs nokkurs, fyrsta styrimanns á hvalfángara skipinu 'bogahaus.' Mun það satt vera, og mun fitharaldur einnig hafa fryllu tekið.*

[My native says that the policeman 'Walker' (*'gángari'*; from *'ganga,' 'to walk'*) is now married to a native woman named Unalin, formerly the concubine of a certain Long, a mate on the whaling ship 'Bowhead.' This is true, and Fitzgerald (*'fitharaldur'*) also has taken a concubine.]

Walker tells me that when a whitefish was killed here this fall pieces of the skin were given to "everybody," i.e. to each native or family on the beach. The same is true when an ugrug is killed, but not of a small seal. For waterproof soles whitefish skin is best, and ugrug comes next.

SEPTEMBER 23 [. . .] At noon I had dinner with the police—Sgt. Fitzg., Mr. W., Capt. L. and myself—and it was as fine a one as I have seen here—oyster stew, caribou steak, french fried potatoes (in perfect condition), pear, bacon and coffee with cream and sugar—excellent bread.

After dinner I secured measurements 21–22 and 23. Kabheahek ("22") is Roxy's half brother by an exchange of wives, Roxy's father and another man's wife. This is seldom more than one night at a time, and seldom except upon the two families meeting after a protracted separation. After another separation this may be repeated. This practice seems to be seldom indulged in except by close friends, partners, sort of blood brothers. Roxy says the Nunatama custom is the same. He says that even when a man has two wives (this applies to Kagmalit, he does not seem to know Nunatama custom), and a traveling friend who has none arrives, they never lend him one of the wives. (Though from their general freedom, I suppose a traveler could get one if he tried hard—that is my sure opinion.)

I notice that most of the natives (excluding kept women, and also those on the Narwhal, of whom I know nothing) who are now staying at Herschel Island (perhaps fifteen grown men all told) are Kagmalit. There is no one whom I know to be anything else than Kagmalit. They seem to be depending largely on the seals they catch in nets.

SEPTEMBER 25 [. . .] Sunday night I saw an ula-hula in one of the Mesinka houses. Several dancers followed one another. There was scant room for three (one woman and two men) to dance, and that was the largest number. Much of the time there was no one, while two danced only occasionally, one man being the rule. There seemed to be two or three slightly different ways to beat the drums, but different dances were also danced to the same tune. Each dance was only from two to four minutes long; but when a dancer once was up, he usually danced from one-fourth to one-half hour. One old man, a doctor (Kagmalit—in fact I heard the affair called a "Kagmalit ula-hula" and all those dancers whom I knew were Kagmalit, though several whom I knew as Nunatama looked on) danced until he was so exhausted that his motions, which had been exceedingly lively, became those of a man half asleep. The other dancers moved their heads, bodies and arms in a manner to make one who did not see their feet think they were jigging. Usually, however, the motion was at the knees, and one or both feet were kept nearly still. [. . .]

The old man rushed about, shook all parts of his body apparently to the dislocation point, and roared and shouted hoarsely. Occasionally, he dashed into the crowd and seized a certain young man by the head, shaking him. The spectators laughed and the young man took it coolly. I was told afterwards that the old man was making the young one a doctor, for fun. This meant, so far as I could understand, that the present generation was having performed for its amusement a ceremony that had been serious formerly. No one appeared to be very serious. Two young men who took care of Roxy's tent during his stay at the dance, passed the time by singing Church of England hymns. One of these was Eskimo [. . .] .

A game of handball Sunday afternoon was played as follows: The crowd was divided into two parties, usually this is the men vs. the women, but this crowd was promiscuous, a few men helping the women's side. The ball is thrown to any member of one's own side and by him to anyone he chooses. The game is to intercept the ball and to get it into play on one's own side. I was told there were no prohibitions. You could even take the ball out of an opponent's hand by force. This I never saw done, but pushing, etc., was frequent. This game, I was told by Roxy, was played at Kupik before whites came.

Many seem expert jugglers, especially the women. They will keep three stones in the air with one hand, or keep one ball in the air a long time with the toe of one foot, kicking it several times in the air.

Blanket-tossing a woman, and jumping springboard are favourite amusements. The blanket-tossing I have not seen; formerly a big seal hide with handles was used. The woman tossed kept on her feet if she could, and was thrown twelve to fifteen feet in the air, it is said. Broken bones and dislocated joints were often the result. I have seen women who have been pointed out as having broken arms [. . .] .

Capt. Leavitt assures me that Oaiuk's father was as real a chief at Kupik as there ever was at Point Hope or Port Clarence. He himself has paid this chief toll and could not get deer hunters except through him. If personally offended, he would compel all the Kagmalit of his village to boycott certain ships and sell meat to certain others, even when the boycotted ships offered a higher price. Displeasing other natives had no such consequences. [. . .] .

SEPTEMBER 27 [. . .] Close to Sabine Point the rudder came off, and we got our first serious scare. Oblutok who sat amidships, was too excited to be able to push down the centreboard and I left the bailing to do this. Roxy soon got the rudder on. For the rest of the way the blows of the waves kept shoving the rudder up and it had to be frequently hammered down. Mrs. Roxy was about as cool as anyone and attended to stacking the sail, which Roxy either trusted her to do without orders, or forgot to do—

I don't know which. We got under way again without taking in any water just then. We were running all the time under a full sized storm sail.

Just before coming opposite the whaleman's house at Shingle Point the boat began dipping her nose into the billow in front, and was taking in waves on both sides, both forward and aft. A few minutes later all the people of Shingle Point—except Mr. S. (probably too dignified)—saw us about this time and came running to the beach, expecting us come ashore. I had ¾ of a mind to advise this but left it in Roxy's hands. He said he would run ashore if the boat was his; but said if we did escape that way Stein would never stop growling, besides we had a good chance of being lost, and would surely lose both boat and contents. So I told him all right, we would try for the end of the sandspit—a mile farther.

Ijiktjak and Roxy's two boys ran along till the end of the sandspit, which we rounded in terrific breakers, for the lake is shallow. When we came just inside the point a little water was coming in through the centreboard hole—we shoved this down just at the moment of rounding the point. I was cold and wet, and so walked home with Oblutok, who was also soaked while Ijiktjak and the boys took our places. [. . .]

Roxy says six years ago fifteen Kagmalit died at Herschel Island of pneumonia, and in one week seventeen at Kupik. Ever since he remembers Kagmalit have been dying fast.

Soon after passing Kay Point yesterday we saw by the angle of the Penelope's masts that she had gone ashore. We found her high and dry ca ¼ mile from the houses. She had had only the big anchor out, and had dropped it. She went ashore Sunday night.

Most of the Huskies seem fond of cards, though I have seen no gambling. Often the women play, and Roxy and his wife frequently and their little girl often with them play casino. Many of both sexes are also fond of checkers, but none play chess, so far as I know.

SEPTEMBER 28 Last night Oblutok, and some of the rest of our folks, had an ula-hula in the next tent until after 12:00 at night. [. . .]

Roxy tells me that when he was a boy they had various jumping tricks, one to kick a stick over their head with both feet, landing on them again, another was to tie a thong around the neck and just above the knee of one foot and drawing the knee close to the chin and kicking with the free foot.

He showed me tonight various scars on his legs where he had been cut when swollen there, and water came out. He says if cuts had not been made the swelling would have turned "all the same bone" as they did in the case of a man he cited.

Today I got from Roxy about 60 words of the vocabulary on parts of the body. [. . .]

SEPTEMBER 29 [. . .] Roxy says at Kupik they had a special whale house. This house was used for no other purpose.

OCTOBER 2 [. . .] Sunday work on Stein's house was suspended, but Roxy kept on fixing his, and moved in towards evening. Monday Oblutok moved into the house also, so there are now ten in it. Later young Roxy and his wife, whose tent has been moved near the house, will come into it also. In order to get the necessary room the beds are arranged steamer fashion.

Besides having gonorrhea young Roxy appears to me to have consumption also. I was therefore afraid to go into the house. Mrs. Roxy's consumption was bad enough in a tent, but the two of them in a house rather scares me, so I arranged with Stein to take me into his house. This puzzled and worried Roxy a good deal, evidently. This led to a talk last night as to our past bargains. I reminded him that he agreed to keep me without any furnishing any grudge, and to take me to Eskimo Lake, all for a 4 pt. blanket and "some tea." But that I had already given him a sack of flour I got from Harrison and intended to give him ten gallons of molasses and 40 lbs. of pork, besides the three piece of pork I had already given him. This he declared was not enough, and he wanted more some time. I told him I would give him no more, but he told me with such apparent sincerity, that while I had nothing he had intended keeping me for nothing but that now I had grub he wanted some, that I decided after leaving him to give him another sack of flour, and I carried this to him later in the evening. But, like Hall in his book, I have had something of a change of heart concerning the Eskimo, that I am not sure it is well founded.

Yesterday and today a large wood-shed has been added to the NW side of Stein's house—and I have spoken tentatively of buying it (the house) next year "in case certain things happen." I have helped in the work at intervals. [. . .]

Roxy tells me that when he was a boy of about 12 years of age fights with weapons were frequent between Kitigari and Kupik—Kitigari being only about six miles E from Kupik. As I understand, these were sort of impounded fights between individuals or small groups, the fight sometimes followed vendettas. He says that men of one village often picked up things which men of another claimed belonged to them, and fights resulted. In these spears, clubs, snow knives or anything else were used, and men were often killed (cf. Firth's account). But about the time Roxy was 18–20 years old, these inter-village fights came to an end; apparently simply because people began to see they were silly.

When he was a boy he says there were seven houses in Kitigari of the type of his own house at Shingle Point only they were larger, most of them. These housed, on an average, six families, he says. There were also small huts of skins on a frame like a smoke house, "perhaps two, perhaps four," in which certain unattached persons lived (orphans, though mostly old people). He does not remember how many houses there were at Kupik at the time, though there were more houses there than at Kitigari. Kupik, besides, was a trading centre for the people to the east as far as Liverpool Bay, and beyond and to the west as far as Herschel. The fights do not seem to have prevented this intercourse. They were more in the nature of quarrels or brawls, and seem to have occurred especially at these meetings.

In scraping skins the women use both iron and stone scrapers, the stone scrapers seem to be preferred with rough skins at the first scraping, or rather, in beginning the scraping. On small skins, as muskrat, I have seen only iron ones used. [. . .] . Tulugak's wife rubs the inside of rat skins with a paste of flour and water; Stein says that at Point Hope they take a little white, chalk-like stone, burn, and powder it, using it to rub on skins. Though she is a Kagmalit she may have learned this from her husband's people, who are Nunatama. [. . .]

The lampwick used by Oblutok is composed of moss. By the side of the lamp is always lying a little round stick which is left in the oil and lighted whenever they need to look into dark corners. This torch is also used for lighting pipes, etc.

Mr. and Mrs. Tulugak sleep at night with their necks and upper part of the body uncovered by the bedclothes, when the house is so cold that with two shirts on I find the double 4-pt. blanket scarcely enough covering. It is to be noted, however, that they suffer continually with cold, and deep coughing all night—though in the daytime they cough but little.

OCTOBER 3 [. . .] We can see from here that someone is living on the sandspit, 5 miles E. Tulugak thinks it is the old member of Iaki's party—the one with the white hair and enormous white and green labrets—the one that would not let me measure his head. [. . .]

OCTOBER 4 [. . .] Roxy has told me two things of considerable interest: First, that "170" years ago, when his father's father was a small boy he could barely remember seeing the last of a woman's labret which had been in fashion before that time. These were single labrets, of stone usually he thinks, worn in a hole in the middle of the lower lip. They made the lip stick out "like a shelf," as he indicated with his hand.

The second was, that a greyish stone was "all the same gold" among his people formerly. This was soft and stood fire perfectly, and was used for labrets, lamps, etc. It came from Prince Albert Land. He showed me a pair of labrets of the material, and it seems to me the same as Klengenberg's lamps.

Of pottery Roxy never saw any, but his wife had seen some fragments brought from the west, and he had been told by western natives of its manufacture and use.

OCTOBER 5 [. . .] Stein and I went after "grouse" in the forenoon and secured ten, four of which went to Roxy, as I had his gun and seven skulls. With these I killed only three; two with Stein's gun before he went home and two after he took home the 8 we had killed and my empty gun. The meal (soup) we had of the six this evening is the best I have had since dining with the police—a dinner previously extolled, I believe.

The nail hole in the sole of my foot (received at King Point when tearing Stein's house down) healed up ca. the 26–29 of September but is even now a little painful, though I haven't walked lame the last 7–8 days.

Roxy tells that when a man of his village killed a whale (as boat-steerer) he wore a crowskin with beaks and claws across his back for some time after. It was also usual to tattoo him with two lines running from the corners of the mouth to the angle of the lower jaw below and in front of the ears. His father killed a whale about in October and wore a crowskin until about April. When the houses had all been fixed and all preparations made for winter, he sent word out that there would be eating and ula-hula at his house for the intended tattooing because of the whale he had killed. The house was filled with guests, and during the celebration the two lines were tattooed.

Formerly the women and men of Kupik used to tattoo a line diagonally down from the nose. He remembers seeing one old man and two old women (all very old) who had the tattoo. Boas shows tattoo works carved up from the wings of the nose, so I shall make further inquiries, for Roxy assigns both the name "tummitok."

In an umiak the man who steers is "umialik" while the boat-steerer is "niuyakti." The crew range from three to six besides this, and often consisted in part of women.

Roxy had previously explained that the wearing of feathers, etc.,was for purposes of identification. He says that the same sort of feather, or other insignia, was also tied to snow knives, or any other article of value that was likely to be left lying around—to show at a glance whose it was.

OCTOBER 7 [. . .] Today the woodshed was finally completed by putting on doorposts and a door. The place looks comfortable for winter now. This evening I finally secured Roxy's women folk's consent to have their heads measured.

Roxy corroborates, in a measure, Capt. Leavitt's statements as to chiefs at Kupik. He says his own father (Itaarktjiak) and grandfather were chiefs there. When his father died, Oaiyuak's uncle, Kaxalik, became chief and remained so until (six years?) ago, when he and seven other members of his household of eleven died of the black measles—among others his two wives and his eldest son; a younger son lived (who was too young to be made chief, besides he didn't want the post). Three years ago "Mr. Frith made Oaiyuak chief" (by giving him tea, etc., apparently). Some time later a trader at Red R. made another Kupik the chief in a similar manner—by making him his trading representative, or Katatje.

"Long ago" the chief had much power. No one could sell deer meat without the chief's permission. This agrees perfectly with Leavitt, and Roxy explicitly says that Kaxalik had this power, though the chief has no such power now.

In Kagmalit dancing [. . .] , a stick six inches long, called "Kattuk," is used to beat the drum, which is half rotated with a tambourine motion and a blow is struck on each edge alternately.

In stretching the drum, it is "tuned" by tapping with the fingertips around the edges. If the sound at any place does not satisfy, the skin is readjusted at that point. The material is usually deerskin.

The balls used in play by Kagmalit were kicked with the foot and were some three to five inches in diameter. The outside was often of white fish skin and the stuffing was fine wood shavings or whalebone.

I am told that Mrs. Oblutok's father, who lived at Kittegaryumiut sometimes, always spent his winter at the S. end of Eskimo Lake, near where our camp is supposed to be. [. . .]

Both Roxys agreed last night that if they saw a man too far away to know his race they would speak of him as "innuk." But they didn't seem to see any reason in the world why a man near whom you were should not always be called Kabluna, Tamik; or subluarana if he were white.

If I understand Roxy right, dancing was sometimes in the nature of contests between villages. Persons danced as representatives of certain villages, and sometimes men not belonging to a certain village might be chosen to dance for it; say, if all the crowd were Kupik, certain men might be told "you be Kittegaryumiut." Whether these were contests of strength, endurance, or what, I do not know. [. . .]

OCTOBER 8 [. . .] Roxy says that so far as he knows, nose rubbing was never a general form of salutation, but was indulged in practically solely by old people who saw their children after a long separation—perhaps after believing them dead.

I described to Roxy Hanbury's louse remedy for sore eyes, as he saw it. Roxy says that he has been told that the Nunatama run a hair across the eye in some cases, and also that they sometimes make a hair fast to a louse to "make him scratch" the eye. His people, he says, use a sharp, bent nail and make a little wound inside the eyelid with it. When the eye clouds, I understood him to say, they occasionally scratched the eyeball.

For snow blindness the Nunatama, he says, cut the tip of the nose, and prod sticks up their nostrils; the Xagm. cut on a level with the eye and an inch or inch and a half back of the outer corner of the eye, and also on the top of the head above each eye just in front of the tonsure or even across the front border of the tonsure. Cutting, Roxy says, is their only "medicine," and is not done by the doctor, but by anyone at all, often by the patient himself. They cut for everything. I believe I have already noted that Timmiuni, whose eyes are now well, was cured by cuts on the top of his head, and that Tsitsak was cured of earache by a vertical cut an inch and a half long and about an one-eighth inch deep, an inch in front of the ear, the middle of the cut being on a level with the opening of the ear. The small of Roxy's back is practically covered with scars, and he has them all over, even on his fingers. They emphasize that it is not so much blood, as water, that comes out, and this water must be gotten rid of in some way.

Sometimes the doctor is called. He works in the patient's house, and his treatment consists in songs and dances. While he is at work no one must leave the house, though the doctor himself often goes out, goes around the house, and comes in again. The dance ordinarily lasts from about 7:00 P.M. to 1:00 A.M. Occasionally it may be longer. Sometimes, too, there are recesses of a few minutes, when people may leave the room.

The fee is proportioned according to the severity of the disease, and ranges from three to five foxskins, to a finished umiak made for the doctor of from five to seven whitefish skins. If a man is poor, people join in and give the doctor anything they feel like, one a knife, another a foxskin, etc., regarding these contributions as much as a matter of course, as giving a destitute man food.

If the doctor makes a cure, or if he fails to cure but the patient lives, he keeps his fee; but if the patient dies soon after treatment, the doctor comes back with whatever he has received and refunds it. Among the Nunatama, Roxy says, the doctor got no pay until the benefits from his treatment were evident.

In the time of Roxy's great-grandfather (paternal) his people lived in two villages about one mile apart, Kupik and Kingnirit; but the filling in by the sea of the places where they used to kill whitefish induced them to move some six or seven miles, where they founded Kittegaryumiut and Tsannirak; these last places being about one mile apart. In Tsannirak there were two kajigis and in Kittegaryumiut three. But these have all fallen in ruins and been burnt, and there are now no kajigis on the coast. [. . .]

When dancing was on they sometimes danced a whole day without eating; when they ate they had to go to their own houses for the food. In the spring the kajigi was used as a workshop for repairing umiaks, etc. [. . .]

The kajigi had the same sort of an entrance as an iglu, was lighted and heated comfortably with lamps and had windows of whitefish skin.

The three–four weeks ending about "New Years" were almost continual dancing, R. says. The month was called the "dancing time." There appear to have been eleven "months" in the year, counted from each new moon—a bit of these is "in the vocabulary." Probably there were ten "moons" and the moonless summer time filled the remaining three. Roxy puts it that they "left August out."

OCTOBER 9 [. . .] Roxy drew for me a map indicating the position of the old towns Kupik and Kingnirit and the newer ones, Kittegaryumiut and Tsannirak. The people at Kingnirit moved to Kittegaryumiut and those of the Kupik to Tsannirak. This was in Roxy's great-grandfather's time. The Kopuk men, both while at Kupik and later at Tsannirak, hunted up the Anderson River while the Kittegaryumiut people hunted towards Richard Island. The result of hunting up the Anderson was frequent fights between the Kupik men and Itkillik, who were thus traditional foes.

The last "fight" with Itkillik came when Roxy was a small boy—he does not remember it. His mother and his brother and cousins were in an Itkillik house of which they had taken uninvited possession. The Itkilliks, who were eight in number, tried to drive them out and a fight ensued. Roxy's mother killed two with a knife; four others were killed, and two escaped—a boy of 12 and an old man. This fight occurred on the Peel and is probably the one of which Firth tells (see notebook no. 1). The Itkilliks used to come down as far as Tunurnak.

I noticed today that young Roxy wears a young hawk's wing feather suspended by the "near" end by a string around his neck inside his shirt. I asked him "why" and he said he didn't know—someone gave it to him long ago and he always wears it. Roxy explained that this was a remnant of the "marks" he had explained to me before—worn as unquestioned as we wear our Xian names, be they William or Van der Möller. Young Roxy produced two white weasel skins fastened together at both ends. These were to be worn as a wreath, only more on the back of the head than the classic. There was a string to tie these under the throat. Y.R. said he would not sell them for any money. Roxy said he had a wolverine head skin split so as to fit as a fillet on his head, but that he disposed of it many years ago, for he got to see they were no use. Whatever may have been the understood meaning of these things once, Y.R. seems to prize it much as a gift—as we might be unwilling to part with a spoon sent us at teething time—they seem to have no present idea of their mystic value or significance, but only regard it as a matter of course that they must be treasured.

OCTOBER 10 [. . .] Roxy tells that the "Kagmalit singing," a [. . .] continuous and softer song, accompanied evenly on the drum, which is half rotated in the hand and struck on alternate edges, came from the east lately, reaching Kittegaryumiut only some ten years ago, and Shingle Point later.

In the "Kagmalit dance" which is now at all events, not always to the Kagmalit song, only one man and one woman take part at one time, being followed by another pair when they are tired; in the Tuyormiut form, the most common at Herschel, any number of either sex take part. In the Kittegaryumiut kajigi there was usually one big drum (say, three to four feet across) and this sufficed, but the Tuyormiut often had as many as five drums.

When a visitor came from another district it was usual to dance as long as he pleased before eating. Roxy has heard that "long ago" there were fighting games, but his information on the point has been vague.

He gave me the following information for coast Huskies:

Tuyovmiut = Shingle Pt. to Herschel
Nolouganmiut = McKinley Bay
Kagmallialuit = Baillie and around
Kagmalit = Langley Bay

At Herschel if a sled came from the east it was always said: "Kagmalit are coming!"

At Kittegari they did not use nets for whitefish but speared them from kayaks. Roxy thinks there were as many as one hundred kayaks. A good hunter, if he was lucky, sometimes speared ten in a day.

OCTOBER 11 [In Icelandic:] *Skrælingi sá er hjá steini [. . .] býr lætur sér lítt bregða þó hinn reiðist og tali illmannlega og drjúgt.* [The native staying with Stein is undisturbed although the other gets angry and speaks proudly and in a brutal manner].

It seems they look upon such things with indulgence, regarding it as the white man's idiosyncrasy [. . .]. [In Icelandic:] *Hann sagði brosandi við mig í dag að steinn talaði rétt eins og hann væri Kapteinn.* [He said to me smiling today that Stein spoke as if he were a Captain] [. . .]

Roxy's wife saves the feathers of the birds eaten, and uses them as swabs whenever it is thought necessary to wipe a pot, or some mess off the floor. Feathers are occasionally used to wipe the hands after meals.

Succession of chiefs. Roxy says when a chief died his eldest son became chief; if he had no son, his brother became chief; if no brother, some relative in whom the people had confidence. If the son was mentally or otherwise unfit, the people would decide that fact and then the succession took effect. If there was no brother, popular opinion decides which of the relatives should become chief. [. . .]

Kajigis: As before stated Tsannirak had two kajigis and Kittegaryumiut three. The doors were not like the iglu's [. . .] , but were something after the white man's style. There was a whitefish skin employed to close the door when necessary. When a dance was to be held, no fire was lighted that day, and the house cleaned just before the dance—normally this began between 4 and 7 P.M.

Kaxalik vs. Whittaker: Roxy gives the facts of this quarrel as follows: K. offered Stringer a whiskey bottle to drink from; S. handed it back; K. offered it to W. who smashed it. He says K. threatened to kill W. but does not know if he would do it.

Attempt to kill Whittaker: A Husky whom Roxy names went into W.'s store house to see what stores he had. W. ordered him out roughly.

OCTOBER 12 [. . .] Commerce at Kittegari. For copper, lamp stone, tutak stone, etc., the Kagmalit paid in skins and blubber, paying as much as five whitefish skins for a copper skin scraper. The place seems to have been a trading center, as was Kupik.

OCTOBER 13 Waterproofs. They had a waterproof garment made after the manner of a union suit, with hood and boots attached. It had a slit of a few inches down from the neck in front for putting on, and was made large, to go over artegi, water boots, and everything. [. . .]

Trade with Point Barrow. The first man of whom Roxy knows that came from Point Barrow was one who arrived in a umiak at Herschel a few years before Roxy was born. He stayed there until after the freeze-up, when some Shingle Point people took him home with them. Later he was taken to Kupik by a resident of that place, and finally he got as far as Baillie Islands, where he married and turned back with his wife, who was a cousin of Kunaslik's grandmother. After this Point Barrow people frequently came as far as Baillie, bringing tobacco and labrets which they exchanged for copper and stone for kodliks.

Kaxalik: R. says K. was made chief by Firth: Roxy's father was the last real chief apparently.

OCTOBER 14 The tents of the Kagmalit were made conical on a frame of ten or more sticks tied together at the top in the manner of the cooking tripod. They were preferably of moose, though seal and deer were also used. It was the Nunatama who introduced the dome shaped tents.

Kagmalit-Nunatama disagreement. Four years ago the Kagmalit delivered the Nunatama a sort of ultimatum to the effect that if they did not stop using poison for animals they would have to leave the country. This the Nunatama seem to have taken to heart.

OCTOBER 15 Yesterday noon three Nunatamas (one of them Iaki's son-in-law) came from the East with pack dogs. Their camp is five sleeps away. They have killed 68 deer since they went inland (ca. September 6) and brought some meat on pack dogs. They will sell Stein some, on credit till the ships come. Roxy, Tsitsak and I are going with them. I take Stein's sled and six dogs. We may stop a few days to hunt. I take a regular sled and Roxy a toboggan and we start probably Wednesday, October 17. Stein has lent one of them his sled that is at King Point and he is getting it today; returning tomorrow.

OCTOBER 19 [. . .] Thursday I left Shingle at 6:15 A.M. and got to Escape R. at 7:30 catching most of the folks in bed. We started at 9 with 5 sleds and 1 toboggan—Roxy. Our party is: Roxy and Tsitsak, who go to hunt, Mr. and Mrs. Tulugak, who will join with the camp, the three Nunas who came down to get their sleds, and an old man, Ijiktjak, who has been at the Reef since left there by Harrison's party. We made 4–5 miles and camped. Iaki is to let the "Son in Law" go back to the Reef for his tobacco. [. . .]

OCTOBER 21 Saturday we had heavy traveling—up hill all the time, going along a ravine where the sleds dragged on the stones. About sundown Tulugak camped, his dogs being tired. An hour later we got to the top of the ridge, and half an hour later camped at a deer cache of our Nunatama friends: meat slightly rotten. Have been eating kirktjak the last few days. [. . .]

OCTOBER 25 Camp. Yesterday we picked up another deer, leaving, however, some of the meat for me to take going back. At 6:00 P.M. we arrived at the camp. It consists of two oval brush and moss houses, the larger about twelve by twenty-five feet and eight feet at the top of the vaulted roof. There are three women and four children in the camp. The men left in charge had killed 11 deer while our companions were absent.

Shedding teeth. A little girl who had just pulled out one of her milk teeth, wrapped it in a piece of meat and gave it to a dog. This, I was told, the Nunatama always do.

Candles. The Nunatama have always used candles, one I saw being about two inches in diameter. [. . .]

Traps. Yesterday, we stopped to make a wolverine trap. The beast has to reach in through a door for the greased end of a long stick, on the outer end of which a short stick is pivoted to support the roof.

OCTOBER 26 [. . .] At supper tonight we had a mess made by stirring together a quart each of metted deer and finely minced meat. This we stirred with the hand in a ten quart pail, and in half an hour the pail was full of a puffy creamy stuff. It tasted fairly good, but is too rich for a white man's taste. The stuff is called "akuttok" by the Nunatama. [. . .]

NOVEMBER 1 After two more sleeps we got home last night at 7:15 P.M. going from the river near where we had the third sleep going up—making 3 days in 1. We got up at 3 A.M. and started at it, two hours were spent also in climbing the hill from the river. At dark (4:30) we made a small cache in the river bottom 2 miles from Escape Reef. At that point I shot a dog who had followed [. . .] . He would have stayed to eat the meat had we left him.

Home life, Kagmalit. Tonight Roxy's wife was unusually sick, head, back, etc. The manner in which he sat by her, held her hand and forehead and rubbed her back, was exactly in the manner to be expected of a "civilized" man who had great affection for his invalid wife.

Nunatamas. Social life: It seems one reason why natives prefer [. . .] women who have lived with whites is that they "savage" more—are up to white men's ways in trade, etc. and can work after their fashion and advise them in dealings with whites. I am told so and I am seeing, believe it to be true that at the hunting camp both Ninquaktjiuna and Apokork defer in everything to their wives when trading with whites. N.'s wife, for instance, advised him against selling me deer skins for less than 5^{oo} for she knew they sold for that this summer at Herschel. She makes a mistake, for skins will be cheap next year, but the case is in point. Of course all wives have considerable influence, but these have a special one in dealing with whites.

NOVEMBER 2 *Property Marks:* Roxy's family property mark for generations in the male line was carved on sled toggles, spears, bows, etc. Clothes, etc., had feathers or skin stripes.

Infanticide. Stein tells me of two cases of infanticide last winter, a Point Barrow man and Nunatama wife; one Kagmalit woman who left her white husband. He has known of many other cases, usually girl babies.

NOVEMBER 3 Gave a birthday feast today. All Roxy's house came except young Roxy and wife. R.'s brother, Shapodaitok from Herschel, and a boy, also came. We had boiled, fried and raw deer meat, boiled and fried pork [. . .] , hot baking pound's bread, apple cake and coffee—plenty of everything and everybody apparently satisfied. [. . .]

NOVEMBER 8 [. . .] Wearing boots: The Nunatama wear their winter boots on alternate days on a different foot. The Kagmalit wear same boot on same foot all the time, as we do.

Dancing: Among the Kagm. where any dance is done the dancer may touch anyone present—man or woman—whose turn it then becomes, to dance at least one dance—a sort of "tag." [. . .]

NOVEMBER 17 [. . .] It must be considerably below zero today, but up to this it has not been cold—never more than—10°, I feel sure.

This morning I saw the first evidences of the sunrise—sunshine on the ice front to sea—at 10:15 A.M. [. . .] .

NOVEMBER 20 Today it is blowing the first blizzard of the year—equal to an ordinary N.N. blizzard, but not a star performance [. . .] . Stein came in it, arriving from King Point at 1:23 P.M. [. . .] Stein, etc., was stormbound 21 day in a good miner's cabin on Roy Pt. Bay, or near it on the river. Took them much to get to Herschel—Roxy went through ice twice and Stein and Tsitsak once—had narrow escapes from drowning. Followed coast all way, except cut across from King to head of Kay Pt. Bay—beach impassable.

NOVEMBER 23 Wednesday evening the patrol came—Corp. Haylow with David for guide [. . .] . No letters—none had come from the "outside" as the "October scow" had not connected with the Coingley. [. . .]

DECEMBER 9 [. . .] Thursday night we camped at Tunurnak, the first Kagm. village site on the way E. Had hoped to find people here. Dogs on one fish ration, for the loss of Sunday and Monday had put us behind in grub. [. . .]

Boy's first game. T. showed me a place near Kittegaryumiut where he shot his first duck. His parents invited all the neighbors for a feast with plenty of tea in honor of the event. [. . .]

Snowshoes. Typical Kagmalit snowshoes are of two pieces of driftwood sewed together with thong or whalebone at heel and toe; toe sharp and turned up. Nunatama are of two okpeks, spliced at the toe, rounded toes and turned up rather less than K. Have seen them made of one okpek around the toe.

House at Kangianik. Similar to Roxy's at Shingle Point. Four kodliks, one at each main post, kept burning all night, supplied with oil from a bunch of blubber suspended by a stick above and behind the flame. Wick is a pile of wood scrapings like sawdust. Kodliks are all of iron. House heated by stove also. Window of a white whale stomach. Ventilator always open. Rather warm inside, but no bad smell. Diet: fish and tea. [. . .]

Feuds. An old man here, whose father killed three men and wounded three more in one night with a knife. A man near here somewhere who killed two men with a rifle two or three years ago, one of these Roxy's cousin. Police have not been told.

Hand wipers. Both sexes employ considerable time in making shavings like fine excelsior with fistfuls of which one wipes his hands and mouth after eating.

Rate of growth. Tsitsak is said to be seventeen years old and to be full-grown. Roxy says boys are full grown at sixteen and seventeen.

DECEMBER 10 Surgery. Saw an incipient boil on a girl's back slit with knife today. A bunch of excelsior was put on as an absorbent.

Water holes. The one here has a windbreak of snow about three feet thick. There is an ice pick with a point of iron and a sort of spoon of wood with a blade about four by six inches, handle about seven feet. The water here has a faint trace of salt [. . .].

Cleanliness. Today they scrubbed the floor carefully with warm water and rags. Floor is partly of hewn, partly of round logs or poles. The little girl washes to excess, and most, if not all, wash their faces in the morning. The women comb their hair daily. There is no bad smell in the house. Have seen no signs of lice. [. . .]

Nursing children. The three-year old girl here today is not weaned yet.

DECEMBER 11 Started today at 10:20 from Kangianik for Tuktuyaktok [. . .] . We had two teams, one of them ours, and the others pulling a bob sled with a Nunatama style sled for load. Company: Auautok (of Kittegaryumiut—took his picture at MacPherson with Roxy, Oaiyuak, etc.), Añusinnaaux (Kaxalik's son) of Kangianik, Tannaurmik and his wife of same place. Find many signs of the "chief" about Oaiyuak—will write of this later. House is modified Kagm. style—no wings but a room to the side at left of entrance (as you enter) in which I am to sleep. [. . .]

DECEMBER 14 [. . .] Oaiyuak set 5 isibyuat for a wolf that has been prowling around. [. . .] Oaiyuak's clever wife (Roxy's father sister) is Amaratjiak, the younger Illrok.

DECEMBER 15 Amaratjiak has a single horizontal tattoo line on each arm [. . .] about over the upper neck of the humerus. [. . .]

Kajigi. Oyanginna says the Kagmalit the other side of Baillie make a snow kajigi every winter.

Xagmallit. The people here make it plain they do not consider themselves Xagmallit. Those are the people to the east.

Fishing: Formerly no one of Koukpagmiut hooked fish while sun was down. As it is, only Oaiyuak is doing it. [. . .]

DECEMBER 16 Left Tuktuyaktok for Kangianik with a company of Huskies to meet there Oaiyuak's boy from Singyok with my instruments so as to measure the Kit. and Kang. people who are all at Kang. [. . .]

DECEMBER 17 Notice here, as with the Nunatama in Stein's house, that tulurak (raven) is used to scare children when naughty.

Childbirth. Notice no peculiar practice in regard to the newborn boy. Mother in some pain yesterday, everybody grieves over the child, as among kablunas. Mother eats only boiled fish as, I believe, the sick do usually.

Oaiyuak's sled failed to arrive last night so I lose the opportunity of measuring Iuitkuna, etc. [. . .]

Oaiyuak's sled arrived today from Singyok at 11. Measured 14 persons.

DECEMBER 18 Went from K. to Tok. 9–12 December [. . .] . Met Roxy midway, gave him a little scolding at parting. Gave away 15 plugs at K. and 13 at T.—tobacco all gone. Took 15 head measurements.

DECEMBER 19 Dance. Last night saw the best dance yet. Agnalluak, who has incipient consumption, danced first a long time with her back most of the time to the audience, and with no violent movements. She occasionally said something, i.e. how her cough started (audience, "too bad!"), that she hoped it would stop soon ("amen"), etc. Then Oaiyuak began dancing alone sometimes playing one of the drums, sometimes merely with his gloves in his hands, or nothing. He was stripped to the waist. His movements gradually became very violent [. . .] . He now began making excited and earnest statements (or questions) to which the audience replied. Occasionally, he jumped down into the doorway, dancing there sometimes with his back to the audience, sometimes his breast, continually exclaiming and asking questions. Both here and on the floor, he made complicated passes with both hands. He seemed near dropping from exhaustion at one time. At this point he went out of sight into the passage. I did not see just the movement when he popped up into the doorway again, but believe he came into it backwards. At least someone held up a drum in front of my face at the moment; when I saw him he was dancing there again with his back to us. When he turned, there was blood running out of his mouth at the labret holes. This trickled to his breast, but soon stopped flowing. After this he mostly walked (sort of cake-walk, stooped forward) in a circle, beating one of the drums. At the shouting points of the dance, the drums beat violently and most of the people sang the accompaniment. At the speaking parts there was silence, except for the responses. These remarks came in bunches, between which (perhaps about a minute) the drums beat softly, stopping just before O. began to speak again. Near the end of the dance he ceremonially drank a cup of water, holding it high with his right hand, and striking a dramatic upward and forward attitude, while with his left hand he held the hand of a decrepit old woman [. . .] . During the performance everyone was very serious. O.'s part of the dance lasted about forty-five minutes. Dancers seem to want to have something in their hands–usually gloves, either grasped or put half-way on. [. . .]

Gambling: Have seen no gambling or betting, the ship's natives play cards or checkers for tobacco, etc., in the manner of the whites—probably in imitation—and I have heard of such games being played in iglus. I have heard gambling proposed, but the crowd has rejected the proposal (3 times so far).

Tricks. One boy showed me twenty-two tricks with a string, called tuktu, kimmek, amaox, etc. He said there were others. The H. say these are "all the same as writing." [. . .]

DECEMBER 20 [. . .] Anderson arrived last night also with wife, child and brother. As always, no hurry now, we may start December 22. I should have liked to start on the shortest day of the year—but the others may prove short enough.

Polygamy. O.'s two wives seem to get along well. The older is evidently boss, though she seldom uses her authority. Certain things, as piptje and tea she has in her charge and deals out to the other one. She seems as fond of the children as the mother is.

Physical characteristics: The men have nipples better developed than I remember seeing them on whites. There is uniformly a spot of about one inch diameter, slightly conical, of a dark brown color, and looks about as the palm of one's hand does under a low magnifier. The nipple itself is about one sixth of an inch in diameter, cylindrical, and about one fifth of an inch high, about like an empty 22 cal. "BB." cartridge inverted. The accumulation of flesh, too, beneath the skin simulates a woman's breast to a considerable degree. [. . .]

O. continually sings about various exploits, his and others,' at which everybody laughs. [. . .]

Beginning a sealing article.

Say that experience is the best teacher, many advocating learning by doing; but I have always been a great believer in having few teachers on my backs. In my time there were no books telling how seals should be hunted, but I had good teachers in the Eskimos. [. . .] But even better teachers than the Eskimos were the seals themselves.

DECEMBER 21 Commencing a new diary book on the shortest day of the year offers a rather propitious opportunity for becoming Hall-ish and philosophising a little.

The first part of the winter has passed rather pleasantly but quickly and not unprofitably. It has not been noticeably colder out-doors than in Dakota and the Husky houses are comfortable—free from odors of any very pronounced type and free from lice, though otherwise not over clean. Appetite and health always good, and always plenty to eat—cheerfully given. [. . .] The knife-fork-and-plate prejudices have left me and my fingers have been fork and dish for some time now. The fish diet does not pall at all—and Anderson brought some salt, which improves it. The people are always friendly and jolly—Roxy is the only one who has given me reasonable cause for dissatisfaction, and that can be set down to his sophistication aboard whalers.

Of course the repeated delays in reaching H's camp are annoying a bit, but they may prove for good, for they keep me among the Kagm. where I wax in wisdom day by day. Occasionally, however, it is not easy to keep from reflecting on how much more pleasantly and profitably it could be spent had I only a dog team of my own so as to be unhampered in my movements. [. . .]

Tonight a Kotzebue Sound Kalelik who lives some 15 miles inland, came walking in pursuit of one of his dogs which arrived this morning—ran away.

Pulling milk teeth is practiced—tonight a girl had one pulled that had become loose. A loop of sinew was used.

DECEMBER 22 To continue the moralizing of yesterday—my experience with Husky communism is likely to make me a convert (at least, a mild sort of one) to the general doctrines of communism. The system is certainly admirably adopted to the conditions here. The seemingly very strong objection to C.—that some are lazy and will become parasites—seems to have little force in the actual life of the H. Some [. . .] are more energetic than others, and accomplish more, but all try and all do something. The fact that one works harder than another worries neither of them, nor the community in general. Of course, a complete communism might not work so well as this modified one.

It seems probable to me that the H.'s ideas on sexual relations are largely a product of their communism.

Both in conduct and in talk they are "shameless"—in the Adam-and-Eve-in-the-Garden sense. Children up to, say, 8 years (both sexes) frequently appear naked and among men and women the full-dress idea has been considerably developed—to the waist. [. . .]

DECEMBER 23 [. . .] Childbirth, Nunatama. The mother immediately after birth presses the baby's head firmly before and behind with her hands, but once only. Anderson says he believes the Kagmalit do not do this, while his people, Kotzebue, do as the Nunatama do. [. . .]

DECEMBER 25 Blood mixture. The habit of the Nunatama of coming to the sea every year at various places for trade or fishing made intermarriages with various coast people frequent, so much that careful inquiry almost always shows impurity of blood; Kuwax and Katotox, for instance, had a Kotzebue father. [. . .]

This is a pleasant enough Christmas, though I had hoped to spend it with Mr. Harrison and should have spent it still more pleasantly there. To know that he is only a short day off makes a week's delay more irksome. If this or Christmas is no less pleasant, the chances seem that the 2–3 years of arctic life will sum up agreeably. [. . .]

DECEMBER 28 [. . .] *Nunatama: Former home:* This country had no trees (merely okpek), no rabbits, few fish in summer and none in winter but plenty deer—formerly. Now there is no deer, and only a few N. are left there.

Rabbitskin blankets. K.'s wife has made two for the children to sleep with; woven "all the same knit," K. says. She learned how since coming here, though the Kagmalit do not practise this. I can't find out from where she learned. The skin is slit in quarter inch strips, twisted so as to bring the hair out, and then looped; for which a wooden needle (4 in.) is used. [. . .]

1907

JANUARY 1 [. . .] At the beginning of the year our plans for the rest of the winter are already roughly formulated as follows: Mr. H. and I leave here ca. January 17 (this place is called Kangianik) for Toker Pt. There we will have a sort of headquarter [. . .] . Then we proceed to Shingle Point to get some of my things there, and to get some observations in the Delta, if the weather permits. Returning, we shall come by way of Mr. H.'s boat and Selakotok's, to get some of his stuff and my oil, cocoa and salt. This should bring us back about February 15 and give us 2–3 weeks rest for the dogs before starting for the East early in March. We aim to go to the Coppermine, if the game supply permits, by the interior near the tree line, and to return *via* the coast and Baillie Islands getting back by sled if possible, to H.'s boat, where Kunniax (who stays here probably to take care of Kokatu's kids—his wife will probably go with us) is to have all our stuff before the snow leaves. Then we will spend the time till the steamer arrives at Iglupuk in mapping parts of the Delta. Our prospects are in every way brighter than they were last fall, though more portable provisions would be an immense help. We expect to buy a load or so of dry fish on the coast to take with us as dog fodder. We are getting about 60 fish a day now, but afraid it may not hold out—they are a sort of white fish averaging a little over 2 lbs. each. [. . .] We also have some apples, syrup, salt and spices—are, on the whole, very well off.

JANUARY 6 Time passes pleasantly here. Just finished "Farthest North," which I have found interesting [. . .] reading. Mr. H. has Pager, Nordenskjold, Richardson (besides Collinson and McClure, whom I have read), and I shall go after them, for I am usually ignorant on arctic subjects. I am, on the other hand, not doing much in the Husky line this week.

Fishing. Nets set under the ice here are first placed by cutting a series of holes eight inches in diameter about six feet apart, and two holes two feet in diameter at the net ends. The net line is passed from hole to hole under the ice by means of a bent stick, a tuperk willow. [. . .]

JANUARY 10 [. . .] Our daily routine seems hardly worth commemorating in ink—unless it be to become Nansenic. We get up at 6–7 (H. sometimes earlier), breakfast 6–8 (fish, one pancake or its equivalent in bannok, and coffee). Then H. does some "computation" work and I read arctic novels or write Eskimo stuff. In the forenoon I get three small spruces (go for them ca. 200 yrds. on my snowshoes) and H. chops them and carries in, while I get water and fill the lamp. Then we make tea for our lunch which comes ca. 12 or 1—fish and a pancake. The afternoon is spent in reading and writing while H. "computes." After supper (fish, pancake) at ca. 5 we play 2–3 games of chess, then I read or write while H. usually goes to bed. On certain nights we sit up—occasionally all nights we sit up for calculations (latitude, and error of watch). [. . .]

JANUARY 15 *The sun* returned today—I saw its upper edge on coming out at 11:30. It was behind a hill some miles away (by the lake) which rises perhaps 1° above the horizon. Above this hill we saw half the sun at noon. [. . .]

JANUARY 26 Yesterday Mr. H. and I, with the company of Kalelik's sled, went to Imnaluk where we stayed over night. There are two houses—Alualuk's and another in which Ivitkuna seems to be the leading man. I took a few measurements. The population is more numerous than shown by my census of a few weeks ago, but seems to be "floating"—many who have been starved out of the Kuraluk.

Kalelik has agreed for 2 sacks of flour and some other grub, to take me to

Herschel Island. He said he couldn't do this unless he could trade an old sail he had for fish. [. . .]

JANUARY 28 Burial customs. A. says he has laid out several dead persons in the sweater he still wears while most people throw away the clothes they have worn on such occasions. He also told me that when a man lives alone in a house and dies, he is usually left there. [. . .]

Sickness. O.'s baby, the one adopted of Tirktirk, has been sick for some time. One evening he "spoke," to cure the child, a series of exclamations, declarations, and questions responded to by the company every now and then. There was neither dance nor song. The day before yesterday he built a snowhouse; I was told so that the baby's rest would not be disturbed by the noises of O.'s house. [. . .]

Anatomy: The expression "Misu maluk" is accompanied often by a gesture towards the stomach or chest, indicating that as the seat of the thinking faculties, seemingly. [. . .]

FEBRUARY 1 [. . .] Incantations. O. indulged in a long one after bedtime last night, sitting at the head of his bed. He demands good winds and little, small cold, good going, plenty of various goods at Herschel and cheap, the generosity of his son-in-law, Sander's mate of the Narwhal, and good health and good luck for us all four and the dogs. [. . .]

Shifting population. Auautok and family, who were at Kittegaryumiut, lived a while at Kang. and are now at Imnaluk. Alualuk's wife is his sister and Neviluk's at Shingle Point. One of the younger couples counted here before now is at Imnaluk. Jimmy's mother who was here (Kangianik) in December left with Anderson for Kiglavait this morning. A. himself was the first part of the year in a house he built near Kun (near Husky Lake). There are many people on the coast now starved out of Kuraluk. Mongilaluk the half-breed son of Oblutok's wife, his wife another halfblood, neither speaks English, is at Imnaluk and Jimmy has gone to Richard Island hoping for both fish and deer. Okilliak moved from his and Kunniax's house to Auautok's some distance S.E. Then he and Anderson's brother Oyuliak to Katotox's, thence Okilliak back to his house and Oyuliak to Tuktuyaktok, intending to go later to Imnaluk, and so the story might be long continued. This shows the uselessness of trying to get the census by localities or houses. [. . .]

FEBRUARY 3 Tonsure. Kaxalik, three and a half years old, O.'s son, has just had his first tonsure and the full adult haircut.

Cleanliness. Today, as also this morning, we left Tuktuyaktok. O.'s younger wife washed her face in fresh urine [. . .] .

Language. Mangilanna spoke with Capt. Amundsen's (King William Sound?) "Kagmalit" last winter and thought some words strange in form, but had no difficulty in conversing with him. [. . .]

FEBRUARY 4 [. . .] Washing. O. used today a method I have seen among Russian immigrants, sipping and spitting into his hands. [. . .]

At 1 P.M. we met Ibuktuok and wife and baby going to Imnaluk. I gave him fish blubber, though he maybe is [. . .] thief and liar.

FEBRUARY 9 *Diet* is quite varied on this trip—fresh fish (sometimes boiled) rotten fish piptje, kilalua aktjuk and meat and whale oktjuk—all of which I eat on equal terms with the rest [. . .] . With our tea at noon we have some poptje and whale okljuk—the rest warm.

Endurance of cold: Yesterday O. sewed a rent across the entire sole of my boot (while I had it on) with both hands bare and no apparent discomfort. It took about 5 minutes. My face would have frozen badly in that time turned to the wind, and he sat sidewise to it—of course a little shielded by me, who lay at elbow rest. [. . .]

FEBRUARY 12 Arrived Shingle Pt. (Tapkaruk) at 12:45 NW wind (ca 3) and temperature here recorded at −50°. Very cold; froze both upper lip and chin under beard, as well as nose and cheeks. O's wife froze upper lip and baby (in my sleeping bag and blankets facing away from wind) froze both cheeks. Worst day I have traveled so far—our course square against wind. Dogs occasionally barked from cold and wind—some snow drifting.

My ship is said by Roxy to be but 5 sleeps from Herschel—they had their men at H. before Xmas. Shall learn more at Herschel. [. . .]

Our trip, as a whole, was very cold, though the wind was never very high. [. . .] Our snow houses were large—ca 8 x 10 oval and 6 ft. at vault—and consequently froze a little—just enough to make the frozen fish right for eating. Most days we cooked fish for our meal—eating raw fish for the 1st course even then. This usually mornings. En route, I finally overcame my aversion to white whale blubber (fairly rotten) and ate a good deal of it the last days. It is fatter than whale—more smooth to the tongue and porky—not stringy and does not get into your teath like whale. Whale tastes better (probably because fresher), but I can easily believe the H.'s statements that fresh it is very much better than whale [. . .] . Some of the larger fish we ate had sardines inside them—undigested sprinti. These are esteemed a delicacy, and I found them very good.

The effects of cold on our dogs were quite as pronounced as upon ourselves which the H. understand. [. . .] The sled was lighter, of course, yesterday than ever before, and the wind blew the rime away so it should have dragged easier than on past calmer days which were fully as cold, but the wind seemed to chill the strength out of them so they could not be urged beyond a very slow pace. [. . .] .

FEBRUARY 14 Stein says it took Leffingwell and the sailor with him over 30 days to reach Herschel from Flaxman Island, where the "Duchess" is—they fed 2 of their 4 dogs to the others. How they could use up all this time is quite incomprehensible to me. But I shall get details at Herschel, doubtless. [. . .]

FEBRUARY 15 [. . .] Beliefs. Kataksinok, Stein's wife, was greatly disturbed by my handing Annie, her two year old child, K.'s cup to drink from. Stein says she does not mind who drinks from her cup, except now, while she is pregnant, the child is due soon. O.'s wife shows the same prejudice, but whether she is pregnant I do not know. Her last child was born at McPherson about July 20. [. . .]

FEBRUARY 18 [. . .] Left Stokes Pt. ca. 9: A.M. and got to Herschel ca. 1—ice fair, though we had to curve a bit towards shore. Put up on "Narwhal"—a very pleasant place to stay.

My ship's people—Leffingwell and a sailor—Sturgis?—were here ca. a week and left a day or two before Thanksgiving—in good time, therefore, to catch me at Shingle Pt. L. wrote me a detailed letter, with Corp. Haylow, which he evidently entrusted to Shapodaitok and which he lost *en route* to Tuktuyaktok. [. . .]

Deaths: There has been one death at Stokes Pt.—"Cape York's" wife—consumption.

Births: Two births this winter at Herschel.

Population: Capt. L. counts 65 natives and half-castes on the island, *plus* 6 (Pt. Clarence and Dione) on the ship. There are 16 Nunatamas and 49 Kagm. [. . .]

Childbirth seems frequently to come as a surprise to natives. Oaiuak's daughter had child today, was planning to go E. with father next Thursday, but will now stay until April. Sgt. F. says that unless a birth is expected in a few hours the woman's abdomen is continuously kneaded by other women. As today labor is seldom severe, the doctor said last spring half-whites were often born with difficulty. [. . .]

FEBRUARY 20 Childbirths are said by Capt. L. to frequently cause rupture among Husky women. This often due to the kneading of the abdomen.

"Modesty" in the exposure of the sex organs is said by Capt. L. to be far greater among the men than the women. In examining them for rupture, for instance, the women make no attempt to cover the sexual organs, but the men almost always do.

Beads have no value here now for trading, and Capt. L. has just given all the ship's beads to the children, as they were worthless to him. [. . .]

Portugees and *American negroes* are said by Capt. L. to consider themselves each racially superior to the other in the Herschel Id. fleet—each resents being called by the name of the other—Americans prefer "caon" to "Portugee." [. . .]

FEBRUARY 21 [. . .] *No mail* came from the outside with the Dawson patrol, but surely the news that a big mail was coming down the Mackenzie, due March 15. Mr. W. is going to the fort for this—his orders to be at the fort by March 25. [. . .]

FEBRUARY 23 [. . .] [In Icelandic:] *Frylla Gángara, lögreglufjóns, mætti okkur í dag [. . .] . Sagt er þó að majórinn hafi fyrirboðið Gángara að halda hana í lögreglustöðinni.* [The concubine of Sgt. Walker met us today. . . . It is said though that the Major told Walker not to keep her in the police station.] [. . .]

FEBRUARY 28 *Whale meat* from a 8–10 years old whale on the NW shore of Herschel was our dog food on the trip. The meat was moss grown and looked a good deal like hard-baked hay, but seemed to do well for the dogs.

Pregnancy customs. Mr. Stein gives the following with reference to his wife, who is expected to have a child in a few days. She is a Nunatama. A pregnant woman should not use the "chamber" in the house, though his wife occasionally does. She has not done any sewing for the last few days, and won't until the child is born.

At Point Hope he says, pregnant women could not work at whaling, because they must not urinate on the ice, and the whaling is done some miles from shore.

Menstruation customs. S. says at Point Hope menstruating women were under the same restriction in regard to ice-work as pregnant women.

Whale hunt prohibitions and customs. At Point Hope lead could not be safely cast into bullets within the "village limits" while the whale season was on. Skins must not be worked in the house of the husbands of the women working them if they are engaged in whaling, probably this restriction applies rather to the houses of the whalers than to their wives. Skins are worked in the house of someone not an active whaler, or else in a tent, etc., or in a white man's house. The owner of the house seems the one likely to suffer injury.

In launching a canoe for the first time each season there is some slight ceremony of which I could get no clear account from S. It seems to consist of passes and incantations by the men as they sit in the newly launched craft.

After a death in his family, a canoe belonging to its head, or, probably, to any member, must not be launched for whaling till the first whale has been caught by a member of the village. The same prohibition probably applies to engaging in whaling by men who are not owners of canoes.

At the Point Hope village the spirits of the graveyard were fenced off from the whaling grounds by a fence of stones, or pebbles, set on edge, ceremonially by old women "doctors." The fence was not a complete enclosure of the graveyard, but merely one side, a curve or bow-shaped fence.

Childbirth. Stein's wife (Kataksinok) had her child at 9:15 P.M. tonight. We had the first intimations of its coming at about 8. At 8:30 she asked that I leave the house till the birth was over, and that Roxy's wife come. About 9, Roxy's wife came home with the report that the child would not come before morning, so I went home and was in the house when the child suddenly came. She did everything for herself and the child, but came near fainting about half an hour after the birth. By 11:00 she was sitting up and chatting and laughing as if not indisposed.

Apparently there was no superstition behind her request that I stay away—merely a reluctance to have a comparative stranger present [. . .] .

MARCH 2 *Foreign words* seem to be used by the N. more freely than by the Kagm. [. . .] On the other hand the K. have borrowed from the N. a great deal more than the N. from K.—Ellopa, are you cold, etc. In fact, I know of no Kagm. word regularly used by the N. [. . .]

Childbirth customs. Kataksinok says she must not eat frozen fish now. How many days that will last I don't know. She must not eat fish heads, a great delicacy. Her cup must not be washed. She wipes it with a cloth and wraps it up Eskimo fashion. She treats her other eating appliances similarly, except the plate on which food is brought her, equivalent to the old "iliniak."

The child's first excrement must be burned or else the child will suffer from a hardening of the rectum. The burning was neglected with her first child, Annie, now twenty-two months old, and she has suffered; so the present youngster must be protected, and S. had to burn it today, made a fire in the woodshed. Could not burn it yesterday, so it was kept carefully wrapped in paper till today. [. . .]

MARCH 4 Young Roxy and I (Naipaktuna) were to start today for Pokeik's place up the Mackenzie but they think the weather too bad. [. . .]

Migrations. Stein tells the following: [. . .] the father of Tulugak's wife was born of a tribe who lived on Langley Bay. When twelve to fourteen years old he came to Kittegaryumiut. When a grown man he married and went to Langley Bay again and found no one. Beyond Cape Parry he later found a stone lamp belonging to his father and farther east campsites and remains which indicated to him that the whole tribe had moved east. Nothing has been heard of them since and I suppose they went either to the Coppermine or Prince Albert Land. He was therefore the only survivor of the tribe. He died at Cape Parry about 1903–4 and seemed to be about forty then. [. . .]

MARCH 5 Naipaktuna's going with me to Pokeik's [. . .]—he is afraid he may be taken sick en route—and I am afraid he might (some venereal disease I believe). [. . .]

MARCH 6 Childbirth: Kataksinok, whose boy was born the evening of February 28 was up yesterday, she seemed to be worried by staying in bed so long, but was ordered to by Stein. She never seemed sick, but for the semifaint a half hour after the birth, from loss of blood and exertion in washing the child.

[In Icelandic:] *(Dreinginum stóð við fæðinguna. Stein segist hafa sjéð þetta áður á öllum (2) drengbörnum fæddum hér (þaug voru hálf-hvít).*

[The boy had an erection at birth. Stein says he has seen this occur in the camp of all (2) boys born here (half-white).]

Marriage relations. It seems to be customary that the man who marries the youngest or only daughter, must attach himself to the parent's family. If he is later unwilling to go where they go, the girl nevertheless goes with her parents (cf. case of Tsitsak and Pannigyuk, she is to go with parents to

Kittegaryumiut and he does not want to go, so has already gone up river to Pokeik's).

MARCH 7 [. . .] Starvation. Ovayuak brings the report that a Nunatama arrived from the mountains a few days ago with tales of hunger. Omigluk has plenty of deer on the Herschel Island River and the next camp E. from him has gotten fifteen deer since New Year. But farther E. there were no deer and most of the dogs are dead and the people are said to be en route for Herschel so enfeebled that it is feared some will not get there. Kurugak, Ninagsirk, Apokork and Tuluga, with their crowd, are said to be about the hungriest. They were farther E., had proceeded some dist. S.W. from where we visited them last fall, and then had to fall back. [. . .]

MARCH 16 Still at King Point. This is my first real experience of being storm-bound—the days at Kangianik early in February were at a pleasant house. This Amundsen's house is better than a tent, but cold and not roomy. The door, which Roxy and Ovayuak fixed last time so as to open in, can be opened only from the inside [. . .] . We had to enter through the roof. [. . .]

MARCH 19 [. . .] Thick storm in our faces all day. Gave Kunaslik Uglan to use and left her at the snow house. Froze my right eyelids—first case of this. Face covered with ice crust all day. Kept only left eye open most of time. The nearest to being played out I have ever been. [. . .]

MARCH 22 At Herschel still. [. . .] Starving natives. It seems Ovayuak's account of the starving Nunatama was grossly overdrawn, at least; the sum known here is that they had enough for themselves, but scant dog feed at the end of the dark days. [. . .]

Religion. Capt. Leavitt, who has seen many natives approach death fully realizing it, says he has seen no one afraid so far. They take it better than whites, on the average. [. . .]

APRIL 14 Last night saw some human tracks in the snow on my way to investigate the flag pole.

Here we were told the ship was only a few hours travel farther, and further that she is leaking [. . .] and is expected to sink in the spring, so everything has been taken ashore. But worse news still is the statement that Mikkelsen, Leffingwell and a 3rd man started off on the ice one and a half moons ago and have been given up for lost by the ship's company, which now consist's of 5 men [. . .] .

Mr. *Arey's house* is a native iglo, though not quite of any type I have before seen. It took him a week, single handed, to build it—split logs, etc. Ar. has lived in it 2 years.

For an *interpreter* Mr. A's boy Gallagher, is the only native I have seen who apparently speaks English well enough to be relied upon. [. . .]

APRIL 30 [. . .] . Camped just west of cut bank which is a little way W. of Humphrey Point—the same we past about 10–12 P.M. April 10, *ca. 14 miles*.

A Christian grave (native) is on the shore nearly opposite our camping position on the sandspit—it is of logs in the ordinary style, but has a large cross.

Native graves are said by Mr. Arey to be numerous around Barter Island—on the sandspits. [. . .]

MAY 6 [. . .] Found Narwhal out of deer meat and grub rather short, though all are on full ration. Capt. L. intends coming into Herschel about August 25, preparatory to going out.

No "outside" news came with the mail. [. . .]

MAY 14 Could not start from Humphrey Pt. for fog till 7: A.M. yesterday; camped ca 5. [. . .] Some house ruins near. We mistook this for our cache of April 29 at a distance and made for it—our cache was similarly marked and none of us saw this place before. [. . .]

Intermediate time in large note book to be sent to Peabody by Capt. M. [. . .]

AUGUST 10 Found Peter Ross (widower) with Thompson and 2nd wife, and 3 children—one Ross and 2 Thompson's by first wife—all girls. [. . .]

"Tjiglik" (not Tjiglit) is common word for all Eskimo among L., Ross says. Knows also Nunatama Tj., Kagmalit Tjiglik and Kavane Tjiglik—those around Anderson River.

Head measurements: Measured my crew before, and Ross and Thompson today. Ross says he was measured before—at Klondike rush by man called Storm, who went over Portage and down Porcupine. Woman and children unwilling to be measured, but rather wanted to be photographed. [. . .]

AUGUST 15 Wednesday, rain during night and all day. [. . .] Have pain in chest [. . .] which bothers considerably. [. . .]

Friendship of Itkillik and Huskies: Enoch told me a few years ago (ca 10) a

Husky boy was named after Itkillik who died—nitte—thus the name Ovayuak calls Roxy by for a joke—Roxy displeased. [. . .]

AUGUST 16 [. . .] Overslept account of warm sunshine. Fairly severe frost last night—boots I took off last evening still frozen at 9 A.M. in edge of my bed. [. . .] Willow and scattered spruce appear almost as soon as we cross divide. [. . .] Mountains everywhere remind of Iceland. [. . .]

AUGUST 19 [. . .] At this point the boys [. . .] claimed Enoch had interpreted me as saying I would give them 35^{oo} each for tracking my canoe half way up the Rat. and later that I would pay them something extra for tracking the La P. portage instead. Now they wanted to know how much. I told them when we left MacPherson it was understood they would either make the portage with me accross the bend of the Bell, as Mr. Firth recommended, or at any rate go around the river to that point—the Salmon Cache. Joseph said he was willing but Willison would go no farther. In the case I told them I would pay the 4 dollars a day each for the six days they worked for me. This they accepted and I wrote Firth accordingly, giving Joseph the tent left with the police at 15 skins on his wages. Got started today 11 A.M. [. . .]

AUGUST 23 *Hallucinations:* Night before last night I saw smoke in the ravine coming in from the right as one enters the narrows through the mountains—first 3 shots to attract attention. Last evening saw smoke on left bank ca. 3 miles below abandoned cabin—again 3 shots. [. . .] Both looked strangely blue. It is the tale of the wish and the thought, probably. This journey is getting monotonous. [. . .]

Home has never seemed so far away as it does moping down this infernal river on a headstrong and lazy raft. [. . .]

Below rapids long NW stretch of river, slow current.

Have decided that if I see no Indians tomorrow I shall leave the raft, take a pack load and walk. At the present rate I shan't get out in time to head off Wrigley. [. . .]

AUGUST 27 I landed with great difficulty (easy for cause) a ¼ mile below village at ca 7:30. Found all houses deserted, and slept in one [. . .] . As I finished eating, a man came up after seeing the smoke of cooking. This man I had never seen before, but when I got to the village I found there the minister who took Stewart down last year. He agreed to take me to Rampart in his canoe [. . .] that will carry 2 men. We started ca. 12. [. . .]

There were 4 men, 6 women and some 8 children at the camp, most of whom I got on a photo. They received me very well—the man who came to see me at breakfast asked for tea and tobacco, neither of which I had. Besides this there was no begging, though I gave them several things—odds of grub that pleased them. [. . .]

A pain in the chest which has been troubling me since a day or two before reaching MacPherson is worse today—had been better last 3–4 days. [. . .]

Illness: My chest hurts now so I can paddle or pole the raft very little—getting to look serious. [. . .]

Our boat today kept leaking so we had to go ashore every hour to "patch up," with no apparent effect. However ca. 10 A.M. we got down to Black Creek where we found a white man, Archie Sinklater (Indian wife) and some Indians. With him I came on a raft to Rampart, arriving ca. 3:30. [. . .]

AUGUST 29 [. . .] Mr. Codzow tells me he has found the Huskies as good each as four Indians. When Indians starve they come in and stay around till you won't feed them anymore; the Huskies last winter stayed only a few days till their starved dogs got some strength, and before Indians would have been fairly off hunting they were back to pay in meat and skins for the fish given them to start on. [. . .]

AUGUST 30 Started from New Ramp. at 11:15 A.M. in a 28 foot boat made by Sinklater [. . .] , got to Old Rampart (30 miles) ca. 6 P.M. This is a village of cabins and tents with total population 23 (permanent). The leading men are Joe Albert and his brother who is a trader and is now at Fort Yukon getting goods. Their house is 2 large rooms, clean and well furnished. We are to sleep in it tonight. [. . .]

The women, though they have not exactly the free attitude of the Husky are by no means so subdued as is taught to expect of Indians or behave about as "lower class" whites might do if a "troy" person were being entertained. [. . .]

SEPTEMBER 3 [. . .] Got to mouth of Salmon River at *9:50.*

The Indian men here, S. says, usually make breakfast—was so in Albert's house. Men do all sorts of women's work on occasion. Women do not row in boats when traveling. Moving across countrymen usually went ahead while woman brings camp to appointed place. When men travel by small canoe women move camp along bank sometimes. [. . .]

THE STEFANSSON-ANDERSON EXPEDITION (1908–1912)

Largely at Mr. Rood's suggestion, but partly also because I feel like it, this diary is begun Wednesday November 20, 1907, in New York City.

1907

[. . .]

NOVEMBER 20 Last evening at the house of Mrs. Davidge, 62 South Washington Square, I met at dinner Mr. W. V. Moody (whom I have long admired for his poems and who is red faced, bald and prosperous), Mr. Torrence who has written successful poems I have never read and a play recently accepted by Henry Miller, Mr. Ghent, a socialist writer whose name Moody took for his play "The Great Divide," and another young man whom I liked and whose name I have forgotten. The women were Miss Chrystal Hearne whose play, "The Step Sister" (one she played in) recently failed. [. . .] Another woman whose name I forgot was too good looking to be sensible, at least, unless she is an exception to a rigid rule. Dr. Kelly, a middle aged physician, was a very attractive person, a woman of refinement and brains. The fourth, whose name I have also forgotten, was very pleasant too—she was my table companion. Mrs. Davidge was, of course, bright and friendly but impalpable (an adjective chosen after deliberation). [. . .]

NOVEMBER 27 Last evening Mr. A. asked me to dinner with Ellsworth Huntington and his brother.[. . .]

Ellsworth H.'s lecture in Mendelsohn Hall was a success—some remarkable pictures, but nothing new to one who has read his "Pulse of Asia"—it is out only some two weeks and I have read a chapter only. [. . .]

1908

APRIL 18 Left New York (8:30 P.M.?) for Niagara Falls. [. . .]

APRIL 21 In Ottawa. Arranged with MacDougall, Minister of Customs, for customs exemption on everything but ammunition. Lunch with John. G. Foster a consul general. In afternoon interview with R. W. Brook. Agreed to have expedition known as under his auspices and Museum's etc. [. . .]

MAY 7 Left the Landing ca. 2: P.M. in 3 scows. Made about 13 miles (one mile beyond, road, on west bank, leading to Calling Lake) before stopping ¾ of an hour for supper on E. bank (5:15 to 6:00). Then made some 3 miles more and camped 7:15 on East bank. *Distance ca. 16 miles.*

[In Icelandic:] *Töluverður drykkuskapur að lendingunni. Nagli kaupmaður var færður óvilja og bröltandi um borð miðvikudag. [. . .] Sumir indjánar drukknir.* [. . .]

[There was much drinking at Landing. Merchant Nagle was brought aboard struggling against his will. Some Indians were drunk.]

JUNE 25 *Consumption:* Both Vale and Johnson told me they are doing all they can to get Indians to live in tipees as much as possible—difficult matter when they have houses. [. . .]

JULY 3 Passed through the Sans Sault rapids ca. 9:30 A.M. and tied up ca. 10 P.M. on account of high hard wind in the Ramparts.

Indian camps numerous along river through Ramparts and just above. Most camps are below the bank, on a ledge some ten feet above the water. [. . .]

JULY 4 On way to Red River. Hunting has been poor at Good Hope. The Indians ordinarily live largely on rabbits. [. . .] But this and last year no rabbits [. . .]. Many dogs starved and they are now high in price. Indians had been living mainly on rabbits for "last ten years," Mr. Gaudett said, but these last two there were none. [. . .]

Huskies had come in some numbers to Red R. but most of them were gone towards this coast. Most of the Indians were in, so we saw the largest crowd we had seen so far. [. . .]

JULY 22 Pulled into small river 1 or 2 miles from salt water on account of sudden springing up of northerly wind with fog clouds—rather nasty it must be at sea today.

In afternoon Ilavinirk, Aguk, Punjuabluk and I went on an exploring expedition in my whaleboat up the river we anchored in, in the hope of finding it connecting with "The Husky." Went ca. 10 miles before fair (NE) wind and found source in a biggish lake—no connection with "Husky" apparently.

JULY 23 Deaths. Kunnullak and wife and young girl (about 12–14) of another family died Tuesday of this week at Ninagunuag, apparently of kilaluak poisoning; had eaten of kilaluak day before they became sick. The common belief seems to be they died because they worked at skins (deer, seal) just after a kilaluak was killed.

AUGUST 1 Tuesday afternoon we got a land breeze and boats began leaving. Ca. 5 P.M. the police—Sgt. Selig, Const. Pearson, with Roxy for guide—arrived and ca. 6 P.M. they and we started. They struck straight for Herschel, but we rounded Kay Pt. to go to Flanders Pt. where I wanted to camp. The wind fluctuated a little and we went ashore three times, finally getting to Flanders about noon Wednesday. Here we found several Nuna tents [. . .].

AUGUST 17 "Karluk." Started from Flanders Point the evening of August 15 (ca. 5 P.M.) and by 10:30 camped S.W. Sandspit. [. . .] In boarding the "Karluk" I fell overboard and was nearly drowned.

AUGUST 31 *Near Point Barrow*. Much has happened since the last entry. It blew strong from the east Sunday, Monday and Tuesday and the ice loosened off the coast. Wednesday the ships came in—Beluga, Bowhead, Belvedere, Thrasher, Narwhal, Jeanette. They had fought ice from Point Hope but were longest delayed at Icy Cape. [. . .]

SEPTEMBER 14 [. . .]. Natives finished sled and 4 dog harness: Stork made stove; Mamayauk today as before busy sewing—snowshirts, duffle boots, etc.

Child teeth. Noashak had two pulled with a string today and they were thrown away. Mamayauk reminds me that Kogmollik feed teeth (enclosed in meat) to a dog, but Ilavinirk says his people throw them away.

Beliefs. When he was young some women of his people scraped deerskins the same day an ugrug had been killed and eaten. Later that same summer, some weeks later, an epidemic ("dry throat," he calls it) came, killed many people, among them some, but not all, of the women who had been concerned in scraping skins. This epidemic came because of the skin scraping; Ilavinirk still believes this (Kotzebue Sound). Has known many similar cases, among them the deaths at Niagunuag this summer.

Why dead seals, etc., must have fresh water. In the boyhood of Ilavinirk's grandfather there were at one time many hunters (as usual) at the kilaluak station of Sishulik. One of them, Kaiaaitjuk,was one day capsized in his kayak, but was not drowned for two kilaluak placed themselves one under each arm and he swam off with them and lived with them some time. By and by, he became a little homesick and they took him back to Sishulik. When they came to the surface he saw all the tents were gone, all the people had left for their homes. K. began crying (weeping) but the kilaluak said, "Never you mind; come stay with us all winter and we will bring you here next summer when your friends are here."

K. accordingly stayed all winter and at the proper season was taken to Sishulik by the kilaluak. When the hunters saw them they came in innumerable kayaks (there were both Nunatama and coast people) to the hunt. The kilaluak told K. to keep between two of them and not to go near any kayak for fear of being harpooned. The kilaluak soon found themselves in shoal water and many of them were harpooned. Finally Kaiaaitjuk saw his chance and came out of the water. When he appeared people at once said "There is Kaiaaitjuk," for they recognized him though his outfit was somewhat changed. Over the deerskin coat he wore when he went away, he now had a waterproof coat of intestines (ugrug?) and his kayak was now pure white, like the skin of a kilaluak. But what people wondered at most, was that while Kaiaaitjuk held his paddle level and dipped neither blade in the water, still his kayak flew ahead faster than anyone could paddle. When people saw this they feared he would go away again, and all gave chase to try catch him. One of them was so placed he could head off the fleet with kayak, and got his hand on it as it went past him. At his touch, the kayak became an ordinary one and thereafter moved only to the paddle, as other kayaks. Kaiaaitjuk now went ashore with his friends, but was scarcely able to go into a house or stand near anyone, or he said they smelled so bad. They brought him food such as he had been very fond of

FIGURE 14. Dogsled. Drawn by Fearless (Uyuliak), one of Stefansson's informants. The diaries, March 16, 1909. *(Courtesy of Dartmouth College Library.)*

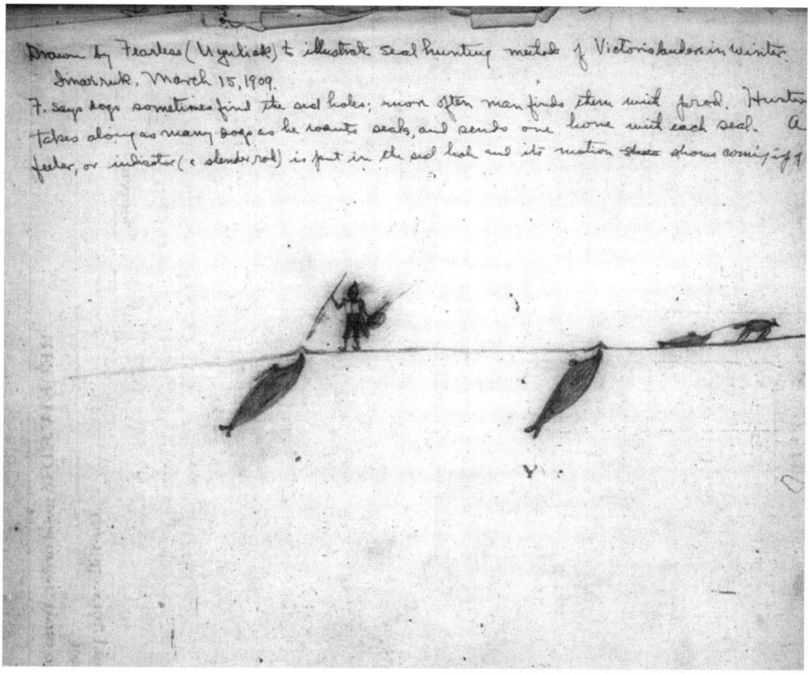

FIGURE 15. Seal hunting, Victoria Islanders. Drawn by Fearless (Uyuliak). The diaries, March 15, 1909. *(Courtesy of Dartmouth College Library.)*

FIGURE 16. Dress. Mamayauk's self-portrait. The diaries, February 19, 1912. *(Courtesy of Dartmouth College Library.)*

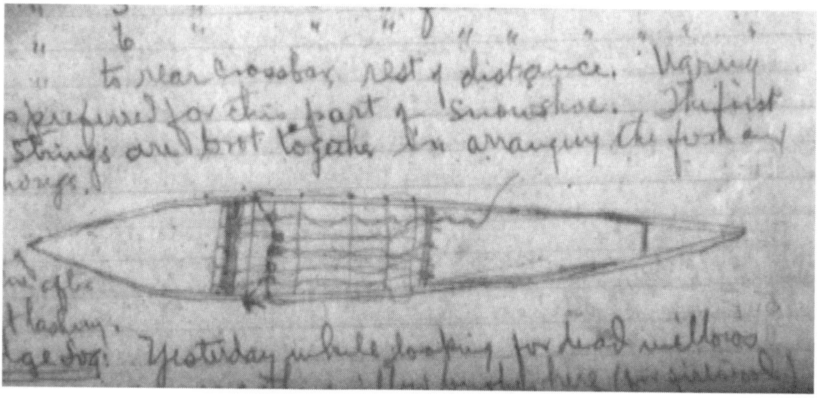

FIGURE 17. Snowshoe. The diaries, October 10, 1909. *(Courtesy of Dartmouth College Library.)*

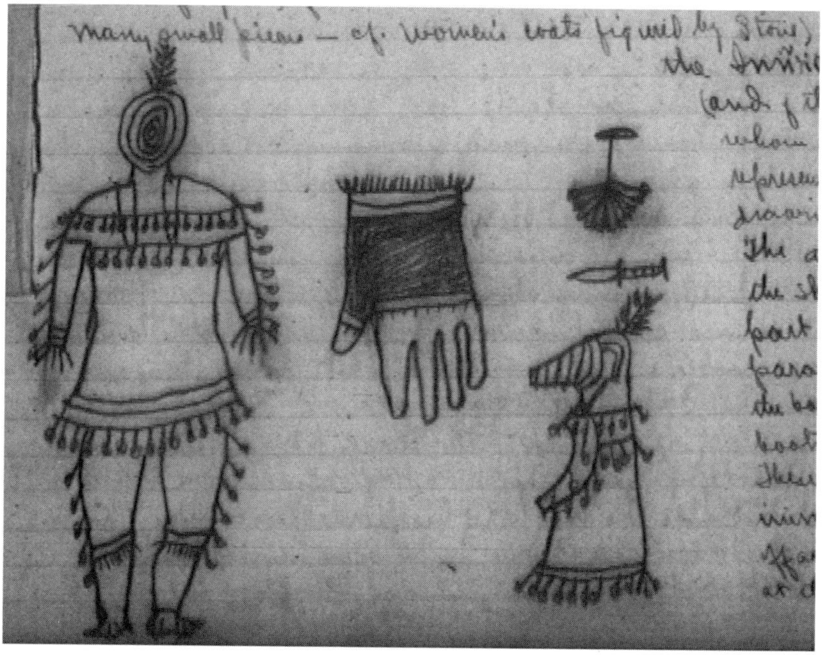

FIGURE 18. Guninana's dress. The diaries, March 13, 1912. *(Courtesy of Dartmouth College Library.)*

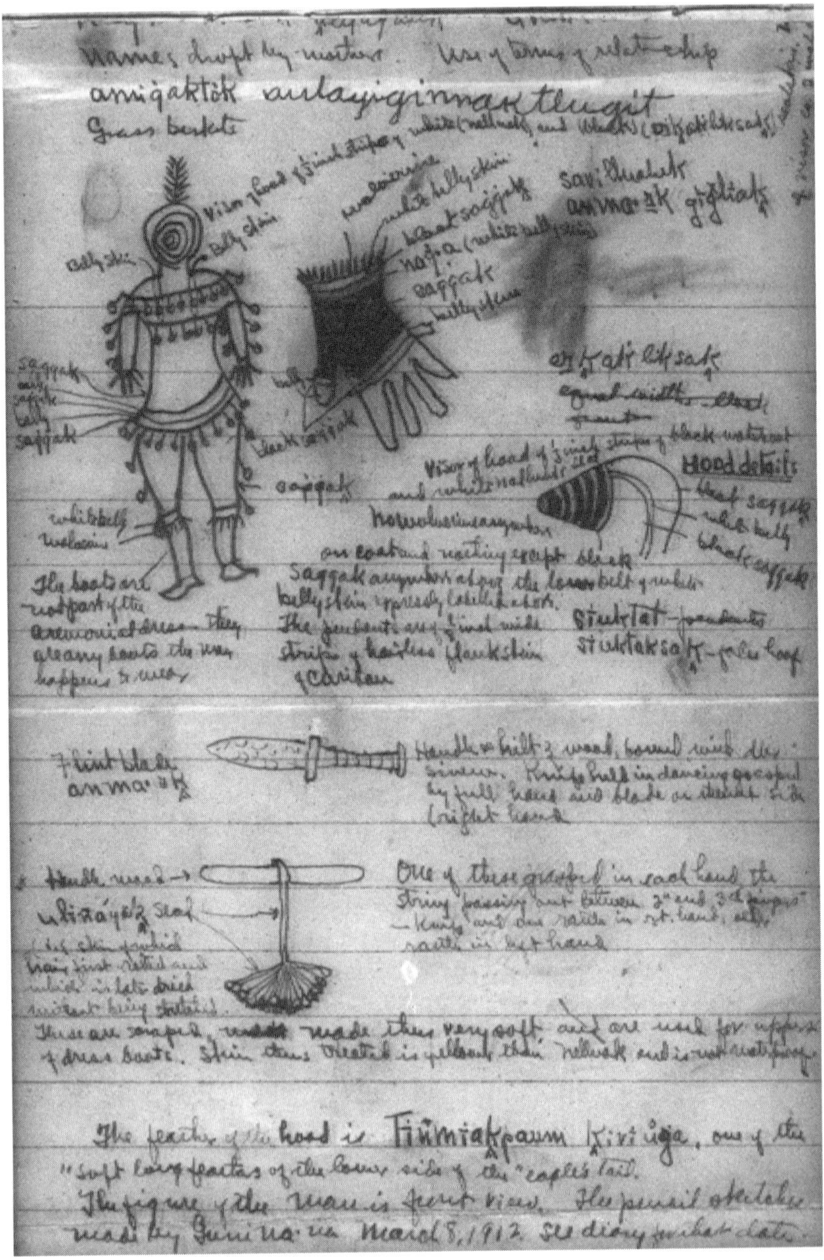

FIGURE 19. Text and illustrations with dress and tools. The diaries, March 7–8, 1912. *(Courtesy of Dartmouth College Library.)*

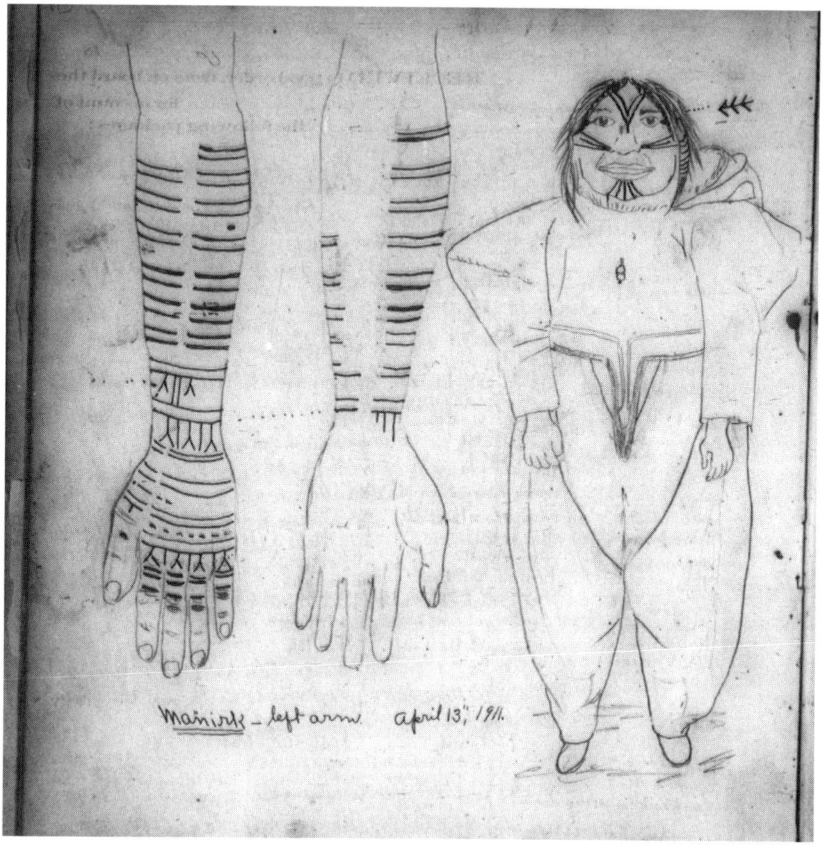

FIGURE 20. Tattoo. The diaries, April 13, 1911. *(Courtesy of Dartmouth College Library.)*

FIGURE 21. Writing in the field. *(Courtesy of Dartmouth College Library; CAE/SAP 026 #7/8.)*

FIGURE 22. Copper Inuit pose for the camera. *(Courtesy of Dartmouth College Library; CAE/SAP 019 #35/36.)*

FIGURE 23. A young boy with fish and spear, June 30, 1916. *(Courtesy of Dartmouth College Library; MMS 229 029: 35/36.)*

FIGURE 24. Woman carrying a cumbersome load, June 29, 1915. *(Courtesy of Dartmouth College Library, MMS 229 021: 10a/11a.)*

FIGURE 25. Umiak sailing in ice. *(Courtesy of Dartmouth College Library, MMS 229 007: 2/3.)*

FIGURE 26. A group of Copper Inuit. Canadian Arctic Expedition. *(Courtesy of Dartmouth College Library, MMS 229 061:11/12.)*

FIGURE 27. Winter camp and dog team. Canadian Arctic Expedition. *(Courtesy of Dartmouth College Library. MMS 229 055:33/34.)*

FIGURE 28. Copper Inuit men, one with snow goggles. Canadian Arctic Expedition. *(Courtesy of Dartmouth College Library. MMS 229 062:14a/16a.)*

FIGURE 29. Koukpagmiut women and child wearing ornate hooded parkas. The Anglo-American Polar Expedition (1906–1907). Lantern slide no. 6. *(Courtesy of Dartmouth College Library, Stef Mss 226).*

FIGURE 30. Interior of a snow house showing cooking area and sleeping platforms. Tuktuyaktok(?). The Anglo-American Polar Expedition (1906–1907). Lantern slide no. 8. *(Courtesy of Dartmouth College Library, Stef Mss 226).*

FIGURE 31. Missionary school students, women, and priests, along the banks of the Mackenzie River. The Anglo-American Polar Expedition (1906–1907). Lantern slide no. 27. *(Courtesy of Dartmouth College Library, Stef Mss 226.)*

FIGURE 32. Inuit women crossing the prairie. Canadian Arctic Expedition (1913–1918). Lantern slide no. 180. *(Courtesy of Dartmouth College Library, Stef Mss 226.)*

FIGURE 33. Playing drums and dancing by an up-turned umiak. Canadian Arctic Expedition (1913–1918). Lantern slide no. 711. *(Courtesy of Dartmouth College Library, Stef Mss 226.)*

before, but he declared it stunk, and he could eat only a trifle at first. Finally he got used to everything, however, and was thereafter as other men. After his return K. told that the kilaluak and other animals that live in salt water, are really tarningit (sing. "tarnik") and that whenever a seal, ugrug, walrus, kilaluak or bowhead was killed he should be given fresh water on coming to shore. (This water is brought from some house, not any particular one, and maybe river, pond, snow, or sea ice water, providing it is not salt.) Ilavinirk says maybe the people lied who told this, but his own grandfather saw Kaiaaitjuk. Anyway, Ilavinirk always gives seals, etc., water.

SEPTEMBER 17 Tuesday morning found me pretty sick—vomiting all night. The evening before we had bread which all of us thought [. . .] had a tobacco smell to it. I alone ate this, for it was hot and tasted all right while the others preferred some cold bread we had. I suppose it was this bread made me sick. Ate nothing but a spoonful of malted milk and 2–3 biscuit Tuesday. Wednesday felt a little better and went with Ilavinirk on scanting expedition to NE to see how the ice was. [. . .]

SEPTEMBER 18 *Started* ca. 2:30 P.M. today for Flaxman Island, or wherever Dr. Anderson may be.

Guests arrived yesterday in the shape of three sleds, two with umiaks (bound for Point Barrow and some sixteen people. Measured all men and one woman—rest of women and children unwilling. These were some of the people we met Wednesday. One of them was the man whom the ice party two years ago encountered on their return, on an island just west of Pingak, he says. He gave me map with location of some families in the Colville this winter. [. . .]

SEPTEMBER 24 Sent Stork and Ilavinirk to ship to see if she was abandoned. They returned 5 P.M., Capt. Mogg aboard "Olga" frozen in ca. 3 m. off shore. Will leave vessel next Tuesday for Barrow, taking all hands. Had trouble with 1st mate (Portugee) and deposed him. Anxious to see me about ethnology collection which he wants to sell to American Museum. Shall go to see him tomorrow probably.

SEPTEMBER 25 Aboard the "Olga." The "Olga" is lying ca. 2 miles off shore from the outside sandbar among ground ice. Some of her staff is being put ashore, but most is being cached on a cake of ground ice a few rods from the vessel Capt. M. stuck here Sept. 11. [. . .]

The people of Prince Albert, Capt. Mogg estimates at 800, 250 of whom they saw. They are in the estimation of himself (and crew, including natives) a very superior class of people in honesty, resourcefulness and intelligence. Extremely hospitable. In winter they live on the ice. Seal are so abundant that at most abandoned winter camps one finds "tons" of blubber either cached or left lying around. They have no fish nets, kill bears with spears, every man and dog turns out, and deer with bow and arrow (tartar bow). Spears and arrows copper and bone tipped. Only Banks Island people heard of are towards Mercy Bay, called "bad" by Prince Albert people. [. . .]

SEPTEMBER 29 *Tradition:* Island 2 is said to be the place (by Kunnaullak) where some people were besieged by a party of Pt. Hope people. The besiegers, who were on the mainland E, starved to death. The place has since been called "Tigiraiminut."

OCTOBER 15 Got to Flaxman Monday forenoon—found Andersen and rest all well. Have stayed in Leff's house. Yesterday got 3 seals: today Ilav. sick (stomach) and Akpuk fixing sled so no one hunted. Dr. Anderson and I getting our mail ready. [. . .]

OCTOBER 21 (Today) started 10:30. Camped 3:30 where we made tea at 1 P.M. Oct. 11th. Met Oyarak about where we met him on the 11th—this time going with one boy and a load of meat (gave us 2 front legs with shoulders) to Flaxman—3 dogs and a sail, for our SW breeze today has been barely enough for a sail. He had killed six deer (between Shaviouik and Sarvanaktok?) and seen some more (four or more). Had left family camped a little way this side Putularayuk's cache. Started from there this morning and will make Flaxman. He was feeling good over the prospect for the winter and will apparently delay his Colville trip indefinitely. If he gets along, so should we, though he is called a good hunter. Was going to Flaxman after cartridges and 4 days later he was out of ammunition. [. . .]

Flaxman Island. A daughter was born the night between Saturday and Sunday (17th and 18th) to Akpuk and Shungauranik. Shungauranik danced furiously in our house at a general "ula-hula" the evening before, and has been able to walk behind the sled with the child on her back since we started. The child is apparently in the best of health, has black hair half an inch long, and thick—"a full head of hair." [. . .]

OCTOBER 28 *Moose.* Akpuk says, were formerly occasionally killed in the delta of the Colville and plenty of them inland. Now, he believes, more come to the sea and they are scarce even for inland.

Fish is very plentiful in the Colville in the fall while the ice is still thin—running up stream. At that time the Nirrlik are, however, looking for deer, and little fish is put by. If they tended to the fishing then, starvation could probably be avoided. When they do fish, Akpuk says they often make traps of willow in the smaller streams. [. . .]

Our prospects are looking worse with only old tracks where we saw plenty deer a little over two weeks ago. In fact, we seem to have seen the only deer in the country, and to have driven them away. They may have gone east or west, but probably went south towards the mountains—which seem only a little farther off here than at Flaxman, though they recede rapidly and disappear just about south of here. [. . .]

OCTOBER 30 *Barrel Point.* Deer driving was much employed by the Colville people, especially up near the mountains, Akpuk says. He remembers one only, however, when he was about eight years old (say twenty years ago). At that time about fifty were killed, and it was a small drive. Kayaks were used, and okpek stakes in convergent lines to represent men. The driving was towards small lakes and seldom towards a river, if at all. The bucks often fought with their front feet against the kayaks. Deer were killed by his father, Billy says, about two days' travel from Cape Prince of Whales. Billy never saw any there. A whale skeleton Akpuk knows about and has seen on the bank of the Colville about two days' journey from Oliktok. Some has by now caved into the river. People say that formerly there was sea extending to this place and a whaling village located here. [. . .]

NOVEMBER 8 Started 8:45; camped 3:00; near Itkillik, saw tracks of sleds gathering willow. Place we stopped called Tuluraluk, on right bank. After starting yesterday, we followed left bank except not going into some small streams, until we came to a point about twelve feet high. After that we kept "main road" pretty well. Saw a grave about six miles from our camp. Opposite (west of it or N.W.) is a point of an island (its south end) high and with small pingoks. This is Peshiksharvik, a place so called from frequent fights and many being killed there. E. or S.E. of this on mainland, high pingok. [. . .]

NOVEMBER 9 Started 8:30: Camped 1:30 at "Miners' House." At ca. 9:30 we arrived at some tents (four) whose caches were in sight from our camp. Found that there is a large number of people in the neighborhood. Stayed with these some three hours and then moved on. One house (willow) is located just by the Miners House—only the women (of two families apparently) were at home—the men where? [. . .]

The people we have seen so far are disappointingly sophisticated, though they do not seem to have much use for "civilized" food. Akpuk's whole family seems to be around here—brothers, sisters, mother. One of his brothers (Ayaunirk) came to visit him last night and Akpuk goes to see him tomorrow, lives some few miles south. Panniulak is the name of our neighbor here. [. . .]

NOVEMBER 14 [. . .] Akoblak's boy has delayed us about one hour today with nose bleeding. He had another attack just after we got into our tent for the evening.

NOVEMBER 15 Akoblak says there are trees on the Itkillik, but not on the Kupik branch of the Colville. He lived among the trees one winter of the five he has spent on Colville (comes from country behind Kotzebue, wife of Colville parentage and birth); at that time (four years ago) some deer (formerly plenty) and moose, fish, rabbits, and ptarmigan; in mountains sheep and some places bear. Now no deer but still some moose in tree country. Some miners occasionally and one expected next year, has horses, and has been on Itkillik before. Have been miners also on upper Kupik. [. . .]

NOVEMBER 20. [. . .] Preparing deer legs. Akoblak's wife is doing a pair as follows: After cutting them off the hide she dried them and then rubbed them soft with a brick-like (pumice?) stone found on the Kupik near Atoakotak's house. She then plastered the skin side with a mush made of boiled deer liver and whale oil. When thoroughly plastered with this each leg is folded like the closing of a book (lengthwise). [. . .]

NOVEMBER 23 Started 7:30, camped 2:30, [. . .] made our first camp going east. Akoblak's family slept in the other house. Both houses have considerable fish (the kind caught at Shingle Point) and are catching them now. They also have a smaller fish, looks like Norwegian herring. They expect the fishing to stop about the time the sun comes back. [. . .]

The sun failed to clear the horizon (the 22nd). It was his last appearance for today he did not even peep up. So he will be away a little over 50 days. [. . .]

NOVEMBER 26 In camp. [. . .] This day is probably the feast of Thanksgiving. [. . .]

NOVEMBER 29 Started 9 A.M. Camped 2:30 P.M. in a house built this winter by some Barrow people who have left it temporarily. Found stove, lamp, etc, in position and blubber on the rack—took some for our dogs. [. . .]

DECEMBER 5 [. . .] Dec. 4th came down to Brower's to stay a few days; take physical measurements and get linguistic notes from Dr. Marsh. Today taking language notes from Marsh. [. . .]

DECEMBER 8 Cape Smythe. Practice of abortion. No disgrace, so far as Mr. Brower knows, ever attached to either voluntary or involuntary abortion and the former was practised until a few years ago, especially by young girls who considered it too early to assume family cares. Treatment was by kneading the abdomen and was done by doctors or by old women. Two or more doctors often worked together in other cases and Mr. Brower believes, but does not know, that both doctors and old women worked together on abortion. No secret was made, he thinks, of the time and place of treatment although he never heard of it till afterwards, except in the case of a young girl who told him she was going to have it done pretty soon, and later told him that now it was done. He never knew death or any serious illness to follow voluntary abortion, though he has known of serious illness after a miscarriage. Treatment was occasionally by hitting the stomach smart blows with a flat stick, though kneading was the usual way. There was no question of "confessing abortion" for it was made no more secret than childbirth. Twins were not desired, but were no great misfortune to the women who had them. Two could not be cared for, however, and one was exposed, usually but not always, the girl, if the children were one of each sex. No secret was made of either the birth or the killing. The sex of a child is usually correctly foretold by the mother after five or six months of pregnancy. Mr. Brower knows of but few mistakes, and in his own wife's case there have been none, two girls and four now living and two girls and one boy dead. He thinks they tell partly by the amount of movement of the foetus, boys move more. Preference for boys is the rule, but in many cases girls are desired. Mr. Brower can give no rule as to under what circumstances girls are wanted, but thinks that in most cases parents prefer to have the first child a boy (cf. Mackenzie River). He has never heard of any magical or other treatment to control the sex of the expected child. Pigmentation among Eskimo varies from that of whites in this general way that the parts lighter than the rest of the body among whites are darker than the rest among Eskimo—cf. *linia labe*. The genitals, nipples, and abdominal line are usually, if not always markedly dark (Dr. Marsh).

Whaling practices are better known to Mr. B. and Mr. Hadley for Point Hope, for the natives were already somewhat sophisticated at Barrow when they came here (some 22 years ago). *Deerskin* clothes with sealskin waterboots were the only ones allowed on the ice. (A few days before going on the ice at Pt. Hope the first year all Mr. Brower's clothes were stolen and he never saw them again. He was immediately presented with a full outfit of the best deerskins). *Cooking* on the ice was forbidden. If near shore the women brought out cooked food occasionally; if too far off frozen meat only was eaten. Mr. Brower says deer, seal and whale meat were eaten, but Mr. Hadley says that four years ago he was the only man who was allowed to eat deer meat—the others refused to eat when H. offered to share his meat with them. Twenty three deer had just been killed and the natives could have had all they wanted. He was told no whales would be caught if they ate the meat, but it made no difference what a white man ate. This is different from the practices 20 years ago (Mr. B. says) for then they used to go ashore, kill deer, and bring them out on the ice to eat. (Perhaps they refused Mr. H.'s meat because it was cooked?).

In Mr. B.'s time at Pt. Hope (over 20 years ago) no tents were taken on the ice and clothes must not be dried, mended or even turned around (as sacks, e.g.). The only thing ever mended was a torn boat sail. Both at Hope and Barrow no deerskin must be worked on the beach (only ca. ½ mile inland) during whaling, but (at Pt. Hope) when the men could stand their wet and torn clothes no longer (3–8 days) they went ashore and there the women mended their clothes anywhere. If a man fell in the water or got his feet wet, he was not allowed to take off his boots or clothes to wind them but went straight home to change if he could not stand the wet. When whales were plenty people did not go home sometimes till their boots were fairly falling off their feet. Sometimes they stayed at home only a few hours, sometimes one night or even two. No pounding was allowed in the whalemen's houses during the season. In the early days they believed whales could be caught only with their old stone gear. [. . .] No ceremonies in the boat while chasing a whale though often many before the season started, or in the middle of it if they were having bad luck. Immediately after the first pokes were fastened to a whale there was a song to make him die quickly—several kinds of song were used, one kind now, another kind or the same kind with the next whale. The singing was not by the one who struck the whale, but by the man in the stern—the owner, or *umialik*. When the whale was dead the blowhole (a hoop of blubber) was cut out, as well as the two carrars off the flukes and laid on the ice, and sometimes pieces of his fins—all in the position and direction they would occupy if the whole whale were on the ice. Pieces of the blowhole blubber and two slabs of whalebone were usually placed in the bow of the successful boat ("for luck" Mr. B.) and kept there the rest of the season. The pieces put on the ice (as above) belonged to the owner of the successful boat. He got his share of the big whalebone, and in addition the small bone near the "rib ends" [. . .] and his share of the meat and blubber came out of the small (just in front of the flukes). Out of this [. . .] he was expected to give a feast to his crew sometime during the dark days. Immediately after the whaling was over there was the "blanket-tossing-dance" and at this the flukes were cut up and divided among those present. The younger people usually ate up their share right there but the older sometimes carried theirs home (the old people). The meat of the whale was kept in ice houses all summer—frozen solid. [. . .]

Doctors at Cape Smythe used to make their living entirely through their "profession."[. . .] There is one still living (The Little Doctor) who has not ever done anything to support himself besides shooting ducks. His "practice" came to an end some four years ago but now he lives with a son-in-law. He is not Christian yet, but four years ago, out in the country his drum and medicine gear (what gear?) were forcibly taken from him and he warned not to practice "devil driving." The drum is nowadays used for "harmless dances" only, and never for charming. Dr.'s fees used to be pretty high, if the man was poor, he promised to pay later (cf. Mackenzie River—different practice). No fees were ever refunded.

"Murders" were occasionally done by the doctors. One case was the following (told by Mr. H.). A young man had been out on the ice whaling and got a severe headache. He sent for a Cape Smythe doctor. When the Dr. came he took between his fingers a pinch of skin just behind the end of one eyebrow and ran his knife through (making two holes). When the bleeding from these did not cure he made a similar double puncture behind the other eyebrow, and, when that failed, another on the top of the head. When this proved of no use he said: "I'll cure you now" and jabbed his knife into the top of the man's head, killing him instantly. Some days later Dr. Beaupre and others exhumed the body, had a post-mortem which showed the murder clearly; and tried the doctor for his life in the station house. They found him guilty but did not dare execute him and merely warned him. Mr. Stevenson, the missionary, disagreed with the "findings of the court" and said that if the doctor killed the man at all, it was unintended. [. . .] The white men were: Dr. Beaupre, Hadley, Kelley, Stevenson, Hopson (and others?). This was in 1892 when Mr. B. was "below." [. . .]

Death during pregnancy: One case of this has come under Mr. B.'s observation—at Point Hope. The woman was carried out as usual. Later four women went to the grave, cut open the abdomen, took out the foetus and buried it. One of the women fainted while at work. The reason assigned for the operation was that no whales would be caught while the foetus remained inside the woman. [. . .]

Restoration to the sea is known to Dr. M. in the case of some of the finbones of each whale. This is done by the whole village at a festival during the dark days. The bones are dropped through a single hole in the ice. [. . .]

Supplementary notes: Mr. Brower: Something like fifteen years ago a woman whaling at Pt. Hope refused to go home when her courses were about to commence and when told to go home by her husband (probably the views of white men made her think she was doing no harm). Her husband killed her by beating her brains out. When the news spread her father came from another settlement and killed the husband. All together 15 were killed in the feud. White men [. . .] did not interfere.

When Mr. Kelly was in charge of the station (in 1891) at Cape Smythe the wife of one of his men had a child on the ice: she then went ashore with it. The whale community was greatly excited, ceremonies of all kinds were performed to pacify the whales, and Mr. B. believes the woman and child would have been killed had it not been that they were working for whites, and the people were getting used to white men breaking all rules. [. . .] Mr. Kelly had forced the woman to stay on the ice. The universal belief was that dreadful luck would beset the whale village (no whales for how long? and other things), the husband would certainly catch no more whales forever, and no one catch a whale that season, and the husband would die soon. The season, however, was about the best ever known, and the husband himself (owner and stern-man of a boat) got six whales. This went far to destroy the whaling beliefs and practices in general.

DECEMBER 9 [. . .] *Inheritance laws:* (Dr. Marsh) When the husband died almost anybody in the village would come around and take what he wanted, leaving the widow destitute. No suffering was caused, however, on account of the general communism.

(Mr. Brower) When the husband died the family property was taken by the husband's brother and relatives if the man's children were young; if his sons were grown they would take the property; If the widow kept her children together the husband's relatives looked after them in a general way [. . .]. All these statements admit of exceptions—held only loosely. Sometimes if the brothers were doctors or old and influential, they got things the sons wanted out of the inheritance. Usually, as in the case of a boat, the one of the heirs (son or brother) who needed it most, got it. The husband of grown up daughters had some claims, but not so strong as sons.

Marriage customs: Mr. B. knows of no case of a man marrying his brother's widow—thinks it was looked upon as a sort of incest. A man did not marry two sisters, or if he had intercourse with his wife's sister it was looked upon as contrary to good usage—almost as incest, if not quite. A man often married for a second wife his wife's grown-up daughter (by another man). If he also took a second daughter it was looked upon about as whites do prostitution [. . .]. If she allowed it she "lost character" more or less.

Exposing children: Mr. B. has known of no real (old descent) Cape Smythe or Pt. B. people exposing infants. (The only twins that he has known of this parentage were one pair born since missionaries came here. Both of these died apparently against the mother's desire and of illness). He has known of it, however, being regularly practiced along the coast west, and by inlanders. One woman whom he knew before she had her first child (a Colville woman) has told him she has had 15 children and exposed them all. She said she found it impracticable to carry them following the deer in winter, although she would have liked to bring up any of them. She is now bringing up two adopted children—adopted at an age when they could almost take care of themselves. The last child exposed near here was a twin in 1898 by Wainwright people (people who had formerly lived at Wainwright). They were Xian. [. . .]

Killing the old. Pt. B., Cape S., and all Eskimos Mr. B. has known have in time of need deserted old people on the trail—walled them up in snowhouses. Normally, if not always, the people so treated took it without protest—it was the natural end, and expected by all who attained old age. Two cases have happened on the coast here as follows: An old woman from Point Hope who had three daughters living at Cape Smythe was walled up. At that time food was plenty in the village. Mr. Herendeen who was here then broke into the snow house and kept the woman a year. She was then a year and a half at the station (Mr. B. there too). She was a splendid worker and sewed all the clothes practically used by the station. At the end of a year and a half at the station she died. The other woman walled up was a cripple, middle aged [. . .] at Pt. Barrow. She died in the snowhouse. Mr. B. never heard of a person walled up trying to break out of the snowhouse. [. . .]

Photographs: A woman whose memory goes back ca. 20 years says in her childhood some people feared cameras and some not. Believed spirit gotten hold of through picture. Spirit controlled equally their *hair, old clothes,* etc, and she thinks perhaps finger parings also. [. . .]

Medical customs: Dr. Marsh: Returning fee: In his earlier years here Dr. Marsh used frequently to see someone marching through the village with a piece of blubber (whale always?) on the point of a stick. This person was on his way to a "devil doctor" to give him the blubber as a returning fee.

Size of fee: The fee was demanded after treatment but was returned only in case of death soon after—say, in pneumonia. The doctor gauged his fee by a man's ability to pay and sometimes took practically everything he had. If the man was poor he "went in debt" and sometimes pledged his services for years to come.

(Mr. B.). The largest fee ever taken, so far as he knows, was when the doctor took practically everything a well-to-do man had except his umiak, and got his services for two years besides. The man worked out the two years faithfully and engaged another man to run his own boat.

Taboos: A growing boy must never eat any sort of liver before puberty—it would make his muscles soft.

In treating diseases a doctor often forbade the eating of certain things, arbitrarily and with no discernible relation to the disease—i.e. he might forbid fish in one case of pneumonia, ducks in another, seal in another, etc. Occasionally taboos other than food.

Medicine: The only thing in the way of medicine was the administering of soapstone scrapings from a lamp. These seem to have been taken in the manner of a drug in certain cases. (I believe oil may be considered another "medicine"—vs.). [. . .]

Forbidden food: the head, forelimbs, back and internals forbidden. What the patient eats may be cooked or raw, however.

Any woman coming in contact with the blood, or any of the afterbirth, would be barren after (further penalties also?). Therefore a woman must do everything for herself at childbirth. [. . .]

Childbearing is often limited to one child, he thinks, because women work and travel too soon after delivery [. . .].

Name-giving: The child is named after some dead ancestor. Only one child is usually named after each ancestor, but there may be duplication if children that live are numerous. If child dies, another may be named after the same ancestor. Informant (women at Dr.'s) had not heard of naming child after living or dead friends, or after recently dead people who were not ancestors. [. . .]

Marriage: Girls were occasionally forced by will. Some of this still, though missionaries refuse to "solemnize." This involves betrothal by parents. [. . .]

Sealing: The people of Oturkarmiut (Icy Cape) and Wainwright Inlet shout tremendously after the killing of an ugrug. This is a charm, but the informant (woman before referred to) does not know the details. No such yelling by Pt. B. or C.S. people, to whom she belongs.

Physical measurements (stature, spread of arms, sitting height) were taken today in the church with the assistance of Dr. Marsh. There were 33 individuals from seven different localities. [. . .]

Childbirth customs: (Mr. B.) When the child was born the woman cut the navel string with a stone knife. [. . .] She then wiped the child with deerskin (or other suitable material?). When all was finished, and not till then, an old woman entered the snow house (tent, if summer) and took the deerskin (with afterbirth, etc.) on which the child was born and carried it far inland to throw it away. In case of difficult delivery an old woman (sometimes the girl's mother) stood outside the tent shouting directions to her, and in extreme difficulty the doctor performed outside the tent, but no one entered until after the child was born and cleaned, or else the woman dead. For about a month after the child's birth it and its mother stayed in the birth house. The woman frequently came out but never entered her own house or anyone elses. Occasionally old women (and perhaps others?) used to visit her in her little house, however.

(*Mr. Gordon*) For a certain time (a year probably?) after childbirth or miscarriage the woman must not *see the water* just before or during whaling. [. . .]

Puberty and menstruation: At Point Hope (Pt. B. too probably) a girl during her first periods was not allowed to drink water out of the same cup as others, and usually, if not always, she was not even allowed to dip her cup in the common water pail. [. . .]

In travelling once with a party along a river a woman having the monthly flow was allowed to ride on the sled but must not put her feet on the river. If she wanted to walk someone carried her to the bank and she walked along the river on the land. When they came to lakes she was allowed to walk on the ice. (Mr. B. does not remember whether she was allowed to walk on the sled tracks—cf. Indian custom). [. . .]

Taboos: (Mr. B.) Certain individuals were prohibited from eating certain animals, and others from certain parts of certain animals—as deerhead, deermarrow, etc. and squirrel, grouse, etc. These prohibitions he understood were prescribed by a medicine man for each man when he was young. Occasionally, he thinks, doctors removed the prohibition—knows case of man who began eating deerheads five years after Mr. B. came to

Smythe. Thinks special prohibitions placed for each whaling season—fairly sure of this, for one season a man would refuse to eat deer liver, another year shoulder, another year marrow, fat of deer or flippers of seal, etc. [. . .]

For the first few years of Mr. B.'s stay at Smythe there were "two old hags" with whom boat owners and others who steered a boat were supposed to have sexual intercourse just before the season commenced. This was strictly adhered to by the "older men" but not by the "younger generation." These women dressed in special designed garments made after the fashion (the pants) of childrens' clothing. One side of the opening was trimmed with wolverine skin, the other with wolf. (These were the "main totems" Dr. Marsh thinks of the Cape Smythe people). The custom gradually fell off and when these two women died the practice died with them (Mr. B.). [. . .]

DECEMBER 12 *Communism* seems disappearing fast among the people of Cape Smythe. The most striking phase is that where a few years ago every man received bone if he was in a canoe that got a whale, and he was then free to sell as he pleased. Now they get no bone to handle; the employer takes it all and pays in the maintenance, to the best of his ability, of the family of his employee. An incidental consequence of this is that people who were in debt (to Mr. B. say) are permanently unable to pay. [. . .]

DECEMBER 17 A fairly thick blizzard and cold. Had 2–3 days of calm and variable airs, and now the NE is with us again.

Dying childless: Mr. B. was formerly often told, both at Smythe and Hope, by young women, that if they should die childless "they would never come back" after death.

Naming children: So far as I can discover, naming at C.S., Oturkarmiut and everywhere to the westward was from dead relatives only. If all dead relatives "were used up" they might be used over again. So soon as child bearing a name died the name became free to use. [. . .]

The soul: Oturkarmiut and Barrow people seem to have thought of body as having one soul only. When man died, body went to sleep and soul went away. People a short time dead often have the spirit come back again and thus become alive once more. Story: A certain Nunatarmiut died in the evening. The next morning the soul came back and the dead man answered when spoken to. Later in the day the soul went away again and man has been dead ever since (told by Kopak—Oturkarmiut).

Doctors used to steal men's souls and kill them that way. When a doctor told a man he would take his soul away the man usually died soon after.

(Mr. B. corroborates this). The only way was to engage a more powerful doctor. If powerful enough the doctor could prevent the soul's leaving the body, and some could even follow the soul after it had left, overtake it, bring it back forcibly and return it to the body, which then became alive and well. The Oturkarmiut and their relatives (Kang. and Nun.) did not have so many doctors as other peoples because the raven had told them now to do most things and they could help themselves. Had doctors, however. (Told by Kopak).

The reflected image: When children were caught looking in water to see their own face they were made to stop and told doing this would twist their face onto one side of their head. (Fear of losing soul?).

Hunting customs: If the entire skin of a game animal were taken out of the country, the hunter would get no more animals of that sort. For that reason a small piece (often from the nose) is cut off and thrown on the ground near where the animal was killed or skinned. *Kopak.*

Tannigvik: The first men Tulurak made he called Tannigvik. The Eskimos had never seen them, but T. had said they would one day see them. Therefore, when the whites came the Eskimo thought they were the Tannigvik of whom Tul. had told them. Therefore they are called "Tannigvik." *Kopak.* [. . .]

The great bird "Mitiravik." This is a great bird that carries off people, white fish, and even bowhead whales in his claws. A certain man named "Kitirriuak" was once carried off by this bird: Mitiravik put the claws of either foot under the man's arms and around him, holding him tight but without injury. When they were very high up, the man stabbed the bird under its wing. The bird gradually settled as its life blood ran out and finally died when near the ground. Kitirriuak then walked home. This is not an old story. Told by Kopak.

Kopak is a man perhaps 60 years of age, but fairly robust still, and exceedingly fond of telling "the old stories" to anyone who listens with interest. He says he has heard many versions of certain stories he knows, but he tells them exactly as his own old people told them, because he cannot vouch for accuracy [. . .] of any but his own people's stories—partly because he never took much pains to remember any other. Many of the stories he heard first from his mother, who was a great story teller. His people, on both sides, he says, were Oturkarmiut—living at Icy Cape and inland from there. He has now lived a long time at Cape Smythe [. . .].

DECEMBER 18 *The raven and the loon:* Dr. M. has been told that the creator of the land at Pt. Hope (pulled it out of water with spear) was called "He who has a loon's beak on his forehead" and the loon's beak is sure enough worn by dancers as far as Victoria Island. But Mr. B. says that during his first years north he several times saw a head dress of raven's skin (wings, tail, head) worn with the raven's head over the forehead of the dancers. Mr. B. has never seen a raven or crow at or near Barrow [. . .].

Taha told me last night (Dec. 17th) that the Utqiaguigmiut knew nothing of the raven's having created the world—in fact, knew "almost no stories" of the raven—until recently (in his own time) his people got them from the inlanders—Nunatarmiut.

White influence on Eskimos is seen here pretty clearly in many things, but in nothing more clearly than in money matters. The incident of the above *Taha* is perhaps an extreme case. It is worth regarding—as follows:

Taha is by a good many years the oldest living Utqiaguigmiut, conspicuous for being well informed on "all old" things and fond of telling them (or has been). He says, and others say so too, that he knows a good many stories which no one else knows, and the knowledge will probably die with him. Taha lives down (south) along the coast a day from Smythe. Mr. B., Dr. M. and Mr. Hawks had all told me how delighted he would be to tell me tales. But three days ago he came up, and day before yesterday Mr. B. asked him to come over and tell me some stories. He seemed "tickled to death." Yesterday, however, he came to see "how much I would pay" for stories. I was sleeping and Mr. B. said he "chased him out of the house." Mr. Marsh asked him over to his house last night. He came and told us a short story of how the deer were made. Then he informed us that that story wasn't much good and so he had told it for nothing. He knew many good stories, he said, such as that of how the earth was made, but he would tell good stories only for pay. Half an hour before he had told us he might have heard sometime how the earth was made, but if he had, he had forgotten all about it. Now he asserted he remembered all the details clearly, but would not tell them, except for pay. Dr. M. pointed out we merely wanted to preserve the stories so they should not die with him, but the argument did not seem to affect him remarkably much.

It is said that some Eskimos here will not feed a hungry white man nowadays without pay: a few years ago their custom were similar to those of Mackenzie river. [. . .]

F in Eskimo: I cannot recall hearing the sound of "f" spoken by Eskimos, and certainly most of them are unable to pronounce such name as "Fanny," "Fred." Last night, however, *Taha* clearly sounded the "f" repeatedly in "tafruma." [. . .]

DECEMBER 21 *Weather* has been calm since evening of Dec. 19th where a fairly severe three day's blizzard came to an end. Dr. Marsh says it was the severest he ever saw, but it was mild compared to those to the eastward, and Mr. B. says they have had much worse ones, though they are not frequent. [. . .]

Naming children: Pannitjiak has heard the Unalit (S. of Yukon) name children after dead people other than relatives sometimes. When an umialik dies a great many children are usually named after him—sometimes 20, she has heard. These children get no [. . .] assistance from the chief's relatives (inheritance, sacrifice, gifts; compare contrary custom given by Boas). If child dies, another [. . .] gets the same name.

Whaling customs: Shortly before the season began, the crew of an umiak had a sort of ceremony meal together. The staple of the meal was maktak.

Early in the morning some children in the village would go out and start singing. As they sang they would march from one house to another and at each house the children, if any, came out and joined the singers, till there were a great many children marching and singing. Finally some woman would come out with a large pan of black skin chopped in small pieces and scatter these among the children who scrambled for them (as street boys after a handful of pennies). This ended the performance. The narrator herself took part more than once. (Told by Annie Kudlaluk.)

The name spirit: Pannitjiak says she has "heard that some people" think that there is a spirit with (or in) a name and that the child that has been named has two spirits. She has never heard who it is if child has two, three or more names. "Some of" her own people and "some of" other people she has known believe this. (I suspect the "some of" is because she is ashamed to admit having believed this herself.)

Tooth pulling was done by members of the family—often women. Pannitjiak was an expert. Tooth "yanked out" with string of sinew. (Mr. B.) [. . .]

Initiation of strangers: [. . .] Both at Point Hope and Pt. Barrow a stranger was made to "run gauntlet"—the villagers, men, women and children, lined up with clubs, etc. and stranger had to run between them towards a house which was his haven. There was more scratching and pulling than there was beating, however, and the women trimmed their finger nails to a point just before the event so their scratches should tell. The man frequently had his clothes badly torn and sometimes they were literally all torn off him. (Mr. B. never knew of clothes being replaced by new ones though he saw village women mending (the torn clothes) them.)

If a man, however, got unseen into some house in the village he was safe there for several days. Finally, however, his trial would come. If he was a man noted for prowess he wrestled publicly with the young men of the village till someone threw him. Mr. B. knows of one Pt. Hope man who threw every man of Cape Smythe without being himself thrown. This was the beginning of dislike (envy to start with) of him which ended in his killing some 2 years later by a man whose head he had smashed pretty badly in a drunk. This man—a port Clarence man—shot him in the leg in the dark and an unknown man stabbed him to death afterwards. (Told by Mr. B.) [. . .]

DECEMBER 30 We started from Cape Smythe at 12:N. Arrived at Tarak's house 4 P.M. fast going. Distance called 25 miles. [. . .] All of us slept in Tarak's house, which is ca. 16 x 18 and has a sleeping platform for eight. Some slept in the entrance passage. Four or five sleds were expected invited to the dance at Icy Cape. SE wind [. . .].

JANUARY 1 Kilavirktarviarou(k) (Place where black geese shed feathers). Got here 3 P.M. today.

Names. A small boy (about four) in this house was born a short time before his uncle died. After the uncle's death the baby became very restless and became quiet only after he got the uncle's name. This was given him as a second name and he at once became quiet. He had been crying for the name. Formerly, when a child was very restless and cried, a medicine man was called in to determine whose name he was crying for, when the right name was found the crying stopped. On being questioned, all the people of the house (three) agreed that not only did the child want the name, but "in all probability" the name was equally anxious to get into the child, i.e., they seem to think of the name as an entity—a soul. [. . .]

Started 10 A.M. Arrived at house of Akebiana (Point Franklin) 4:45. There are six houses here, but only two have people just now, the other four families are at Icy Cape for the dance.

Tattooing. A woman from Nogatogmiut (Napaktok) says girls of her time (she looks forty) were told if they did not tattoo the chin, the chin would grow long to disfigurement.

A "Kagmalit" woman is Akebiana's wife and she is Roxy's and Ovayuak's cousin. She has been around Barrow about twelve years and has forgotten most Mackenzie words that differ from Barrow.

Humor. Two jokes "sprung" last evening may be called typical Eskimo jokes. The loose root of a badly pulled (broken) tooth, came out. Someone said I had twisted it out in trying to pronounce Eskimo words. George said when he was small he cried for another name. His wife said she guessed it probably was worms.

JANUARY 3 Started 10:10 A.M., stopped 1:30 P.M. in vacant house (stove, etc.) at Sisdravuit (Point Belcher). Two inhabitable houses here. About half is house of Portugee Jerome Lope who three years ago last fall went into prison at McNeill's Island, Washington, for "Statutory Rape," living with woman under sixteen.

JANUARY 7 Perpetual frost. At various times in the past I have found in speaking with Eskimo that they consider solid frost as the natural condition of the earth to an unknown depth, the layer thawed in summer is the only part not frozen at that time. They have asked me how far one would have to dig in my country and in the negro's country to get down to frost, after it was explained that in Africa it does not freeze in winter or summer.

During time of no entries in diary have been taking folklore stories most days. Dates on them show pretty well what has been done each day. [. . .]

JANUARY 12 Takpuk is said to be going insane. He is so restless that he has to be traveling or moving all the time. Got tired of waiting for crowd of dancers (who hang around Wainwright four days) and came back to his deer herd. Behaving as he does would not be remarked among the whites, but is considered abnormal here. [. . .]

JANUARY 16 *The school situation* on this coast is complicated by various things. Mr. Lapp. (the resident superintendent he may be called though he lives in Seattle) is over ears in his work, apparently, and has the best intentions, but looks upon the people as miserable wretches (of good natural qualities nevertheless) who need all sorts of help—which help seems to me to amount essentially to pauperisation. People that have been independent for a thousand or so years are to be taught by all the subordinates of the department the essential superiority of white men's food, clothes, houses, etc. over the native variety. [. . .]

FEBRUARY 19 It is in the opinion of Dr. Marsh and all the other white men here that all the old people and most children prefer the native to white men's food—i.e. being deprived of seal, whale and deer would be a much greater hardship (though they had plenty bacon, corned beef, etc.) than being deprived of all white men's food, even including tea.

Mr. Brower's step daughter Inyura (ca. 9 years old) is typical. Mr. Brower sets an exceptionally good table (prepared by a chef formerly of one of the Fall River steamers) the food is varied and the materials expensive. Yet Inyura never much more than nibbles at it, while between meals she eats huge meals of boiled seal, frozen fish, black skin, etc. She has been brought up on white men's food. Her mother is the same, as are all Eskimos I know. Annie Kudlaluk, after being 9 years in Pennsylvania (ca. 10 years old when she got there) is inordinately fond of frozen fish, black skin, etc. [. . .].

A native trader arrived last evening from Kotzebue Sound. He is said to have $500 in money and some "civilized" shoes, sweaters, socks, underwear. He pays $300 in money for white fox; other prices in proportion. [. . .]

FEBRUARY 22 [. . .] *Men off the ice* don't seem to cause much excitement. One went off from Pt. Barrow last Thursday and got back on Sunday forenoon. White man say there have been cases of men in sight [. . .] and no attempt at rescue. Cases also of umiaks put out to help. [. . .]

"Fearless" (Ilavinirk's "brother") who was with Mogg last winter gave me some items concerning the people today. Fearless says people had a distinctly lighter complexion than any Eskimo he ever saw. Saw some whose skin (face) was as light as mine, several with hair ranging from mine to Mr. Hadley's (which is dark, but not black). Hair was, too, not so stiff as ordinary Eskimo and children's hair averaged lighter than grown people's, a thing true of whites, though I have seen no variation from the ordinary black among Eskimos except in newborn children.

It seems entirely out of the way to suppose that these facts can be explained by white blood mixture from Collinson's and McClure's vessels, in view of the fact that no such changes have been wrought at Pt. Barrow in over half a century of definite contact.

Fearless says the complexion differences are carried out in the eyes, for he says the white of the eye was like white men's and not like Eskimo's or Indian's. [. . .] Some of the people had eyes as light as mine, Fearless says (though McIntyre says he saw only one as light and Baker (engineer) says he saw two). Fearless agrees with white men in saying average stature of the people up to that of Nunatamas.

Scarcity of women is marked. There were no single women but several single men; no men had two wives but several women had two husbands. Exchanging wives is practised and little or no sexual jealousy. Large proportion of children (contrary to Klengenberg's story).

Movements of people. People hunt in Banks Island sometimes. Whenever they cross sea it is by sleds, for they have no umiaks and but four kayaks among people whom Fearless saw (Capt. Mogg says about 150 visited ship and F. saw an encampment of twelve houses besides those 150). They sometimes hunt where there are trees (not willows) and have their bows, etc., made of these and not of driftwood. They know of people (Eskimo presumably) who have white men's wares, but these are hostile. Know of Indians also.

Copper not much in evidence among people Fearless saw, most had knives from Klengenberg's ship of former years. Some women had ulus of thick tin from Collinson's ship.

Mr. Brower knew of one woman a daughter of an officer of McGuire's ship. No trace of white blood is apparent in her full grown son who now lives at Point Barrow, woman long dead. It may be said, therefore, that all trace of McGuire's wintering has disappeared. Mr. Brower has seen only one case of light eyes in half-whites here, and knows one case of light hair. All half-caste children I have seen anywhere (Eskimo) have had black hair, have seen thirty or thirty-five. F. says beards no more marked than among other Eskimo. This is negative but he also says beards were as light or lighter in shade than hair. [. . .]

MARCH 10 Started 8:45 A.M., camped 6 P.M. in one of three snowhouses (deserted) on next sandspit west of Iglorak. Biggest (the center one) house had evidently been lined with canvas for permanent habitation, but canvas recently removed and big holes left open in roof of house, about three feet square. The (west) one we slept in was a temporary camp but door and stove pipe hole closed and all in good shape. Did not look into easternmost house.

Snowhouse building seems a lost art. It is said the people formerly made the dome houses, but nowadays they use a handsaw, cut the snow into huge blocks (say eighteen inches by forty), build the house in a rectangle with the walls perpendicular and the gables highest in the center, log cabin shape. A ridge pole of wood is then laid and block laid resting one end on wall and other on ridge pole. If no wood is available the blocks are said to be leaned together at the top. This sort of roof will evidently sag in mild weather. It is said some half dozen men at Cape Smythe and Point Barrow know how to build dome houses.

Inlander combination houses and tents are thus made: The ordinary dome tent is put up. On top this snow is shoveled. It must be soft; if there are chunks they are pulverized or thrown out. When the tent is covered about six to eight inches (patted down with flat of shovel), a fierce fire is built inside. This forms ice in the snow outside. In course of use the tent dries. A space is left between the tent and snow (now part ice), by the first thawing. This acts as insulating space all winter. We thus have practically a lined snowhouse. If the tent be removed the snowhouse remains, unless broken.

MARCH 13 Started 6:40 A: stopt 6:15 P. at Imagruak: I slept in Kunagrak's house and Billy and Uyuliak in other. [. . .]

MARCH 15 *Takok and Arnatulk* are the middle-aged couple living in the other Imagruak house (besides Kunagrak). They have a boy of ca. twelve. Their daughter (or his, at least) is Kenoranna, daughter in law of Akowaks: their (or his) son is Niako(k) a young married man [. . .]. Takok says he is very grateful because I last summer gave a sack of flour to Akowak's party in which was also his daughter Kenoranna.

Another starving family [. . .] came to Takok's house just after Xmas. The man so weak he could not sit on the floor [. . .]. Takok fed them for about a month: they are now housed with Kunagrak—Kunagrak was at C.S. when this happened.

The inland people Takok says, never give each other food when they starve in one house and have plenty in another. In this he says they are markedly different from coast people. [. . .]

The starving Ikpikpik family came January 19th (by a cross in the calendar). Their names: Pillyalla; Kirrnok his wife: child Nirak—a boy ca. fifteen [. . .].

MARCH 16 [. . .] The starving couple who came to C.S. are in mind again, for the couple who deserted them are staying with Kunagrak—Turñrak and Ulorra with girl baby ca. 1 ½ years old (seems sick—consumption?). Turñrak is the brother of the woman whom (and her husband) he deserted. Both are children of Panniulak, my neighbor at Itkillik. Son as well as Panniulak is evidently Christian—he says prayers at meals [. . .] and carries a lot of Sunday school pictures. I asked him how long he had been Xian. "Many years." So this, the most inhuman desertion ever heard of at C.S. in at least 20 years was done by a convert to the blessed faith. [. . .]

Polyandry. A Point Hope woman, Aksiaktok, had two husbands, the earlier Nayukuk; the one added later, Ukullina (a Kuwormiut). N. is from Point Hope and later lived at Point Barrow. Ukullina has now been divorced. All are still living, woman and husband at Point Hope. (Told by Uyuliak and Billy in concert.)

MARCH 18 Seemed cold today. All of us but the boy kept freezing our faces continually. My chin must have been stiff twenty times, and cheeks and nose less often. No harm, of course, to any of us.

Tents of walrus or ugrug gut were, Billy says, sometimes made for summer use at Port Clarence. [. . .]

MARCH 21 In camp to rest dogs and build cache—I am in a hurry to get east to see Anderson and load is too heavy—took so heavy a load because I agreed with Mogg to let Uyuliak travel with me. [. . .]

MARCH 23 [. . .] A lesson in fountain pens may be had from my experience here. March 21st I thoughtlessly filled my pen brimming—before that I had always been careful to leave a space. On taking it out last night (I did not use it Mar. 22nd—too cold in our tent—roofed snow house) I found the "spoon" under the pen pushed forward by the freezing ink to project beyond the pen point. Perhaps I can fix it later, but won't try now. The moral is: in cold weather never [. . .] fill your pen, and keep it point-end up while it freezes. [. . .]

MARCH 29 *Dr. Anderson* had been to Flaxman 3 or 4 days and had gone back to Ulahula again. The following is a *summary of his letter* to me: [. . .]. Beside own party, five others were along (Anktalik, Akorak and party). Had short rations for a while but soon found deer—entire crowd got 63 caribou and one moose. Hunted 75–100 miles down into foothills on south (along branch of Chandlar?). Had killed 15 sheep in November. [. . .]

Distribution of people: Of whites. Capt. Wolki and crew and Mr. Storkerson are at Flaxman, as also John Gruben Island. [. . .] Shariawanna lives here [. . .]. Mikshrak, Ojarayak and the widow Pannigabluk are here also. [. . .] Kugranak, also Igloon, Kashunirk, Oyarak, with families—except Igloon whose woman is at Island: the rest are on the Ulahula except Kunnullak to the west.

Loss of life: January 9th Henry Tanner, 2nd mate of the Rosie H. went on ice for seal. Warm weather (warmest day of winter—Stork says it rained in Smith Bay), wind blowing snow a little along ground. Did not return. Lights hung in rigging at night. Next day vain hunt. Supposed carried off on ice. Early in March body found by Shariawanna west of the E. mouth of Kugurak 6 or 8 miles east of island. Had apparently mistaken mainland for island. Tracks showed he struck coast a little E. of island and walked E. Was sitting, frozen. Apparently died first night—it got colder, but not cold towards morning. Strong man, many years in Arctic, used to sled trips. Easily fell asleep always—on chairs, on sled resting on trips, etc. Probably dozed off and got too cold at morn. Buried on island in grave into clear ice.

Two Eskimos were carried off on ice on New Year's Eve—were sealing. [. . .] Ice carried off clean from beach—did not come back. All new ice now.

MARCH 30 [. . .] *Shall stay here* till Dr. Anderson comes as he gives his date of arrival as April 1st and might easily pass him on the road up the Ulahula, or even between here and Barter Island. Besides, our dogs are pretty tired and sorefooted. If dogs were in good shape I should probably make the trip to Herschel Island for the mail—though Sgt. Fitzgerald will send it up if any Eskimo comes. [. . .]

APRIL 1 [. . .] Work: Since coming to Flaxman I have copied what folklore stories I had with me and am today starting on what is intended as a magazine article on Christianity among the Eskimos.

Gallagher arrived ca. 2 P.M. and said he and Billy left Ned's yesterday morning but Billy lagged behind with Terigluk (Pannigabluk's brother) who is coming from Mts. with load of sheep meat.

Akorak and Kiirroya (Oyaragak's son) arrived ca. 6 P.M.—say Dr. Anderson and party are probably at mouth of Ulahula. They brought in some fish; and are sleeping in our house (Storkerson's rather).

APRIL 3 76+ ϕ (Pannigabluk, widow, Father Kuraluk, mother Port Clarence—184–141–142–140 No lober [100+]

APRIL 9 [. . .] *Billy* and Pannigabluk returned ca. 10 P.M. last night. Had been long encamped Collinson Point shooting ptarmigan with Pannigabluk's shot gun. Terigluk, wife and 3 children left behind on sandspit ca. 10 miles E. of Flaxman. Had been with Billy at Collinson, left there yesterday A.M. and got tired and camped. They came in today against wind (2 P.M.). *Akorak* left this A.M. and with him Oyarak's Kiirroya, a big lazy young man. Akorak seems a fine fellow. [. . .]

APRIL 14 [. . .] Thefts are numerous this year. We have lost from the cache here 1 spy glass, 1 pair deerskin boots, I skein red yarn, about 10 lbs. tobacco, half a tin matches, etc. Others have lost similarly. Whole community very religious. Thefts formerly rare. *Bought an Umiak* today from Shariawanna for a wolf skin (Billy's), Red fox and 2 packages (bunches) matches. It is a large umiak, but many of skins are good for one summer only. [. . .]

[Icelandic:] *Um Giftingamál: Mamayauk sagði oss i kveld að Ikkayuok hefði sagt sjer að Kunasluk og kona hans ætli sjer ekki að gefa dóttur sina festarmanni hennar (Niníox) nema ef prestsonurinn ekki komi aftur—hún er nú geimd honum i von um að hann komi a sumri. Iglevox sagði mér . . . að stúlkan sje lofuð Guðs manninum, enn Miklaskál segir i kveld að Oyarak, og Iglevox sjeu einnig að geima dóttur sína í von um að Kunasluk kunni að verða barnshafandi og þess-vegna þóknist ekki gusðmanninum.* [. . .]

[*On Marriage:* Mamayauk told us tonight that Ikkayuok had said that Kunasluk and his wife do not intend to marry their daughter to her fiancé (Niniox) unless the priest's son fails to return—she is reserved for him in case he will arrive in the summer. Iglevox . . . told me that the girl is engaged to the religious man, but M. says tonight that Oyarak and Iglevox are also reserving their daughter in the hope that Kunasluk might become pregnant and, as a result, would not be acceptable for the priest. . . .]

[Icelandic:] *Miklaskál segir mér i dag: að prestssonurinn hafi sagz átta sér að halda fryllu næst þegar hann kæmi norður; að hann hafi ráði sér (Mikluskál) til að taka fryllu i vetur—hafi sagt sér að gera það þvi að honum (prestsyni) þætti svo vel farið. Synist að báðir hafi gleimt að Mikliskál var i minni vistum ekki prests-sonar. Áður hefur M. sagt mér að þetta og hitt hafi prestur sagt sér að gjöra þegar hann hætti að vinna fyrir mig (i vetur). . . . Jeg trúi ekki á alt þetta. . . .*

[M. tells me today that the priest's son had said he would get himself a concubine the next time he would come north; that he advised him (M.) to take a concubine this winter—he had told him that he (the priest's son) found that quite appropriate. It seems that both forgot that M. was employed by me and not the priest's son. Earlier M. told me that the priest's son said M. should do this and that when he quit working for me (this winter). . . . I don't believe all of this. . . .]

APRIL 28 [. . .] Camped on account of Moacak sleeping cold on sled.

Our cache had been robbed of dog food—apparently by Kunasluk, who camped there 2 or more nights evidently—a seal and some whale tongue missing. Gave Akpuk a sack flour, some tea, sugar, bacon and [. . .] promised him 30 yards drill for a tent—all this as mixed charity and blackmail, for Ilavinirk says "people will speak badly of us" if I don't pay Akpuk (—for what?). . . .]

MAY 7 [. . .] No sign of Anderson so our trip serves only to take dog feed here. Purpose of trip was to arrange to get cooperation with Anderson's crowd in moving our stuff east. Left letter for Anderson at Oliktok asking him to come west to Smith Bay at once. For some reason he has failed to do so. [. . .]

MAY 23 [. . .] Bringing up children. Talked with Ilavinirk tonight about the fact that Noashak is a pretty bad little girl. When we travel she is always on the sled, when we stop she is over all creation tumbling and capering.

He said if she were a boy, he would make her walk. Told of the harmful results of speaking harshly to children. Said when he himself was small his father spoke harshly to him occasionally and he feels the evil effects still. [. . .] Besides, he wants her to have as easy time as white children. Travelled once with Mr. and Mrs. Lapp and children to Point Hope; neither Mrs. Lapp nor children walked a step.

MAY 24 [. . .] *Misers:* Ilavinirk says Shutiauravik told Mamayak some of the wealthy Coleville people used their coats for bedskins though they had racks full of deerskins—for sale. [. . .] Made us turn in to Imnaluk as we had seen *Anderson's* sled track going that way. We thought he had come to the cache and merely gone back again, but at Imnaluk I found following letter:

Imnaluk, Smith Bay.
May 23rd, 1909

My dear Stefansson:

We have transferred all goods from main cache to this place and from this place to an old house ca. 15 m. NE along coast. We move camp to that place with last load today.

At main cache we left seven sacks flour, two bags sugar, 50 lbs. shot and all the coal oil (two cases), as per your instructions.

Sledding has been rather heavy and hard on dogs.

Yours sincerely,
R.M. Anderson

Leaving here 8:30 A.M. [. . .]

MAY 25 Started 9: P.M. last night with 3 dogs and 200 lbs. to see Anderson. Got there 13:30 A.M. today just as they were through supper. Billy was snowblind today so Anderson and Pannigabluk took load ahead—to our camp of March 26 which they call 10 miles from the 2 houses where they now are. Otherwise Billy and Anderson usually trips while P. tends camp. They made 5 trips between cache and Imnaluk and 4 from Im. to 2 houses. Of their 5 dogs none is good and Sport (Ilav's pup) no good. The stuff (incl. camp gear) they are carrying comes to about 3,000 lbs. [. . .]

MAY 26 Started ca. 10: P.M. yesterday for our cache. Arrived there ca. 2:30 A.M. today. Arranged and labelled stuff we are leaving there for Mogg,

Storkerson, Konosik and Atokotoak (Anton). Dug snow out of whaleboat and found some old valuables. [. . .]

Goose: saw one grey goose—first of year. [. . .]

Length of stories. Ilavinirk says his father knew one very good story. It was so long it took about a month to tell it all. Of course, he says, they did not sit at it continuously. His father might go looking at traps one day and hunting another, but always when he came home and had eaten he took a seat in middle of kajigi floor and started where he left off. [. . .]

Methods. Pannigabluk found some small dead bed-willows at Imnaluk, stuck them in the snow, and snared ptarmigan among them.

Religion. Ilavinirk the other day repeated his assertion that before missionaries came Eskimo were bad. Now they are good. The first time the story was that they lied, stole, and worked on Sundays; now they lie and steal but don't work Sundays. To this he now adds that formerly "doctors" used to kill men by magic, but now there is none of this, thanks to fear of Hell.

MAY 28 [. . .] *Hunted* seal between 5 and 9 P.M. Saw two. First one came; he went down at ca. 250–300 yds. Second shot at 100–125 yds. Aimed at shoulders. Blood spurted profusely but seal flopped into hole. [. . .]

JUNE 7 *Doings:* Anderson oiled guns and made himself gamebags today: Pannigabluk made 3 gun covers.

JUNE 9 *Started* ca. 12:30 P.M. with 2 sleds (3 of us) to cache stuff on island ca. 2 miles SE of this point (Coufort?). From there Billy and I went forward SE with light load to explore to SE, for sky looked bad there—black and green water clouds. [. . .] Meanwhile Anderson and Pannigabluk had hauled another load to island according to plan. This was wasting work, and it was for that reason Billy and I cached our load so near house [. . .].

Women's tapsis at Port Clarence and neighborhood were decorated with deer teeth. Pannigabluk says she has not seen this at Barrow or among any of the eastern peoples. [. . .]

JUNE 16 In camp sleeping off, loading shotgun shells, etc. Anderson skinned both fawns shot yesterday. Billy got first eggs of season—willow pt. nest with 9 eggs and bird. Anderson of course took shells for specimens. [. . .]

JUNE 19 Beliefs. Pannigabluk tells that two years ago her brother Alekak wanted to stay at Rampart House as Kurugak did, but could not because their mother (hers and Alekak's) "did not want to die among trees." Why did she not want to die among trees? "That was her idea not mine. I don't know what she thought."

Anderson's trip did not turn out a particular success. Today was the only fairly clear day they had: A "big" river just west of their camp prevented hunting SW or W. Billy had hunted SE and seen no signs of deer.

JUNE 23 *Started* 10 A.M. with all belongings in umiak except dogs which ran along shore. Anderson walked, looking for nests. Paddled seaward and landward along crooked channels and finally got into too shoal water at first point, ca. miles E. from camp. Wood at hand so moved ashore 12: N. and camped.

Last night Pannigabluk could not sleep, and wanted to go off duck hunting at 1 A.M. I had just been out to stop a dog fight when she told me so. I suggested her cooking instead, and she had grub ready at 4 A.M. Meanwhile I hunted but got no game—saw one ptarmigan (willow) evidently just off nests, but could not find nest. [. . .] Woke Anderson and B. at 4: A.M. They had slept only four hours and P. and I nothing.

Goose eggs: While we slept in afternoon (4–8 P.M.) Pannigabluk hunted eggs and found one goose nest—five eggs, fresh [. . .].

JUNE 24 *Started* 3:45 P.M. (after sleeping 16 hrs.) (Anderson and Pannigabluk 12 hrs.). Arrived at extensive mud flats (compelling going off shore) at 8: P.M. tried to advance but mud water too shoal between flats and ice. Got back at 11:30 to place where we were at 8:00. Camped.

Mosquitoes have appeared a "blue letter" day in the Arctic. Out hunting eggs tonight saw one only—the precursor of millions. No doubt they have obtained inland for some time already. [. . .]

Eskimo medicine. Have seen this winter several cases of violent squeezing of the chest to relieve pains there. The patient holds up his arms above his head while the strongest man available stands behind him, puts his arms around his chest and grasps one wrist by the other hand and squeezes about or below the nipples. Apparently he squeezes as hard as he can, while the patient does not seem to swell the chest to resist. Usually the patient lifts his feet off the ground and is thus held up for perhaps thirty seconds, when the pressure is relaxed.

Childbirth. The old women tell the young girls to be sure to get their first child early, as otherwise childbearing will be difficult. Shortly before the time of delivery pregnant women are advised to court violent exercise as "it will loosen the child and make it come easy." This advice Mr. B.

blames for the death (about April 30) of his nurse girl, Flora—miscarriage. She brought a sled out to the flee over rough ice and worked hard on it, against B.'s directions, because old women had told her to.

JUNE 25 *Started* 2: P.M. with half load in umiak for Nirrlik or some other channel mouth of the Delta. [. . .]

Deer: all over the Delta we have seen numerous tracks of deer but no droppings. Tracks not new—probably last year's or so Pannigabluk says though Billy says he does not know. [. . .]

JULY 1 *Started* 7 P.M. Nirrlik arrived there 11:45 P.M. [. . .] Keruk's boat took part of our load and Paniulak's boy Innuohlurak rowed in ours while Pannigabluk walked around with dogs and Kukkarp with her as well as one of the men (name?). People catching about enough fish to eat.

JULY 2 Measured heads today with Anderson's help, twenty-eight in all. Measured all but two grown people (Atokotoak who is sick and his wife) and eight children, mostly small, though some six or seven years. Paniulak gives the number and distribution of the other people, who frequent Nirrlik to trade [. . .]. One old man, Ikakshak, has parts of his skin turned about "white men's" color—not tallowy albino.

JULY 3 In camp at Nirrlik. Some of the people were across the mountains, so far they saw no mountains where they were; supposed they were near the Kunkpuk (Yukon). Saw no Indians, but saw two miners who told that the country was now full of prospectors up to the divide, that Carter had "struck it rich" and also the Jap "Cookie." The Eskimo (five tents) killed seven moose and about twenty sheep to the tent, and some deer, but starved in spring.

Paniulak tells that formerly when a man killed a wolf he ate no warm food four days, if it was a male wolf and five if it was a female. When he got into the house after killing the wolf, he would take a stone hammer (an old one preferably or necessarily) and shout four times in the fireplace or near it, "O-ho!" Four times if wolf a male; strike five times and shout five times if a female.

JULY 4 [. . .] Saw a crane ca. ½ mile W., so set Pannigabluk to cook tea while Anderson and I looked for crane's nest. Saw only one crane: from behavior may or may not have had nest. I shot red-throated loon and later found her nest. [. . .]

At Nirrlik were eight umiaks:—Atokotoak, Neakoyuk, Alak, Paninlak, Keruk, Katteruak, Kaiyan, Aksiaktok, Aiakkerak, Alualuk (arrived as we left). Turñak had his boat up on the Ekallukpik; Puya and Kirinirk have each an umiak and are on their way now with them from Oliktok by the river. Nutarksiruak and wife and two children are in the mountains, not coming to sea this year. Had umiak when he went up, but may be dismantled now. There are not known to be any others on the Kupik or its branches, have deserted either to Barrow or Kotzebue. No one this summer on Itkillik. People at Nirrlik do not seem to hunt at all this time of year birds, eggs, or deer, but fish exclusively. This is the easiest, as mosquitoes don't bother so much. Mosquitoes do not seem so bad anyway at Nirrlik as elsewhere inland, probably because situated on a high cutbank not far from the sea, and because several tents divide attentions between.

Paniulak and family are going to Barrow by the first fair wind. P. says Colville is too uncertain a country for food. Though he did not starve last winter, he came near it, after giving food to those who were starving.

Kutox's fiancée (Oyarak's daughter's) is now well married and will not go to Flaxman. This is said to suit O.'s plans, as he wanted K. to marry Gallagher. [. . .]

Indian feuds. In general the relations with the Indian in the tree country seem semi-friendly. I was told, however, that the father of the girl Dukkayak (Innuohlurak's, Paniulak's son's, wife) was shot by an Indian while he was hunting deer five winters ago. Seems to have been and to be regarded rather as a murder than a warlike act, though quarrels are always admittedly likely to occur. It is said that a few years ago when Omigluk (now of Herschel) crossed the mountains on the Ulahula, he "nearly had a fight" with some Indians he met. [. . .]

The Nirrlik people seem to be pretty stingy. P. was told that Neakoyuk and Alak had flour and Paniulak a little. Paniulak used his for his children only, but the others are said to have cooked for themselves. Neakoyuk also had coffee and shared with no one. After Paniulak got the sack of flour I owed him and the five pounds tea for the copper kettle he did not spread himself much. In fact, the only public tea drinking was at our house. Several women, however, brought us cooked or uncooked fish at different times, and one brought us two good meals of mashuk roots, locally called mahu. These were sacked inland up the Itkillik north of the mountains. They were very pleasantly sour, had been merely boiled and sacked without further preparation. [. . .]

JULY 5 Pannigabluk had breakfast ready at 12:15 A.M. but as Anderson had skinning, eggblowing, specimen packing, etc. to do, we did not start off at once. [. . .]

Pannigabluk who had to go a mile back for her dogs, which had become bewildered and had stopped on the other side of the river from us and behind a bend. [. . .]

JULY 6 Did not get up to sleep before 2 A.M. today and awoke again at 7: A.M.—a short sleep after being up 26 hours. Pannigabluk got up to cook but some of us dozed along till breakfast ready at 12:30. Dogs had been aboard umiak and stolen some rotten fish given us for dogfeed at Nirrlik. [. . .]

JULY 12 Travellers: Pannigabluk yesterday heard 2 gunshots, I heard one—probably some travellers (Pt. Barrow traders?) in the Delta west of us. [. . .]

JULY 28 Diseases. Woman today complained of her heart being so bad it hurt her ribs, and said she got that way after most meals, first her heart would get bad, then her liver, and both "wanted to come up in her throat." In connection with this I asked Pannigabluk about Keruk on the Ekallukpuk River who complained to us her coughing had broken a rib that morning. P. denied the incident, and so did Billy, for they must have heard us amused over the matter. Later today P. told a woman how Keruk had broken her rib one day she was with us. [. . .]

AUGUST 3 After sleeping two hours awoke at 5:30 to find dead calm. Started P. cooking (she had slept five hours). She was sleepy and fire died out once or twice. Breakfast finished 6:30 and off at 7:10 A.M. with faint SW wind which soon changed to NE and then fell calm. Paddled outside Shaviouik Island: ate lunch there 12: to 1: P.M. NE wind now freshened and rowed and sailed till ca. 5 P.M. got in thick lagoon ice floes and took down sail. Paddled and rowed. Got out of ice ca. 6:30 and landed ca. 8: P.M. near place where we cached tent, etc. March 28th. [. . .]

AUGUST 7 [. . .] *Cold:* For first time in the Arctic I have caught epidemic cold. We all have it. Irregular and little sleep possibly responsible. Throat sore, headache, etc. [. . .]

AUGUST 25 *Aboard "Karluk" off Nelson Head.* Got to Herschel August 19th. Afternoon August 20 "Karluk" arrived. Agreed to take us aboard.

Started for Baillie August 21. Delayed August 22nd by sighting whale [. . .] moderate gale in evening and have to all night and till noon next day. Capt. decided not to run into island, and passed it late August 28th. [. . .] Has been too rough for me to write much—seasick too most of time. [. . .]

SEPTEMBER 2 *Ethnology*. Pannigabluk plucks out, whenever they appear, any hairs from her armpits. Looks as if there would be quite a growth there if not plucked. Have heard many whites say Eskimo have no hair there but this is evidently wrong, though the hair may not be so abundant as with whites.

Vandalism. The three Eskimo families who lived at the "Alexander" the year after wreck, mashed everything they could not immediately use, or threw it overboard—cases of windowglass, [. . .] ropes, skylights, portlights—not one whole left. Apparently smashed with a hammer—no attempt to take them out. Cases of clothes, shoes, oilskins, etc. are drifted ashore and half-buried in sand—probably were on ice near ship when thaw came, as these were of too much value to throw overboard. All sorts of stores in cache ashore and in the three-chambered board and canvas house ashore such things as mirrors, coal stove, etc. [. . .]

Gave sick man (besides 6 opium and [. . .] acetate pills) about 30 lbs. deermeat, 1 lbs. tea, 3 boxes biscuit, he gave us fish net (old but good condition and long) and as much half-dried fish as we gave him meat. Gave (present) Paniulak 10 plugs tobacco, 2 lbs. tea and a small cup of salt. (Besides lending us flour he had taken care of our stuff at Itkillik when river flooded the house.) [. . .]

SEPTEMBER 5 [. . .] It is so wintry today that I started off about 12 N. to see from hills N. of here if ice is not in, these westerly winds, if extensive, should bring it. Just after starting, however, it got so thick with snow that I was about to turn home a mile from camp when I saw under the shelter of a rock what I took for a rabbit. The one we saw last week was white. I approached to about fifty yards and fired—no move; fired again, same result—concluded I was shooting too high and aimed lower. The thing jumped up and rolled over. On near approach found a very old human skull with two neat holes in the center of the top of the head and a third through the temporal bone. The grave from which this skull came was about twenty yards away. [. . .]

Ethnology. Pannigabluk tells me Mary Thrasher is now a "bad woman." "In what way?" "She scolds all the time. Most women who live with white men get into the habit of scolding, contradicting and quarrelling."

Pannigabluk's opinion of the Indians, whom her parents used to meet often each year, is that they are "nagomiut," excellent people. [. . .]

SEPTEMBER 6 *Archaeology*. B. and I dug up another grave in forenoon—the complete writing up of it must wait on more liesure [*sic*]. [. . .]

An anniversary. It was Sept. 6th last year we froze fast in Smith Bay. [. . .]

SEPTEMBER 12 [. . .]. . . Snow on high land ca. 2 inches at sea level, though some had fallen at sea level—mostly rain, Pannigabluk said (she got home last night after dark). [. . .]

SEPTEMBER 18 Sent B. and P. with umiak and stuff to whaler's harbor to cache in house, but hunted E. to see if any deer on flatland in that direction. [. . .]

SEPTEMBER 23 [. . .] *Aklak beliefs:* Pannigabluk says Kuwuk women are forbidden to taste or cook for others brown bear until they have had two children and none but the oldest women would skin an Aklak. The same restrictions apply at Cape Pr. [. . .] among Noatak Nunatarmiut, Colville peoples, etc, though none are quite so afraid as Kuwok women. [. . .]

OCTOBER 1 [. . .] *Mittens* are made "for rough use" by Pannigabluk with thumb sticking straight out from one side so they fit either hand equally well—or badly. Theory: when hair falls out from inside of palm mitt can be worn on other hand. [. . .]

OCTOBER 4 [. . .]. Pannigabluk sewing clothes and Billy making snowshoes from old (beef?) barrel staves. Finished first pair yesterday. Takes him best part of three days to make a pair.

Immaculate conceptions. Pannigabluk says Eskimo women frequently have children that have no father. Sometimes they die at or before birth, sometimes they live. When they live they do not differ noticeably from people that have fathers. Some women are afraid of these fatherless children and kill them at birth. One instance of this is the woman Aklaatjiak who lives in one of Brower's "iglupauraks." A few years ago she had a fatherless female child. She buried it at once alive. Another Cape Smythe woman, Iñiavina (she is bald-headed though not old) had a fatherless child. It died when one or two years old, of sickness. A Kuwok man who is now wealthy and a trader is fatherless. His name is Kaxri. She knows of two Unalit women who had fatherless children. One had a boy and a girl (not twins), and the other a girl. Kaxri's mother's name was Imosirk. She was a widow when he was born; she had had a girl before, whose father was her husband. Some women who have fatherless children are virgins at the time, some have had a child before, some are widows. Pannigabluk herself has had a fatherless birth, an abortion [. . .] last spring when she was on her way west with Billy and Anderson. The foetus was about three inches long. She never had connection with a man since the death of her first (only) husband—a full year previous to the abortion. People do not suspect of lying, she says, women who say they have fatherless children, for they know that it often happens. Sometimes, perhaps always though people don't know it, some "doctor" is magically responsible for the child. [. . .] It is not only in recent times, Pannigabluk says, but it has been "always" (nutirn) this way, that women had fatherless children.

Abortions. At the abortion above referred to, Pannigabluk says she had no great pains but lost much blood. She seems to feel no reluctance in telling of the matter.

Dreams. Pannigabluk says when she dreams a river with a swift current, a strong west wind follows; if she dreams the ocean rough with waves, there will be a strong nigirk (easterly wind). If she dreams of making "slap jacks" (but not other kinds of bread), the next day some traveler will come; if she dreams of eating deer-ribs boiled, deer will soon be killed. "Sometimes I dream well (true) and sometimes badly (untrue)," she says. She has heard of people who always dream true. Dreaming a swift river means east only to a few people, it means this or that to others. And so with other dream signs.

Boots. Pannigabluk made herself [. . .] the first boots I have seen made from the body skin of the deer. She says some people want only boots from deerlegs, others like boots from the body skin anywhere. Of course, the latter kind are always worn hair in. She says her husband Alahuk never would have socks made of anything but the upper half of the legskin of a caribou fawn, reindeer would not do. Upper half, skin from knee or hock upwards to where the hair gets long. Anderson would, however, wear any kind of boots.

Obscure entry. The entry for Aug. 29th, I noticed today, is obscure—or incomplete, rather in that it fails to note that on the forenoon of that day we were engaged in moving our stuff ca. 400 yards south from where Fritz landed us to the house built by the Eskimos from the wreck of Alexander. While we were unloading the first load the surf became so heavy that among the boulders by the house the umiak was in grave danger of breaking.

This diary. [. . .] Somehow I find it difficult to keep in mind the possibility that the record may sometime be worked over by someone other than myself and that entries sufficient for my purposes (if used inside a few years at least) may not be of much significance to another! I have several times in the past resolved to avoid this defect to some extent in the future, and I do so now again. Fortunately, however, it is the account of our doings that is chiefly abridged. The more valuable (the ethnological, etc.) notes are usually more full—I am never to trust my memory in them, though my general experiences will enable me to amplify and clarify most of them when it comes to re-writing—if I ever get back home to rewrite. And although there seems endless work to do here, still I must evidently get home soon to make a beginning of letting known my results—else I shall be submerged in the accumulated mass I shall forget, and I shall be unable to secure continued support from people who for years see [. . .] neither me nor any fruits of my work.

OCTOBER 5 *Ink:* Found half-teaspoonful in bottle I thought empty. Anderson has all our ink. [. . .]

Kagmalit. Billy says that among his people, at least, and in most places probably, "Kagmane" is a less frequently used alternative form of "kavane" (in the east; down the coast). The people living to the east (along the coast only?) are called "Kagmalit" [. . .]. His people [. . .] call the people of Cape Nome, etc., "Shagmanerimiut." Has heard Nunatamas call people of Tapkark, Kotzebue Sound, "Shagmanerimiut." His people never refer to people living eastward inland as "Kagmalit." [. . .] Pannigabluk says Nunatamas call Cape Smythe people "Kagmalit" and Mackenzie River people "Kagmalixihlaurat." The people of the Diomedes are called at Port Clarence "Immarxlit" while people living west of the Diomedes, rather far off, on another island are called "Okiovormiut." [. . .]

Letter to Anderson: Am leaving here a letter for Anderson asking him, if he gets it, to come or send inland to find us in the river—which we plan to follow towards its source looking for deer. I am telling him we expect to come to the coast when we think the sea towards Parry frozen—perhaps about Oct. 25 or Nov. 1st. I am giving him a rough sketch map to find bear meat cache and trace us. We are leaving them several hundred lbs. of deer, brown bear and polar bear meat in the whaler's ice house here [. . .].

OCTOBER 13 *Dogs* stole (two of them—one does not even join in thefts) their fill of bear blubber and meat [. . .] last night. Pannigabluk had inexcusably neglected to move it from sled to the rack. Heard dogs fighting in night but thought all our stuff safe on rack. [. . .]

Aklak skins, Pannigabluk says, are used by Unalit and others for umiaks and make a good substitute, though whether better or not she does not know. On the Colville all umiaks are ugrug or walrus, even on the Kangianik (upper Colville) where some skins come from Noatak, some from Kuwok and some from Cape Smythe.

Wolverines. Pannigabluk says if wolverine knows of meat buried under frozen ground, it will lie down on top the earth covering, thaw it a little, dig away the thawed part and lie down in the hole, thus finally thawing its way to the meat. As for stone covering, they will lift straight upward, if necessary, stones to uncover meat.

Aklak meat and fat, I find, has to me a peculiarly disagreeable taste and smell when even slightly tainted. The meat of the big bear had begun to smell when we buried it, the fat layer, apparently, had protected body from getting cold, though skin and internals removed. When we cut it up and buried it in the rock (covering with stones only) it seemed still to have kept warm so much so that middle pieces of pile were still little frozen when Billy opened the cache to take out meat Oct. 9th. Aklak meat, untainted, I like well, and the fresh fat, boiled, has a very agreeable taste. As fat it is to my idea better than deer fat because it is nearly as agreeable and "goes" twice as far.

Aklak feet are like human feet because aklaks are descended from a woman who, with her two children, a boy and girl, ran away from people and turned into bears (aklak). Pannigabluk has also heard some story of polar bears.

Ptarmigan feathers are here a household necessity. One needs at least a bird a day for wiping greasy hands after eating, bloody hands after preparing fish or meat for cooking, or wet hands from any cause. [. . .]

Fish of the type of these we are getting are easily netted, B. says among his people, but caught with hooks. He is making a hook of a piece of ivory we found at the "Alexander" and a shingle nail. We shall try it tomorrow. [. . .]

OCTOBER 22 Started for meat of deer killed (Pannigabluk and I) at 2:30 P. and returned 5:15 P. Billy not home yet—4 P.M. [. . .]

OCTOBER 23 *Crippled:* Am wearing my left hand in a sling account of a sharp pain in the tip of my middle finger. Felt no pain on going to bed, but awoke an hour later with an ache extending to the shoulder and slept little all night. [. . .]

OCTOBER 26 Billy built rock cache on river ice while Pannigabluk and I fetched meat of buck I killed yesterday. Skinned him for specimen, though badly shot up [. . .]—not very large, but large horned. Billy went in evening to look at his trap (of Oct. 19th). Gave him note to put on stick in river for Anderson. [. . .]

OCTOBER 29 *Started for coast* today at 8: A.M. The river is [. . .] badly frozen as yet, leads south for the present instead of east, and we must go back sometime to get ammunition, traps, etc. from Cape Parry and Langton Bay. Besides, I am a little anxious about Anderson's party. If he never got my letter left at Horton River (Wolki's house) he may think we are in Banksland and may not look for us at Parry nor go to Langton Bay. He will then be short of many things he needs and we short of many we need. Our tent is uncomfortable too—a round wall tent ca. 10 ft. in diameter. [. . .]

Deer lore: Pannigabluk says female killed today (Anderson's specimen) is 3 ½ years old now—in her 4th winter—and that her present fawn—the one killed—is her first. [. . .]

NOVEMBER 1 *Change of plans:* Pannigabluk announced this morning she would like to stay here to protect our meat and skins—and to avoid the trip to the coast, doubtless, for she is no great traveller. The offer was quickly accepted. I had thought of asking it but had refrained as I thought she would consider it a too lonesome job. We shall therefore (unless Anderson's welcome arrival shall change all plans) build a house for her and leave her to sew skins while we go to the coast to look up Anderson's party. [. . .]

Fish. Great excitement tonight over Pannigabluk's seeing two fish known as titalirk through hole she made to get water. She and Billy have been fishing for them most of the time since but have had no luck.

NOVEMBER 2 All three of us started ca. 8:30 to skin deer and get meat. About a mile up the little river leading to the deer we came to fresh tracks of 10 or 12 [. . .]. After about an hour I ran into Billy and Pannigabluk (it was thick fog) who were lost and had wandered about considerably. [. . .]

NOVEMBER 3 [. . .] *A birthday*. This is my thirtieth. It is in some ways more satisfactory than the last, for a year ago Billy and I were on our vain inland chase after polar bear near Beechey Point, without fire in −35° weather. But then that birthday had the advantage of being only the 29th: between the two there lie too few and too small accomplishments, too many miscarried plans and imperfectly accomplished purposes. [. . .]

NOVEMBER 5 Billy worked on house and I got last load of meat from near our camp October 30—the buck cached by Pannigabluk on ice and some other meat I left by it yesterday. No fox thefts. No tracks anywhere—snowing too fast. Two or three inches of snow last night and this forenoon. [. . .]

NOVEMBER 6 Went (B and I) in morning to rack for load of Anderson's specimens and other deerskins. Decided to trust meat on rack to the iced legs and started off again for coast to find Anderson. Pan's house had only frame completed—she will have to find the moss for the roof, make door and window, etc. She has no axe, so will have to burn branches, etc. She has ca. ¼ lb. tea and 1 lb. flour—we none. Salt is all gone. Started 12:15 P.M. and camped ca. 5:30 at our camp site of October 17. [. . .]

NOVEMBER 11 Blizzard: not travelling as it took over half the day to get meat out of the ice house and make other arrangements for going westward to look for Anderson. Something of a disappointment to find no traces of him here. [. . .]

Our camp last night and today very uncomfortable—a white man style tent is no fit shelter from a blizzard. Stovepipe guard torn out of tent during night and we have improvised with a dog chain. Stove red hot but freezing three feet from it—almost nausenesque discomfort in writing with numb fingers. Are feasting, however, on flour and oatmeal with salt—three delicacies we have gone without for some time. There is some compensation in this gorging, but we would both prefer to be back in the river on a diet of "straight" meat. [. . .]

A confession: Lest sometime in a warmer clime the less agreeable memories of the north may blend with the pleasanter into a uniform agreeable haze—lest I come to believe I "enjoyed every day of the year" up here—I will set down now the fact that I don't enjoy today and that I sincerely wish myself in a warmer, more civilized land. Every few minutes I subconsciously make and renew various resolutions (which I shall doubtless break if the opportunity offers) of never going north again if I ever get south from this venture. [. . .]

NOVEMBER 13 [. . .] Trade across Bering Strait. Billy says his father made a number of trips in umiak to Xodlit to get reindeer skins. Perhaps more frequently, however, the Xodlit brought their wares over. B. says in his neighborhood there are many ruins of houses built on top of cliffs for fear of Xodlit attack. This was very long ago; in more recent times visits of Xodlit were entirely friendly. Caribou have for a long time been absent from the rivers inland from Port Clarence, though Billy has seen numerous bones. His father told him he made one killing of twelve deer. This was when B. was a baby; now about 25. [. . .]

Ideas foreign to Eskimo. The value of time idea found currently among "civilized" people seems entirely incomprehensible to the Eskimo. If they can get a sack of flour for two fox skins from a trader two miles away, then if that trader were to haul the flour to their village they would equally expect a sack for two skins. So I found the people of the Kittegaryumiut neighborhood would expect the same price for each fish sold at home as they could get hauling to Herschel where they seldom arrive with over a dozen fish (say fifty pounds) and often with none. So, in trading if they know a trader buys a rifle for ten dollars they consider it worth only ten after he has carried it two thousand miles, spent a year in doing so, and hired many men for the work. They will, however, of course, pay any price for a gun they need, but their thinking is this: "You have the upper hand; you are 'doing' me out the difference between ten dollars and what I pay you, but I must have the gun." One of the results of this view of trade is that the advantage is all with the resident as against the itinerant trader. Those who make long voyages, e.g. for deerskins, lose from hunting the time they travel and usually have to pay what the skins are worth in their home neighborhood. When a man is known to get more for an article than he pays for it, the profit is looked upon after the manner of winnings in gambling, somewhat as we look upon stock exchange transactions. There is, in other words, no such idea as our "legitimate profit."

The wages idea such as they have is quite different from ours. Indeed, this might be considered as our idea misunderstood. If I hire a man for a stated sum or quantity of goods to work for me a year, if the day after I hire him he falls sick and is sick all the year and I keep him. [. . .] and his family and care for them all as if they were my own people, all this is not considered in any way to affect my obligation to hand him at the end of the year the amount he would have received had he worked hard and efficiently for me every day of the year. A concrete instance I know of illustrates a variant of this idea. The man Kumaslik was hired on these terms: he was furnished fifteen (or twenty) sacks flour, besides rice, beans, tea, coal oil, etc., a new rifle, and a thousand cartridges, tent material, etc., and promised certain things at the end of the year, if he should do as follows: trap energetically with (fifteen) traps furnished for the purpose, and deliver all foxskins, half his deerskins and sheepskins, and the saddles of all deer and sheep killed, to his employer. Kumaslik trapped six foxes and sold the skins, ate the saddles of all deer killed, and used all deer and sheepskins, in fact willfully and openly broke every item of his agreement. Now he expects to receive, and his neighbors expect he will receive, the things promised him at the end of the year. These views of wages and bargains have been fostered, perhaps engendered by whalers with other white men who have been so dependent on the service of Eskimo that they have put up with anything. A man who tried to do differently would become known as a "bad man" and the object of an informal boycott. Necessarily this paragraph applies only to Eskimo who have had considerable dealing with whites.

The rigidity of the triangle idea is, so far as I know, unknown to Eskimo mechanics. In lashing a quadrangular frame (as the rear end of a sled) to make it rigid, they will wind innumerable turns about the angles but never use a rope or string as a diagonal. That they never use a stick as a diagonal, I am not sure, though I have seen no case of it. It might be noted here that the Eskimo are the only Americans, north or south, who have ever employed the dome principle of architecture.

The cardinal points idea seems to be absent. There are words currently translated as "north, east wind," etc., but I fail to see they have any but a local relation to our ideas that correspond to these words. Their real meaning is "landward," "seaward," "up the coast," "down the coast," etc. Thus the word "nigirk" means southeast wind at Point Tangent twenty miles east of Point Barrow, northeast wind at Cape Smythe or Wainwright, south wind in Greenland (West Coast—Kleinschmidt) and north wind (sailors have told me [. . .]) at various points on Bering Strait. This fall nigirk with us on the Cape Parry peninsula was a northerly wind. I have found no name for the North Star (though the Dipper is named) and no evidence that Eskimo have noted its peculiarity of no apparent motion. Traveling at night they often shape their course by a conspicuous star, but always make allowance for its motion, as they would for sun or moon. [. . .]

NOVEMBER 18 Started 4:30 A. Camped Wolki's house Horton River 6:00 P.M. [. . .]

Anderson's party has evidently never been here, as letter I left for him this fall in Wolki's store house is there still undisturbed. [. . .]

Freezing: As last year, Billy froze his face sooner than I. He has on his left cheek a brown spot the size of a dollar and a half-dollar one on his chin. These are from the day we left Langton Bay (November 14). I froze my left wrist that day account a bad mitten, but did not freeze my face till a slight touch on the cheek day before yesterday—November 17th.

Bad situation: Day before yesterday Billy discovered when wanting to mend his mittens that he had forgotten his sewing gear at Langton Bay. We are badly fixed therefore. One of his mittens has a badly torn thumb, and four of six boots I have with me are torn and unfit for use. My boots were all in poor shape leaving the river, but I counted on mending them as needed—and counted on Billy to do it. I should of course have known enough to take a needle along also. Billy tried to make a needle of a brass rifle shell with poor success. If the road were good we should be only a sleep now from Baillie Islands where we expect to find people, for some of them told Billy (when they came aboard the "Karluk" last fall) that they intended to winter at the island.

NOVEMBER 21 *Yesterday* started ca. 8: A.M. towards Baillie Islands to continue that way our quest for Dr. Anderson's party. Met them ca. 15 miles west (just at E. end of 5 miles of "Smoking Mts.") of Horton R. about 2:30 P.M.—great rejoicing.

Dr. Anderson reports that storms, runaway dogs, etc. prevented his reaching Herschel this fall [. . .]. At Herschel boxed his specimens for shipment and left in care of police. Left Herschel August 24th with our stuff aboard our and Pannigabluk's whaleboats and Ninaksirk's sloop. Bad weather and various delays. Froze in at Tuktuyaktok 25th September [. . .]. Reports all has gone well except for slowness. [. . .]

Anderson brought ½ year of "*Literary Digest*" which I am reading tonight while house sleeps. [. . .]

NOVEMBER 23 [. . .] *Plans:* Anderson says the more he thinks of it the better he likes the idea proposed by me—to stay yet another year. He agrees with me "it would be a pity not to make use of ample outfit of ammunition, etc. sent us by the Museum" and now lying presumably at MacPherson and Barrow. If he stays it will, he says, give him an opportunity for working thoroughly the entire (practically virgin) field between here and the Coppermine. [. . .]

For me the opportunity would be almost if not quite equally desirable: there are an indefinite number of stone graves evidently on Parry, both from what we have seen and from what ships and Baillie natives say. These are of unknown source and age, and should be very interesting, judging from the little digging we have already done. If we decide on another year, we will try making a short trip to the Coppermine this spring and another next year. To make reasonably sure of getting our outfit, one of us will unfortunately have to go to the Mackenzie (Tuktuyaktok, where our whaleboat is), thence by boat to MacPherson to get the stuff thence, and then to Herschel to meet the ships and get taken eastward to Baillie Islands or Parry. [. . .] We can of course not know whether the Museum will approve of our staying, but that means merely not knowing if they will lend us financial assistance, as they have no power to recall us or direct our movements. If they shall fail to approve we, or I rather, shall have to become personally responsible for some bills with whalers to pay off our native help. These I shall, however, in the first instance make payable by the museum in the hope they approve our plans, having merely a verbal understanding with the captains that a refusal to honor drafts is possible and that I shall then endeavor to make them good personally. I cannot see, however, how anything but a general change of policy can prevent the Museum from supporting for a third year a venture which they have already booked two years. [. . .]

NOVEMBER 24 [. . .] Customs. Ilavinirk says the first time he killed a wolf was when wintering at Horton River (six or seven years ago) with Katotox and Kirrnok. When he came in the evening Katotox's father said he must not eat cooked food or drink tea for five days. When he was going to drink water they told him not to until they made him a cup. K. made him a cup of sealskin from which he had to drink. All this, Ilavinirk says, was new to him. The old man said if he broke the rules he would, if he did not die, become very sick or suffer great misfortune the next year. Ilavinirk says he broke the tea prohibition before the five days were over, but did not notice being particularly sick or unfortunate that year. The old man, however, was much worried about him. (The old man was a Nunatarmiut). That same winter when Ilavinirk came home one day reporting the killing of a polar bear, the old man said he must not work wood (chop wood etc.,) the next day. He was also going to hang up to the roof of the house a crooked knife, but Ilavinirk would not let him. Said that he submitted in the wolf case because there he was ignorant, but that he had killed many bears without more ceremony than a grouse and had suffered no harm and he wasn't going to begin ceremonies now. [. . .]

Food. Ilavinirk says he knows his people ate all the fur animals now trapped except wolves, but then he says wolves were very rare anyway and that it is possible they really had no objection to eating wolf, but none was killed when he was around and so he never saw one eaten. He himself, however, never thought of eating first wolves he killed, did not take carcasses home. Note: He did not kill a wolf till he had been aboard ships many years and had opportunity to absorb white man's prejudices. Many Eskimo are now ashamed of eating wolf, fox, etc., and lyingly deny that they or their people ever did, admitting always, however, that neighboring tribes did. In recent years Ilavinirk has eaten many wolves and likes the meat. Mamayauk has eaten all fur animals and objects to none. [. . .]

DECEMBER 9 [. . .] Both Kunaslik and Mamyauk sick and unable to eat the deerskin and oil to which we had fallen again after devouring the saddle of meat, bearpaws and 5 Canada jays. Both said they would be unable to walk next day unless they felt better. Ilavinirk a little sick too—"all the same tired" and dizziness. I therefore decided to walk to the house and get meat during night and meet them next day if they could travel or else pack the meat to their camp. If a good feed did not make them well it would strengthen dogs and enable us to make some progress next day. Started 8:20 P.M. got to house (ca. 18 miles) at 4:15 A.M. *Sunday*. Found Pannigabluk all well, up and cooking over a cheerful open fire in a cozy house—really a rather pleasant homecoming. [. . .]

Slept till 10 A.M. and started back 11:45 A. with ca. 30 lbs. of dry meat and 5 lbs. backfat of deer. Met sled ca. 6 miles down river. Both K. and M. had felt better, had eaten some skin and oil and started 4 A.M. [. . .]

Wolverine thefts: Pannigabluk had neglected [. . .] the rock [. . .] on which I relied to keep the wolverines down. Anyway, when I got to the rock yesterday I found half a dozen pieces of meat on the ground (neck and rib foreparts), all (3 or 4?) the deerskins torn in pieces, one paw gone off the wolverine, and the wolverine carcass and half (probably) the meat gone. Foxes had helped to eat what was on the ground—the meat off bones—but those pieces of which no bones were left were evidently carried off by wolverines. That the wolverine carcass was gone shows them cannibalistic, even when there was plenty other meat. [. . .]

On being "hungry": It is no more than right that I appologize [*sic*] to my diary for taking so much of its space for this paragraph and for preceding observations on the same subject, for most northern travellers deal too long and lugubriously with this topic, a thing of which I hold a strong and frequently expressed disapproval. But it is a matter concerning which one repeatedly asked, and one after all of some scientific as well as considerable popular interest. This might be no excuse for writing of it at length were it not that I (though in my own esteem not really a liar) have often found on belated reference to my diary that I have told to many men on many occasions of facts and feelings which seems to have been absent at the time of an "adventure" but which have by some mental process attached themselves to it later and have become as vivid as the real facts or have now overshadowed and then even obliterated the facts. Where my contemporaneous record of an event is meager these adventitious elements are bound to remain undetected and to become for me and anyone who believes me, as if they had happened. [. . .]

DECEMBER 14 *Doing nothing*. Ilavinirk installed match tin stove in house. He is a little better but severe headache. We cannot well start after deer till he is able to move. [. . .] Shall probably finish our lamp oil tonight and be in dark thereafter till Anderson comes—though there are a few bones with some fat. [. . .] There is daylight in house and tent enough for about 4 hours sewing each day. Ilavinirk and family are in tent, Pannigabluk, Kunaslik and I in house. [. . .]

DECEMBER 16 Ilavinirk still about as sick. Thought inaction would do no longer so started up river with Palaiyak and Pannigabluk while Ilavinirk moved into house. I started 9: A. and hunted W ca. 5 miles, then S. ca. 5 and then to river. Found no trail there [. . .].

DECEMBER 23 Have made no entry for a week because of no lamp at night. Today I am first in the house during the light hours—except Saturday, when my diary was in Pannigabluk's camp and I at home. [. . .]

DECEMBER 19 Pannigabluk sick stomach. Cannot travel. Hunted W, S, and then E, getting home at dark. Few tracks seen and those rather old going S, but weather worst possible and not much chance of finding tracks. Thick snowing till 12: M. Clear towards evening. SW ca. 25 and soft snow drifting slightly in thickest woods. Hilltops covered with trees and only odd low places bare. Several Indian tipee squares and one lake ca. 2 x 5 miles. Hilly. [. . .]

DECEMBER 20 Pannigabluk still sick but somewhat better and able to travel. Palaiyak sick, but not so severely as Pannigabluk had been. Decided to turn home for these reasons: (a) deer evidently more numerous along river where trees spars than in thick woods, (b) Pannigabluk not able to travel fast, (c) left instructions at home for Anderson to proceed at once on arrival home with toboggan to hunt deer SW into woods [. . .]. I struck home straight across country to get home that night as I feared Anderson might have arrived and might start west. Got home 3:30 P—started 8:15 A. Pannigabluk and Palaiyak proceeded down West River to camp near its mouth. [. . .]

DECEMBER 21 Pannigabluk got home ca. 2 P.M. Both she and Palaiyak better. Had seen recent (half day old) tracks crossing S across West River near mouth and E across main river in 2 places this side West River—all good sized bands. Hard luck my not being with them.

1910

JANUARY 8 No entries since December 28th, 1909, because of never having been in house during daylight, and no lamp at night. Tonight light for first time. Women breaking bones today and we use some of tallow for lamp. [. . .]

JANUARY 13 (8 A.M.) Shall start in about a half hour with Palaiyak and six dogs to get bear grease from North River. At Jimmy's camp shall probably pick up Tannaumirk and his 2 dogs. Taking all dogs in hope of meeting Anderson. [. . .]

The sun came back today for first time, I think. Saw rays on the river cliffs but did not see sun.

JANUARY 22 *At Alexander Wreck, Parry Peninsula. Arrived* here January 21st (last night) at ca. 5 P.M. (the above date is by Anderson's time—by my time it is the 23rd today. He has made daily entries and is doubtless right). [. . .]

Anderson found polar bears had broken open house and eaten all our blubber and spoilt some of our stuff—spilt all our alcohol, among other things. Anderson got sick and was in extreme pain for five days—pneumonia. Since then getting a little better, but has no appetite yet—for anything but frozen fresh meat, of which he can make a good meal. [. . .]

Decided it is up to me to stay here with Anderson. Billy and Palaiyak will start tomorrow for the river—today Billy is showing his trapline to Tannaumirk, who will stay here. Billy takes blubber, tea, cod oil (a little), ammunition and some trifles. If they can get deer they are to stay inland; if not, to come to the fishing lake this side Langton and send a sled to the Alexander. As soon as Anderson and P. are strong enough we shall move to Parry—nearer open water, bears and seals.

Eskimo character: A Baillie man named Kutukak is with Capt. Wolki and considerably in his debt. One day when Anderson's party were over at the ship K. said to Billy he wanted to go inland to hunt deer. Billy asked when they were going and K. said when Capt. W. got home (from Langton Bay). Billy said that was good; they could then travel together perhaps. When Capt. W. came home K. went to him and said he wanted to go inland to my camp to hunt deer—that I had sent him an invitation (through Billy) to come. This made the Capt. pretty angry as he wants to get his money back out of K. and wants therefore to keep him near. Anderson succeeded easily in convincing the Capt. that I had no desire for more people, but he still believes Billy tried to get K. to go. This habit of giving other people's orders for excuses is apparently universal. Practically every broken bargain is explained by "So-and-so told" [. . .].

Turñnrat beliefs. Tannaumirk tells: He has only once seen a turñnrat. A year or two after he began to hunt with a rifle, it happened one full-moon evening that he and another boy went out of the house together. This was at Tuktuyaktok. The clubhouse (kajigi) was still in fair repair but not much used. When they came out of the alleyway door they saw a man standing near the kajigi and took him for one of the neighbors. They did not speak to him as they expected him to come nearer, for theirs was the only inhabited house and they thought the man had come to visit them. But instead of approaching, he turned and entered the dance house. The boys expected he would soon come out and waited, and the man did come out in a few moments, but stopped outside the door and soon went into the clubhouse again. The boys now became curious about what he was up to and who he was, and went to the door and called to him. No answer. They then went in, struck a match, and looked in every corner but saw nobody. They then went to the house and told what they had seen. No one but they had left the house and the people said it must have been a turñnrat. Then for the first time the boys became frightened. Up till then they thought of nothing but that it must be a neighbor. There were no tracks the next morning except their own at the kajigi door. [. . .]

FEBRUARY 6 The 3rd went over to the *Rosie H.* to see if we could get a kayak from the natives there, as we are helpless here without one. Tannaumirk looked at traps (no fox) the forenoon and went with me over in afternoon.

Kutukak promises to make a kayak to sell us as soon as they get two more seals; it takes three fresh skins to make kayak. [. . .]

Home at ca. 4:30 to find camp almost made by Anderson and P., both of whom are now practically well, except that neither can run much. Anderson seems to be more nearly recovered than P. though his illness is more recent than P.'s. [. . .]

FEBRUARY 23 [. . .] Today as usual writing down a few Eskimo words, getting forms from both T. and P.

Fishing methods. In reading Steensby's "Eskimo kultur etc." yesterday, I found the description for East Greenland of sealing through two holes in ice by two men, one watching, the other holding a long spear. Someone last winter (I think it was Kadriviak) described the same method for fall fishing. (*I feel sure I must have noted it at the time, but make this entry in case I may have been careless*). Pikkalu lived on the headwaters of Kuwuk once, but never saw or heard tell of this method.

Inhabitants of Parry. Kutukak and others aboard the Rosie H. told me the other day that the former inhabitants of Parry were one people with the Baillie Islanders and that one summer they all died of disease, except one who thereafter lived at Baillie Islands. Capt. Wolki, however, says this is a new story. [. . .]

MARCH 1 Anderson and Pik. started today to take load to Langton Bay. I was going to send the two natives, but Anderson said he was tired of inactivity and wanted to go. [. . .] Weather was fine in morning but began thickening just as sled was starting and I fear they may have lost way and been compelled to sleep without a fire—hard on them with such poor clothes as they have. One's clothes soon become wretched when no woman looks after them.

MARCH 2 Reading Thalbitzer's "Phonetic Study" and cross-questioning Tannaumirk. Most of Th.'s puzzledom with the Barrow dialect comes from (as I believe) Ray's incorrect transcription of the Cape Smythe dialect. Ray seems to have suffered from the usual English deafness to final consonants in Eskimo. [. . .]

MARCH 3 Reading Eskimo books and cross-examining Tannaumirk as much as I dare. If I get him tired (as I have once or twice done) he becomes careless in his answers and unreliable saying "yes" to anything, or pretending he understands my questions when he does not. [. . .]

Shamanism. T. says a few years ago Taikpauna died and had been dead all day (about twelve hours) when Alualik undertook to resurrect him with witchcraft, and succeeded. Both are still living, Taikpauna, a very old man, and "many people" saw T. die and knew that he was dead all day, and saw Alualuk revive him. Tannaumirk asked me if Jesus was the only white man that knew how to wake up the dead. He said many Eskimo used to know how and do it frequently. Many still know how, but dare not practice, by and by nobody will know because none dare to learn now for fear of not going to heaven after death. When I told him that I doubted if Jesus really did raise people from dead, T. said it was reasonable white men should doubt it if they had no one who could do it, but the Eskimo understood how it was done by others and therefore believed Jesus could do it also. [. . .]

MARCH 6 [. . .] *Ilavinirk,* Mamayauk, Noashak, Jimmy's Boy, Pannigabluk, Ukuk, wife and 10-year-old daughter arrived from fishing place at about sundown. Had been three days coming and had seen Anderson's trail going Langton wards and looking a day old March 4th. Account to that Anderson has made good progress and should be back soon.

Ilavinirk says they had hard times inland before Billy got there. They ate all the deerskins [. . .] down to the thin and all the dried-up leg sinews they had (of about 30 deer). Later they got enough deer and came to the coast, I guess, partly because of Sulk and partly to get white men's grub, which they claim to consider it a great hardship to be without. [. . .] At Okat, the fishing place, [. . .] "there are no fish"—which again, is Sulk's. They are now bound to leave at once for Mackenzie River, and bring word that Billy refuses to go along for any trip eastward. [. . .] I am saying nothing, as I have not yet decided whether to try to change Ilavinirk's frame of mind, or use this as an excuse for telling him and his crowd to go to blazes. I am a little tired of his endless praying, face washing, and missionary-learnt insistence on his rights and my obligations to him, without even a hint of his being supposed to render any return—a feature the missionary has apparently neglected. The whole people here are unrecognizable from what they were in 1906; this happens to be coincident with their mass conversion to the blessed faith. [. . .]

MARCH 9 [. . .] At ca. 10 A.M. Ilavinirk's family and Tannaumirk started with two sleds south (back) for *Okat,* while I stayed behind to wait for Anderson. Anderson arrived ca. 11: A.M. and ca. 3: P.M. he and I with one sled started after Ilavinirk [. . .].

MARCH 11 Started ca. 10: and arrived at our camp at *Okat*. Found they had been catching about 250 lbs. of fish per day with three hooks. Ca. 500 fish, perhaps. Catching them with three-pronged hooks, some unbarbed native hooks of bone and iron, some "civilized" barbed ones—about equally good, though unbarbed mouth—hooked anywhere, most of them, from gills to tail. [. . .]

MARCH 16 [. . .] Eskimo ways of thinking. Ilavinirk told me (I forgot to record the conversation) three or four days ago that he himself is naturally of a skeptical turn of mind. He continually prides himself herein, without good reason. He is really the most gullible Eskimo I know. He had some private doubts of certain añatkok performances. He had made a ring of wood about the size of a napkin ring and had it inside his clothes. No one in the kajigi knew he had it. He made an excuse for going out (to piss) and dropped the ring in the dark hallway carelessly on the floor. When the performance was to begin, he asked to be one of those who held the rope. A long single thong of ugrug was brought, the añatkok tied feet together, hands behind back, a turn over neck and under knees, bringing his chin between his knees. Then Ilavinirk and another man took hold of the rope and braced themselves. Somebody lifted the doctor up and tossed him carelessly down the trap door in such a way as to have hurt any other man, but the añatkok never struck bottom. The line played out with terrific rapidity, so that it took the skin out of the hand of Ilavinirk who was going to try to "hold the doctor." When the line was about all payed out, the strain ceased, and they hauled it in hand over hand till they brought the añatkok, bound as before, up through the opening, and behold (!) Ilavinirk's wooden ring was on the rope, just behind the shaman's back. He had made himself so small he had gone right through the ring and thus threaded it on the rope. He had turned natural size before they pulled him up through the scuttle. Ilavinirk concludes that though certain doctors may be frauds, this one certainly was not, and most doctors are not. In fact, no genuine doctors are frauds, but some unprincipled men pretend to be shamans when they are not. One such is Pannigabluk, as witness: When hungry at the river and impatient for me to come back, Pannigabluk said she used to have seances for Alashuk's deer hunting, and it never failed to bring him deer. Ilavinirk says he knows "doctor business" is wicked, but they were in such straits that no means were to be neglected. He told P. therefore to go ahead. He and Mamayauk took part in good faith (i.e., did not work against P. by doubting her) and she announced at the end that her spirits (Alashuk and a white man) had talked of eating deer tongues tomorrow evening and had said Dr. Anderson and I would come with our whole party in two days. Ilavinirk was to kill deer next day. No one arrived for a week. "We know now what sort of a woman Pannigabluk is, and we'll not believe her in anything she says. If she had spirits she would have told the truth, for spirits know everything and never lie." Ilavinirk explained further he thought it was too bad spirit-driving conflicted with religion but as it is, everyone must quit them for everybody wanted to go to heaven.

MARCH 17 [. . .] *My watch* stopped just in time to allow Anderson to take along west—a deerhair in the works, doubtless, on account of the broken glass. There is now no watch in the party.

MARCH 18 [. . .] Women's tutaks. Both Mamayauk and Tannaumirk remember seeing tutaks that were said to have been women's center labrets and that have been sold to the steamer people at McPherson. They know the "common report" that women wore them once. They are said to have always been inserted from the inside. The largest he has seen, Tannaumirk indicates to have been about three-quarters of an inch in horizontal diameter as worn in the lip, one-fifth or one-sixth of an inch in vertical diameter and with an axis of about half an inch. Those he has seen have all been of white stone. Neither of them has heard any reason assigned for these tutaks going out of fashion. [. . .]

MARCH 25 [. . .] *Eskimo medicine:* Tannaumirk says that if there is found late in summer or the fall or winter an egg that has been sat on but that has failed to hatch, this egg is "excellent to cure sickness"—but thinks it is about equally good for all kinds of sickness, and does not know how it is used—eaten, ribbed ones, broken or what not.

For insomnia, the Kit. people eat Aklak excrement, which is said to cause the eater to fall into a long and profound sleep. [. . .]

Anñroak (chosen, medical) are also fragments of a deer killed by walrus, the about-to-be-excreted excrement of a moose (killed by men), and lice of Indians (Itkilliks) (Kittegaryumiut).

If a person has been unable to eat (no appetite) for a long time, the best medicine is the head and stomach (or either) of a faegen gull hung about the patient's neck under the clothes with a string (Kit.). [. . .]

MARCH 29 [. . .] *Incantations:* B. and Tannaumirk both know of "evil songs" that have power to kill. T. says that if a man was to be killed the song would be "sent to follow him" by someone at a house or place from which the intended victim had gone away (on a journey usually or always). Many were killed in this way T. says. Tannaumirk knows and B. has heard that swans were often killed with songs. When the song was chanted one of a flock of flying swans (who were often almost out of sight when the song was concluded) would fall to the ground dead. Billy has learnt one of them songs and tried it but it did not work. T. has never tried it because though he has asked people who know them to teach him, they have always refused. Both Ovayuak and Alualuk know and use them and Taikpauna is especially adept in this manner. [. . .]

MARCH 30 Billy to skin deer I shot Monday; P. to set traps. I started out with intention of going only a mile SE to where Tannaumirk has one trap—account of my sore feet. (I put on woolen socks, which do not overheat the feet so. They worked very well in this case. Unfortunately I have only two pairs left, both practically worn out.) [. . .]

Prospects: Everyone is cheerful here now but I, who am deeper in the blues than I have ever been in the Arctic. With only three poor dogs it seems we shall be unable to make use of what is otherwise the "best" opportunity we are ever likely to have of getting to the Coppermine. Billy and Tannaumirk are both eager to go—hardly less so than I—but without dogs it would be foolish for us to start, for we had to eat up all our light food in the Cape Parry stay consignment upon Anderson's and Pikalu's illness. At the time of Ilavinirk's muskox hunt a few years ago he came back along the coast for over a week (in early May) without seeing a deer, seal, bear or muskox—not any food animals but rare squirrels. I doubt we could pull a week's rations on the sled, and it would take us two weeks to cover the distance Ilavinirk did in a week. Besides, when one intends to live by hunting one must not spend all his available strength on pulling a load. I suppose, therefore, we shall have to put for going till next year, and by then I fear I may have lost Billy, my only good man for such an undertaking. Besides (but that is a minor matter) I should like to try meet Melville and Hornby if they get to the Coppermine as they plan to this spring. [. . .]

Eskimo physical characters: The Eskimo have no name for the "Adam's apple" [. . .]. I have heard them comment upon its appearance in "some white men." Today they [. . .] spoke of the voice box as being "probably the same thing as one was sticking out on the necks of some white men." In the deer it has a name: kokak (Kittegaryumiut).

Turñnrat beliefs: Ilavinirk tells that a man of his place "long ago" went off along the coast walking in search of material for an umiak mast. [. . .] Coming around a point he saw two human figures at a distance. They had head gear different from Eskimos and he concluded they were turñnrat. As they approached they kept up a continuous moaning noise and never allowed his hands or any part of his body to come to complete rest, as any part or function of the body that stops in the nearness of turñnrat is liable to permanent rest—i.e. if one becomes silent, one becomes dumb, if an arm stops it becomes permanently stiff. When the two figures came near he heard they were shouting at him. At this he took more fright and ran for home. When he got home he was almost dead from running. He reported having seen the turñnrat.

The next day a small invading boat arrived. The people took them to be more turñnrat. The women went to the willows, the men all put on their anñroak (around the neck) and lay down with arrow on string alongside the houses. One old man [. . .] was a little in advance. When the boat landed the men in it began cooking fish. The old man then said he thought they were humans since they cooked fish. He then advanced towards them and remained unharmed thereby. Finally a trade was made of a small saw for a marten skin. From that moment all fear vanished. These were the first white men ever to come to Kotzebue Sound so far as the people of this village knew. Before that they had had knives from the Kohudlit (Siberian natives) only.

Hair cutting: Ilavinirk says that his people used to cut their hair short all over the head, some of them, when the weather got warm each spring—especially those going inland frequenting. Some wore the tonsure cut always. Some, again, never cut the hair—wore it "like women." Ilavinirk's father wore his hair long all over the head and braided it in two braids "like a woman." When traveling he pinned the braids coiled on the back of his head. He cut his hair short first when a very old man—then on account of headaches—"his head was always hot so he cut his hair short." Tannaumirk knows there were different styles of hair cutting at Kit. but does not know the details. Young men he has seen with long hair untonsured, but not braided. Never saw an old man untonsured unless his hair was shortcut all over the head.

APRIL 2 (10: A.M.) Intend starting this afternoon for Parry, trusting to traps to protect our meat still outlying. There is still faint hope of going towards Coppermine—and I am going to proceed as if that were still our program. There is therefore need of hurry. [. . .]

Started for Parry ca. 3: P.M. with our three dogs, Ilavinirk's 3, Pannigabluk's 2, Taunnaumirk's one and Pikalu's one. The only good ones are Pannigabluk's 2. [. . .]

APRIL 7 As sleds had only about 8 miles to go I went inland both to look for deer and to spy out land, as charts make the portage here to Darnly Bay not over 4 miles. It was a little foggy. [. . .]

APRIL 8 Capt. W. says it is either Friday, Apr. 9, or Friday, Apr. 10. Perhaps I have lost a day. [. . .]

APRIL 20 Day spent in foolish quarrel with Ilavinirk over various things. It started by his asking how much tea we should buy next fall. I told him that four of us going to the Coppermine would take but 12 half-pound pkts. and 2 lbs. good tea while I would leave his family of four a case and a half (90 lbs.) and I did not want to buy more. He said he was not used to starving himself and wasn't going to now, and would leave now that I was going to start treating him as a captain does a white sailor. He was no dog to be starved. He would go to Tuktuyaktok and look after his boat. After reasoning with him a long time in vain I was forced to remind him that by white men's law a servant hired for a year who quit work without good cause before his time was up, forfeited his wage and that he therefore had no boat at Tuktuyaktok but that I instead had a boat there. He said that was all right. He had always been a poor man and was willing to remain so. He would go anyway. I stopped arguing then and went to get a trap in, leaving the boatless argument to sink in. When I got back he had bethought himself that I had really always treated him well and that my stuff would all spoil if no one cared for it while I was to the Coppermine. He would therefore stay. He knew that 90 lbs. of good tea was enough, but had merely resented, on principle, that any limit should be set arbitrarily. He was not used to that, he said.

This used up a good, clear day, on which we might have started. [. . .]

APRIL 25 *Trip towards Coronation Gulf:* Started with Ilavinirk, Palaiyuk and six dogs Thursday, April 21 at 1:45 P.M. Mutual "best wishes" with Capt. Wolki in the morning before he started off on yet another search for his catch of aklak meat. [. . .]

APRIL 26 *Sickness:* Tannaumirk, who had been sick since the day they got to Lyon, is no better. I don't think he is shamming though he is evidently afraid of the Nagyuktogmiut and would be glad of an excuse to stay behind. I think his case is bad indigestion. [. . .]

Food tastes. Tannaumirk eats only ugrug (bearded seal) when both it and bear (barren ground) are cooked. He says it does not taste so very bad, but he can't stand the smell. Old John, a German sailor with most of such men's food prejudices, says it is the "best meat in the Arctic" for it "tastes and looks just like pork." He does not like caribou, saying it is "watery" and prefers salt beef every day to deer meat even once a week for a change. All of us here prefer bear to ugrug except Tannaumirk. This is the first barren ground bear he has eaten, except some tainted and moldy bear meat he ate and liked at Langton Bay in January. He has eaten many polar bears and is fond of their meat. All the rest of us prefer barren ground bear. [. . .]

MAY 1 [. . .] Tannaumirk relates: In former times bull caribou when fighting would often get their horns interlocked and die thus or be killed. This interlocking may sometimes have happened naturally, but he knows that it was often caused by some chance watcher giving a twist to his hood; i.e., throwing the hood back from the head and giving it a complete turn with the hand, as one would twist a wet cloth in wringing it. Pannigabluk adds that her mother once saw bucks fighting. [. . .]

Pannigabluk, in making a short cut where the sled went farther off shore, came upon a ruined village on a sandspit. She did not count the houses but thinks they were over twenty. There were numerous sticks upright, some the remains of racks. She says the village looked older than that at Flanders Point on Herschel. If our camp was yesterday at Roscoe River, then these houses would be about five to eight miles east of it by her account. Driftwood in large quantities at this village site, she says. Saw two or three "up-ended" stones inland.

Sleds. On seeing accidentally the picture of a "kutchin" sled in the frontpiece of Richardson's "Second Journey" Pannigabluk and Billy both said it was like a Kuwormiut sled, P. said "just like"; Billy said he had seen most of them with the rear end a little lower in the runner bend than the front end. He has owned one sled bought in the Kuwuk "for a rifle, when rifles were yet valuable." It was longer than any sled he has seen at Herschel, though some of them must be sixteen or eighteen feet long. Kuwuk sleds never had sled runners, neither did they, he says, ever shoe them with ice or ice them even slightly. The runners were of [. . .] canoe birch. It was the best sled he ever used for snow, but very poor crossing ice.

MAY 3 *In camp* account of fixing and making spring footgear. We started unfit in this respect, and I find Pannigabluk gets ahead with it only slowly when we travel every day. Besides, as we do not intend to return before fall I am not in any hurry. [. . .]

Eskimo cleanliness. Certain remarks and deeds of Pannigabluk's today prompt me to enter certain things about Eskimo cleanliness, etc. *Some light may be thrown thereby incidentally on our own.* (*If I have written some of this before, no great harm will come of it. I should be sorry to lose anything throwing light on this subject.*) Pannigabluk will clean dog excrement off a sole of a pair of boots with her ulu, wipe it casually with a rag that may have had as bad uses a dozen times before, and then proceed to eat with the ulu or cut up with it food for cooking. She will not use the same spoon twice in a half hour to stir her own tea without wiping it between times with the same rag, if it so falls, with which she has just wiped the ulu. Most of the Eskimo I know will pick up and eat without concern a piece of blubber, cooked meat, raw meat, fish etc., that falls on the floor, no matter in what state the floor is, but most of them would throw away a piece of bread that dropped in the same way. I noticed this especially in Roxy's house. He has been with the police a great deal, and seen them throw away such pieces; naturally, they less often would drop meat, etc., than bread, besides meats are native foods and the customs with regard to them are of long standing. In times of scarcity they will eat their own foods to the last scrap and take pride always in a clean picked bone, but I never saw a bacon rind eaten, nor even shaved close in time of necessity. I gave bacon to Kunaluk's starving family last spring, he threw away nearly a fourth of the bacon with the rind. Most Eskimo wash religiously every morning. Usually, they soap profusely and leave it unrinsed on the face. Few of them seem to care if the water is dirty. In Ovayuak's house up to twenty would wash from the same water or until the dish was empty. Then the towel passes around, the same for months, and occasionally a nose blown into it incidentally.

On my telling Pannigabluk one day that certain water was dirty she said that was no matter, she was just going to wash the teapot inside with it. I am considered a sort of renegade because I insist on the teapots and my own cup remaining unwashed. I have often heard my natives tell strangers that with many good qualities I have the failing, differing thus from most white men, of caring little for cleanliness in my food utensils. That I prefer manifestly dirty dishes to apparently clean ones in an Eskimo house, is considered a curious eccentricity; some seem to think it is "put on." Pannigabluk will sometimes wash a pot thoroughly with an ancient dish rag and then use the water to make soup. She will hook with the dirtiest finger to the bottom of a cup of tea or water to get a deer hair, of which she conceived me, in common with "all" white men to be in horror, in spite of my protests that I rather am fond of hair in my food. I have known no Eskimo to contract the white man's horror of hairs in food. As with us, white cloth garments must be washed, a dark one may be as dirty as it will. [. . .]

Songs. Eskimo songs seem to need explaining. Tannaumirk knows a great many, most of them composed by Ovoyuak or others he knows. When he sings them he always explains after the song what it means—"what it says" (i.e., gox). Then he sings it over again after telling "what it says." In needing explanation these songs resemble the old Icelandic and "scaldic."

MAY 4 [. . .] Sled. Billy improvised out of the bearskin a sled of a type new to me, except from hearsay. He merely laced it into a bag and attached the bag by the head-skin to the rear end of our sled. On level snow its two hundred pound weight can be pulled by a small dog; on glare ice it is a bit sticky; in rough going its weight comes in play, of course. To have this behind the sled rather than on it may or may not increase the average hauling weight, but it is a convenient way, and I am afraid of two hundred pounds more on the sled, a breakdown would be serious. [. . .]

MAY 5 Started 11:45 A., camped 7: P. with 1:35 out for lunch. Camped because sled began to drag very heavy as snow froze with lowering sun—shall throw away skin here and pack meat on sled, as not over 75 lbs. left by tomorrow morning. [. . .]

The land: Shall not commit myself as to where we are, by the chart. [. . .]. . . Ca. 5 P.M. saw an aklak just E of the delta making W straight for Pannigabluk, who was taking a short cut. We had plenty meat, but thought bear might harm P., so B. and I went after him. His heading for P. was evidently accidental, for he soon turned off on sea ice. Having started, I followed him, while others proceeded with sled. He made off to seaward at an angle of about 15° with the coast—seemed merely [. . .] aimless [. . .]. Walked at rate of ca. mile per hour and occasionally lay down for a minute at a time. [. . .] Near shore the bear sighted and headed for Pannigabluk, who had lazily dropped a quarter mile behind the sled. She shouted and ran for all she could. The sled people heard her (I was too far behind to help) and shot the bear at ca. 50 yards. When they cut in between Pannigabluk and the bear, the bear seemed to first see them, though they had been approaching each other (all on run) at an angle of 90° in plain view on level ice. When bear saw them she turned to run at full speed away. An old female (by teeth, old) not much larger than cub killed last fall—lighter color, too than any I have seen—probably a different sort of bear. [. . .]

Hare parasites: There are still visible on Pan's arm as small dark spots (six or so) the bites of hare lice she received April 29 in skinning one killed by Billy. She says their sting is very painful. [. . .]

MAY 8 In camp, using a bad day to make boots for Tannaumirk, whose two sealskin pairs prove unsatisfactory. The only good boots this time of the year are oiled deerskin, with hair in, and ugrug or whitefish soles.

Songs. Pannigabluk sang today a song [. . .] which she says she learned when young among the Unalit. This song has an irresistible tendency to suggest the music of "The Darling of the Gods" which I suppose to have been based on Japanese melodies. I have noticed before that she sings songs much resembling the one Indian tune heard all along the Mackenzie. This, too, she says, is Unalit. [. . .]

"Meaningless" infixes: "*Uvvalaraluok*" (and the same attached to a large variety of expressions) seems to have no meaning in Pannigabluk's speech, except to slightly soften or lessen the force, as any circumlocution does in any language—as with us a sharp "no" is the most emphatic possible negative. [. . .] There is seldom a sentence heard without it, except [. . .] words spoken in anger, and the like. This gives a peculiarity to these dialects, as if the mouth were half full of small pebbles.

An analogous case is *-araluk* in Mackenzie. This really means "old" in the sense approximately of our "you *old* scamp" (in friendly, half-jocular sense), but it is used so often as to destroy its force, as Nukkaralura, my younger brother (nukkara); ovayuaraluk, Ovayuak; Kouliraraluk-put, our lamp (used entirely without reference to its being in reality old (or new), good, poor, large, small, or any other quality). [. . .]

Victoria Island language: Heard Tannaumirk the other day say (to Billy and Pannigabluk) that it was curious that the Victorialand people speak a language very similar to the keyukokat (the familiar spirits of the shamans) [. . .].

Traces of people. At almost every place where we have camped or cooked we have found sticks, split pieces of sleds, etc., but all uniformly very old, any or all might have been half a century or more. Have found two bed planks from a snowhouse and about the last of April or first of May, a single stone tent ring. Tent might have been round or square, and about eight feet in diameter. On thinking about it, a log evidently chopped by white men seems rather mysterious. We found it May 7th. [. . .]

Today, at camp time, we came upon the first fresh signs of people, numerous choppings with a dull adze into pieces of wood, logs, etc., apparently to test their quality, as if searching for sled or bow material. Consequently everybody excited and in good spirits. Marks seem to be of last summer. One would suspect they were made by Victoria Island rather than Coppermine people, for they were evidently in search of material for artifacts.

MAY 10 Started 1:00 P.M. and camped 8 P. on what may prove to be Pt. Young in which case our last camp would be Pt. Wine. [. . .]

Victoria Island. The morning clear, and from the top of the cliff at our camp last night (ca. 200 ft. high) we had our first sight of land accross the sea. Have spied carefully for Clerk Island but seen none of it. [. . .]

MAY 12 Started 2 P.M. (flogged my watch 2 hrs. today and one about a week ago) and camped 7: P. at Cape Bexley, which is low, and broken rack chiefly. Crossed nearly point to point. Ice about as yesterday.

Saw tracks of two men with a sled getting wood from Point Hope. Camped tonight at a deserted snowhouse village. There are over forty houses, how many more I do not know; part of the village is completely snowed over under the cutbank. All seem to have had skin or gut windows, the window directly above the door, and the door usually facing south, though in some cases north. Every window about twenty by twenty inches. Were in one house, about seven and a half feet high inside, ten feet in diameter, and with a U-shaped bend along walls, facing door about fifteen inches high. This, Tannaumirk says was the support for the bed boards laid across the house. Seal and ptarmigan leavings; food plenty as sealskins lying around, dogs would eat them if hungry. People evidently came for wood, from Victoria. Houses about two months old, or less. One sled trail fresh, not over two weeks. It comes from the east and follows main trail north towards Victoria Island.

MAY 13 Started 2:30 P. on trail of people leading towards Victoria Island after moving Pannigabluk who did not want to go and then camped east about half mile to some wood. Main trail perhaps two months old and hard to follow, but one new sled track, about two weeks. At about 4:30, some eight miles from our camp came upon a village [. . .] which showed by fish spears, etc. that people intended returning. From roof of one house saw with glasses three men, some three miles northwest, sealing evidently. Headed for nearest. Before getting to them, saw a deserted village about in our former course, 320 by compass, some five miles from one first seen. Getting near first man B. and I halted team while T. went ahead to try not to frighten him by all approaching. The man sat on his snow seat bent forward as if watching for seal, occasionally raising his eyes only, not his head, to T. When T. got within some paces man suddenly stood up, seized an iron snowknife that lay on the snow beside him, and poised himself as to receive an attack or to be ready to spring forward. This scared T. and he went no nearer, but started to talk. The other never smiled or paid attention for some time repeating monotonously (about twenty times a minute, as often as one breathes) ha-ha-ha-ha, etc. Evidently he at first understood nothing of what T. said, but he soon began to. Then he began talking and T. did not understand. T., however, knew from Kalakutak (who was both with Mogg and Klengenberg) a Victoria Island phrase; *alianaituaraluit* (they are good) which he then used, and showed by lifting his coat he had no knife. After about five minutes of parley Iglixsirk laid down the knife and soon after began an examination of T.'s clothing, which seemed to satisfy him we were harmless, he had probably heard of "calico" from Victoria Island people. He then told T. to tell B. and me to follow a little way behind while he went along a line of sealers to tell that we were *alianaituaraluit*. We came near, forgetting to remove our goggles. If we had, I don't

MAPS AND PLATES

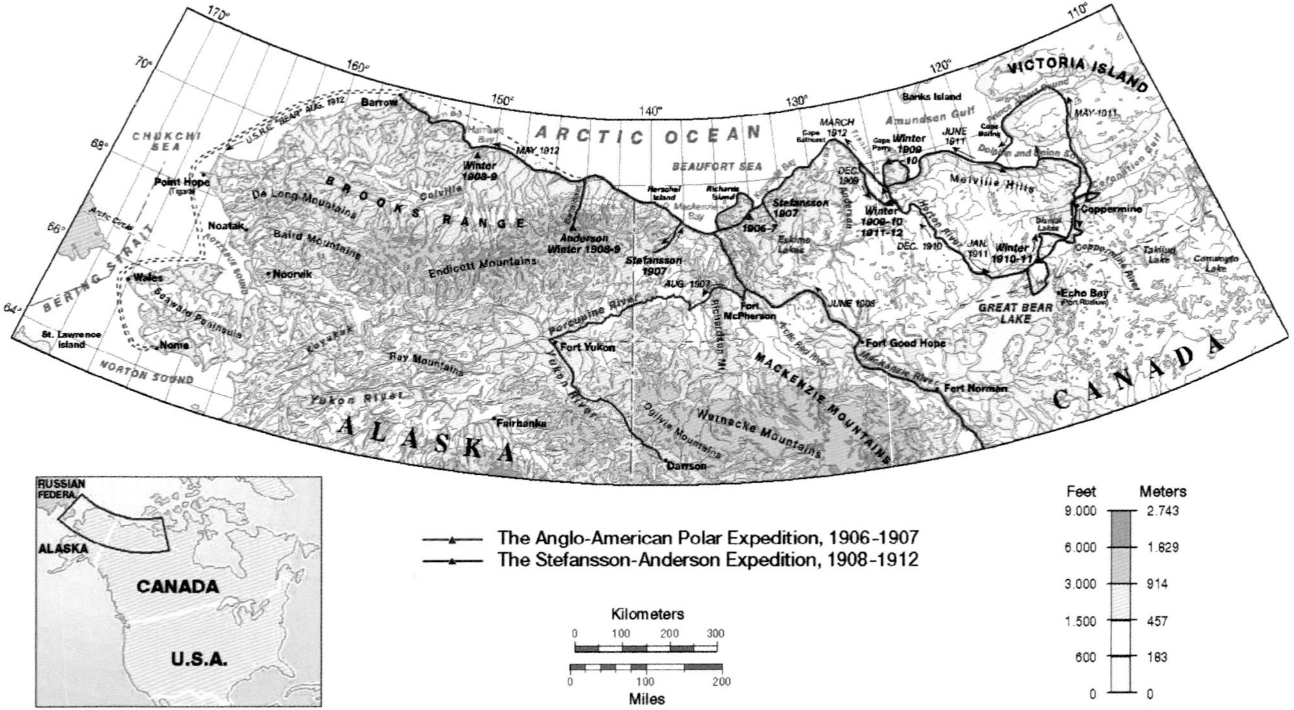

PLATE 1. Map: Stefansson's ethnographic routes. Map drawn by Lovísa Ásbjörnsdóttir. Based on V. Stefansson, *My Life with the Eskimo* (New York: Macmillan, 1913).

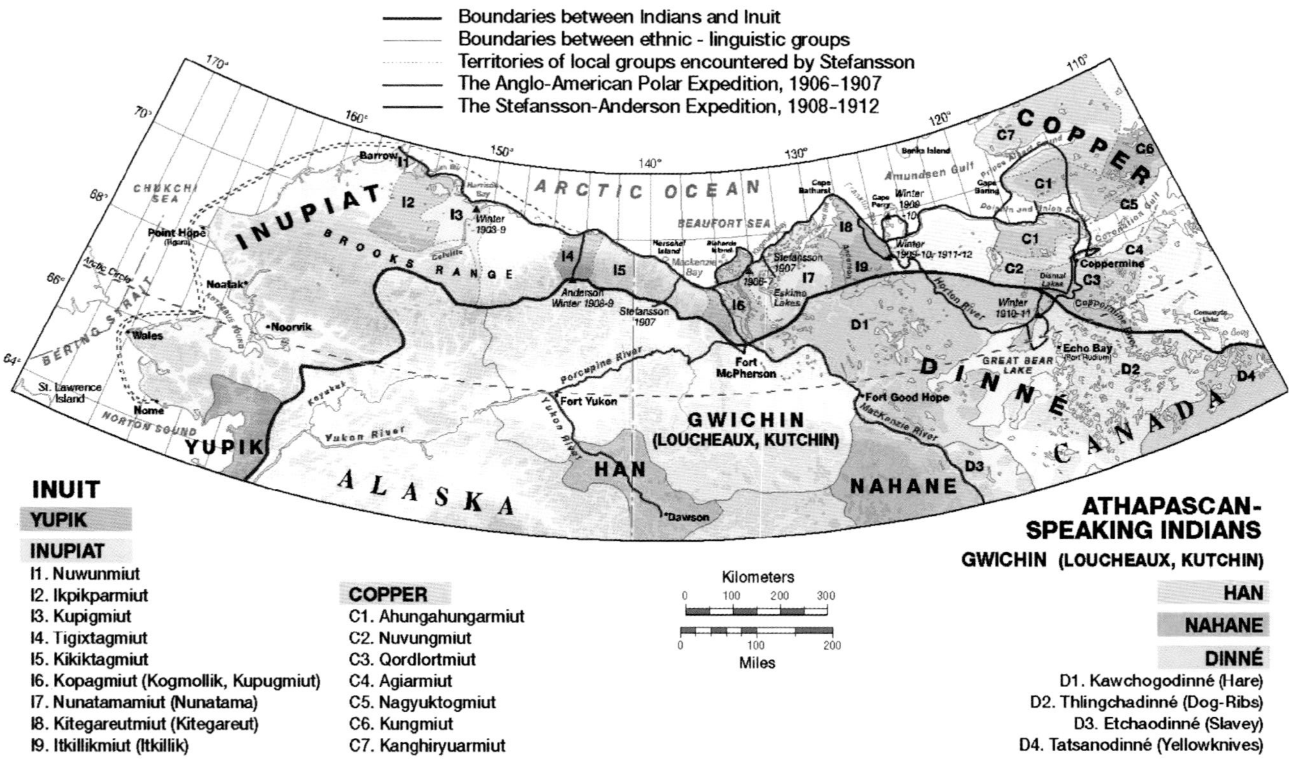
Boundaries between Indians and Inuit
Boundaries between ethnic - linguistic groups
Territories of local groups encountered by Stefansson
The Anglo-American Polar Expedition, 1906-1907
The Stefansson-Anderson Expedition, 1908-1912
ARCTIC OCEAN
BEAUFORT SEA
CHUKCHI SEA
INUPIAT
YUPIK
COPPER
BROOKS RANGE
ALASKA
CANADA
DINNÉ
GWICHIN (LOUCHEAUX, KUTCHIN)
HAN
NAHANE
Barrow
Point Hope
Noatak
Noorvik
Wales
Nome
St. Lawrence Island
NORTON SOUND
Arctic Circle
Fort Yukon
Fort McPherson
Fort Good Hope
Echo Bay
GREAT BEAR LAKE
Dawson
Yukon River
Porcupine River
Mackenzie River
Horton River
Coppermine River
Coppermine
Amundsen Gulf
Banks Island
Cape Bathurst
Mackenzie Bay
Eskimo Lakes
Anderson Winter 1908-9
Stefansson 1907
Winter 1908-9
Winter 1909
Winter 1909-10, 1911-12
Winter 1910-11
I1
I2
I3
I4
I5
I6
I7
I8
I9
C1
C2
C3
C4
C5
C6
C7
D1
D2
D3
D4
INUIT
YUPIK
INUPIAT
I1. Nuwunmiut
I2. Ikpikparmiut
I3. Kupigmiut
I4. Tigixtagmiut
I5. Kikiktagmiut
I6. Kopagmiut (Kogmollik, Kupugmiut)
I7. Nunatamamiut (Nunatama)
I8. Kitegareutmiut (Kitegareut)
I9. Itkillikmiut (Itkillik)
COPPER
C1. Ahungahungarmiut
C2. Nuvungmiut
C3. Qordlortmiut
C4. Agiarmiut
C5. Nagyuktogmiut
C6. Kungmiut
C7. Kanghiryuarmiut
Kilometers
0 100 200 300
0 100 200
Miles
ATHAPASCAN-SPEAKING INDIANS
GWICHIN (LOUCHEAUX, KUTCHIN)
HAN
NAHANE
DINNÉ
D1. Kawchogodinné (Hare)
D2. Thlingchadinné (Dog-Ribs)
D3. Etchaodinné (Slavey)
D4. Tatsanodinné (Yellowknives)

PLATE 2. Ethnographic map: Inuit and Indian groups. Map drawn by Lovísa Ásbjörnsdóttir.

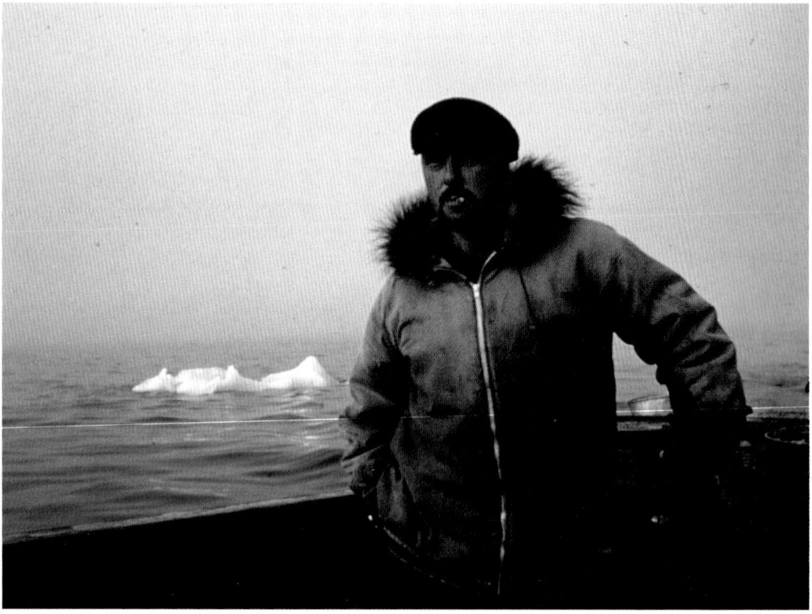

PLATE 3. Alex Stefansson aboard a boat, Mackenzie Delta, 1955. Photo: Dr. June Helm and Dr. Richard MacNeish. © Robert S. Peabody Museum of Archaeology, Phillips Academy, Andover, Massachusetts. *(Courtesy of the Robert S. Peabody Museum of Archaeology.)*

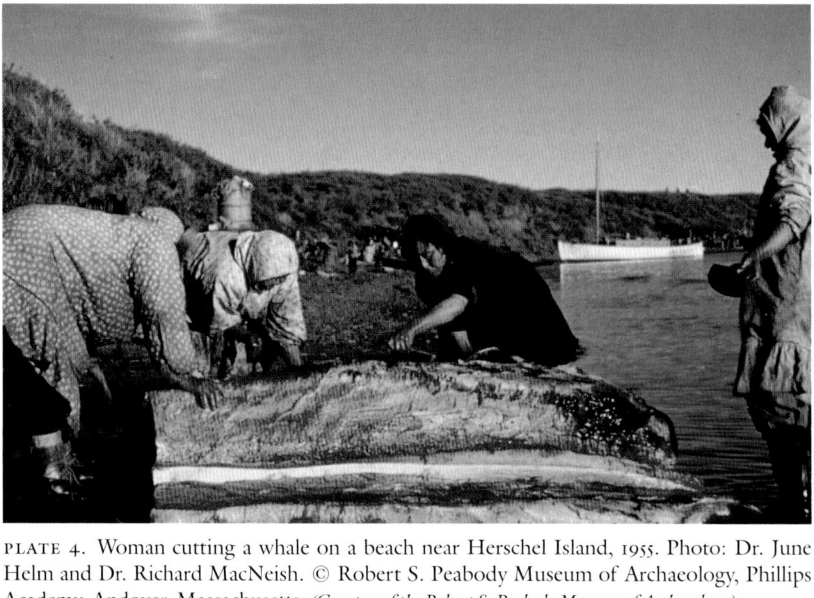

PLATE 4. Woman cutting a whale on a beach near Herschel Island, 1955. Photo: Dr. June Helm and Dr. Richard MacNeish. © Robert S. Peabody Museum of Archaeology, Phillips Academy, Andover, Massachusetts. *(Courtesy of the Robert S. Peabody Museum of Archaeology.)*

PLATE 5. Frank Stefansson at Nunaluk, the camp of his grandparents Stefansson and Pannigabluk, July 2000. Photo: the author.

PLATE 6. Rosie Albert Stefansson demonstrates one of her parkas at Inuvik, July 2000. Photo: the author.

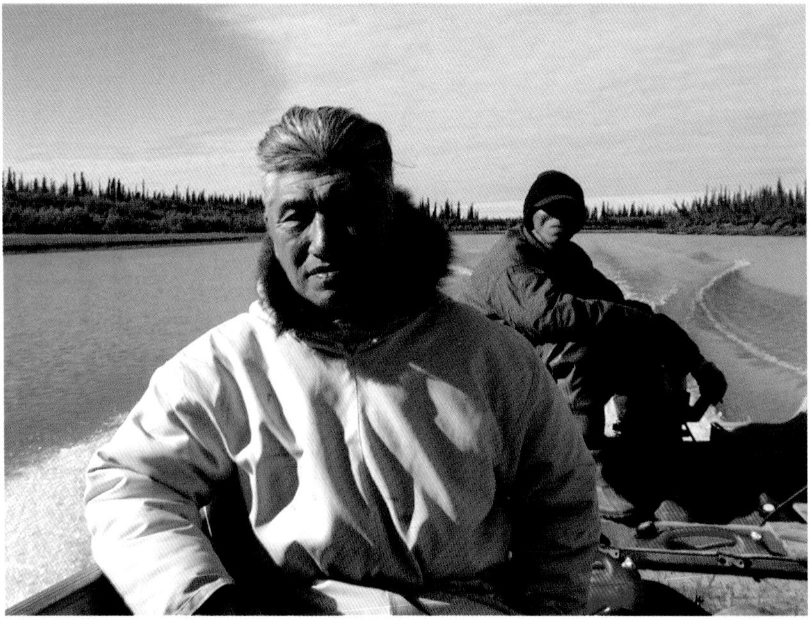

PLATE 7. Frank Stefansson (left), Mackenzie Delta, near Aklavik, July 2000. Photo: the author.

PLATE 8. The editor (second from right) interviews three of Alex Stefansson's children: Rosie Albert Stefansson, Shirley Esau Stefansson, and Frank Stefansson, at Inuvik, July 2000. Photo: Hákon Már Oddsson.

PLATE 9. Stefansson on a summer hunt. Canadian Arctic Expedition, 1914. Lantern slide no. 63. *(Courtesy of Dartmouth College Library, Stef Mss 226.)*

PLATE 10. Copper Inuit fishing group, June 1916. Canadian Arctic Expedition (1913–1918). Photo: D. Jenness. Lantern slide no. 126. *(Courtesy of Dartmouth College Library, Stef Mss 226.)*

PLATE 11. Copper Inuit hunters. Canadian Arctic Expedition (1913–1918). Lantern slide no. 129. *(Courtesy of Dartmouth College Library, Stef Mss 226.)*

PLATE 12. "Blond Inuit," 1909. Photo: Lomen Brothers. Lantern slide no. 134. *(Courtesy of Dartmouth College Library, Stef Mss 226.)*

PLATE 13. Copper Inuit at Coronation Gulf. Canadian Arctic Expedition (1913–1918). Lantern slide no. 176. *(Courtesy of Dartmouth College Library, Stef Mss 226.)*

PLATE 14. Group of Copper Inuit, Victoria Island. Canadian Arctic Expedition (1913–1918). Lantern slide no. 181. *(Courtesy of Dartmouth College Library, Stef Mss 226.)*

PLATE 15. Inuit mother and child, 1916–1920. Lantern slide no. 215. *(Courtesy of Dartmouth College Library, Stef Mss 226.)*

PLATE 16. Fannie Pannigabluk and Alex Stefansson. Canadian Arctic Expedition (1913–1918). The caption in the files of the Stefansson Collection reads: "Puningabluk, forewoman of those employed to make clothes for the ice party, and her little boy Eric, 18 March 1914." Lantern slide no. 186. *(Courtesy of Dartmouth College Library, Stef Mss 226.)*

Plate 17. Stefansson's field diaries. Photo: the author. *(Courtesy of Dartmouth College Library.)*

Plate 18. The Mackenzie Delta, July 2000. Photo: the author.

think our first meeting with these people would have gone well. The village proved to be southwest about three miles, we had gone past it. When we arrived within a hundred yards of the houses, they asked if we would camp near them, or a little way off on account of the dogs. We preferred to be a little way off and as many as could get at it turned-to to make us a snowhouse.

Snowhouse building differs here somewhat from the Kittegaryumiut who build in a regular spiral from the ground up and cut the snow usually outside the house. Here the snow is probed with a probe about four feet long to see if it is good quality down to the ice and the ice level. Blocks are then cut from the floor of the house first, and so as to have their transverse diameter vertical. The Kittegaryumiut are particular about the size of the blocks having them about uniform. These cut blocks any shape and size, some like a "four square" timber and anything from a foot to four feet long, some squares, some triangles, etc. [. . .] The wall is not started in a spiral [. . .]. When the roof part is in construction the blocks are more regular in shape and of more uniform quality. There was not enough snow in the floor for much more than half the house, a few blocks were spoiled for the snow was not good. The house was about circular and about eight feet to the dome, diameter about ten feet. Outside to a height of about three feet, a second wall is built outside the first, about eighteen inches from it, and soft snow thrown in between. [. . .] When house was finished this was walled up and a new door, shaped about two and a half feet high, cut in from entry. The sleeping platform is built of the pieces that break and of new blocks passed in to front it, with loose snow shoveled over. In our case the platform is about eighteen inches, but I have seen it two and a half feet, in which case it consists of a horseshoe-shaped bench left or built around the wall and boards laid across. All the people seem to carry with them dwarf willow for bedding and their skins are polar bear, seal, and deer. The lamp is on a platform usually of two parallel bars two feet above the floor and resting one on a piece of snow on edge, the other [. . .] on a bar at right angles also stuck through the wall. This is about eighteen inches above lamp stand and from it is swung the pot, while above is frame for drying socks, etc. In front of the lamp is a sideboard from twelve to twenty-four inches wide on which rest the ulu, dipper, pieces of meat to be cooked or that are cooling, parings of blubber trimmed off too fat meat, etc. When this gets pretty well littered it is scraped clean, the litter being pushed over the hack edge of it and falling in a pile about under the lamp. This is periodically gathered up for dog feed.

When our house was built and the bedding in place, some half dozen men had sent to their various houses for contributions of cooked, or if there were uncooked food. When one discovered we had forgotten our primus-stove—this was a serious thing, as our plan was, for we expected to spend a week if necessary in following up the trail. It was at once declared we must not think of eating in a cold house, and we were taken each to a separate family—for no house is large enough to comfortably accommodate three visitors and the family—the house is always as small as the family justifies. After we had all filled up on hot sealmeat and blood soup we went home, to find that a good stove lamp and plenty blubber had been provided. After entertaining for an hour about fifteen men and five women, we were left to sleep. [. . .]

MAY 14 Tannaumirk and 2 men went ashore to get primus, and Pannigabluk if she wants to come. *The ice* is comparatively smooth out here, and is said to be so to Victoria Island, except near the shore of the two lands—mainland and Victoria. There is a small pressure ridge perhaps every mile, but nothing to delay a loaded sled 10 minutes in the hour. The ice is said to be so all winter. These people live on it ¾ of year.

The people [. . .] look clean as compared with Baillie, for instance, and are models of good behavior. In fact, have manners towards strangers such as I do not suppose any white men have ever honored themselves by showing to any branch of the Eskimo race. There is interest, but no forward curiosity shown with regard to all the strange things we have and do; no laughter at a dialect which must seem funny to them; the greatest courtesy in everything, the best seal for the visitor; the first choice of food; continual expressions of friendship; no questions as to why we came. No spitting out and calling "bad" food we give them to taste, though all say "We are not used to it and do not like the taste." The same with smoking. "We do not expect people from far away to have no manners different from us, so go ahead and smoke," but several have had to leave the house when T. and B. smoked together. Continual invitations to come and eat though they are short of food, got three seals yesterday for thirty-eight people, an average catch, and continued bringing presents of blubber for our lamp and meat to cook, small pieces, for there is little to give. The snow today keeps melting in holes from sun, and each house is carefully patched as it appears, our clothes are carefully brushed of the least particle of snow in entering a house. One could particularize endlessly, but the sum is courtesy and good breeding with generous kindness.

At Cape Bexley last winter there were three groups of people joined, these, who hunt in summer invariably south from Point Hope "toward a lake that is like the sea for size," a Victoria Island group bound up the west coast this spring (they are supposed close now), and a Victoria Island group (now "far away") who belong off the mouth of the Napaktulik (Coppermine River). No one here has seen the Nagyuktogmiut, but they say they are excellent people, which encourages our party. There must have been over two hundred people at Bexley, to judge by the snowhouses.

There is probably not a single copper implement here, though some ulus etc., are nailed with copper rivets. Their iron comes from the "Ualinarmiut," whose location is not yet clear to me. They have iron pots, frying pans, snow knives, etc. The knives are all made by themselves, apparently. One woman and perhaps other, has seen white men, though they do not seem to recognise me as one—perhaps because my speech is from their point of view, not much worse than Tannaumirk's and I believe better than Billy's. The language resembles Kittegaryumiut more than any other dialect I know, yet some things remind more of westerners [. . .]. I have this advantage, too, that when B. or T. identifies a word, he at once changes its pronunciation into the form of his own dialect, while I try for the local. That I speak something like T. is shown by the fact that they were unanimously agreed T. was my younger brother, and that he was not full grown "because he is so much smaller than you, and brothers are often similar in size."

The women do not braid or apparently tend the hair much, but I have seen only one woman (no man) who apparently is lousy. The men cut the entire top of the head close in a horizontal line a half inch above the ears, and wear the back hair loose. Both sexes use the hair frequently for toothpicks, in manner of "toothsilk." This I have never seen before. The women, most or all, tattooed. The lines down the forehead are (the two) everywhere equidistant (about ¼ inch) from each other, go half way down the nose, and are, the inner, one inch, the outer 1½ inch, apart where they end at the roots of the hair. The only old woman here has her forehead bald an inch or two back, and the lines end where her hair formerly ended. The eye design varied. [. . .] The cheek lines I have seen did not vary. They extend from nostrils slanting up to ear, meet at nose and are about quarter of an inch apart at ear. The chin lines I have seen varied from five to seven and equidistant in pairs.

The clothes are of the general style of those I got from Mogg (Victoria Island—Prince Albert Sound) but vary greatly, no two being quite alike. The swallowtail is usually to knee and never below calf of leg, and from six inches to fifteen inches wide. Some coats are cut about as our "frock" coats I used when teaching school. One has almost a horizontal lower line and reaches almost to knees. The sleeves are generally short and the mittens not quite to wrist, leaving the wrist bare, all but snowhouse-building gauntlets. The pants and coat barely meet in front, typically, and when one reaches arms above head the abdomen and chest are bare from an inch or so below the navels to above the nipples, for the coats are very badly cut at the shoulders—for a man about a foot broader than the wearer. On some women's coats the shoulders are nearer the elbow than the shoulder. Outside their pants, the women wear two huge pairs of leggings fitting loose around the thigh suspended from a belt. They must fill with snow in a blizzard. Both sexes wear slippers over leggings. Two men froze to death last winter, old men following the trail behind a party. It is a wonder half of them don't freeze to death.

Tattooing. The most common number of chin lines is five. The lines are in general quarter of an inch apart at top and half an inch at bottom, being all curved but the middle one. They begin about one-half inch below edge of lip mucous and end where they would disappear from the view of a person whose eyes were on a level with those of the wearer. The hand designs seem to be unlimited in number and form. [. . .] Have seen no tattoo on men.

The complexion is a good deal darker than our two men, who have been much outdoors, though the ice may sunburn more than the shore. Some are as dark as half-blood negroes.

The hands are typically Eskimo in general, but one woman (twenty-five or thirty years, approximately) has the long fingers that I have seen only in half-bloods. She has no other readily apparent non-Eskimo characters. "Kablunak" is used here for "white man." This is the first locality I have been where it has an apparently respectable standing. The western people know it only as slang, on a par with taksipuk. Tannaumirk, who has never worked on a ship, did not understand it when used to him last night, and only when I explained it today when he did not yet get its meaning from their talk. [. . .]

"Modesty." Have seen no signs of the "sexual hospitality" which Mackenzie Eskimo have told me was part of ordinary courtesy to a guest.

Sores: Several persons have sores now, mostly on the hands, though some on eyebrows, forehead, and one in the scalp. He has hand sores too. When this man's hand sores have healed there are little elevations, almost like warts and lighter color than rest of back of hand, about color of palm. The one now open is circular, like a conical pit, about one cm. wide and half a cm. deep. It is red, perhaps from plucking off scab, which seems a habit. It is not apparently a "running" sore, nor yet is it dry, about as moist as our lips.

Names are given here with a freedom not found to the present to the westward even among people who have worked on ships. Among Kittegaryumiut people, the name is never given you by the man himself when you ask him, but always by a bystander, here each as he first sees you says: "I am

So-and-so; what is your name?" When we arrived here, Tannaumirk had to repeat his name to every man as they went along the line of sealers, each sealer giving his own name in return. After we got to the village, those who had not seen us before always gave their own names before asking ours. [. . .]

The voice is kept much lower and the manner in telling stories, conversing, etc., is quieter than that of any group I know and contrasts especially with the Kittegaryumiut. Contrary to all groups seen before, they speak favorably of all those people of whom they have any knowledge. They seem to have no knowledge of Avoak or Kittegaryumiut. Of the Itkilliks they know, but they say "we do not know what sort of people they are, for we have never seen them."

Our sled got back in the evening bringing Pannigabluk. Some of our stuff left in cache on shore. Dance house built today in our honor.

MAY 15 Dancing. [. . .] The dance house has its floor on ice level, is about fifteen feet in diameter and eight feet high. It is full six feet in height a foot from the wall, i.e., the roof very flat. In building it, two temporary doors were used on opposite sides. As with all houses, the door faces south. The hallway is about half the usual length, about five feet. The door is a trifle higher than ordinary. There are no seats or benches along walls. People stand in complete circle, some boys in the front row, "so they can see." All the men and about half the women present. No special place for the women. A circle about five feet in diameter left for the dancer in center. There was no drum, but their bewailing its absence showed they ordinarily use it. They said: "We almost never dance. We have no drums any more." This would imply the dancing on decline. The dance now was entirely perhaps at Billy's instance.

Most of the dancers assumed being very tired or overcome with languor from heat, they cast their eyes down and the hand dangled lifeless at the wrist. They sang in general with the chorus, there were words to three fourths of the song and in some cases the dancer used words while others accompanied him without words [. . .]. In a half dozen cases the singer made a mistake, used words when he should not have joined the words of the chorus, etc. In each case he was "jogged" by one or another, and one who failed to hear first correction was tapped on the shoulder to draw his attention. This was all done in a jocular way, each mistake causing laughter, corrections given and received about with same spirit as in a "set" at a country dance.

One dancer Iglixsirk, danced about in Kittegaryumiut "doctor" style. His movements quick and often violent, his facial expressions at times diabolical, his shouts earsplitting and evidently intended to frighten. At intervals he would suddenly face someone and ask: "Who am I?" [. . .] "Am I a good man?" etc. [. . .]. Occasionally, however, he dropped the dance manner and smiled as pleasantly as his Mephistophelian face allowed. At a set point in his song, everyone joined him in a half dozen movements bending at hips and knees. Both my own knowledge and Tannaumirk's verdict show this performance to be one not essentially different from the Mackenzie River type.

Trip to Victoria Island. After the dance we had supper of seal meat and blood soup and then started in search of the Victoria Island party that was supposed to be near. One man, I can never remember his name, one of the prominent men, came along, saying, "When you come near, I will run ahead as a herald (kivrarniaktuña) and tell them you are good (harmless, friendly [. . .])." Leaving at 9 P.M. ("We always travel at night in the spring," our companion said. He did not want to start earlier than we did.) We first struck east about six miles when we found a deserted camp. The trail from here led north about five miles to another abandoned camp about a week old. Here the trail was a trifle north of west about five miles to the present camp (four houses, three with sealskin roofs, one all snow) which lies about two miles east of Tulugak some ten yards from shore on a low bit of coast. We had therefore traveled in a U-curve. When a half mile off we stopped the sled and our friend ran to the houses. He darted into one after the other, and in about two or three minutes the men began to come out. After a few words, all started looking to the dogs, securing those not already tied. Then a shout was raised for us to come, and our friend came running to meet us. When about two hundred yards off the village, men and boys, all in line (not in file) started slowly forward to meet us, holding their hands above their heads and calling out at intervals, "ilyira-naitturut," "namnakturut" [. . .]. "We are made glad by your coming," etc. When near, we each were asked to pass along the line from (our) right to left. As we came opposite, each in turn he gave his name and we then repeated ours. This was done even with boys not over eight years, though the boys were fallen out of line before the introductions and being introduced to them seemed more or less optional. A snowhouse was then built [. . .] and we cooked some milk. (They had all been asleep and the seal meat frozen, so they said they would not be quite ready yet.) We were then taken each to a separate house, where we introduced ourselves to the women (they giving name first). The meat was cooked, we had a sort of midnight supper (had arrived 3 A.M., it was now 6 A.M.) and then all went to sleep again. [. . .]

MAY 16 [. . .] The village is about N. from Cape Bexley, or a little west. The crossing from there is not over 20 miles [. . .].

Personal appearance: I now understand why the Stapleton people take me for an Eskimo. There are three men here whose beard is almost the color of mine and who look like typical Scandinavians. As Billy said: Three of them look like fo'c's'le men, and aren't they huge? And one looks like a Portugee [. . .]. In the mainland partly I had noted that a large number of men have a few brown hairs in their moustaches and (more rarely) in the chinbeard, a few there have moustaches to be described as dark brown. This I have never seen on Eskimos to the west. Here, however, are men with abundant (3 inch long or so) chin beards (reaching a trifle beyond the corners of the mouth), a full brown in its outer parts but darker near the middle of the chin. The faces and proportions of the body remind of [. . .] sunburnt but naturally fair Scandinavians. (They are very much alike, though no two have same mother, and resemble closely one Icelander I know, Sigurjon Sveinsson, of Mountain, N.A., as he looked about 1885. They resemble, too, picture I have seen of Dr. Anderson's father.) The one that looks like a Portugee has hair that curles a trifle at the tips—about as much as mine. One woman has the delicate features one sees in some Scandinavian girls and that I have seen only in one half-white girl to the westward—and there to a less degree than here. I know over 20 half-bloods, and none of them resembles a white man in particular—most of them could pass among either Eskimo or whites as Eskimos if there were no particular attention drawn to them; no one could fail to be struck by the European appearance of these people (cf. accounts of [. . .] Klengenberg and of Capt. Mogg and his crew, both white and Eskimo, as previously noted in my diary). I am exceedingly glad we fell in with these people: it has enabled me to verify previously received accounts, and to establish, to my own satisfaction at least, a very interesting fact. More will be written of their eyes, etc. after I have had better opportunities of seeing them.

Relations with other people. There is living here a man belonging to the Nagyuktogmiut. Several of them have brothers and sisters living now with the Stapleton group. They have, at present at least, less to do with people along the west coast, the first of whom are now supposed to be, as they habitually are, on the ice of Prince Albert Land. These will hunt the summer to the north of the Sound. [. . .]

Knowledge of land. This group has names for all points and rivers on the mainland to Cape Lyon, but not beyond. They also name several points on Banks Island (including Nelson Head?). Banks, they say, is uninhabited, though. The Prince Albert Sound people occasionally spend the summer there, crossing by sled in spring and fall. [. . .]

Cooking. There seems to be very little uncooked meat eaten. I have seen two cases among Stapleton people of a single man at end of a meal asking for a piece of frozen meat because he had not had enough cooked meat. Tannaumirk has seen one meal where frozen meat formed "a course." Today our dogs were fed cooked meat, "for," they said, "meat frozen hard is not good for a dog." [. . .]

MAY 17 *Cephalic measurements* taken today of 15 of the 17 here—two small boys afraid. [. . .]

Presents: To follow many an illustrious example among "explorers" I decided to present each of the five women here with three needles. This would have been small pay indeed for all their hospitality, for they all have iron needles (which they evidently value higher than factory made ones, for they have doubtless found them brittle—a bad quality here, though desired where there are shops on every corner). They would not hear of the "present" part, and all brought gifts in turn—fancy mittens, sleeves, boot-soles, etc. all saying they were "honorable people and would not be shamed by having a gift unreturned."

MAY 18 [. . .] Counting. I have heard of Eskimo being unable to count beyond six, but this is my first meeting with that fact. There are seventeen people here and after careful conference they showed me on the fingers of three hands (do not use feet as Mackenzie do) there were fourteen. They had no name for this number and on being pressed, none could count beyond six. [. . .] A half hour of trying by Billy and me could not induce them to count at all, unless objects were in question (as our dogs, or theirs, the size of their families, etc.). (They would not count their fingers, deeming it useless, I suppose, their number is well known.)

Entering a house, everyone (except members of the family) utters a series of sharp exclamations from the time he stoops to enter the alleyway till his head is inside the door proper. The first to come to our house each morning always comes singing loudly; also, when no visitors known to be with us, while yet at a distance.

Skin roofs and snow walls are used in the spring by the Haneragmiut. Have been in use since they came ashore here some eight or ten days ago. There is a ridge pole some three feet shorter than the long diameter of a slightly oval house, supported on X sticks and lashed to them. These sticks incline a little, in pairs, toward the center of the house. The rest of the rafters, of which the ice pick is always one, are either from the wall to the ridge pole, or from wall to the X sticks, whose end sometimes, and sometimes not, sticks out of a hole in the roof. [. . .]

MAY 19 Misinformation [. . .]. Billy misunderstood the other day that a woman who was telling about the two-masted umiak had been to one of the ships. On close inquiry we find neither she nor any other of them was, but they have all their information from the Kanghiryuarmiut, some of whom were at the ship. It seems the Kanghiryuarmiut seldom come down here, they probably made a trade expedition after meeting the ships, who, as is whaler habit, immediately glutted the natural market, expecting later, I suppose, to create an artificial one for tobacco, matches, firearms, flour, and perhaps whiskey.

Outside influence on Eskimo. Outside influences seem to be as slight and indirect here, therefore, as one can find among the Eskimo or perhaps anywhere in the world. This would be a good place to stop therefore, and we might do so.

People to the east. [. . .] All of these are about equally untouched, and the Akuliakattagmiut are on our home road to be easily seen again.

Dogs are not numerous. Most people have two dogs and the largest number I know of is four. They are on an average about fifty pounds if in flesh but are rather thin now, though not skinny. They seem to get nothing but bones and blubber and not much of the latter, judging by how greedily they eat when fed, a dog soon is satiated with blubber. At Haneragmiut there were fourteen dogs to five families. Here I have not been able to count them. [. . .]

Western people. One woman says her mother was from far west along the coast of the mainland, this side Lyon somewhere, I suppose.

Starvation. Pannigabluk has heard of two people who starved to death "aipani" "when there were no seals in the winter." Two old men froze to death this winter, possibly (we suspect) partly from hunger.

An accident. A man here, Kudlark, when shooting at deer last summer, shot past accidentally and killed his younger brother, an adopted son of Aialuk (the Aialuk living with Akuliak). [. . .]

Misunderstanding: B. also misunderstood that one of Haneragmiut was originally from the Nagyuktogmiut. He had not even been to their country.

Left Akuliakattagmiut camp at 4:45 P.M. and got to our camp about 6 P.M. Their camp is about eight miles from the northwest corner of the Cape Bexley peninsula (the land one reaches first from Point Hope) and bears about 300° magnetic. Since leaving shore (some time after the sun came back) they have had three camps, the first about miles east of the present, and the other some four miles farther north and half way between first and present camps [. . .].

Cephalic measurements taken of all women when they came for present of needles and most of the grown men. No boys came at my call for all the village, and I did not want to press it. They all seemed restless after novelty of first few measurements wore off, so I did not venture to try their patience on stature, etc. Photos of group worried them too, so took no individuals.

Brief entries only will hereafter be made of other things than ethnological information, geological or geographic and other things that concern the purpose of our trip to the Arctic, for I am becoming worried about the capacity of my two notebooks, especially if we should stay all next winter, as I at present feel inclined to do. Hunting, mishaps without serious consequences, "whys," short or long mileage, etc. will be left to take care of themselves largely. [. . .]

What I know and what they know leads me to think as they think, that neither they nor their ancestors (Akuliakattagmiut or Haneragmiut) have come in contact with any of the middle-century explorers. I think it worthwhile, therefore, to give more space than already given to a description of their manners, etc. The same freedom from inquisitveness, as at first shown, continued to the end of our stay. I was beginning to suspect this really an apathy or lack of interest, so I showed a few of them some of my things, and explained them—partly to test them and partly to prepare for similar inquiries of them, as my business unfortunately does not allow me the same non-inquisitiveness as characterizes them. They were immediately not merely politely but genuinely interested, though they showed no such interest in the wonders B. and I had to tell of faraway things that were not on hand. When I presented some needles to the women they all wanted to pay. This I declined on the ground our sled was too heavily loaded already (as it is); I told them that when we go home I should be glad of anything they give me. Pannigabluk and Tannaumirk had, however, received while B. and I were in Victoria Island several presents of sealskin, bootsoles, slippers, etc. Their interest in us continued to our leaving, though only the men (all I think) came to see us off, helped load the sled, etc. B. and T. had explained when people parted as good friends they always shook hands, so of course it was up to me to shake hands too. I regret having been forced to plant here the seed which I hope may not sprout of this to them thoroughly foreign custom. We had great trouble in getting any information out of them. They are far from garrulous. Our many inquiries as to where the Nagyuktogmiut are and how to be found, brought an invariable "We do not know, we never were there." It was an accident we found out that three of them did know the way by winter; straight down the middle of the strait. Either these had not been present when we inquired, or they had been silent when those who did not know spoke up, I think the latter is the fact. The others must have known too, by hearsay, but in every case, we got, "We do not know" as an answer when they had not themselves actually seen the thing (except information as to their ancestors). This character I have often noted in Eskimo to the west, but never so marked as here. They will also agree with you in anything. After telling us in a body of three islands known as "the hares" [. . .] they at once agreed with Pannigabluk who said they were only two in number as a woman had told her who had been there. This is a place where people habitually cross the strait, and no doubt many knew positively how many there are, but they immediately agreed with Pannigabluk that there were only two. My chart shows three islands (Listen and Sutton) and I have no doubt there are three. Similarly, after telling B. that the Nagyuktogmiut consider the Itkillik bad people, they at once agreed with him when he said they were very good people. (They had previously said to me "We do not know what sort of people they are, for we do not know them.") While they probably once had an organic connection with the people towards Cape Lyon (and one indeed has a mother from "far west") their present movements seem to be restricted to less than fifty miles of coast and to the strait ice just north of them. Some spend an occasional summer in Victoria with the Haneragmiut or the Puiplirmiut farther east. This is a very confined sphere. Perhaps this has had a strong influence. At any rate, after allowing for their not well understanding our speech, I am inclined to consider them far (certainly somewhat) less intelligent in general than any I have before seen. Eskimo everywhere are little interested in the outside world; these show practically none. But as their intelligence is less, so their general kindliness and good breeding is far beyond anything I have before seen. Of course, I have seen only "civilized" and mostly Christianized people heretofore. I do not think the social virtues so prominent *because* of a lack of intellect, but it seems clear that greater intelligence does not predicate a greater fitness for living in harmony with their neighbors.

Their generosity was always prominent, and the expression of it was monotonous. Perhaps because of difficulty of conversing and a distaste for remaining silent (considering it impolite) they kept constantly repeating "We hope you are having enough to eat." "We want you to be content (not lonesome) while with us. We are therefore trying to feed you well, for a man with a full stomach is seldom discontented. He is well off who is well fed," etc. These were endlessly repeated. I believe some of their phrases have a status similar to our proverbs, for their phraseology was almost never (if ever) varied. Whenever one of these sentences was uttered, most or all present acclaimed with "iyarrl," which we do not understand exactly, but which clearly is akin to our "amen," "so it is," "so be it." When we left we took with us a number of small pieces of meat, presents, and their last words were inquiries if it was enough and urging us to speak up if we wanted more. (It has been noted that they have little themselves, especially since they have neglected sealing largely since we first came. When we were not five miles off they were spread all over the ice, hunting in earnest for the first time since we came.) Modesty is not among their conspicuous virtues, however, for as often as they expressed friendliness (which was about every five minutes) they would say "ilyranaitturu" "kiyanakturut," "nagoyurut tamapta" and when they spoke of other groups, "they are excellent people, just as good people as we are." They are as monotonous in this self-praise as in their good wishes to us, etc. It is to be noted, however, that the connotation of these phrases is not so much that they are an excellent, superior people, as that they are harmless, friendly, not to be distrusted. A phrase much used by the Haneragmiut and occasionally by the Akuliakattagmiut is "namnakturut," literally we are easily seen, easily discerned from afar, but which I suppose denotes "easy to see through," [. . .] "not treacherous," "really as we appear."

Their kindness to their dogs, a uniform trait I believe of all uninfluenced Eskimo, is even greater than I have ever seen before. One of the dogs will every few minutes come and stand with his head in the doorway. He invariably gets a bone or piece of blubber. They can spare no meat now, but they do not clean-pick bones as western Eskimo do, and if someone tries to drive him off, another member of the family will protest "You cannot expect a hungry dog not to beg for food," "Drive him away with a bone and not a stick," etc. The dogs wear their harness all the time, and when they fight they are not beaten apart, as is the custom farther west, but pulled apart by the harness, which seems to be left on for this purpose. I saw one dog struck with a small stick, but he was an inveterate trouble breeder.

Measuring their heads, I saw neither lice nor nit, though this gave me a good chance to see any there were. I do not think them quite free, however, as I saw one or two women feeling for some such thing inside their coats. They were never successful in their search, which bad luck seldom attends a similar quest in the Mackenzie. They probably never wash but I know from experience one gets no dirtier after the first few days.

They showed no fear of head measurements and of being photographed, at first. But B. officiously explained the photo process which seemed to make them uneasy and I dared not go beyond two group pictures, for we expect to have considerable to do with these people later. They made no inquiry as to the nature of my operations in photographing them, possibly not to show ignorance, or perhaps for some other reason. B.'s explanation was gratuitous. [. . .]

I made a grave blunder. Wanting to see them shoot with bows, I thought it a happy introduction to the subject to show them how to shoot. I therefore set up a small stick at one hundred yards and fired at it. Two of the apparently prominent men went with me at my call for volunteers to see the effect of the shot. Unfortunately, I had missed and wanted to shoot again, but this they earnestly begged I should not do, saying they were unused to such things. I regretted my foolishness in starting this, but seeing it was started I thought it better to show we occasionally did hit, and B. and I each fired once, both hitting. The repetition seemed to rather reassure them. Two bows were then brought out at our request. The range seems to be about one hundred yards and at twenty-five yards they hit within a foot of the target ("bulls eye") about four out of five times. Doubtless these two were the best bow men. Evidently the bow is a more satisfactory weapon for deer than I had supposed, yet it surprised me that they should have given up the method of spearing, which has everywhere, so far as I know, been the mainstay of deer hunting. They told us that the deer were no longer as formerly. In the time of their forebears (sivullivut) they were very plentiful, and are growing, in their own time, fewer from year to year. This probably explains why they have given up the kayak and spear method—it accords with the caribou situation everywhere, and is not, I think, a mere "golden age" belief. Only a few of them have really good deerskin clothes and some help themselves out with seal and squirrel [. . .]. Their houses have no bad smell noticeable to me. They doubtless smell somewhat of seal oil, but so do our houses smell of the things we eat and use, and we don't consider them therefore vile. They are very careful that their lamps are trimmed and I have not yet seen a snow roof with traces of lampblack evident, and it would soon show on snow, ours was fairly black in a week, but then we don't understand lamps, except Tannaumirk.

The lamp and stone pot are a pretty satisfactory cooking apparatus. A lamp takes perhaps double the time of a "primus" to boil water, but it can be left for hours unattended, and if one wished (but this they probably never do) one could leave a pot on going to sleep and find boiling water in the morning. It seemed to me those who used stone pots took less time in cooking than those who had iron or tin ones (over half of them), but this is perhaps because the stone ones are long to fit the lamp flame, the iron ones are round and therefore with less heating surface. I have heard of Eskimo merely warming meat to eat it. These always comment unfavorably on a piece that is a trifle rare and I have not seen one eaten that would not be considered "medium" or "well done" if a beefsteak in a grillroom. In fact I have never seen Eskimo eat partly cooked meat so bloody as many steaks I have seen devoured in cities—when they cook, they usually cook well. Besides, I have tried boiling seal more than the Eskimo do and found it toughened the meat, unless you boil it an hour or so, when it softens again but has lost its best flavor. I prefer meat put unfrozen in cold water and taken out about five minutes after the water boils. At this season of the year I much prefer seal to deer meat, if fresh.

At meals the couple of the house and anyone else who cares to, usually an old or middle-aged man, sit on the edge of the bed platform with their feet hanging over; younger visitors stand, as do the children who typically come in from play to eat and dart out again when done. When the meat is considered cooked, the woman takes it out of the pot, using a handle-less musk-ox horn dipper in her right hand and the fingers of the left hand. The pieces are put on the sideboard in front of the lamp and left to cool. They are occasionally felt of, and when comfortably cool to the hand, the woman takes a piece, squeezes it between her two hands to squeeze out any water that might drop on the floor or one's clothes, and rubs off the blood [. . .]. Then the woman hands out the pieces to those she pleases. In our case only, who were guests of especial honor, the husband took the piece intended for us, usually felt of it and the other pieces to see if it was really the best, squeezed it again and rubbed it to make it drier, and then handed it to us, saying their meat was not much good, but this was about the best piece. In all cases blubber was carefully trimmed off, until they found that I liked to have some left on mine. Most of the people hold the meat in both hands and do not use a knife; some use an ulu, eating in the ordinary Eskimo fashion, biting into the meat and then cutting just in front of the teeth. After eating, the hands are wiped on a birdskin. I have seen ptarmigan, gull, and swan used. Then any fragments that have dropped on the floor are scraped under the table with an ulu.

Of ceremonials I saw no trace, nor of charms, though they probably have both. Tannaumirk took a leather thong worn over shoulder and under arm across the breast and back, to be a charm, but I think it was to carry the knife. It is worn between the two coats. [. . .]

MAY 21 Started 11: A., camped 4 P. acct. deer killed. [. . .] *Distance 5 miles.* [. . .]

My Eskimos, especially Tannaumirk, have the unpleasant habit of being superior to the people they meet down here. T. keeps talking about how their houses smell bad (which item he alone of us all noticed), how they are ignorant of this and that, and how there is great need they be taught that and this—to use guns, matches, flour, tobacco, and to pray. Pannigabluk and B. have the superiority to some extent though B. not much.

The Akuliakattagmiut and Haneragmiut all have iron snow knives, though one Akuliakattagmiut has a copper one too. All the women have iron ulus, only one has a copper one, but she has also five iron ones. They have whittling knives, crooked knives, and needles, all of steel. Their tools are all sharp. [. . .]

One of songs [. . .] was characteristically different from any Eskimo song I had previously heard. It had both rhyme and a scaldic assonance as in the Njáls saga: [Icelandic:] *"Spara ek ei god gjeija, grei þikkjir mjér Freiya"* [I don't wish to blaspheme the Gods but I think Freyja is a bitch]—or more like some others, whose words I can't remember—very short lines and frequent rhyme [. . .].

MAY 22 Started 1:45 P., camped 6:15 P. Point Cockburn. [. . .]

Introductions. Each man of Akuliakattagmiut or Haneragmiut usually explained the meaning of his name or made some pun on it at time of introduction. This I took to be to help us remember the name. Each seemed to have a stock phrase, for some must have had a dozen occasions to repeat their names and always used some set accompaniment. Some made no comments on their names after first introduction, and a few not even then, simply repeating the name two or three times. [. . .]

MAY 23 *Snowbunting* heard this morning outside tent. [. . .]. Had seen from camp before others woke up what appeared to me a snowhouse window just south of the two little islands (north end of northern one 46° from camp, south end of southern one, 50°). Had previously determined to cross to Victoria Island south of Listen and Sutton Islands to look for the trail of the people who wintered with the Akuliakattagmiut as Pannigabluk claims a woman told her that they always travel along the Victoria Island coast after passing these islands. Either Pannigabluk misunderstood or else the woman did not know, as this snowhouse soon proved to be one of seven and the trail lead about 80° or 85° towards mainland, and this must be the party in question. Followed trail till 10 P.M. and passed three camps after the first one, four in all. Trail about two weeks old. [. . .]

The "windows" I have spoken of in previous entries are not windows, but holes cut in the snow wall to pass out bedding, etc., at time of breaking camp, to save carrying through alleyway. The hole is naturally over or near the door, as the woman could most easily stand there passing things out. It is never to the left of the door, but rather often to the right of it, because, no doubt, lamp occupies left of door.

The Ak. did not understand "umialik" and could not seem to get the idea from explanations of B. and T. T. believes they do not know what an umiak is, but they spoke of the ship (K.'s or M.'s?) as a two-masted umiak. It is possible they got this word from Kalakutak, [. . .] but I think they understood "umiak" originally. They speak of tuktuwok and napoktok, but have seen neither moose nor tree. T. thinks (but strangely I failed to notice it) they use "*k*" for "t" [. . .].

MAY 24 Started 11 A.M. and at 1:15 P.M. after several stops came to place where trail led inland. This is not at a river mouth proper, but at a tiny inlet at the bottom of a V-shaped small bay. [. . .] The trail led about 140° over several small ridges about three miles to where we found two tents and seven people. The other sleds had moved farther on. There were two men, three women, and two boys (see cephalic measurements at back of book). They had fish only for food and say that they have never had quite enough to eat since they came. They, however, at once presented us with about ten pounds of boiled salmon trout. They consider themselves Akuliakattagmiut though they often hunt here [. . .].

Though only women at home they seemed far less timid than others seen. A woman who had been fishing stopped on her way home to wait for us a half mile from their camp. Nevertheless, we halted and sent Pannigabluk ahead to confer. We then pitched camp about a hundred yards west of them on the ice. The dress in general is the same as Akuliakattagmiut but two of the three women have a twelve inch long, one and a half inch wide tail in front also [. . .]. A young woman whose child died soon after birth a few days ago has a tiny tent to herself.

A boy is named "Nyer" which is said to be the name of a kablunak who lives far away by the sea; can't find out just where. We met the same name in a woman of the Akuliakattagmiut, but it was not explained to us.

They have songs which they sang for us which they say their ancestors got from the Ualinarmiut very long ago. They were surprised to find neither T. nor B. knew them. Brown hairs in eyebrows and moustache (no beard) of both men. Hair cut of men Akuliakattagmiut. Two men and one boy have front hair braided, two small braids, apparently to keep it out of eyes. One woman and ten year old boy have back hair wound in two bundles with hairless thong. House furnishings much as Akuliakattagmiut.

They have sledded some wood, for fuel, which they burn with blubber, of which they say they have plenty. They gave us both for cooking. [. . .]

This group appears to better advantage than others seen, seem more intelligent, answer questions readily, seem far better informed about their neighbors. They tell us that we can cross here readily to the sea by following the trail of their companions to their camp, from which the sea can be seen. [. . .]

MAY 25 In camp till evening. Left eye paining badly and Tannaumirk snowblind both eyes worse than my left. [. . .] Cephalic measurements of all—seven in general not much suggestion of Scandinavian or European type. They say they never had skin scrapers of copper or iron, but only horn and white and brown bear bones. [. . .]

The Puiplirmiut are said to be inland in Victoria Island from the Listen-Sutton group of islands. Have just moved in, they think. They are called more numerous than the Akuliakattagmiut by a good deal. [. . .]

They call the Indians, Irksinaktut, bad, or rather, to be feared.

Amaratjak has some sores on one leg (did not see them) and he showed me scars of sores from sole to knee open last winter. Size ten cents to dollar and leg as a whole swollen, slightly swollen now. Sores chiefly or only on feet. He is the father of the baby that died at birth a few days ago—perhaps syphilis?

The first case of anyone asking for anything was that of a woman today who asked for a spoon for her boy who asked her for it. We refused as we have only one each. [. . .] They are evidently not nearly so untouched by outside influences as the Akuliakattagmiut, though they call themselves the same people. Perhaps they are a division of the Akuliakattagmiut who have long acted as intermediaries between them and those farther east [. . .].

MAY 26 Started 11:15 A. with Arnatulk to introduce us for camp of his former companions who, he said, were on a lake not far off. Got to the lake ca. 3. P.M. and found they had probably camped only a day, and then gone seaward. [. . .]

The kabluna Njer, Ner, or, Nerk [. . .], as variously pronounced remains a mystery. Arr. told me he was an excellent man, "just like us." I could get no idea of where he lived "by the sea," but not by the Haneragmiut, Kanghiryuarmiut, or any group whose name I knew. He was "lost" (a word used here of people who freeze or starve to death on trail or out hunting) "and when he was lost we gave his name to children." [. . .]

The Haneragmiut are more numerous than those we saw. Arr. asked if we had seen "Taktok" when at Hanerag. [. . .] Apparently we saw only half the Haneragmiut who may therefore be estimated as thirty-five to forty. Where they were I have no idea. That no one at Akuliakattagmiut or Hanerag said a word about them is an interesting fact.

MAY 27 Started 2:30 P. and came in sight of Coronation Gulf at 5 P.M. on a low ridge having an Eskimo cache, a pile on ground covered with stones, fish spears, clothing, etc., showing owners intended return before fishing season. 6:45 P.M. came to two caches, a rack and a pile on the ground. The rack was about four feet high, two boards on two columns of small flat stones. At just 7 P.M. we got to the salt ice and the trip we have hitherto called "towards Coronation Gulf" has become "to" it. I had hoped for and looked forward to for some years, the pleasure of rounding Cape Krusenstern into the Gulf, but that has been denied by the pleasant happening of finding this portage route. Shortly after striking the ice we saw numerous fishing holes and some fresh footprints. A little later saw a woman fishing, and then three tents. Billy went ahead to confer, and at about 8 P.M. we pitched camp about two hundred yards to east of this camp, which is on the north shore of a narrow inlet running into a valley. [. . .] Had seen band of deer in forenoon and while others camped I went about eight miles southwest but saw nothing.

Home at 2:15 A.M. Gave people saddle of meat, all we had left. They gave us a dozen tomcod. People seem more sophisticated than others, are evidently getting more so continually as we go east. They seem to take our coming about as we would a visit from next door, not to be considered anything out of the ordinary. Their clothes, speech, etc., same as last camp. Two deerskin tents, one house of snow with skin roof.

Say no people yet at Bloody Fall, only after river breaks up. [. . .]

MAY 28 [. . .] Copper is said to abound near Dismal Lake. I bought a copper snow knife this morning and saw a piece of copper [. . .]. The copper piece was rudely triangular about five by seven by nine inches and half an inch thick. It had been partly melted either to break it from its native bed or to break it from a larger piece.

The people we left this A.M. are said "aipani," to have killed with a spear (or spears) the husband of the Haiyuxuk whom we saw with the Akuliakattagmiut, now wife of Itayuk. They sometimes speak of the Akuliakattagmiut as Akuliakattagmiut sometimes as Nogatogmiut, so they seem to be only half and half real Akuliakattagmiut, perhaps the man killing causes them to live apart from the group. As noted above, they are the most sophisticated, forward, and inquisitive people we have met. They also declared themselves well informed of the ways of white men [. . .]. They offered no pay for needles I gave them, the first not to offer pay. As Hanbury was not in the habit of giving gratuitously, they probably have from Hudson Bay the idea that white men do not take pay for such trifles (only for flour and whiskey). [. . .]

People here asked to taste the salt we put in soup, and after that firmly refused to taste any of our food, at previous places all have tasted the different sorts we have, pemmican, milk, and triscuit. Brought us seal meat after seeing us eat, evidently thinking we must be hard-pressed for food to eat such stuff. Plan to go with them to island tomorrow. [. . .] The "ten" this morning denied that their knives were from the Ualinarmiut, but said they were from the Akuliakattagmiut.

They seemed to know nothing of the ships (Mogg and Klengenberg) in Victoria Island nor of Richardson [. . .]. Did not seem to know of the episode of the camp desertion at Bloody Fall, though they profess to know well all those who summer there. [. . .]

MAY 29 From our camp (a low, gravelly point) the next point S. bore 142 ½° (Cape Kendall?) and the E end of a small, dumb-bell shaped island off Cape Kendall, 131°. [. . .] On this island some years ago "most of the people belonging near here" starved to death in the winter—continual blizzards and no seal. Eider ducks (Pacific?) seen by us first today but seen here some days ago, as well as big white gulls. Snowbuntings, first since last entry. Snow thawed on top island (dark basalt rock) for first time enough so people got water from hollows in rock. [. . .]

MAY 30 [. . .] *Started* off 11: P.M. to find trail of people supposedly bound for Dismal Lake, as I have decided to try summering there—to be nearer Langton Bay, and possibly to have base there to sled loads of museum specimens to Fort Norman.

MAY 31 Crossed Back Inlet to island northeast of Point Mackenzie and camped 4 A.M. [. . .]. Found here two weeks (?) old trail of three sleds which I take to be those we should follow. It leads to Point Mackenzie. [. . .]

People here not properly Akuliakattagmiut, though they speak of them occasionally as Nogatogmiut. Brown hairs in beard, eyebrows, etc., least numerous of any people seen, more like Eskimo proper though all look more or less so except some Haneragmiut. They were last winter at Cape Bexley to trade. [. . .] Always brought contributions of meat at each meal though we had plenty seal, ate with us, and we occasionally with them. People east here much smaller eaters than Mackenzie and west, perhaps because they often starve. Speech here differs somewhat from Akuliakattagmiut but clothes, tattooing, hair cut, etc., are the same. "*Black Brant*" seen today first—two, flying west. Also first *grey geese*—7 or 8 flying SW. Snow buntings now common. Warmest day so far—snow melting fast. [. . .]

Ceremonies of meeting. Noted, but did not understand that [. . .] the man we first met stroked Tannaumirk's clothes over with downward motion. Hala did the same the other night and we now understand this is connected with turñnrat belief, to remove evil influences. Apattok fed us each with a piece of raw blubber which he would not let us touch but himself placed in our mouths. Possibly simply hospitality, more likely to ward off evil influences, or to see if we were human and not spirits. (Some of my folklore tales from the west imply blubber fatal to spirits, kills them.) Fear of our guns not shown since by Akuliakattagmiut, probably through Hanbury's Igliki telling of them. [. . .]

An old man here Ekallukpik, says he was a child when white men were here. They were ferried in kayaks across this river at camp about half a mile nearer sea than present camp. They have heard that formerly they used to meet the Ualinarmiut for trade, before white men ascended river. Ualinarmiut said to be excellent people, possibly Baillie Islanders, or only Cape Lyon people. They never meet the Akuliakattagmiut now. [. . .]

JUNE 2 *Started* last night 11: P. and ca. a mile NE of tents picked up half a deer of three deer killed by B. in the morning [. . .].

Camped 6 A.M. at Point Mackenzie to wait a day for promised coming of Kirkpuk and family who are going towards (but not to) Dismal Lake. It seems no one going this year to the lake. If they do not come today, we shall strike for woods up the Coppermine and return to Bloody Fall "when the mosquitoes come" which is when people are said usually to go there. [. . .]

JUNE 5 No one since Akuliakattagmiut has shown fear of our guns, but have on the contrary all urged us to use them on game (expecting to share feast, doubtless). On the whole I somewhat regret not either staying with them or proceeding along Victoria Island either North to Kanghiryuarmiut or E to [. . .] Nagyuktogmiut and beyond—in spite of our very unsuitable preparation and outfit for a woodless country. I had hoped by establishing a base at west end of Dismal Lake to make easy either sledding specimens to Fort Norman or to Langton Bay. [. . .] The first people we met in the Gulf (Basil Hall Bay?) were half starved, and told us that a little way off shore the seal would be on the ice now in number. It seems therefore there either is taboo on hunting seals crowded on ice, or else they consider themselves unable to secure them.

JUNE 6 Shall start today packing up stream ostensibly to hunt but secretly hoping to get to people eventually—those who hunt the Napaktulik summers. Taking 70 round my rifle (leave 100 here), 260 for B. and T., 100 for Pan's rifle which I shall use if my rifle burns out, ca. 100 half-size bullets, primus and ¾ lb. pounder for ptarmigan (all we have of that sort of ammunition). Taking only pocket diary as fear getting this wet. [. . .]

JUNE 13 Ekallukpik the other day took triscuit for whale meat on seeing them first. He took my light hair as a sign that I was a very old man, saying, "You and I have lived a long time, our white heads show it." [. . .]

JUNE 19 Pannigabluk says Kuwuk people hang afterbirth in a high tree. Among her own people a woman with a child on her back (i.e. less than about five years must not eat kaksrauk (black-throated and redthroated loon), if she does her child will be unable to walk or be at least a poor walker.

River fell perhaps 2 ft. last night. It is now ca. 6 ft. lower than winter ice level. Ice cakes 10 or 11 ft. thick are here over 50 yards inland one granite bar 10 or 12 ft. over water—ice water have been same 20 ft. above present level [. . .]. Pannigabluk says river was "very high" one morning when she started cooking, but when she woke us for breakfast it was down again—jam I suppose. Have seen driftwood up over 50 ft., perhaps 40. Must have been jam. [. . .]

A serious misfortune, the first of the summer (though being East of the river was against all calculations) has come in the form of Billy's illness. He is in great pain continually, his voice is feeble and a whine, his left eye is practically blind (i.e. a hand held in front of it is seen as a faint shadow) and his right, though not paining, is so dim that today when a wolf came near camp he could not see the sights to shoot. This alarmed him much, as he had supposed the sight still good as ever. The pain, he says, is most of the time in the eye itself, but always continuous "in the nerve that leads to the brain" [. . .].

Our plans are perforce modified greatly by these circumstances. I must give up hope of reaching people up river, as I suppose them somewhere about south of their winter home near Gray's Bay. We have about 10 days meat ahead, so I shall start with Tan, and 3 dogs tomorrow for a six day round trip along river and back across country, thinking it barely possible people may be near. If we do not find people (and probably though we find them, unless they give us certain information of very abundant deer elsewhere in the fall) we shall continue moving towards Dismal Lake slowly, as I have now become considerably worried about our prospects for the winter. Burdened with a sick man we must move slow. Tan, though old enough, is in fact a mere boy without enterprise and unused to hunting as he comes from a non-hunting community. I am therefore myself the only food provider, and in a strange country I feel insecure. If we reach Dismal Lake we have the chance of the fall deer migrations upon which Bear Lake Indians depend, and in case of bad luck are nearer than anywhere else to sure food supplies (on Bear Lake—whites and Indians always have plenty fish there), while we are all afraid of the seacoast in winter—none of us know ice sealing and when the natives starve almost every winter and frequently die of hunger, our chances there are not good—would become a burden there on the natives. If our fall hunt turn out well we (Tannaumirk and I) can perhaps make a fall trip to the coast to trade off our stuff for ethnological specimens, and then get to Langton Bay along the treeline—or if we must, to Bear Lake and Norman. As things have turned out, our far best plan partly from point of view of an ethnologist and of man afraid of hunger would have been to turn back at Coppermine [. . .].

JUNE 23 Home 1 A.M. and to sleep 3 A.M. [. . .] Started 8:30 A.M. and turned towards home about noon as our time is up and no fresh signs of people. Old signs are plenty, a tent ring and firewood leavings on top almost every one of the big hills along river. Hill tops average over a mile apart. Most tent sites seen on very pinnacle of hills. [. . .]

JUNE 27 Billy's eye does not pain as much as when we left, and he can see with it what pages in this diary are blank and which have writing. Other eye a little duller than before sickness—he can shoot if light is just right, but not so accurately as before—this means more waste if cartridges, as he is bound to hunt. [. . .]

Two months gone since Cape Lyon. Though hot here, travel still good along Victoria Island coast. Wish we were there, or with people somewhere. Victoria Island could easily be circumsledded from a base at (or E of preferably) Cape Parry between April 20 and July 15 [. . .]. In the inactivity here I cannot help dreaming of various such things I should like to do. I now plan to move our camp 15 or so miles S. to our deerkill and the fish lakes and then go with one man to Bloody Falls to see if people are there this year. [. . .]

JULY 8 A tolerable day in tent and slept with intermissions—14 hours. [. . .]

Eskimo habits of mind. When we first saw robin redbreasts the other day all three agreed they were kiyirk (the name for blue-jay) and fond of meat. When T. and I found first nest he said he now saw they were not kiyirk, as the eggs were different, but he is now evidently back to his former view, for he agrees that he and B. yesterday had found a kiyirk nest with three eggs. On reasoning the matter over P. concluded they might be kayotak, [. . .] not kiyirk. From this B. violently dissented, saying kayotak is not found here. The mental trait illustrated is the same with both, however. Each identifies the bird positively with a bird they knew before, though I do not know kayotak the difference between robins and jays is great. This trait is noted in diary in reference to snow geese, sulupaurak (arctic trout?) and aklaks (land bears). One must bear this trait in mind in reasoning about Eskimo prehistoric migrations on the basis of animal names, a source from which I now expect less light than I did before I understood their laxness in differentiations. (Cf. also the Nogatogmiut-Killirk, et. al, belief, that doe never fawn two years in succession). Last winter we repeatedly killed a solitary doe and fawn, when the doe carried an embryo, also often a fawn broke from a band and returned to look for its dead mother (who had embryo). This last fact Kunasluk admitted was very strange in view of the known fact that if a doe had embryo, that proved she had not fawned the past year, fawn's return probably being accidental. When single doe and fawn are together, he called that accident, too, as any two deer might be found together, that the doe had milk in her udder did not seem strange to him, perhaps because Eskimo women give milk five to seven years after bearing a child. Typically an Eskimo is very different in advancing an opinion based on his own observation, but rock-firm in adherence to views he gets from others "for people would not keep saying it if it were not so." The fact that many Eskimo here have names of white men (Nerk, [. . .] etc.), B. and T. refuse to regard as strange, as "the people here, as we used to, no doubt have white men for turñnrat (familiar spirits) and name their children from them, as we used to." When I pointed out that the name "Nerk" is characteristically non-Eskimo, they said that was natural, as turñnrat who were white men naturally spoke like white men and had white men's names. I pointed out that Arnatulk had told us the Kablunak

"Nerk" had been averse to eating seal-oil; that too B. and T. said was natural, as many turñnrat have strong food-prejudices and B. personally knew of several turñnrat that would not eat seal oil; T. contributed that Alualuk's turñnrat would not eat seal-oil. B. added that being a white turnnrak, it would be especially natural he would not eat oil. The only thing that seems to them strange is the fact that "Nerk" is said to have died. They do not know of turñnrat dying, but say that, come to think of it, it would be but natural they should die, though people naturally are not likely to become aware of this circumstance.

Both B. and T. are Christian, though B. admits he is not well posted on Christianity, T., however, is a sort of deacon, and missionary last year to Baillie Islanders.

B. the other day after singing what he "mis-knows" of the hymn "Rest beyond the River" explained that if one was Christian, when one died he would have to cross a river and could not rest at all after death till he got across, by which time he was in many cases very tired. This explained, I suppose, his misunderstanding (with additions) of his Sunday school teacher's (Port Clarence) explanations of the symbolism of the hymn. [. . .]

JULY 12 [. . .] Pannigabluk making tallow of bones. [. . .]. Sun, I think, due to set tonight, though it has been hidden at midnight by hills some time. I have never been so glad to see it come in winter as I shall be to see it set this summer, and the nights get dark and cool. [. . .]

JULY 14 [. . .] Now that deer are getting fat, none of us miss the things we haven't, except that Pannigabluk and B. will hanker for tea a while—Tannaumirk and I don't care. [. . .] Pannigabluk says inland (deer hunting) people say horns and bones get swollen when deer gets very old. [. . .]

JULY 24 Made camp at Hanbury's "Willowgrown Islands" [. . .].

Lice. Pannigabluk says "annirut" come out, as child at birth, from a man's body in at least three places she knows of, at the nipple, under the arm, and near the upper inner part of the shoulder blade. [. . .]

JULY 27 People found and our hopes therefore realized. Our old acquaintance Apattok with wife, two sons, daughter-in-law and her baby girl. They are the people we left at the island off Cape Kendall. The other three, Kirkpuk, wife, and child are said to have attempted to follow our trail (we had talked of summering together) and their whereabouts are now not known. They may, I think, but Apattok thinks not [. . .]. They say a large party, the

Kogluktogmiut, have just gone south up the small river we were on yesterday [. . .]. They are said to be now, as habitually on Imaernirk Lake, a common name among Eskimo for lakes notably larger in spring than fall. This is said to be "near" from here but no one can tell just what that means. Shall try to keep in touch with people hereafter, though we cannot stay long here as only two deer have been seen since they came here "a few days ago" (ikpuksak). These both they killed with bows, though they have kayaks; otherwise they live on squirrels and ptarmigan which they mostly shoot with bows; we cannot afford this, as our ammunition would soon run out and must therefore find deer. The camp is, I believe (though they do not know) situated about where Hanbury found "Igliki's" camp. Extensive innukcuit (deer stockades) both on lake shore and on land. [. . .]

JULY 29 Found on reaching lake people gone. Have gone "south into the woods and are lost till they make sleds and come out again." Ap. says it is hopeless to try to find them but I shall have a look around tomorrow and the following day [. . .].

JULY 30 The "lost" people of yesterday prove to be visible with our glasses from our tent about four miles off on east side the southern part of the lake. Shall move there this afternoon. The two women are very helpful to us, cutting out sinews, helping cook, sewing, etc. without our suggesting it. They use all three principal tendons of hind leg for sinew, ours only two. They and Kittegaryumiut people skin deer head by splitting from nostrils to eyes and horns, westerners cut up middle face and make Y-cut from between eyes to horns. In boiling heads, westerners cut off nose, split rest of head, and boil brain loose (if not eaten raw). Kittegaryumiut people cut off nose just below eyes instead of above nostrils, split skull but allow it to hang together so that it retains the brain in boiling; on eating it is opened oyster fashion and brain eaten as oyster from shell. I have not yet seen a head eaten here, but the bones show they split whole head, nose to foramen, without removing nose. They crack marrow bones with stone on stone without scraping off membranes; ours scrape off membrane with knife and crack with back of knife.

Moved about five miles and camped on account numerous deer seen. Got to them just in time to conflict by our scent, with deer-driving plans of resident people so neither got any. B. approached the only person we saw near, expecting to apologize, but she took fright when she saw B.'s strange clothes, and ran for home, abandoning deer-driving operations [. . .]. Later B. got five small deer, three females, two young bucks, and I two, a female and a large buck. After shooting latter I was approached by a stump-legged man (feet frozen off) wife and small girl, who said this was their buck, had wounded him this morning. I gave him the doe besides. (Ap.'s people had by this time arrived at village and news of our harmlessness were carried to hunters.) [. . .].

Caps for mosquitoes are worn by most, though Alyirk had an addition to his head that extends it well forward. Caps are usually squirrel and are tied, bonnet fashion under the chin. [. . .]

AUGUST 2 Learn that Kirkpuk who followed our trail last spring and was lost to his family (Apattok's) is camped some four or five miles S. of here, having come around by way W. end Tahierpik, where he went looking for us.

"Black flies" troublesome first time seriously yesterday. They crawl all over one inside clothing and hide here and there. [. . .]

In the afternoon a crowd of eleven (three women) including Kirkpuk came to visit us, the Kogluktogmiut. At their suggestion moved to their camp in the evening, they carrying most of our stuff. [. . .]

AUGUST 3 [. . .] People have plenty of meat and do not seem to care to hunt, expecting wonders from our rifles and modestly refraining, or else shifting burden on us. They dry meat on rails supported by stones three feet above ground. When outside is dry, it is then taken down and piled under sealskin rainshield. Very generous to us, give us more dry meat than we could eat if we ate alone and then insist on our eating with them about five times a day. Boiled meat and blood soup in morning only. Have no kayaks, left them near mouth of Coppermine.

One man at Imaernirk, the footless Aiaki, belongs to Unnumuktok (Arctic Sound—according to Hanbury) and one here belongs to Akuliakattagmiut, whom he left this spring (will return next fall).

Saucers, cups, etc. here from Mogg or Klengenberg. Some are said to be from Kanghiryuarmiut, others from Puiplirmiut. Aiaki says some of his people have rifles; one man here (Huprok) has a new house trap which, he says, came from the Kablunak to the east [. . .]: People more like western Eskimo in appearance and manners than any seen yet, striking difference from Victoria Island. Our people (P. and B.) say their speech is more easy to understand than any other and Aiaki and his wife's best of all. Thus affiliations are evidently closer in some direction other than Victoria Island. [. . .]

AUGUST 4 Suddenly without any foreknowledge of any of us, the camp broke up about noon to move south (compass) eventually to woods which I suppose six or eight miles off in that direction. This is evidently reason why they have not hunted recently, as they are heavy with meat for moving. One family—Natjinna, wife, boy of eight, girl of two, decided to come with us S.W.(compass) where we hope to cache meat for winter. Very glad of their company as one family is about as good for my ethnological purposes as many, for the present. Moved our camp ca. 4 mile SW (camp) to our deer kill of yesterday. [. . .] Clear variable airs, hot.

AUGUST 5 Moved to woods beside small lake. Musk-oxen are said to frequent the district to N. and W. of us along Dease River, which has no Eskimo name, other than Imaernirk River. The first musk-ox signs (of recent years) we saw along E. side of Imaernirk, last winter's dung abundant. [. . .] Watched with glasses native hunt—2 bucks. [. . .]. Not space to describe hunt. [. . .]

AUGUST 7 [. . .] B. hunted west with no success. Apattok, son, and son-in-law and the three families moved to us today. Say Huprok killed two large bucks in one day recently, several other deer killed.

AUGUST 8 Natjinna's and Uluxsrak's (Akuliakattagmiut) family moved on farther S. today and we have only Apattok's family. Imaernirk is abandoned, all people now S.E. and S. of us. Said to be people scattered here and there all the way to the coast, as well as E. of the Coppermine. [. . .]

AUGUST 9 People here evidently don't know much about Indians as they call the tipee frames occasionally found Kablunak tent-frames. Natjinna and others evidently fell in with Melville-Hornby party (about four miles S. of our present camp) for they tell of meeting six (some say eight) white men there two years ago, and Nat. has a shawl ax, file and other things from them. All refuse to believe that any of this party were Indians, though there can hardly have been more than four white men, and the woman must certainly have been an Indian. Have been trying to teach people to eat akpek. Most or all the men and children have tried and some like them. Most of the women refuse to taste them even, and those who taste do not like them. About the only berry they seem to eat is a small black one growing on a low shrub that resembles an evergreen, these berries none of us like, though I eat them when brought me as presents by the children. The name "akpek" seems known to all and some, but not all know an "akpek" by sight. The Akuliakattagmiut couple say they never saw an akpek before, but I think that is merely because they do not pay attention as the Akuliakattagmiut hunt close up to Tahierpik and the woods occasionally. [. . .]

AUGUST 10 Hunted S., saw over twenty deer, three bucks of which shot two, half inch back fat both. B. returned [. . .]. Natjinna and Uluxsrak's families returned. N.'s baby sick, swollen feet, and other parts of body, ears, etc. [. . .]

Billy killed five deer while with Huprok's people eight or ten miles S.E. of here. From there he saw Imarryuak (which is Bear Lake, I suppose) from a hilltop. Huprok told him that once when he was a boy (now thirty-five) his people hunted for some time along the shore, but fled on hearing shooting, which they attributed to Indians. There are only four men (three women) in Huprok's party now, all scattered in groups of one and two families, some gone back, some forward or E. Apattok's family moved back to Imaernirk.

AUGUST 11 [. . .]. Trees (where I found red currants the other day). Some 60 or 80 deer in sight from here—others went after them but I took Pannigabluk and dogs to meat of one of yesterday's bucks before starting to hunt and deer mostly gone when I got there. [. . .]

AUGUST 13 Moved camp SE 3 miles to top of hill where Eskimos habitually camp—no wood but good view of ground frequented by deer. [. . .]

The Unnumuktok woman (wife of footless Aiaki) told Pannigabluk wonderful stories the other day of the Pallirmiut, from whom they get guns and other white men's wares. These Pallirmiut come overland from a country near which white men have big houses. They kill so many deer en route north that they bring sealskin bags full of deer marrow. Their women use a whole deerskin for their hoods, which hang down to the ankles. Only a few of the Umin. have guns as yet, but they have from the Pailirmiut cooking pots in which they cook a whole deer at once. [. . .]

AUGUST 22 After traveling about two miles saw Indians at a distance, three families, one of them man who was with Melville-Hornby on Melville River two years ago. Speaks a little English, says Hornby has house N.E. corner of Bear Lake close to our route yesterday. Hornby is coming back soon, he says, with boatload trade and had sent this man to try find Huskies and establish relations. I am sorry to see trade begin but it can evidently not be long staved off and I am glad to see it fall to Hornby of all those who seek it, I am therefore at Hornby's urgent request (through the

Indian) undertaking to bring them together and took the three men this evening to the next Husky camp about five miles N. and eight from Bear Lake. [. . .]

AUGUST 23 As mutual amities Eskimo and Indians danced; very like in song, loose, stooping attitude, gestures, step, almost as like or quite like Eskimo of Mackenzie River and Coppermine. Six Eskimo to visit Indian camp on condition I go too as interpreter and guarantor. Indians last night and Eskimo today by my request in first case and Indian request in later, left guns and bows respectively at a distance. Indians last night refused to sleep till we lay down on each side the three as sort of guard. Very amicable towards last today. Indian insists on making many presents contrary to my advice. Bought three Indian dogs from Eskimo for two knives and an old coat. Ulus (iron) for plates and jack knives, snow knife for poor butcher knife. [. . .]

Indians Catholic and swear in French. Brought pictures of Virgin, etc. for presents (to be worn over right breast) and message from Bishop he would build mission at Bear Lake if Eskimo good. Indians say winter time they use drum in dance, and from gesture today the dancer carries and beats it Eskimo style. [. . .]

AUGUST 25 Indians moved to habitual camping place of Jim; two miles west. [. . .] On invitation took some meat to Indians to be dried in tipee. [. . .]

Jim's father killed by bull moose, hooked under shoulder blade. Was on trip to mountain Indians to trade tobacco, etc. for the company. Caribou heads never boiled, roasted by fire with tongue in, kept rotating till all baked but nose, then placed on plate with nose to fire a few minutes, then jaws opened and if underdone, placed gaping toward fire. Bear Lake people, he says, do not eat boiled meat if least bit rare, but eat slightly rare roasts, i.e. tongue of roast head. Half-dry and dry tongues boiled, dry meat usually pounded before eating. Lines of braided deerskin, flat, half-inch wide. In winter travel always, tent at night, do not sleep by fires, as the Cree. Use old tent frames which are numerous on all usual routes of travel and on favorite hunting grounds. Slept with Indians. [. . .]

AUGUST 27 [. . .] Fort Rae ("Jim Hislop place") is called seven sleeps from S. side Bear Lake and some Bear Lake people occasionally go there Christmas. Fishers (no deer) called "sometimes hungry" at head Bear River, but "people never hungry" east of Lease or along E. shore Bear

Lake. In winter Jim says much gambling (song, drum, sticks in closed hands, à la Cree). Use head straps in packing. In cooking, head cut as at Kittegaryumiut, and hind leg dismembered similarly. Udder and kidneys usually roasted, liver "not liked," (perhaps as Loucheux, think it poisonous, or have it taboo). Thin, cut meat dries in a day, then placed in pile under pillows fear of dogs. When "plenty" will be cached on a rack. If legs of rack of stout logs wolverines will not climb, they say. [. . .]

AUGUST 28 Brought to Indian camp most of our meat from creek bottom N. a mile. Wolverine had stolen from our rack one backfat and some meat. Indians Catholic service; say do not hunt Sundays, but went for meat, Jim Hislop saw two moose, one large, in comparatively woodless country. [. . .]

AUGUST 29 Built rack for our meat near Indian camp and started homeward along treeline [. . .] making this long curve to look for Hornby or someone who has seen him. Camped where valley curves eastward, beginning of our branch of the Dease. [. . .]

AUGUST 30 [. . .] Home before sundown. Met party about twenty Eskimo going west to camp near our sleeping place of last night. No deer east, they said; a few families gone seaward to fish along Coppermine. Natjinna and Uluxsrak's families gone, took without asking three quarters of our meat, about eight caribou, and cached it by their future sled-making place. Took, too, about twenty deer sinews and two deerskins of ours without permission. An old woman Aialuk, left by the food caches. Many have cached meat at sled-making place. This woman had one breast frozen off last winter and it is tied with a string Pannigabluk says. [. . .]

The Indians learned to hum B.'s most complicated song (Pihjuulirktuna or puna?), after hearing it two or three times. B. and T. learned this at Akuliakattak and it took them longer it seems to me. Evidently songs of Eskimo not essentially different from Indians. I don't think a white man could learn it in hearing it twenty times. [. . .]

AUGUST 31 [. . .] Pannigabluk says Kagmalit habitually use water pails and cooking pots as receptacles for urine. [. . .]

SEPTEMBER 6 [. . .] Pannigabluk says Nogatogmiut, Killirk and Kuwok people, and perhaps others cooked mountain sheep and caribou in different pots on different fireplaces when cooked at same time. If cooked at successive times, the pot, if they had only one, was carefully washed with water between times. Some people never ate caribou and sheep the same meal, others ate both together. Women did not eat sheep of any of the four legs or front of the rear line of the shoulder blades. If they did, their husbands would become sick "inside" (i.e. lungs, liver, stomach, etc.). Prohibition did not apply to women past childbearing. Of the shoulder vertebrae, the women might eat the meat above the line of the ribs, but not the fat and meat facing into the thorac cavity (below the rib line). People that ate sheep and caribou same meal, washed hands with water between the two courses.

Old men, and they only, often wore pants same style as women, socks and pants one piece. This "because they had ceased to make long journeys." [. . .]

SEPTEMBER 13 Hunted N. and shot 4 bulls ca. 5 miles from camp. Soon after spied [. . .] a mile NW of deerkill and found there Melville and Hornby's camp. This was a meeting to which I had been long looking forward—since meeting Jimmy late in August. [. . .] B. had failed to come home owing to exploding about pound wet powder he was drying while smoking a pipe. His whole face badly burned and both eyes so swollen closed that one cannot tell if his good eye was seriously injured or not. [. . .]

Got the first news since May 12, 1909—King Edward dead, flying accomplished, English channel [. . .], Peary-Cook dispute (which all of us have discounted in advance), Rasmussen's proposed expedition to Eskimos, Mark Twain dead and Harriman had heard by police from Herschel that Anderson and I had both left the Arctic—gone home (by whaler, presumably). [. . .]

SEPTEMBER 17 Hornby and I to his camp-cache at last rapid, Dease River. Hodgson and family there, building log house. Lives in combination tipee and wall tent. Hodgson says at Peel River Eskimo always carried knives in hand all day, in store trading, etc., as late as 1896. In 1885 Indians between Porcupine and Yukon River usually hunted moose with bows (though they had guns) and a few still wore the old type clothes (pants and socks in one piece like Eskimo women) though had cloth. Loucheux more afraid of Eskimo than vice-versa, as it is here at Bear Lake now. [. . .]

Very marked break in language between Loucheux and Good Hope but nowhere else till one comes to Cree to south. No great difference from Loucheux down Yukon as Hodgson knows. Diary book given me by Melv.

and another by Hodgson so I can write more freely than before—no more fear of paper famine. [. . .]

SEPTEMBER 25 At Hodgson's. At Trout Lake, eight days west from Providence, are twenty-five or less hunters who trade alternately at Providence, Vermillion, or Liard. They are pagans. They come, some of them, every year about Christmas to Providence. They are called more enterprising than any others who trade at Providence. They speak a dialect of Slavey. They live in a good game country. They do not visit other Indians, nor do families of Christian Indians hunt among them for a year's visit, as other groups do with each other. Women never come to the trading posts. Occasionally a few come in canoes down Beaver River twenty-five or thirty miles S. of Providence and go home up Yellow Knife, about eighty miles, north of Providence. This is outlet of Beaver Lake. [. . .]

SEPTEMBER 27 Pannigabluk has been told that the people who hunt here to the woods every year make various articles of wood, beyond what they need, for trade to the Puiplirmiut. [. . .]

SEPTEMBER 28 Pannigabluk relates that Noatak, Kuwok, Kangianik, Kagmalit and affiliated people used to use in summer when traveling by umiak or camped on streams, a tent resembling an Indian tipee. It was a rectangular pyramid with only the four corner sticks meeting at the apex. A foot or two below apex was a hoop much like the frame of an Eskimo drum. To this there were (fastened) willows (large number) running to the ground. Some four feet above the floor four crossbars made a rectangle strengthening the corner posts and willows. The largest tents were about the size of Bear Lake tipees (36 caribou skins). There seldom was cooking done inside and the vent in the top was for smoke used in smudging mosquitoes. Meat, clothes wet from rain, etc. were sometimes dried in tents, a fire being then used. [. . .]

Dog language. Dogs are never addressed imperatively in first person, always in third. Lie down, akuvilli (let him lie down), not akuvittin (you lie down). A dog is forbidden to do a thing by words which, if literally translated (or if applied to a man) tell him to do it. Uyoriun, don't fight with him (literally "fight him"); nerkiksran parkittutin—you have found something you must not eat (literally "you have found something meant for you to eat"). Ki, ki, kilamik (literally, come, hurry up!) is often used by my Eskimo to dogs who will not stand still when their pack is being fixed. It really equals our "be quiet."

SEPTEMBER 29 P. relates: The irrigak is a turñnrat that lives in the woods. They are very numerous in some localities. She has never had a front view of one, but has seen one walking away from her. It looked much like a man and was about as tall. It had a coat on, probably of squirrel skin, and it was so torn there were only shreds left, and P. could see the bare back and ribs (kattigak). It had no hair, but so far as she could see skin like a man. It is a very troublesome turñnrat in that it steals squirrels and ptarmigan from peoples' snares and traps. She has had it steal squirrels from her snares. The squirrel was always replaced by a little earth, moss, or grass; that's how she knew the irrigak had been there (and that it was not merely a case of the squirrel having escaped). B. contributes that once he was out snaring ptarmigan with an old man. They got very few. The old man said that was no wonder as they were in a locality infested by irrigaks. B. pointed out he had seen no strange tracks in the fresh snow. Naturally not, the old man said, for it is one of the characters of an irrigak that it walks without touching the ground. When seen they seem to be walking on ground, but as a matter of fact their feet never come nearer than about six inches from the surface of the ground or snow. B. has never seen one.

B. says his people (when on the seacoast) sometimes used to live in tipee-shaped houses made entirely of driftwood. If big, the sticks were split, but most of the sticks round. They were fitted closely together. At Kittegaryumiut T. says rough houses were used such as I have seen with big spaces between logs and used to smoke-dry fish. People sat in these by the fire, but had a regular tent besides.

The Copper Eskimo have repeatedly told me the cheap butcher knives I brought for trade are fine knives because they bend easily. My own knife none of them care for because it will not bend. Hodgson says the Porcupine and Yukon Indians had exactly the same test for the goodness of a knife. At Barrow and Mackenzie, now at least, they will not have a knife if it bends. They don't like anything lighter than a Wilson nine-inch blade (at Barrow at least), which they cut down with a file to seven inch drawing. [. . .]

T. says that while camped on the hill on the river bank above (91 mile S.) our present camp the Eskimo sometimes killed as many as four deer in one day per man, i.e., two or three men out of eight or nine hunters frequently reported three or four deer killed that day when they came home at night. Some days no one hunted. [. . .]

Have abundant paper now and promise of more, so shall when time allows—make fuller diary entries than heretofore, and include many things I have been habitually omitting. [. . .]

Peary-Cook: M-H. gave me September 1904 copy of manuscript with Greely's "Discoverer of the North Pole." From this, and from what M.-H. tell from the papers, there has evidently happened exactly what all of us thought would happen when it became known Cook had gone north. That hardly anyone doubted Cook would come back claiming the Pole was a source of worry to all the better-informed of Peary's friends then, and even isolated as I am here it worries me considerably to find our fears come true. I don't know Cook, and what I know of him (though chiefly to his detriment) is all hearsay largely from Alaska and Seattle (Mt. McKinlay); I know Peary slightly, like him well, and know nothing to his serious detriment. But my concern is hardly a personal one, nevertheless, but regret that a man of worth and much accomplished good work should be placed in Peary's position. [. . .] As for Cook's heroism and sufferings (a la Greely)—and Peary's for that matter—those who know anything know that's chiefly rot. What Peary deserves credit for is not the mere achievement of the Pole, but consistency and persistence through a quarter century of hard labor under trying conditions; what Cook deserves credit for, if anything, is waiting till just the right moment to step in and snatch deftly the wages of another man's toil when that man's work was done and his payday had at last come.

Though it is not unreasonable to hope that Ambron's work and my own will advance knowledge along our lines as much as Peary's has along his, we are nevertheless fortunately inconspicuous enough not to precipitate any such unpleasant things as Cook and Peary have done. Melville tells me of a Danish Expedition to the Perry Islands, but if they gain laurels they will not be stolen from us, though they are entering our field, for we are having our chance and shall retain what honours we earn and deserve. [. . .]

OCTOBER 2 Yesterday to the sled-making place, expecting to find Huprok, but found instead Nirak Talik's crowd, five families in three tents. Huprok, they said had started north two sleeps before we came, carrying their sleds on their backs. [. . .]

OCTOBER 8 [. . .] Beliefs. Pannigabluk told some time ago that "Kadzom nunani inopta," (the winter I was at Kittegaryuit, when several families in the mountains south of Shingle Point had to retreat on Rampart House where Mr. Kadzow outfitted them, the same families whom I visited in October, 1906), they at one time had nothing to eat but a little caribou fat. They used to make tea, of which they had plenty, and then boil over the steeped tea leaves in a little water and add the grease (much as we did with seal oil in December, 1909). Kunaslik and his son Pikalu alone would not eat this mess for the missionary had told them not to eat tea leaves. When taxed with having eaten tea leaves before, they said that was before they were told by the missionaries not to. I asked Pannigabluk why the rest of them ate tea leaves when they knew this from Kunaslik. She seemed to think the question silly and replied shortly that it was all right for them to eat the tea because none of them had ever been forbidden to do so (i.e., K. and P. took the missionary's simple statement that the tea liquor only was meant for consumption, to be a personal taboo inflicted on them individually by the missionary and having no force for anyone else. In December 1909, when we were hungry, Kunaslik was the only one of our party who did not eat tea leaves soaked in oil, but took the oil "straight." I did not attach significance to this then, but understand it now).

Pannigabluk also tells that it is dangerous to leave a sleeping child alone in a house, even for a moment. She has known one case. One spring two large parties had met to dance and trade, the one Kuwormiut, the other Indians. An Indian mother, who probably did not know of this danger, was dancing when she heard her baby begin to cry. She went to it, gave it the breast and it soon fell asleep. A little while later she went out to get some meat from a stage at the tent door. She was only gone a few moments, but when she came back the child was missing. The people stopped dancing and searched all day but found no signs of the child. It was not old enough to walk, besides no one had entered or left the tent by the door, as the mother had her eye on the door all the time (as Indians usually do fearing dogs). The people all agreed the child had gone up to the sky to Jesus because of being left alone. Both Indians and Eskimo were Christians. [. . .]

OCTOBER 14 Pannigabluk says of mother who lost child, noted above, that it happened before she was born, but she knew personally several people who had been present at the dance. Her own mother was one of these. People did not know until this occurrence that it was dangerous to leave a sleeping child alone, but since then they have known it.

Tannaumirk says Kittegaryumiut had no horn dippers, either musk-ox or sheep, except spoons for scooping ice out of holes in setting nets, etc. These were usually musk-ox, sometimes deer horn or even wood. Never used "snowshoe-like" type I have seen among Kuwok, Nogatogmiut, etc. Mrs. Hodgson tells that when she was a little girl at Fort Norman her father used to spend all summer with the Company's scows and she lived with her uncle (mother's brother). Each group then kept very strictly to their own hunting grounds and only in extreme need followed game into a neighbor's territory. Once her uncle, she does not know why, decided to hunt farther west than usual. Though they were near the western boundary of their proper district they went three short days' marches farther west. On the third day they found a stage with dry meat and fish and plenty of baskets and stones from which they inferred the owners had no kettles and boiled their meat in baskets with hot stones. They saw no iron at all, although there was plenty of household gear. They were all thoroughly frightened, and immediately turned back, but by a different way from the one they had come. On the march children were usually allowed to play in the rear of the party and to straggle along as they pleased. In this case they were not allowed to play at all and were cautioned to silence; on the retreat they walked ahead, instead of behind, the stoutest bringing up the rear. They traveled far into the night, and finally camped without a fire and without chopping or making any noise. The dogs were all tied and each fed more than usual so they would not howl. Long before sunrise they again broke camp and marched till dark, when they first made fire on reaching their own ground. The Loucheux, she says, seemed to be a bit freer than the rest in their wandering. In recent years none seem to fear visiting their neighbors or wandering about freely except to the northeast of Bear Lake where there is danger of falling in with Eskimo. [. . .]

OCTOBER 17 This diary forgotten at Melv. Hornby Friday, October 7 when I left them to go home. Slept at Hodgson's and home October 8. [. . .]

OCTOBER 21 24 pages of report to museum and half a dozen letters finished. Ice does not yet bear a man on bay behind island here—no ice outside island. [. . .]

Animal heads. (Hodgson tells of all Indians of the Arctic) do not like to allow animal heads taken out of country—fear scarcity of animals.

OCTOBER 22 [. . .] Melville tells that until Maccallum started a crusade against it, Bear Lake women had separate (usually brush) huts at time of monthly periods. No woman may step over a fish net or go over one in a canoe. It brings bad luck to the owner of the net. A man who carried a deerhead on his back must not walk along the trail, must walk on the side of the trail. If a bearskin is carried across Bear Lake it spoils the fishing in the lake. This applies to sleds; M. does not know if it applies to a canoe. Woman during menses must not walk in the trail. When a boat passes a spot where an Indian has been drowned, they toss a little tea and tobacco into the water. A priest at Fort Good Hope once caught and kept a live caribou, since then there are no caribou at Good Hope. [. . .]

OCTOBER 23 *Melville:* When wind on the lake is too strong for fishing or for hauling, a woman who has a child at breast goes out-doors and squeezes her breast so as to send a squirt of milk up into the air. This stops the wind, though not always promptly nor on the first attempt. [. . .]

OCTOBER 31 [. . .] *Careful observation of nature:* T. told me today that hares have large fore paws and small hind ones, and showed me hare tracks to prove it. The tracks [. . .] prove T.'s contention. He must have seen a good many dead hares (we killed two last spring) and a good many hundred dead rabbits.

Windows. T. tells Kittegaryumiut never used ugrug or beluga intestines for windows, used by preference the gullets of gulls. P. says she has seen at Baillie Islands gullets of the various loons in use, but if these were not, they used fish skins of anoxlirk, ekaluakpuk, and others.

Snares and hooks both used at Kittegaryumiut to catch gulls. Snares for feet set in a roofless house that had meat bait in middle of floor. Hooks always set in water.

NOVEMBER 1 T. back to fish lake with pack dogs—deerfat, skins, etc. I to build cache here. [. . .]

Spirits. While alone the other day P. heard pounding in the woods north of camp. She took this for Indians camped near and chopping wood. Later, she heard the noise from all sides as if a man had walked slowly in a circle a hundred yards outside our camp, pounding the trees with a rod as he went. There were no tracks so Pannigabluk knows they were turñnrat. [. . .]

NOVEMBER 10 Started 8:55 A. [. . .]. Course 264° for a conical peak just east of a "mountain" [. . .].

Beliefs. Eskimo as elsewhere noted, from Point Barrow to Baillie at least, believe that in winter smokeless powder is "not strong" and will use only black powder guns if they can, 38–65 and 40–82 preferred. Bear Lake Indians uniformly believe that a black powder bullet "gets cold" in winter soon after leaving the barrel, that great speed is necessary so bullet may reach its mark before it "loses speed through getting cold." 38–55 are said to be the worst and it is claimed that in very cold weather the bullet barely penetrates the skin of a caribou at fifty yards. 45–90 guns are said to be the best of the black-powder kind. This caliber can hardly be given away now to Eskimo.

Western Eskimo (Pannigabluk, Billy) believe eating a caribou windpipe, whose rings have not been split, will kill a dog. I have seen B. split windpipes of small animals before feeding to dogs. Bear Lake people say there is no danger in windpipes but ribs are deadly and must not be fed dogs. In every camp one sees long bundles of ribs hung up out of reach of dogs. This belief is unknown to Eskimo, and windpipe belief is unknown to Tannaumirk. [. . .]

NOVEMBER 17 Started 8:40, camped 4:30 on east side river. [. . .] If only we knew that Anderson is where I asked him to be—which he will be if he has been able to make it—we might now hope to get to him in three days. Dogs getting slower and weaker daily and so are we. [. . .]

Takes me some effort of will to write much. [. . .]

Started 5:30 A., camped 4:30. Short distance partly due to Indian's insisting on "boiling the kettle" during the morning—at sunrise the dogs were yet going well. He seems to think it a great hardship to go without fire and tea for over four hours. [. . .]

On account of the many "human uncertainties" about Anderson's whereabouts, I am becoming badly worried. If he is not in the river we shall have a "run for our money" or for our lives, rather, if the scarcity of game continues. The nearest sure source of relief is the Eskimo settlement at Baillie Islands, about 15 days distant as we are travelling now, if we follow the river as we practically have to do on account of the Indian who has neither the clothes nor the disposition to fit him for the open coast. [. . .]

NOVEMBER 22 Billy came home unsuccessful late last night. To double our chances of deer I had the Indian take the two sleds on down the river and hunted myself the E side while B. hunted the W. Regret to give up the survey, but our dogs have now been 5 days on a single caribou skin and we have no more skin except our clothes. We have ourselves been five days on a ration of two tablespoonfuls twice a day of flour each, and ⅛ lb. tallow each per day. I don't know how the others felt, but I have felt continual nausea the last three days and getting depressed and a little weak.

B. had no luck today, and it fell to me to save the situation temporarily by killing one of a band of four deer—saw three "bands" of one, seven and four respectively. Could have killed all four with my rifle but misjudged distances for the black-powder gun. Could also have killed deer I badly wounded [. . .]. As all pretty hungry I chose to pack home 50 lbs. meat. Got home about midnight. Dogs had gone well and Indian had made 12 or 14 miles, so I had a tiresome journey home.

Lost my prismatic compass today, the property of the Geological Survey. The case had been buckled too loosely and the compass fell out doubtless when I was running after deer. Did not notice the loss till night, and unfortunately the snow is drifting so my trail can not be followed tomorrow. I shall have to make with a pocket compass [. . .] likely to lead to errors. I hope the survey will consider the bearings I have set down from their instrument to be worth the price of it. [. . .]

NOVEMBER 23 I do not remember feeling so disappointed as [. . .] today—there are no traces of Dr. Anderson, others of our party, or any people whatever in the river. [. . .] Caribou are numerous and have been for some time past, so it is not lack of game that has kept Anderson away. Something has gone wrong, it is beyond me to tell what. I feel more blue than ever in my three years up here. This has been a hard trip for all of us, men and dogs and has accomplished the last of the things we promised to try to do—the tracing through the greater part of its course of one of the larger rivers of Canada—and are here where we had a right to expect at least a camp stocked with deermeat to find no one, and the caribou season almost over for this section of the country. We can do but one thing—camp here and try to dry enough meat to take us back to Bear Lake. The Indian dares not go to "Salt Water" and I am none too anxious to take him, as neither he nor his short haired dogs would be suited for the coast. [. . .]

Placed notes for Anderson at our old house and at Cool Creek, came back along east bank of river. [. . .]

Today B. brought home meat of these two deer. When he came home last night he told us he had killed the deer SE of camp, that it would take more than a day to get the meat, and about 5 miles up stream from here—at a small creek we know. [. . .] He had struck his homecoming trail of yesterday and was following it. It turned out finally that he had killed the deer about 5 miles from camp, 4 miles *down stream* and had been this badly lost though yesterday was fairly clear. This, in my experience, is typical enough of Eskimos, though they are commonly supposed to have "a compass in their heads."[. . .]

NOVEMBER 26 B. and Indian making cache for meat, icing broken toboggan, etc. [. . .].

My work up here, I have been fond of asserting, entails few hardships. But just now it is pretty hard work, and has often been so these three years. To be five or six miles from camp every morning at daybreak and about that far from home at the last daylight, to carry home heavy loads over rocky ground when successful and still heavier loads of disappointment when unsuccessful—this makes a monotonous—and a trying life. The continual nervous strain of a hand-to-mouth existence, where there is not even the shelter of a poorhouse in case of failure, has a telling and cumulative effect. Without in the least relinquishing my hopes of many more years of arctic work, I continually feel more strongly the desire to be so well equipped in future that I shall have at least a year's supply of food somewhere awaiting me to tide me over a season of failure. Just *knowing* of such a reserve if one never had the comfort of a month feel of it to vary one's diet would lessen by half the strain of the winter. This is a hard country for a hungry man. [. . .]

NOVEMBER 27 Started down river again: broke camp about noon and stopped at faint day light about 2 miles N. of last year's home. It feels queer to be back to the old place and find not a track or trace of humans. I feel unreasonably resentful, or rather hurt, at someone, I don't know whom, who is responsible for this absence of welcoming friends.

The Indian peevish and whining his last grievance that he has had to do "women's work" (cut up meat to dry) though it was at his own suggestion he stayed at home to do it while we hunted. It would be little use for him to hunt anyway—his eyes are poor and his glasses poor, and his step too slow to take him in daylight far enough from the river to have chance of game—there are almost no tracks less than 5 miles E of the river. [. . .]

NOVEMBER 30 [. . .] Last winter (1909–10) was the first when starvation was general among Good Hope Indians on account of failure of caribou (i.e. in the district mapped as the basins of River Macfarlane and River la Roncière) (Johnnie). [. . .]

When Johnnie some fifteen years ago crossed the mountains west from Simpson toward Telegraph Creek (just after Christmas) there was plenty game, chiefly moose, except for three days crossing the crest of the mountains, where there are no sticks. Game chiefly moose.

Bear Lake people, for crossing the lake in winter, wear caribou skin pants with hair in à la Western Eskimo.

Bull caribou skin in the fall is stronger than moose skin for shoes (Johnnie). Billy's grandmother remembered the last fight between the Kaviaragmiut and the Kohudlit of East Cape. She was so old when B. was a boy that "her skin was not like human skin, but hard and black," and "she had almost come to nothing" (our "shriveled-up" nunupiuriktok). B. found some arrows of the battlefields. The East Cape ones were of iron and had a very slender shank just below the head, but shafts otherwise about size of Eskimo arrows. [. . .]

DECEMBER 3 Langton Bay. Arrived about 1 P.M. today. Our last night's camp proved to have been about 5 miles true south from Whalemen's Harbor and we struck the brow of the Melville range 3 miles too far west—at our Aklak River of last year. The wind blew a terrific gale behind us down the mountain [. . .]. On the sea ice we at once found sled tracks not older than a week or two, and a mile from the Harbor came upon fresh tracks—evidently of people tending traps today. Tracks were large and small Eskimo size, but later saw larger track which B. and I agreed was Anderson's. This was almost too good to be true—the best I hoped for was a letter telling where to find him, for Whalemen's Harbor is a place without native resources—game, fish or firewood. A half mile west of the Harbor we came upon Palaiyak with a fox on his back and later caught up to Anderson and Ilavinirk coming home from traps. [. . .] Capt. Bodfish had carried Dr. Anderson from Herschel Island and Dr. Anderson spent the following two weeks at Capt. Wolki. [. . .] Dr. Anderson with our entire outfit was landed at the Harbour August 27, and September 9 he was joined by our Eskimos Ilavinirk and family who had been hunting caribou for skins for clothing all summer. He had secured 47 good summer skins and had dried 500 or 600 pounds of meat (on weight) and had over 300 pounds of fat. Dr. Anderson had while yet alone discovered the carcass aground and had killed a polar bear on it and made a specimen of the skin. Since this time (including this bear) four polar bears, one barren ground bear, five wolves, and about 50 white foxes (six of these caught by Anderson and skinned for specimens, as well as the brown bear, a cub bear killed by Ilavinirk in the spring, the polar bear and two red foxes).

There has been no sickness this summer, and there is none now. Everything has gone better than usual with us and everything looks well. The only discouraging thing is that the reports of our work received by the Museum up to their writing us in May (13) 1910 lead them to believe that in spite of our "earnest and energetic" efforts, which they don't doubt, the results do not seem to be as large as they could get in other fields with a similar expenditure, and they ask us to come out "as soon as possible," which meant this past summer. Anderson very generously wrote them to the effect that he could not possibly abandon all the things I relied on his doing while I was still in an unknown place and unknown circumstances in the east and no one could tell when or how I might come back. It appears now that we might have been in a very bad plight indeed had we found no one here, even with no caribou I have every confidence all three of us would have reached Langton Bay alive, but I doubt our working Baillie Islands from here with the Indian on our hands, for he is a baby, and hard to tend, in bad weather. [. . .]

DECEMBER 4 Spent last night till 2: A talking with Anderson and the rest of the night writing report of our Horton River trip to the Geological Survey. Today have written a personal letter and spent the rest of the day over plans with Anderson. We have decided as follows: Billy, the Indian, Anderson, and I will start for Dease River so soon as our dogs are rested up a bit (perhaps a week—they are very thin and weak). We will make there the best zoological collection we can—caribou, wolves, foxes and wolverines, etc. We will at the same time make the best possible collection of ethnological things, and send all with Melville, Hornby and Hodgson. We will then come up here along the coast in the spring in time for my spending the spring in archaeological work on the Parry Peninsula [. . .]. If we can then get our stuff aboard ship we shall try to go out with our collections. [. . .]

DECEMBER 7 Writing letter, etc. Talked with Anderson about future. We agree it would be unwise to abandon the fine outfit we have—which is ample for 2 years, without using it. With such an outfit and the whale for light and food one can do good work here free from the anxiety for food that has been constant up to now. Am writing [. . .] offering to stay another year and urging this point.

DECEMBER 8 [. . .] *Eskimo and Indian relations:* Ilavinirk says that at the Yukon mouth Indians and Eskimo had a sort of jargon for talking together [. . .]. People [. . .] on upper branches of Colville [. . .] could talk with [. . .] Indians pretty well. [. . .]

DECEMBER 18 [. . .] Apparently I keep underestimating distances. Sometimes I pace them, allowing 2000 paces to the mile and then I find my previous estimates low. [. . .]

DECEMBER 21 Anderson lost ink bottle today, but a little ink in fountain pen. [. . .]

DECEMBER 29 Dogrib feast. Johnny says that "when Dogrib Rae Indians make a big feast for plenty people to eat," they take a small piece of meat, fat pemmican, bread, and any other food they are about to eat, then a cup is taken and a little grease and bouillon is skimmed off the top of the pot in which the meat was boiled. This cupful is spilled into the fire and then are thrown in the pieces of meat, pemmican, etc. This must be done before anyone starts to eat. "This is Dogrib fashion; Bear Lake don't do like that." [. . .]

1911

JANUARY 2 Started 7:00 A. camped 2:05 P. east bank river. [. . .] Hills getting a little lower, [. . .] rock and crops rarely [. . .]. Several places saw tracks of the *three* bears female two cubs I hunted several days ago. [. . .]

JANUARY 5 *Billy* tells: In the neighbourhood of Cape P[. . .], both at the coast and inland, grass is worn both summer and winter but never inside the stocking—always between sock and boot. He never heard of any sort of hair being used to take place of grass [. . .]. The wearing of grass insoles was [. . .] not learnt from the Lapps who came with the reindeer. The Lapp custom differs in that no sock is worn.

The Lapps have all left Alaska so far as B. knows, except one who married an Eskimo woman [. . .]. This man has no reindeer, but is nevertheless well off. He came a young man but nevertheless speaks Eskimo poorly, at any rate as to pronunciation. All the other Lapps had Lapp wives. [. . .]

JANUARY 21 Old Tom's wife and daughter refuse today to let me measure their heads. Melville says he has often tried but never been able to get a photograph of the daughter and took the mother when she did not know what was being done. [. . .]

JANUARY 22 [. . .] *Ideas of Eskimo and Indians:* The Eskimo generally (Tannaumirk, Pannigabluk, the Coppermine people, and generally all Eskimo I have known—Billy is an exception, now at least—do not seem to understand that caribou ever frequent the woods, or can be expected there. They seem to think if the animals are in the woods it is accidental, they are passing through etc., while the barren is their natural habitat. Tan, last summer asserted they were never found in large numbers but on the seacoast—not even on inland barrens. This was controverted by Pannigabluk whose experience is that of the inland barrens (upper Colville). If caribou *are* in the woods, they seem to think it next to impossible to find them, except accidentally. In the thick wood west of Horton river the fall 1909 I tried vainly to get Billy to follow, or to follow with me, fresh caribou trails—he went systematically from high hill to high hill and plied the spyglass—which was of practically no use, as only rare spots are bare of trees.

This and following entries made at various dating to fill up vacant pages of this diary and so save space in current one. The Indians, conversely, think the caribou are on the barrens only in summer and in mild weather in winter coming to the woods for shelter in bad weather (evidently the Indians have here put themselves in the place, expecting caribou would behave as Indians would). [. . .] Telling of "Caribou Point" Johnny said: "The caribou that come there stay while the weather is cold; the woods are *thick* there" (underscore indicates how he emphasized the wood). In telling about how he fared when last from Bell's party he said: "I saw plenty caribou that day but I could not kill any—there were no trees." (This by no means shows that Indians never kill caribou in the open, but that they consider absence of trees a sufficient excuse for not getting in range and it is, with their hunting methods for they walk straight at the deer, upright and always dressed in funeral black.) [. . .]

My own opinion is that neither Eskimo nor Indians have a reasoned and reasonable theory of the movements of caribou, nor only based on sufficient (more than over sided) observation. Neither seems to account rationally [. . .] for the whereabouts of caribou when they do not actually see them—a sort of mystical or miracle-postulating view they have instead (as also neither of them have an idea that caribou lessen by being killed in great numbers, both say of the scarcity of caribou: "they have gone away to some other place"). [. . .]

B. explains (Pannigabluk confirms for her place) that usually a newborn child cries. It is that a turñnrat makes it cry—the child is crying for the name of this turñnrat or dead man. When the child gets the right name he ceases crying. Sometime people make several wrong guesses and so child has several names. In some cases right name is never found and child keeps on crying. B himself ceased crying at the second name, which is "Iumaktua luk." Some children never cry—they do not want any name. These are called "atkittok." (But a child always gets a name if there is a near dead relative who has not yet had a child named after him. The "atkittuat" had no such relative pressing by needing a name-bearer). [. . .]

JANUARY 29 *Beliefs.* Pannigabluk tells that among the western Eskimos (generally, she thinks) a woman who wished her (unborn) child to be healthy and strong should eat the cartilage between the bones of the knee joint of caribou [. . .] to make a child strong [. . .]. Among the Nogatogmiut and Killirimiut—and other—women at menses [. . .] were not allowed to eat caribou heads. [. . .]

JANUARY 23 Left Hodgson's at ca. 6: A. At 10: A. [. . .] Left Anderson and B. with instruction to Anderson to follow river till he came to our house. [. . .] *SW* 35 blizzard and very cold—froze face while going before fair wind and sweat streaming down my face. Sat up large part of night for Anderson, who did not come. [. . .]

Race blending. Arrviyunna was the "Eskimo George" of whom Hodgson tells, who was the company's interpreter at Peel River. He is long dead. His wife was an Indian and his three children are living among Indians. One of these three was born with one arm wanting.

Niuittjiak is now living among the Peel River Indians and has an Indian wife. Both these men belonged to the Kittegaryumiut. Iruanna Kittegaryumiok had an Indian husband for some time and lived at McPherson. Memoranna may have had an Indian father. Tannaumirk knows one Peel River Indian who lived at Kittegaryumiut; he was a grown man when T. first remembers, and T. used to call him "Añayura" (my older brother) for no reason known to T., except people told him to do so. This man died while T. was yet small. All, or most of the fingers of one of his hands were wanting from birth. This man was unmarried. [. . .]

Use of bows by Loucheux. As late as twenty-five or thirty years ago (if not more recently Mr. Hodgson says) the Loucheux of Rampart House frequently came to the post with only bows and arrows, though they owned guns. They explained this was "because they were hunting moose," as they preferred the bow for this use. Bows are still in use in almost all parts of the Mackenzie, though in some districts use is confined to women or to shooting birds and rabbits.

Shape of snowshoes. The round Yukon toe is (now, at least) in use on Bear Lake for women. Harry Hodgson says a shoe may be the proper woman's shoe, however, so long as the toe overlaps and is lashed. The men's shoes have this toe (a slight knob and lashing confined to one groove around the toe), as far south as Providence. Loucheux only use round toe for both sexes. Kittegaryumiut Eskimo had the same toe as Bear Lake, but perforated and laced instead of lashed and no knob. Tannaumirk does not think women's shoes differed from men's. At his place B. says (inland from Port Clarence) the men had the sharp toe as at Kittegaryumiut and women slightly rounded. Pannigabluk says the people of the Colville had the round toe (Yukon) for both sexes, but the part of the shoe in front of the foot was generally narrower on women's shoes. [. . .]

Comparison of Eskimo and Indian customs, character, etc. It may be that I am scarcely fitted by experience for a just comparison of the two people, but then a comparison may never have been attempted by anyone better fit. Anyway, the following is set down, with some diffidence as far as Indian character goes; as to hunting methods, camps, etc., here there is little chance of my going far wrong, as I have discussed what I have seen with the Hodgson's, Melville, Hornby, and the Indians themselves. Johnny Sanderson, while quarter of white is an Indian in bringing up and in his ideas.

The two peoples as travelers. The Indians carry less impedimenta in winter and in that matter have the advantage. The Coppermine Eskimo, who carry less than any other Eskimo I know, always carry the table and other wooden furniture that goes with the lamp, besides the lamp itself and the cooking pot. They carry no tent in winter, but the Indians frequently also travel without the lodge, making "open camps" in the wood. When tents are carried, the advantage in weight is with the Indians, for the lodge weighs no more than the modern tents of the Western Eskimo and the Eskimo carry the willow framework in addition, bulky and a little heavy. Pitching camp seems to take about the same time with the lodge and the beehive tent. But when the tent is once pitched there is no comparison in comfort. In fact, the word "comfort" is out of place in describing a lodge camp, at least in cold weather. "Cheerful" is about the only term of precise that ever partly fits—the huge blazing fire is cheerful [. . .]. It is almost impossible to dry anything, as steam rises in clouds from the snow-covered ground and from anything in fact that gets warm. Frequently, I was unable to see Anderson's face, though he was my next neighbor, for the steam from the ground. This steam condenses on the away-from-the-fire-side of any garment hung up, and alternately condenses and melts on the fire-ward side, as the fire varies in heat. If one attempts to bank the tent, it smokes, and if one camps in a low place (valley) it usually smokes anyway. This is hard on the eyes (besides the moment's discomfort). Anderson was nearly blind some days and suffered considerable pain. [. . .]

In the matter of which are better long distance runners I have no opinion of one's superiority over the other. There are many white men who state positively the Indians are much better, but these are, so far as I know, men who know only the Indians. It is true that the Indians travel faster and stop more seldom in traveling short distances; but the apparent reason, nowadays at least, is that they are so poorly dressed they have to keep moving to keep warm, while an Eskimo is usually, if not always, comfortably warm on the body and can therefore take his ease anywhere by turning his face away from the wind.

As hunters of caribou it seems to me clear the Eskimo are better men. The Indians have about the same methods of driving deer as the Eskimo and if they differed materially I would not be competent to contrast them as to efficiency. They snare more deer than the Eskimo trap or snare but that is through the advantage of better local conditions. But in "straight hunting" the Indian has but one way (if trees are absent for cover). He walks or runs straight at the caribou, shoots poorly at long range, and depends on the caribou's curiosity and frequent stops to get in range at all. This method is equally used by the western Eskimo (the Coppermine people do not seem to use it), but only in one of two cases; when the weather is calm and the snow crusty, stealthy approach is impossible through the deer's acute hearing; or when the deer have accidentally seen or heard the hunter and further concealment is to no purpose. Otherwise, the Eskimo have the habit of careful approach, and can often get within one hundred yards of a band of deer on even level ground, while if there are several Eskimo their approach to deer is often worthy of the term Hanbury applies when he calls it "a carefully planned campaign." From some point of vantage the ground is studied out (nowadays with the use of glasses) with reference to the wind, the direction the deer are moving, etc. It often takes an Eskimo all day to approach a band that an Indian would be shooting at fifteen minutes after he saw them; but then an Eskimo is about five times as likely to get his deer, and does not scare the animals off the hunting ground to such an extent as the Indians do. The method used by the Bear Lake Indians is well enough where caribou, when they come, come in thousands and can be butchered off hand; but in a country such as Horton River, where one needs to kill a large portion of the deer seen in order to live, they would starve, as indeed the Good Hope Indians have been completely starved out of Horton River, their ancestral hunting grounds. On Horton River we can live well by attending to the hunt at proper seasons. As companions when traveling my experience confirms that of Hanbury (who could contrast Eskimo and Indians from personal knowledge), Pike, Russell, etc. They are always whining when something goes wrong, are always ready to break a bargain, always haggling for more pay, always homesick and worrying about not being able to see their little grandnephews, or other distant relatives. They are afraid to go out of the territory of their own tribe, except along the Mackenzie highways of travel. None of these faults the Eskimo have in general, or at least none of them are so universally evident. Our man Ilavinirk is always worrying about starvation in a strange country, but he has some cause. He has starved, and his health is poor, he has frequently in the past been unable to hunt or travel for weeks at a time. B. and P. have none of the above faults, and T. only some of them slightly developed—is homesick, a little lazy, a good deal thoughtless and very lacking in initiative. The Indians are very much on their dignity, I have never seen an Eskimo who was. Johnny, for instance, felt very grieved at having to do women's work, cut up meat to dry, find spruce boughs for flooring the lodge, etc. There are lazy Eskimo, but I have never known one of them to refuse doing a thing (be it sewing, tending the baby, cutting up meat, or what not) on the ground that he was too important a person to do these things. Few Eskimo will stand being harshly spoken to. They will leave an individual employer or a ship at no matter what loss of pay, etc., promptly if harshly spoken to by the man in highest authority (be the reproof deserved or not). Indians (it seems from Johnny's case and what I have heard) will not only stand sharp words, but will be more attentive and better servants if occasionally dressed down a bit.

Honesty, at least "business honesty," is on a higher level among the Eskimo. The Akuliakattagmiut would not accept the smallest thing without paying for it; the Western Eskimo through long training, have become beggars to a degree, but not as the Indians. But if the Western Eskimo promise pay they will deprive themselves of "necessities" and luxuries to meet their bills. An example were the people to whom Cadzow gave credit at Rampart House the winter of 1906–7. He gave them no more than he was accustomed to give Indians as gratuities, but some of them made a three hundred mile trip from the coast (Alekak, Tulurak) to pay bills of three or five fox skins, and carried fox skins for the settlements of debts of others. They were so far from Cadzow that they needed have no fear of his attempting collecting or even seeing him. It might be that Alekak and Tulurak paid their debts to get more credit; this can't be though of those who sent their furs with these two to pay debts. Most of these, or all, without a remote notion of ever again seeing Cadzow. As a contrast, an Indian at Norman will run up as big a bill as he can with one trader, and then, before that trader's face, take his furs to a rival trader to avoid paying his debts, and then change his trading post for another when he can get no more credit at Norman. Even now Eskimo take no "debt" from the traders at Peel River, though some are often urged to do so, for the traders know that if they can sell to a man more than he can pay for, that man will bring the furs next year to them, whereas they might otherwise go to a whaler. And having brought furs to pay his bill, he will probably bring also the rest, for he won't have the time to go back to the "Fort" and Herschel Island (to the ships) without forfeiting his chances of the summer white whale hunt and the fishing.

I have, however, known cases of misrepresentation, cheating and real "confidence games" among the Mackenzie Eskimo (the details are already down in my other diaries). There are also thieves, but they are few, everybody knows them for thieves, and they are looked down on, a few years ago they would have been killed.

Comparisons of ethnological interest. Tonsure haircutting was (and is even now by old men, Johnny says), practised on Bear Lake. It was Mackenzie River Eskimo style, and not like that of Coppermine. [. . .]

JANUARY 27 Anderson and T. to Hodgson's to get stove we forgot there the 23. B. making snowshoes as his old pair is badly broken. Intended to hunt but found my rifle frozen up (on account of being kept in the house at Hodgson's while we were on Langton Bay Trip). [. . .]

Discussed with Anderson buying rifle from Hodgson for Tannaumirk to use to replace the broken one, but decided we could not afford it, though his being without a rifle may easily sometime mean the difference between having something to eat and not having it. When next we go off from our house we shall have to leave him and Pannigabluk again behind, and caribou are as likely to come here as anywhere. It will be rather bad to have them either starving or making a scant living snaring ptarmigan, if deer are at hand. Neither will it raise our standing in their eyes to find us unable to get rifle when they know Hodgson has them for sale. But the rifle would cost us about 100^{00} (80^{00} for the rifle, plus cost of ammunition) if paid in fox skins, as we should have to pay it. [. . .]

JANUARY 29 B. hunting SW. Should be hunting too, I suppose, but decided to begin the report requested by the Geological Survey of Canada for publication in their annual "summary." They will have to get the American Museum permission, of course, before they can print it, but I shall have done my part to please them when I get the report in shape to print. I do not really like writing anything for publication now in uncomfortable—especially poorly lit for writing—quarters, without reference books, and without facilities or time to properly collate the materials. Then one is distracted by present worries—no signs of game just when we want to start for Coronation Gulf—and we cannot start till we can leave the house sufficiently stocked with food especially now that the man we shall have to leave behind—Tannaumirk is without a rifle. Anderson seems even less able than I to cheerfully face things going wrong, and his gloom is an additional worry. [. . .]

FEBRUARY 9 B. to old tipee camp to get Tan's traps. I writing on ethnological report. Right hand pain considerable from bad frost burns from my rifle while shooting February 5. These burst while I was skinning caribou February 7. One of these had lived 15 or 20 hours after being shot through intestine [. . .]. Foolishly got my hands into this, and have since feared blood poisoning. Though the hand pains now there are no symptoms of poisoning, however, so far as I see [. . .].

FEBRUARY 18 Writing on ethnological report. Tannaumirk visits traps, which are long ago snow covered. [. . .] T. came home before sundown; did not visit farthest trap—one set by Billy at his deer kill of February 10. Gave fear of *turñnurat* as his reason but would not say he had special reason for fear—only that he "felt afraid." Pannigabluk says he has had several such fear-spells this winter. After dark tonight refuses to go outdoors even for ca. moment alone. [. . .]

FEBRUARY 19 Yesterday's gale continues—a trifle milder in afternoon, and a good deal less snow flying—more of it is beaten hard no doubt. Our best dog, Dekoraluk was in good health last night when dogs were fed; today he is unable to stand. [. . .]

Theories of disease. Tannaumirk says either men or dogs may lose their gall. In that case they become ill and usually die; the symptoms are [. . .] inability to close the mouth, unwillingness to eat, staggering gait and later inability to stand up, etc.

FEBRUARY 20 [. . .] Beliefs. Pannigabluk when small was forbidden to eat at the same meal, berries and seal meat, especially if fresh. They habitually ate berries with old seal oil, but must not use fresh. Grown people feared this prohibition less than children. Tannaumirk says he was forbidden to eat bowhead whale, meat, skin, or oil, while his labret holes were healing.

Dekoraluk died this morning. He was the best dog I have ever known. It will do him little good to write him a memorial here; neither can I word my feelings any more than one can do so after the loss of his best friend. He had been long in our service, always friendly, always faithful. We have often worked hard together, he harder than I and more cheerfully; we have often been hungry together, he oftener than I. But though hungry and tired he never shirked, and at a special strain he always had a little extra reserve to put forward—when most men or dogs in his position would have given up. He was almost beyond nature honourable and magnanimous for a dog.

He has refused to steal from a meat cache which other dogs broke open before his eyes [. . .]; he was easily the best fighter of all the dogs we ever had, but never started a fight [. . .]; he was the only dog I could know who would help a dog who was down, though he did that only for his brother Kanivarok who survives him.

It is the hardest thing about our life here to watch the death of dog after dog, who has served you well and been a faultless friend through hardships and thankless toil. I am glad Dekoraluk did not die of hunger [. . .]. His death has taken my courage away for the time being. [. . .]

FEBRUARY 27 [. . .] Beliefs. Pannigabluk says the Nogatogmiut, Killirmiut, etc., believe that if a child "before he gets understanding" (before seven or eight years) is continually forbidden to do things it wants to do, continually *told* "don't do that," "stop your noise," etc., their ears become like dogs' ears and they are stupid throughout life. If a man has big ears, or is stupid, people know he has been forbidden to do what he wanted to do when a child. Tannaumirk confirms this for Kittegaryumiut, but is not sure of the dog's ears, knows that stupid people are so in the degrees in which they have been forbidden to do things. Pannigabluk says it is better to run the danger of a child pricking his eye out with a sharp knife than to forbid him the knife if he wants it and thus have the certainty of making him stupid. [. . .]

MARCH 2 Writing on ethnological report; Tannaumirk hauling home meat. Snow last night, cloudy today, variable faint airs here at house.

Beliefs. One of the lobes of a caribou liver is called "the thumb" (kublua). Mothers that are bringing up young sons should eat this (Killirmiut, Nogatogmiut, etc., Pannigabluk says). When the boy grows a man and hunts deer, the bands will circle about him in a curve shaped like the outside (margin) of this lobe. This will give him a chance to kill many at once, while if his mother had not taken the precaution to eat this lobe, the deer might have run straight away from him. There is a story ("Unipkak") that tells of this, and a song in it about making the caribou circle as if running around the lobe of a (huge) caribou liver, but Pannigabluk knows neither. [. . .]

Migration theories: The door-ward part of the interior of a house is "iglum uata"; the part away from the door is "iglum kivata"; the door-ward part may be called (often is) "ualinirk" but the opposite end is not "kivalinirk" "though that would be correct, if people did say it" (Pannigabluk). The people to the west of another people are said to be "uatani" and are called "Ualinarmiut" in many cases—e.g. the Upper Rae. Most neighbourhoods have a river east of them named "kivalina" or some similar form [. . .]. If it should appear that in other parts of the country (say, east of a given point) "ualinirk" means east or north, say, or south (cf. nigirk = s. wind in Greenland [. . .], E. and here Mackenzie river, etc.), then it may have a bearing on the direction of migration of the Eskimos.

In an animal the head-ward end is called "kjeata" and the tail-ward part "uata" because (Pannigabluk) "that is the way the food goes in and comes out." The same terms apply to the trunk of a man, but not to the legs—i.e., the navel is "innum uatane" but the knee or heel could not be so described (Pannigabluk says). [. . .]

MARCH 4 Pannigabluk tells a few years ago she and a large party of people were traveling in winter. They had gone up the Killirmiut branch of the Colville and had reached the head of the Kivirk, which flows into the Yukon. There were a few trees where they camped the night in question. Among the party was the elderly [. . .] man Kenoranna, his wife Okilaerk, their son Turñrak or Tuyak (a grown man). These pitched camp a little (a hundred yards perhaps) away from the rest of the party. When all camps were made, the rest of the party noticed that Turñrak's party had a fire outdoors and that the old man Kenoranna sat by it, but his wife and their son were inside the tent. Later they heard Kenoranna crying "Let me in, why don't you let me into the warm tent?" Later he began upbraiding his son: "It is only a few days since you ate in one day five ptarmigan I killed. I am not decrepit. I am feeling a little sick tonight but it is nothing serious. I shall not die if you let me in." Later as the strong wind increased (nigirk) the cries became inarticulate, but were still loud and plainly heard in the camps of the rest of the party, for the wind blew that way. Towards morning the cries died away. Everybody knew that Kenoranna was not seriously sick, and people thought it mean of his son not to let his father in, seeing he was not very sick. Kenoranna had another son, Puktuan, who was away hunting deer. When he returned he was angry at his brother for having let their father freeze to death when he was not seriously ill. Kenoranna's wife cried the next day for her husband. Puktaun and Okilaerk are since dead; Turñrak still lives, usually stays with Aiaki (Kanirkpuk) and is probably in the Mackenzie Delta. [. . .]

P. tells on the Ikpikpuk in summer a boat party was traveling. One boat contained a middle-aged woman and her son, who was sick. He was uncomfortable in the boat and urged his mother that they remain and wait for the next boat party which was coming behind, allowing their present companions to go ahead. So they stayed in their tent and their companions proceeded. But when it got nearly dark the mother was afraid to stay alone over night with a sick man, so she started off for the camp (about eight miles away) of the party for whom they were waiting. When she got there she told: "He called after me; 'Mother, don't leave me when I am sick and our friends are sure to be coming along soon in their boats.' But I dared not stay in the night with a sick man." The next morning they all went to the sick man's tent and found he had shot himself in the night. The dead man's name was Irkaark, his mother is Akergavik; they were Killirmiut. Akergavik is now dead too. She was the younger sister of Okilliak. (This happened about ten years ago). (Note): This was in the time of epidemic and five members of the party were already dead. [. . .]

MARCH 7 Tannaumirk and I both sick. Feeling too mean to write much. Cloudy, SW blizzard 40 down to SW 15 towards evening. [. . .]

MARCH 8 Both feeling a little better. Tannaumirk has headache and a sore back and neck. Dark rings around eyes and eyes ache badly. The center of my trouble seems to be the hurt in the pelvic vertebrae received February 22, but there apparently is some complication, for same pain extends down the right leg to the knee. Stomach also out of order intermittent desire to vomit. SW blizzard 25, very cold.

MARCH 9 [. . .] Beliefs. Pannigabluk says Nogatogmiut and Killirk women might not eat the inside membrane of the ribs (i.e., the membrane covering the side of the rib that is towards the intestines or lungs), of mountain sheep or brown bears. They might eat the meat of no part of a sheep that was front of the eighth rib, counted from behind, except as follows: the leg back of a plane bisecting each from leg from the middle of the shoulder blade to the middle of the hoof, and the meat above a horizontal plane bisecting the neck vertebrae from the head to the trunk, i.e. they must not eat the head, ventral halves of the front legs, ventral portion of neck, or any part of the back vertebrae behind the neck and front of the eighth rib counted from behind. They were forbidden also the heart, that part of the intestinal fat that is near the pelvis, and any part of the pelvis itself. They were, however, allowed the kidneys and kidney fat. When eating lungs they must be careful not to eat any of the bronchial tubes. They were not allowed to eat any sheep marrow. A man might eat any part of a sheep. Children of both sexes ate all parts; the first menses put a girl in a class with the women. Women were allowed to eat any part of a caribou, except during menses, when they must not eat caribou heads. [. . .]

Pannigabluk says the beliefs of different families varied among Killirmiut. Her husband believed it was safe for her to eat of only five ribs of a sheep of each side. He told her not to eat of any of the first four or the last three ribs, the ones between she might eat.

MARCH 10 [. . .] Writing folk-lore. Eskimo text. Have finished 2—(Pannigabluk) "the girl who broke the taboo" and (Tannaumirk) "the blind boy and his grandmother." [. . .]

MARCH 12 [. . .] Names of dogs. T. and P. agree that dogs usually have names of dogs now dead which usually belonged to people now dead, most often to the parents of the man whose dog now bears the name. Pannigabluk once owned a team (five or six) all but one of whom had names from folklore stories (unikpak). Of the three we have had, Kañivagok and Ukuñerk had folklore names.

Pannigabluk told me that she learned at Rae River last spring that Natjinna who was with us all summer, one of the sons of Ekallukpik, had been named after the white man who came to Rae River when Ekallukpik was a boy. This information Natjinna himself repeated last summer so both Pannigabluk and Tannaumirk heard, though now is the first I knew of it. "Natjinna" from "Richardson" is certainly as close as Velvinna from Melville and Caunapina from Hornby.

For a test, I spoke Richardson's name as we would in ordinary unemphatic conversational speech. Both Pannigabluk and Tannaumirk heard it and repeated it to me as Natjisin.

MARCH 13 Language. Pannigabluk says the people between the Yukon and the Kuwok, most of them had never heard the word "iglu" and would not have understood it, had they heard it. At that time there came to them (near St. Michaels) a man who was gathering folklore, ethnological specimens, etc. This man told them that the "Kagmalit" spoke of a house as an "iglu." This they would not have believed, seeing it was only a white man who told it, had not her mother spoken up and confirmed it by saying it might well be so for she had heard the *same word* when she was among the Immarxhlit and the Okiovuormiut. Pannigabluk is not sure it was known by the Nogatogmiut, she thinks it was known but seldom or never used. All the Colville people knew it twenty years ago, she says, "for they traded every summer with the Cape Smythe people." South of the Kuwok the word for a house was "tupergruk" or some dialectic variant. Itjaliganrak was the word for a tent (or Kallrovik). Tuperk, covered both houses and tents, a common, nondiscriminating name. Napaktak, a tent similar to an Indian tipee, though hole in top smaller, and covered when it rained, no fire in summer unless meat or fish. Panapkak, was a white man's style wall tent. [. . .]

MARCH 14 Swimming [. . .] was known by two (Roxy) men only in the Mackenzie district when Memoranna was a boy. Pannigabluk says several Cape Smythe men knew it, but she thinks they learned on their trading expeditions to Nirrlik. Both near the Yukon and on the Killirk everybody could swim. Young men and young women often went swimming either in separate parties or together. They used to make a fire to dry themselves before dressing. The maturer girls used to wear breeches, the younger girls and the boys none.

This summer Pannigabluk was told by Natjinna's wife that a few years ago, when they crossed the Dease River, the string broke by which they were ferrying their goods on a raft. There was no man on the raft. Huprok, she said, then took off his clothes and swam (pubraktuak; to wade in deep water is turnmaktuak) to the raft and tied a line to it so the others could pull it ashore.

When looking for musk-oxen, Natjinna's wife said they used to cross the Dease (about eight miles above its mouth) and hunted northwest to the edge of the barrens. They habitually use a small raft, one or two men cross first trip, and after that the raft is hauled back and forth with a line.

Beliefs. Pannigabluk tells her husband spent a year at Cape Smythe before Brewer came there. He told among other things the following. In the spring when they were about to go out to the edge of the floe to begin looking for whales, each umialik (master of a whaleboat) would take a dish in which his wife had placed *some* small pieces of maktak ("black skin," true skin, and say quarter of an inch of blubber) and whale meat. Going to the trapdoor (houses at Cape Smythe had only trapdoors then) he would stand astride the trapdoor with his back towards the door of the alleyway, face towards the bed-platform end of the house, and throw the pieces one by one between his legs through the trapdoor towards the door of the alleyway. [. . .]

Names. At Cape Smythe at one time there were four men who bore the name Appaiyauk. One of these was called Appaiyaugnak, that may have been his name from the first, or it may have been given him later in life to distinguish him from the others. The most prominent of the four was always called Appaiyauk. The remaining two Appaiyauks were given the distinguishing suffixes -hlux and -tjiak. Appaiyauxhlux is now dead but Appaiyauxtjiak is the one still living and at present one of most important men at Cape Smythe. When the prominent Appaiyauk died (but Appaiyauxh-lux, brother of Tagluksrak's wife) still lived the -tjiak was removed from the present umialik's name. He has since been plain Appaiyauk.

At Herschel Island, etc, and at Cape Bexley and east I have heard of no such distinguishing suffixes being applied to men of the same name.

Among Killirmiut: Alahik, Alahualuk and Alahurak; Pannigabluk + puk, Pannigabluk + rak and Pannigablualuk—all were "Pannigabluk." [. . .]

Names. A child is named Keyuk from one of several Keyuks. The one from whom the child is named is "oma atka" (that one's name), the others are not the child's "name," though they bear the same name. [. . .]

MARCH 15 Dr. Anderson, B. and T. arrived about 8 P. last night. [. . .]

Eskimo understanding of their language: It seems impossible for me in any case, now that I can talk pretty freely in their language, to get from any of our three Eskimos an explanation of the meaning of a separate one of the component parts of a word if the word is a complex one, i.e. they can tell you of "iglu puk" that "iglu" = house and "puk" = big. On the other hand, of the word malliktallirk both T. and P. told me point blank that tal and li(rk) had no meaning of their own. Tannaumirk explained carefully and correctly that the word means that one who did not use to follow, began following; and that after once beginning to follow he kept on doing so habitually. But he denied that tal(tak) meant "habitually" and that "lirk" meant "begin to"; denied also specifically that either had a meaning of its own. "The whole word we understand, the parts by themselves mean nothing."[. . .]

MARCH 17 Rewriting text of "Man who married a goose." It is slow work. Today in about 9 hours of writing I did five pages—not only slow [. . .] but trouble to verify text from Pannigabluk who is occupied with other work and easily gets tired anyway. Dr. A working on 4th skin of 7 caribou [. . .] Tannaumirk cleaning his wolfskins: B. hunting NW for moose, Pannigabluk yesterday finished sewing a caribouskin tent cover and now working on boots.

MARCH 18 Last evening B. home at dark. Saw no traces of moose where he saw plenty a month ago. Coming home he saw tracks of three men with two toboggans coming from WE and passing back of our mountain (about ¾ mile from house) in the direction of the mouth of the Dease. These men had seen his morning snowshoe trail, as they stopped on it. One was without snowshoes—large foot prints. Snowshoes of others small. [. . .] Plan to start for Coronation Gulf so soon as Anderson can get his skins in shape to day. Pannigabluk can then have them (dry) in shape for us to take to Melv. Hornby's when we get back. [. . .]

The season is as advanced here now as at Langton Bay April 20 last year. Our ice windows are full of holes though we have little fire. Our Eskimos think unanimously that ugrugs are on top the ice now in Darnly Bay—where as we know from last year that they do not come up much before April 20—none of them seem to have a conception of the season being different here than farther north. This is especially strange of B. [. . .]

MARCH 22 *Started towards Coronation Gulf* 12:50 P.M. Two toboggan, seven dogs, Dr. Anderson, B.T., and myself. Camped 6: P.M. near NW corner of largish lake in wood. [. . .]

MARCH 24 Yesterday morning forgot our ink bottle at camp breaking and left it behind—we have a little ink which we carry frozen. [. . .]

APRIL 5 Were breaking camp about 12:30 P. when the NW wind which had been blowing about 15 miles an hour suddenly increased to NW 35 or 40. Weather so thick that we might easily have passed an Eskimo camp at 200 yards without seeing it so we decided there was no use moving. Made camp again therefore. *Wood* here is all old, mostly broken pieces of small trees and it takes about a ½ mile of coast to supply a night's camp. [. . .]

APRIL 6 Started 11:30, camped 6:45. Distance fifteen or eighteen miles. Followed seaward side of island chain extending with few short breaks about parallel to shore. [. . .] Found autumn snow village of twelve houses on the Limestone Island, seaward side. Saw later autumn track of one sled and found just before camp one footprint by a piece of wood that had been chopped this fall with an adze. [. . .]

APRIL 9 Started 9:45, heading 330° Mag. for the E. end of a conspicuous cliff that forms the S. side of an island in the chain next north of the one we have followed [. . .]. When we had gone 11 or 12 miles on this course, we found a 3–4 day's old trail of one sled, 2 dogs, 4 persons going 20° Mag. Followed trail 12 or 14 miles and camped 7: P.M. in the snow house of the party we were following—house by NW corner of a small high island [. . .]. In evening through closing house too tight, we came near committing involuntary suicide. Before any of us realized that anything was wrong, first Tannaumirk and a minute later Dr. Anderson became unconscious, uttering loud, snore-like noises for half a minute or so and then becoming silent and still. B. and I realizing the danger quickly, broke a hole both in the door and in the side of the house and got out—we tried to go back in to rescue Anderson and T. but B. collapsed by the side of the house and I could not even crawl inside [. . .]. In ca. ½ hour I was strong enough to get back into the house and boil up some malted milk (we had 2 lbs. which were cached all summer on our sled on the Coppermine). This strengthened others up considerably, and by 1: P.M. we were all in bed—only B. and T. really sick. [. . .] From point of reaching Eskimos (April 10, 1911) diary entries are continued in the volume used for Eskimo notes the spring 1910, so as to have those notes all in one book. [. . .]

Range of Ideas. The people east and north of Cape Bexley were probably even in the earliest days among the most isolated groups of Eskimo anywhere, *isolated not only from our world of ships and trading but also from their own kind*. A comparison of them a hundred years ago with the then equally uncivilized Mackenzie Eskimo would probably, even then, have shown in intellectual things a heavy balance in favor of the westerners. However that may have been, the difference in range of ideas today is marked. Unfortunately, the sixteen years of Herschel Island whaling that preceded the writer's first visit to the Mackenzie Delta had made it difficult to determine for that locality what ideas were local there or of ancient introduction, what ones were borrowed recently from the Alaskan Eskimo, whom the whalers brought with them, and what had been absorbed from the white men directly. Nevertheless a comparison will be attempted on the basis of what seems to be local and primitive in the Mackenzie district.

Inability to count in the Coronation Gulf district has a wide direct influence; it is besides an index to their general mental status. At the Baillie Islands and west any grown person can count up to four hundred (twenty twenties); at Cape Bexley, in Victoria Island, and east at least as far as the Kent Peninsula no one can count above five. Even this seems to be a numerical vocabulary beyond their wants. In summer nothing is of so much interest or importance to them as the caribou, yet of all the people we have lived with and hunted with, no one (unless cross-questioned by us) ever used a numeral larger than "two" to designate the number of caribou seen or killed. If there were more than two but less than six they knew how many they were but never told. The expression for more than two was invariably "many" (amihuaryuit). When we pressed them for more exact details they could tell us "three, four, or five," but with impatience as if ours was unreasonable or childish curiosity. If there were over five the answer would be; "I don't know how many, very many." Of certain things, such as the population of a small village, they have approximately correct ideas of number to and even above fifteen and will indicate this by holding up their ten fingers and getting some bystander to hold up as many more as are needed to complete the total, prompting him by "one more finger" till he holds up the required number. Of such a performance the main performer seems very proud and the assembled *always* find it highly amusing. It is probable that it is seldom except when we ask questions that anyone finds occasion to express a number above five. We never heard a man not of our party ask any question in regard to exact number after he had been told "many."

In the Mackenzie district a band of caribou seen is usually reported by exact number if there are less than ten; over that number careful estimates are let suffice, e.g. "over twenty," "less than forty," etc. (It is in fact, usually, exceedingly difficult to count caribou correctly if the band is over ten animals.) [. . .]

APRIL 10 The future. For over a century since Hearne first saw an encampment of them at Bloody Fall the Coronation Gulf Eskimo have made little "progress towards civilization." It was probably after Hearne's time that they first saw an article of European manufacture; later they got a few scraps of iron, etc., by plundering the abandoned boats and gear of the Franklin expedition; Richardson traded the Rae River group a few knives, files, and needles, and so did Rae a little later; Collinson's ships traded with widely separated parties at Cambridge Bay and on Prince of Wales Strait and threw heaps of empty tin cans and other waste gear ashore; McClure's abandoned ship on the north coast of Banks Island may have become Eskimo spoil, though he never saw Eskimo on Banks Island, as well as some wreckage from Franklin's ill-fated ships on the east coast of Victoria Island. Of recent years articles of iron have begun to come in more freely by overland native trade from Hudson Bay. Firearms and the fur trade are known by hearsay, though they have not as yet penetrated into Coronation Gulf proper.

From the present year, however, change will be rapid. Our unwilling ministrations this summer broke down the walls of fear and hatred that ignorance of each other has till now maintained and that has since effectively kept apart the Coppermine Eskimo and the Bear Lake Slavey. The fur-trading post on Bear Lake River (Fort Norman) is the natural market for Coronation Gulf. The white men there are eager for the Eskimo's furs; the missionaries there are no less eager to extend their activities. Both *(or the fur traders at least*) will go to the sea if necessary to attain their ends. The Eskimo, after familiarity with our outfit for a summer, are set on getting guns, fish nets and tools, now that they know the Indians are really a harmless lot and friendly. In a year or two the Eskimo would go to the traders if the traders did not come to the Eskimo. And if neither Eskimo nor trader had the enterprise to seek the other, the Indians are eager to act as middlemen between. Commerce in goods may, therefore, be said to have begun; commerce of ideas cannot help following close behind.

From the point of view of the ethnologist and sociologist the result of these new forces is clear, the rapid change of ideas, institutions and material surroundings. *These need not be considered beyond here in general—they have been considered above or are readily inferred from our preceding discussion. A few of the least evident points only will be taken up.*

Up to the present, three-quarters of the food of the people has been the seal and three-quarters of the year have been spent in its pursuit. The sea has therefore, been their home, the snow hut their dwelling. But the coming of the trader and the acquisition of guns will give the land a lure it formerly did not have and increasingly the people will become land-dwellers seeking furs with which to buy articles to supply their newly discovered wants. At first making a living on land will be easy, for caribou are still numerous. The result will be that the people will live on caribou meat for twelve months a year (some of them, at least) instead of three or four; where they had one dog to hunt seal-holes for them in winter they will now have teams of four or six with which to make long winter journeys (or so it has been in the west of the Baillie Islands) and these dogs also will feed on caribou meat. At present the caribou has in winter a wide zone of safety between the Indians who dare not face the barren ground and the Eskimo who prefer the sea coast. But the Eskimo fear the woodless barrens about as much as a fish fears water, and when the fur trade draws them inland the doom of the last muskox will be not a decade away nor that of the last caribou many decades. This will have its effect on those northern tribes of Indians who are still to an extent caribou-eaters, while the disappearance of the caribou will drive the Eskimo back again to the sea coast. They will then have to get all their living from the water instead of three-fourths of it as at present and will have to dress in sealskins where they now use caribou. By then they will have learned tea drinking, tobacco using, etc., and will have lost their economic independence as completely as have all Eskimo west of the Baillie Islands. They will then be less well fed than at present, less well clothed, richer only in ideas without which they now live content and in wants which their poverty will never completely satisfy. The Coronation

Gulf people look to the immediate future with eager anticipation; so do also the fur-traders at Fort Norman. As a spectator with no material interests at stake the writer feels that the trader is to be congratulated, but not the Eskimo. In closing a chapter on the Eskimo of King William Land, Captain Amundsen says: "My best wish for my friends the Netchillik Eskimos is that civilization may never reach them." It had reached them even when that line was written, or its wants and its vices had, and that is all of civilization that is readily absorbable. It is now about to obliterate the last oasis of economic independence on our continent, the populous district surrounding Victoria Island. I would wish these people the same wish that Amundsen did their neighbors to the east, but I should have to put it in a past tense and should have to add a regret that I had a part in bringing the change about. [. . .]

APRIL 10 This diary was *in cache* of the Coppermine from June 6th, 1910 until we picked it up there all safe a few days ago (see other diary, April 4th). The notes are continued here now so that my observations of the Eskimos E. of Cape Bexley may be in one volume.

Started today at 11:45. [. . .] Enthusiastic welcome—one or two old acquaintances from our summer on the Dease—the Footless (Itigaaittok) family. Say we have narrowly missed numerous parties of people to the west. Report the "Teddy Bear" wintering just E of Coppermine. He had come to Coronation Gulf partly to look for us, they say—sorry he troubled. Some purchases tonight. Sleepy and tired so short entry. Camped in excellent vacant snow-house, fitted up for us and furnished with lamp and drying rack. [. . .]

APRIL 11 Day occupied in taking cephalic measurements of all but one boy (4 years) of the 15 people here and in buying the specimens [. . .]. Prices very different from last spring account of ship's buying. Most who sold garments cut off pieces to throw away—some did not. Bought one dog for knife—cheese knife. Anderson meantime taking pictures. [. . .]

APRIL 12 Some trading, sewing of cats cradles on cloth, etc. Had intended going to next village E. but a man offered to go instead and fetch the people here. This suited us better. The man however got lost on account of the thick weather and the fact that Aialiuk (the man whose trail took us here) had not gone to the village as he went east—the messenger thought he had and followed his trail till he found it lead nowhere, then he came home. [. . .]

APRIL 13 B. with two women, Arnauyak and Anaktak, to fetch people of next village. They went east about five or six miles, found deserted village and trail southwest. Found people by going southwest seven or eight miles and came home from a little west of south at dark. Two sleds came with them and one had come ahead, two boys to pay this village a visit. They had started for here before B. got to their camp. "Igliki" whom Hanbury saw is coming tomorrow. He treated B. especially well and fed our dogs half a seal, the first square feed since they came here. People here and those B. saw starved two years ago a trifle earlier in year than this and lost most of their dogs—have few to spare yet. A white man called Kakcamuna is said to have come to trade a year ago this winter to "our countrymen east" (perhaps to Unnumuktok?).

APRIL 14 [. . .] Did some trading. A dance house was then built by clearing away the Footless family's alleyway, cutting a six feet high arch in their wall where the door used to be, and building a ten by twelve snowhouse so that those that were crowded out of the new house could stand in the Footless house and watch the dancing through the arch. Dancing about two hours when it broke up on account of the visitors being anxious to get back home for a square meal. We had stayed so long keeping people from sealing that the village was out of meat. (They told me they did not want to go sealing for fear of our getting lonesome.) Went with visitors six miles south to their camp, which is (apparently) some ten or twelve miles from the mainland, a trifle west of north true, from the mouth of the Kogluktualuk, which is the place whence comes the material for most of the stone pots and lamps in this locality.

[. . .] Iglihirk and Ulipsinna told me separately that their grandfather had seen white men near the Coppermine but their father never had, nor they themselves except when Iglihirk saw Hanbury. An old woman [. . .] was about six years old when her father saw white men on Rae River, she herself did not see them. I asked Iglihirk if he had heard of ships being broken and white men dying on the east coast of Victoria Island. (He is the first man I have seen who knows Victoria Island has an east coast.) He said no; but he had heard of two ships being broken in the ice offshore east of Victoria Island and all the men eventually dying. Had any of the white men lived a while among the Eskimo? Not that he had heard. People had slept once in this village when B. arrived. [. . .]

Anarak says he really belongs west of Cape Bexley; has often camped with the Haneragmiut but always hunted summers on the mainland with the Akuliakattagmiut or near them, a little west of them sometimes. Iglihirk says just the same of himself. Anarak's wife also used to be with the Akuliakattagmiut. This perhaps accounts for her having more "fancy work" on her clothes and her husband's (*the suit we bought yesterday*), the only man's garments here I have seen with red stripes. [. . .]

This village when we came consisted of one single snowhouse, one double one, and two tents with snow walls. One family from other village came with us (Kaiariak, son of Iglihirk) and built a house, the rest of the village will follow today. Two seals caught today by noon by 2 of 4 hunters who went out—seals into village within 2 hours of time hunters started. Other hunters not in yet (2 P.M.). Anderson taking numerous pictures today and yesterday—I occupied trading and talking to people. [. . .]

APRIL 18 *At the schooner "Teddy Bear."* The 15th was spent buying ethnological specimens taking measurements, etc. The 16th, about noon we started off towards the reported wintering place of the ship, heading about true SW that day and the following night till we came within 3 or 4 miles from shore, when we turned to go parallel to land. At 8 A.M. we went ashore and spent some time hunting for wood but found only one small tree root. [. . .] Got to ship about 9 A.M. today.

APRIL 22 Since arriving at the "Teddy Bear" have been occupied writing letters and reports. Our plans for the summer have been completely changed by the new conditions. The schooner's captain, Joseph Bernard, has offered us assistance which we cannot wisely refuse. It was a disappointment to me to find a ship in Coronation Gulf—I am more glad than ever now that it was not later than the spring 1910 that I got in here. Now that it is here we must profit by its assistance, seeing the assistance is freely offered. [. . .] This leaves me free to start at once from here towards the north to visit people not previously seen. I shall let events decide whether I spend the summer in Victoria Island, Banks Island or on the mainland (with the Akuliakattagmiut) or go back to Langton Bay before the ice breaks. What I most want to do is to circumsled Victorialand and complete the survey of its coast from the point where Hansen had to turn back. It would be a feather in one's cap—and a feather cheaply bought—to finish from here without any of the conventional arctic paraphernalia, a task that Amundsen's well-equipped party had to win back from. [. . .]

APRIL 24 Sled and 5 people came to trade from village a few miles NW. Among these Artigiliok and Kallun whom we saw on Rea River last spring. They say ugrug are on ice everywhere (i.e. here and there) around the islands. They traded 4 fox skins to Capt. B.

APRIL 25 Five Puiplirmiut came over today from not far northwest of here. [. . .]

APRIL 28 Intended starting today but delayed by taking cephalic measurements, etc., of people who arrived, sewing cases for new rifles [. . .], etc. Four sleds arrived—mostly people seen and measured last spring at Rae River [. . .]

APRIL 29 Started towards Banks Island 3:15 P.M. [. . .] At 5:45 came to temporarily deserted camp of people not at ship, kayak and other things, including blubber, in cache. At 6:15 crossed our east going track of about middle of our second day going east along islands, between first and second islands [. . .]. At 8:30 reached second deserted camp, permanently deserted. Camped in one of snowhouses. Most of houses here double. Have been told that usually, but not always, double houses are built by those who are in the habit of exchanging wives. [. . .]

APRIL 30 Started 10:45 A.M. following old trail. In about eight miles found camp not over two weeks abandoned, but could not trace trail by which they arrived there. One faint trail (a single sled) leading northwest, evidently had come overland from Lambert Island way. Did not follow this as hoped to find people off Krusenstern. At the first cape south of Krusenstern found last fall's village, unknown number of houses as snowed over among the big ice cakes. Northeast of this cape, about one and a half miles found village of eight houses deserted three or four months.

In all villages seen on ice far from land, doors faced south; in villages at point of Cape, doors in most or all directions. Rounded Cape Krusenstern about 11: P.M. and camped nearly opposite E. and Lambert Island at 3:15 A.M. (May 1st). [. . .] Headed from Krusenstern for Lambert Island about 3 miles from Krusenstern, came to a locality where in half a mile radius we saw 4 ugrug on top ice (about 1:30 A.M.). Two were at a place 400 yards from us that with glasses looked like ¼ ca. acre of open water. This scared us as we supposed it was current keeping ice from freezing. Probing with knife found water everywhere under snow (on top of ice?). Made carefully for nearest land to SW, and camped. [. . .]

MAY 1 Slept 8: A.M. till 2:30 P. and waited rest of day for cold enough so we could use winter boots—have but one pair *ulitcuilat* and must save them against time when it ceases to freeze at night. Saw from camp an Eskimo village a mile or so east of Lambert Island. Started at 8 P.M., got there at

10:30, slow going account dogs sweating, heavy load (took part of two deer killed) and soft snow, softened by thaw today. Camp consists of twelve snowhouses. People mostly Puiplirmiut, though many others here too. [. . .]

MAY 4 In camp waiting for Kirkpuk whom we have hired to go along with us—for me to have some local person to talk with, and to have benefit of their knowledge of the ways of a woodless country and to have a woman to mend boots. [. . .] The teeth of an old woman here, Havinuk, are worn even with the gums in both jaws and as far back as the eye teeth, molars slightly less worn. Not a single tooth seems to have fallen out. Many younger Eskimo, however, have lost several teeth. [. . .]

MAY 5 *The caribou* band of 7 of which I shot 2 yesterday were all bulls—the horns about the length of their ears. [. . .] One of the natives crawled up on a seal and stabbed at him, but got blood only. The ice was so thin it could be felt heaving under one's weight "and in some places there was no ice probably" they say. Even when crawling flat-bellied towards seals the hunters keep stabbing their knives through the ice to test it. On the sealing ground the ice is in few places over two inches thick and mostly not over an inch. B.'s blunt "skinning knife" went through at every stab. Accidents are said never to happen to men or sleds "for we know where it is safe to go." Could not learn if caribou ever fall in but were told they often go far around to avoid the bad places. B. said also he never saw so many ugrug in one locality as here last summer. It would evidently be a great hunting place with boats in fall and nets in all seasons. The ice was everywhere smooth where the seals were. The seal holes were mostly "as big as tents and some oblong and much bigger than any tent." The current could be heard in most places under the ice and in the holes it could be seen running rapidly west. So far as we can learn it always runs west, though people seem to have paid no particular attention to it, and are therefore not to be relied on.

A ceremonial gift of caribou meat to their dogs was made by Apattok's family the evening we came here. We had given each family about five pounds of meat and this was at once set to cook. I was eating with Apattok. When we were half through he asked his wife, "Have the dogs had any caribou meat yet?" "No. What can I be thinking about," said his wife, who cut off a piece for each dog about the size of a pea and gave it to them. (I take it that this was a ceremony, the dogs look well fed. They have plenty of seal meat on hand, and the pieces of caribou were so small anyway that they were a bare taste.) [. . .] Deer meat was here cooked in the seal pots without even changing the strings they are hung up by, as do the Kogluktogmiut (at least Huprok's family), nor was any ceremony applied so far as I know, not even washing the pots between. Water boots, summer style, are worn by some, ordinary winter boots by others, and by a few sealskin leggings, hair out, with slipper made in the manner of the soles of water boots. [. . .]

MAY 6 *Kirkpuk* since last night had experienced a change of heart. Yesterday "because they thought he would cry" they had left their new-born baby with a woman who was to become its foster mother. Today they had fear the baby was crying after its mother and must return to it. As they were about to start back a woman was seen coming along our trail. This proved to be Aysalik, the foster-mother, coming to bring the baby to Kirkpuk. Now Kirkpuk must go back because someone had sent him word with Aysalik to come back. The real reason of his wanting to go back, I think, was fear of the people on the other side of the Kanghiryuarmiut and fear we would abandon him somewhere. When he wanted to go yesterday he told us he had no tent sticks at all of his own and said Kudlaluk would sell us a set for his use for a knife. I bought these off hand, Kirkpuk saying they were the ones he was then using for his tent—had borrowed them from Kudlaluk. A few minutes later he came again and said the set was 2 sticks short for summer use—his brother Aialik would sell us 2 for a small file. I bought these. Today when Kirkpuk turned home he was going to take all these back. I have no use for them but I would not stand for it nevertheless and asked him for the sticks. Had them brought 3–2 from Aialik and one from Kudlaluk. When I asked him where the rest were he said that was all—that Aialik had given him only one stick (should have been about 10) and he (Kirkpuk) had borrowed the rest from other people. This may or may not have been true: at any rate there had been barefaced cheating somewhere. I sent the one stick back to Kudlaluk with the word that I should want pay for the knife when I come back—this was chiefly a bluff, as I don't really expect ever to come back here.

Started 1:35 P.M. and took course generally true north. At 5 P.M. spied people by shore of Victoria Island ahead of us and got to camp of three houses at 5:35 P.M. [. . .]. People hunting seals only though camp by shore, now three days old. They have had hard luck and have only a day's supply of meat ahead. They are nevertheless very generous with the little they have, more modest and pleasant people than we have before seen. None of them have been to the ship, which explains much [. . .]. Camp is at mouth of Kogluktogmiut River which "used to be a good fishing place but has ceased to have many fish. There are ugrug in its mouth though." [. . .]

One man of about forty-five, Avranna, is totally blind and has been "for a long time." He seems tenderly cared for and goes walking about outside with his cane, guided by the shouts of grown people or children warning him of obstacles and telling him where to go. [. . .]

MAY 7 Houses. Houses here have the land east of them but all have doors facing north, in that direction land is about two miles away. At last village (Kirkpuk's) three houses faced south, one east, and one north. The one facing east was north of a house facing south but there was no house immediately east of it and none farther north or west. [. . .]

MAY 9 [. . .] Visitors arrived about 1 A.M. this morning. Neglected to note yesterday we saw a native village with the glasses a mile or two southwest of the most easterly island off the mouth of [. . .] Forsythe Bay (if Forsythe Bay is the narrow estuary or fjord-like bay and not the wider one west of it). Two of the four families of this village had started inland in the afternoon, following the river. When they came to our trail the rest camped and two men followed us up. They must have known we were not of their people for B. used snowshoes. Probably guessed who we were, though they did not let on that they had. When they heard our names, however, they knew we were the party that had passed east last spring and asked where the rest were. They have been catching plenty seals and ugrug lately, the latter in the river mouth. They are going up the river to fish in some small lakes in which the river heads "not far inland." [. . .]

The Ualinarmiut. Older of two men asked B. if he were a Ualinarmiut. On B.'s replying "Yes," he told us his wife's father was a Ualinarmiut too.

Misunderstood (both of us) they wanted to say that their families would follow them and arrive in a little while. [. . .] Put off more inquiries about these Ualinarmiut till the morning but woke up to find men gone. [. . .] They left probably about 4 A.M. Did not even get the women of these men. [. . .]

MAY 12 [. . .] Hunting with Huprok last summer was a young man (B. tells) [. . .] who forbade anybody to break for marrow bones of caribou he had killed. Both ends must be sawed off to get the marrow. This was because "caribou might all leave the country, if the bones of any he had killed were broken for marrow." This man would break in the ordinary way bones of caribou killed by anyone else. He was the only one last summer who, so far as any of us learned, put restrictions on manner of eating marrow. B. says in his place he heard of people who had similar restrictions as to breaking marrow bones. When B. was young he had pain in his index finger. The doctor then told him that until he was a grown man he must not eat fish roe or he would quickly die. B. kept restriction some years but broke it before grown up. None of his people would eat ptarmigan heads with seal oil for fear of going blind.

MAY 13 Anniversary finding Akuliakattagmiut last year. Saw from our island village on ice bearing 270° from hill on south middle of island. Started for this at 3 P.M. after shooting and skinning one more caribou. Got to people sealing three miles southeast of village at 6 P.M. and to village at 7 P.M. Distance from island about ten miles. Evidently much nearer south than north shore of bay. [. . .]

Reception seems worth describing. The three first approached showed some timidity which quickly wore off and invited us to village. When within half mile they signalled meaning "the Tigmiut are coming" by one man running off to the left from us at right angles to our course about ten yards and back to us again, this repeated twice. A crowd of men and boys then started to meet us, a crowd of women following a few yards behind, because of timidity or because slower runners. When they reached us we were surrounded by a howling friendly mob who jumped around us, pulled at our clothes to attract attention and all talked at once so no one could be heard. They were eager to help put up a tent, but of course were more hindrance than help. When the tent was up seventeen persons besides ourselves crowded into the tent (seven by seven feet square). When first approaching us all ran with upstretched hands, palms forward [. . .], opening and closing of the palm to show there was no weapon held in the hand. [. . .]

MAY 23 The Kanghiryuarmiut. The Kanghiryuarmiut (according to Hitkoak) never kill seals, but live on caribou and musk-oxen. Their land is east and south of the Ahiagmiut. They never come to the sea except as single families visiting other tribes. [. . .]

The stolen primus stove "needle" we found today in our sledgebag. It was taken from its bag in our tent. Thief must have had change of heart, did not want to return it openly, so stuck it in the handle bar bag on our sledge. [. . .]

MAY 30 Got to sleep about 10 A.M. today, after pulling everything today the sun was shining faintly then through cloud. Were waked at 3 P.M. by high wind (NW35) and rain. [. . .]

B. tells when he was young the Ualinarmiut used to come to Port Clarence, with umiaks loaded with nothing but wooden platters, pails, etc. He thinks these Ualinarmiut were mostly or all Unalit. These were bought by the Port Clarence people and carried by umiak the following summer to the Kohudlit who bought them for reindeer hides chiefly, but also for tobacco. The Port Clarence people paid [. . .] entirely in goods received from the Kohudlit, reindeer hides, legs, sinews, and tobacco.

The Kanghiryuarmiut make few of their bows, but get most of them from the Haneragmiut in exchange for iron goods (plunder from Bay of Mercy and goods bought of Ekalluktomiut who get them on the Akilinik) and made and unmade copper.

Tent sticks. Their tent sticks are partly of local driftwood, partly from the Haneragmiut (Cape Bexley driftwood), but chiefly from the Puiplirmiut who get them from those who hunt on the Dease.

Sleds. Their sleds are chiefly or entirely from two sources, the Haneragmiut who either get the wood or the made sleds from the lands or the hands of the Akuliakattagmiut, or from the Puiplirmiut who get them as they do the tent sticks. Of course, a Puiplirmiut sled may get to the Kanghiryuarmiut by way of the Haneragmiut or a Haneragmiut or Akuliakattagmiut sled by way of the Puiplirmiut for these meet every winter to trade.

The Akuliakattagmiut get Bay of Mercy iron from the Kanghiryuarmiut and Hudson Bay iron from both Kanghiryuarmiut and Puiplirmiut, the Kanghiryuarmiut getting it from the Ekalluktogmiut who either got it themselves on the Akilinik or got it from the Ahiagmiut; the P. getting it from the Kogluktogmiut or the Nag. who get it from the Uminnoktok who got it directly from the Ak. (by going for it or from the Pallirmiut traders who come to Unnumuktok from the Akilinik) or through the intermediation of the Ahiagmiut. [. . .]

JUNE 26 [. . .] Langton Bay. People East of Baillie Islands. Ilavinirk learned the following [. . .] on his trip to Baillie last April. [. . .]

At two times many of the people around Langton Bay died, the first time of starvation; the second time of an epidemic. (Both these events seem to have happened between her birth and marriage, say fifteen years). After this the people "because they had become so few" divided and went in three directions. Those with whom her parents went turned west towards Baillie; some went north towards the tip of Parry, some went east to Lyon or beyond. Those who went east probably kept on farther and farther east for they never returned. What happened to the Parry contingent Ilavinirk is not clear. There always were people on Parry. In summer one settlement of them was at the bottom of the bay where I shot the two deer April 7, 1910. I saw remains of racks there but took them to be recent; I now believe them to be of ante-whaler origin as they looked older, if anything than the remains north of Okat which Ilavinirk found so rich in specimens last year. [. . .]

JUNE 28 *Writing on reports*. [. . .] One seal shot by MarxIlauna.

Ilavinirk tells that at Point Hope when he visited the place first with his father, as well as later when he lived there, a very large cold storage house was owned by an old man there (whalers call him "the old chief"). This house had been built so long ago that its owner had no idea of the number of generations. When the owner died the storehouse passed to his son. The owner put into the house all the meat, etc., he had; if there was space left over he allowed others to fill it. In this way the house was used sometimes by two, sometimes by three men. When the owner had a whale he always used the entire house. [. . .]

JUNE 30 Point of view. Monologue by B. with occasional comments by Ilavinirk and Mamayauk. "The Kanghiryuarmiut told me: 'When we want to kill a man we stab him with a knife. We do not shoot men with bows. What is your practice?' I answered him: 'We shoot them with guns.' (Laughter, Ilavinirk and M. as well as narrator). But that is not a good way to kill people unless at long range. When I was a boy we children were playing outside and the people in all the tents slept. A man (name given) went with a gun into the next tent to ours and we heard he wanted to kill the man in the tent. Our parents did not know till afterwards; we did not awake them; it was none of our business. (Of course, it wasn't, chorus I. and M.). The man who entered said: 'Sit up, I do not want to kill you lying flat' (no intention to allow man a fighting chance, merely against etiquette apparently to kill him lying flat). But the man did not want to sit up; he did not want to die, that man (laughter from I. and M.). His wife sat by, she did not say anything. Then the baby (boy about three years old) woke up. He began to cry as he did habitually. He was a great child to cry. Then his father thought he would not like to die for his boy would cry and he could not hear or see him. He sat up suddenly, seized a knife, struck aside the gunbarrel and stabbed the man to death." (Comments by Ilavinirk: "That man had no more sense than a dog that growls before he bites. It is not safe to give warning, except from a distance, when you are going to shoot a man.") Approval from B. and M. "A knife is much better than a gun. Though it does not kill so quickly, the knife, if of any size, will paralyze the stabbed man so he can do no harm, especially if the stab is in the abdomen." B.: "Yes, that is the best place, it is not so easy to hit the heart and a stab in the stomach serves all purposes." Further discussion along same line. B. explained, incidentally that both parties were good men. The quarrel was over a game of cards of the previous day. That he did not care much how matters went is shown by his doing nothing when he expected the man of the house to get killed, and expressing no regret when the other man suffered. No expression from anyone to the effect that it "served right" the one who began the affair.

A story of a theft or of Sabbath breaking cannot be told without expression of horror, nor do lax morals escape severe censure. All these have been condemned by the missionaries and the resulting divine punishment emphasized. It has never probably occurred to them to preach against patricide and murder. The fear of the police keeps that in check but the missionary prohibition would be more efficacious still if he chose to declare himself and assign an approximately severe divine punishment. (I mean no sarcasm in saying this has not occurred to the missionaries. They are not accustomed to inveigh against murder among us and they do not know the need of doing so here. Against exposing children they have preached with good results.) [. . .]

JULY 3 Añatkot belief. B. asserts tonight that he has seen in clear broad daylight an añatkok turn a stone pot inside out and back again without breaking it. Ilavinirk confirms, he has seen it too. Ilavinirk has seen a three inch long piece of file stretched till it was a fathom long; it was elastic and when man gradually allowed his hands to relax the file assumed its original shape and size. B. in turn confirms, has seen it. Unintentionally allowed them to see I did not believe this, both angry. [. . .]

JULY 7 Preparing to start for the river mouth north of Okat. Shall send men thence to get our cache in Darnley Bay by boat up the river, while I dig the ruins there. The house sites here seem barren. Apparently the people had the fortune not to die of starvation, for they seem to have taken away with them all their goods. [. . .]

JULY 11 Sent Ilavinirk, B. and Man. up river to Barnley Bay portage for stuff cache there in June. [. . .]

Had some trouble with my people today. Hav. told me how he had sold his wooden goggles for $2, stone bladed knife he found at Kittegaryumiut for $6, and other such articles amounting $84 at Fort Mackenzie in 1907.

He said he could pick up more stuff than that here in half a day, and that what we have found already could be sold there for $500. [. . .] I had to appeal to them on the grounds of our "hard luck" in the past and that whereas they were engaged to support us by hunting, I had as a matter of fact frequently had to support them with my gun. They gave in finally, but I fear their digging here after will not be very enthusiastic. [. . .]

JULY 15 *The report writing* the last week has brought out a good many things of interest that are clearly in mind still but have failed partly or entirely to get into my diary. This shows the importance to me of getting spare time next week for writing—not only while I have as yet not forgotten, but also which I have my companions at hand to remind me and to verify doubtful points.

Burial customs. Kittegaryumiut, Mamayauk tells: When a man died during the fore or middle part of the day, while yet there was daylight enough for the funeral, he was put away that day; if too late, the body remained till morning. People slept in the house with the dead if the body could not be moved before night. The body was completely covered with the dead man's own sleeping clothes while others slept. When the body was carried out all sleeping clothes (other clothes too, but she is not sure) and cooking gear was carried out just after the body and laid for a few minutes on the snow or on top of the roof of the alleyway. These were then carried back into the house, being carried both out and in through the regular door; the body was not carried through this door but through an opening in the house wall made for the purpose, generally on one side of the real door. Only a few followed to the grave; the dead person's husband or wife sometimes followed, sometimes sat in the middle of the house floor with hood up. They often wept, but only from real grief. The children might or might not follow; some usually did. The sled was always drawn by men, not dogs. The body was usually dressed in new clothes, with new mittens on hands. The body lay on its back always and arms were sometimes folded at right angles to the humerus, sometimes down by each side the body. A knife was sometimes placed in the man's hand; the food utensils and special cooking pot used during the last illness and other articles such as a man traveling might need, were placed outside the grave. The dress was also the full traveling garb, including "tapsi" and was the best that could be afforded. The chief mourner did not go out of the house for five days, sat most or all the time on the middle of the house floor, never lowered his or her hood, and ate separately from the rest of the people. No one in the village must sew new garments (but old ones might be mended) for the same five days. There was no singing, drumming, hammering, or other loud noise. At the end of the five days, the chief mourner took off all clothes, and put on new and the old ones were carried out on the sea ice and thrown away. No members of the family might eat of the heads of any animal of land, sea, or air, until after the first anniversary of the death. At this anniversary there was a sort of celebration and singing and dancing. It was not held at the grave and might be held anywhere. "People feared the dead thinking they might become turñnrat."

M. knows of nothing resembling a soul or spirit inside a man who is well, but a sick man is entered by a sokotak which has usually or always been sent by a shaman's "wishing the man to die." This finally kills him, or leaves him through being driven out by another shaman. She does not know what or where these sokotak are before or after being inside a sick man, or after the death of one they have killed. She thinks only one enters any one man at a time. He is not possessed by two at once. On a good many of these fine points she is uncertain. Those prohibited from eating heads are the surviving husband or wife and the couple's children or adopted children; but not persons attached to the family as a sort of "free servant," the parents, brothers, and sisters of the dead, but not the parents, brothers etc., of the dead person's surviving wife or husband. A grandchild of the dead must not eat heads but the husband or wife of a grandchild may. Adopted children differ from real in that a son, say, must refrain from heads for a year, but are under the prohibition that bind the son. All those under the head-eating prohibition throw away their old clothes and don new ones when the chief mourner does and in the same manner. If the dead owns good clothes they are used by some other member of the family. There is no fear of sleeping in the dead's bed place. The house is not avoided or abandoned because death has occurred, except that occasionally in epidemics where a whole family is dead within the house the house is allowed to cave in upon them.

Ilavinirk tells: At Kigirktarukmiut (Kotzebue) when a man died the body was wrapped in skins and placed on a temporary rack made of two rows of crossed sticks. During the next winter the relatives gradually accumulate a quantity of driftwood or other logs near the grave. An elevation is formed by laying short stubs of large logs crosswise; on top of these a box is built log-cabin fashion sometimes to a height of say five feet (perhaps a three foot pile of logs underneath making the total eight feet, say). The body is then placed in this, and outside the remaining wood is piled tipee fashion, about the grave. In some cases a platform inside the tipee pile takes the place of the box. The body is dressed up for traveling at burial, and what a traveler may need is placed by the grave. The grave is visited twice after this, i.e., twice dressed in fresh clothes after the first had time to become rotten.

When a man was supposed to be about to die all bedding was carried out of the house except what the sick was using. If he died so late that dark came before the house could be put in order, the people either slept without their bedding or else did not sleep. It was seen to that at least one person was always awake. Soon after daylight the body was dressed in new clothes, if they were available, else the best of the available used clothes, was lifted through the windows "for the hole in the floor was unhandy for such things" and taken to the burial place. As soon as the body was gone, the willow flooring was cleared out of the house, new willows replaced it, and the bedding was brought back in. About the same prohibition as at Kittegaryumiut maintained for five days. The people of the mourning house entered no other house and none others entered theirs. After that there were no restrictions, Ilavinirk thinks, except that the mourners ate for a greater or less part of the next year only of food secured by themselves or at least cooked at home.

When Ilavinirk was young he twice accompanied a party which made a long pilgrimage in two skin boats to the place inland on a river where a couple had buried their ten year old daughter, an only child. They each year dressed the body in new clothes and set the grave to rights. So long as they were about the grave a fire was kept constantly burning, so near as could be without danger to the grave. They cooked over this fire when the work was done, but often ate before that, in which case usually of pre-cooked or dry food which was warmed up by the fire. As they commenced eating of some food of which the dead had been especially fond, a piece would be cut off or divided off and put in the fire, the fonder the dead had been of the sort in question the larger a portion was put in the fire. It was said this was food for the dead. If the dead was a tobacco user, tobacco was also burned. When all work was done about the grave and all had eaten what they wanted, the rest of what food had been brought near the grave was burned just before the people left.

Ignirkariaktuat was the expression for lighting a fire by a grave, feasting there, and for the subsequent head- or foot-lifting, if that was to be done. Some time, say, when a number of boats were passing the recent or old grave of an añatkok they would stop, make a fire beside the grave, put into it each family a share of every sort of food they were going to contribute to the feast. Then all ate and the rest of the food was put in the fire. When this was done the listeners usually crouched around the fire on hands and knees to listen to the voice from the fire which was built near the grave of the dead añatkok. Questions were asked by the men around the fire and answered from the fire by the spirit of the dead añatkok through the mediation of the living añatkok who sat outside the circle. "These answers sometimes came true and sometimes not."

Another method which did not necessitate the presence of an añatkok, though one would officiate if he was there, was that anyone at all laid himself on his back near the grave of the dead añatkok and another person lifted his foot or his head by a stick. If the foot was light the answer to any question was "No," if heavy it was "Yes." [. . .] No unburned food was ever left by the grave.

JULY 17 [. . .] The swimming. Swimming at Kittegaryumiut, or rather wading was by both sexes, but in separate places. Both swam without clothes. In one case of three boys bathing, one of them (brother of Memoranna, Jimmy) was drowned in a river about fifty yards wide and deep only in a small hole in the middle. Ilavinirk never knew of both sexes bathing together after they were say ten years old. Only a few really swam and only when grown.

Customs. Ilavinirk tells when a man died the first of his relatives to have a child would name it for him. Soon after this event the dead's nearest relative, a son if there was one, would inquire of the three, four, or five persons who had worked at the first burial of the dead, at making the final grave, or had tended the sick just before death, what they wanted for presents. Generally it was a full suit of clothes where the prospective recipient prescribed the sort of each garment. He would then ask the child what sort of food it preferred. If not old enough to speak, the child was answered for by one of its parents. He also prescribed a suit. If the child asked for caribou marrow the chief mourner often undertook a journey of several weeks to the upper Nogatak to buy marrow bones or shoot deer. When all was ready people were bidden to a feast in the kajigi. The child and those who waited on the dying or handled the dead are placed in the center; the child first receives its gifts, then the others. After this come gifts to those who have sewed the gift clothes or otherwise helped to prepare the feast. In the aggregate the chief mourner gives away a large amount, often all he has but the guns, his other food-gathering implements, and cooking utensils. The bedding from his house is frequently all given away. When the gifts to these are over, outsiders, all nearby are bidden and some from afar, join in the feast but they receive no presents. Everyone who gets a present soon pays for it by presents back to the mourner, though nothing is thought ill of it if they are unable to do so. Those who feast only make presents of food. The aggregate received by the mourner is usually as much as he gave, or more. The mourner always protests against these return gifts, saying he was only paying for services done the dead. Ilavinirk himself has given one such feast for his mother. She died when he was about eight or ten, he gave the feast when sixteen or eighteen years old. One woman who had tended the sick could not be reached, she had moved to another place. [. . .]

Child betrothals. Children at Kittegaryumiut are often betrothed when young, sometimes a few weeks after birth. These are called: "katitarigik." In many cases they marry others, but when they do marry each other the event takes place rather before than after the girl's first menstruation.

Trade. Ilavinirk tells "Talak apa añaña" (Kittegaryumiut form is Apagma) used to go from Kigirktarukmiut in winter (not fall) by sled to the sea near Icy Cape, thence to Cape Smythe, and back by the same route, being home before spring. His purpose was to buy stone pots, lamps, and wolverines. His trade was chiefly Siberian tobacco, but also other Siberian goods. This man was dead before Ilavinirk was born. There are several relatives at Cape Smythe connected with these journeys: e.g., Seravanna and Sagavanna. Ilavinirk's father told him first and later Seravanna and others told him at Cape Smythe. [. . .]

JULY 19 Ilavinirk tells the smallest arlut are a little larger than the common seal, the largest are about equal to the largest walrus. Their general appearance is somewhat that of fish, their teeth are long and interlock; [. . .] they have some black maktak (black skin). They feed chiefly on seals and white whale. When they hunt seal they surround it as wolves do caribou. The arlut get all around the seal while some get below it to keep it from diving. The white whales, for fear of the arlut which prefer deep water, sometimes swim so near shore that they crawl on the bottom while their backs are out of water. People say that wolves and arlut are avariksut ("chips of the same block"), equivalent, alike, equal. When wolves starve on land they go to their relatives in the sea and turn arlut; likewise the arlut when unable to find food in the sea go inland and become wolves. These wolves, as far as Ilavinirk knows, are in no way differentiable from ordinary ones.

The Kigirktarugmiut frequently see the arlut but do not kill them. They tell a story of four brothers of the Imarxlit people who were hunting walrus in a boat. When the elders were not looking the youngest speared an arlut. His brothers reproved him, but nevertheless "seeing it was dead anyhow" took it home, cut it up, and ate some of it. That night several arlut kept walking around the house, weeping as people do in grief, while a multitude of others swam near the beach. The four brothers all died soon after. Among the Akuliakattagmiut the common name for wolf is arluk. They know, however, the word amarak. Ilavinirk never heard of a wolf being spoken of as an arluk when seen at an distance.

Marriage by capture. His second wife, Illrox, was taken "forcibly against her will" by Ovayuak (Kittegaryumiut), brought home to the house, and prevented from going home that day. Later she did not go home "for fear of making Ovayuak angry." Amaratjiak, his former wife, was in the house at the time, she apparently was glad of the acquisition of a seamstress. Illrox had a mother, an older brother, and other relatives present. None did anything.

Young girls were told by the old women: "If you don't marry soon some young man who wants you, some old man will carry you off to be his first wife's servant." They also told a story of a woman who would not marry. Several married men and widowers had had an eye on her for a long time. One day one of them attempted to carry her off, others tried to get her away from him, wanting her for themselves. In the struggle the woman suffered several breaks of bones and died as a result (Mamayauk tells).

JULY 20 [. . .] Taboos. Ilavinirk tells on upper Noatak when he was a boy, caribou caught in snares must be skinned with stone knives only (anmark). The ear cartilage must not be separated from the head, but the skin of the ears must be with the hide. The head must not be cut from the trunk, but the body was cut in halves through the thorax. Ilavinirk does not know how many ribs went with the head part. The meat of a snared deer must not be boiled in any but a pottery kettle [. . .] but it might be roasted or eaten raw. He does not know that women were forbidden to eat certain parts of these deer. Deer shot with guns might be skinned with iron knives and cooked in metal pots. He thinks deer shot with bows in the open might be cooked in metal pots, but those shot with bows in "kañirkat" in enclosures must, he thinks, be cooked in pottery pots. When he was there, most of the shooting was with guns, except bows were often used in the enclosures. [. . .]

JULY 21 [. . .] Aqliktuak tells: A woman with child cooked her food in a separate small pot. Some women when with child must not eat seal. Some women with child became skin poor while others fared well because no allowable food was on hand. After childbirth those who bore male children were not allowed to drink water for four days, but were allowed a little meat broth as part of their food, allowed to eat only a small quantity. Mamayauk when sick was once forbidden by an [. . .] añatkot to eat caribou, another time to eat seal. Sick persons were frequently forbidden to eat fish bellies. "Nerigovinñok, dokonoaktutin." Boys were aglirktut on killing first ptarmigan, deer, etc. Does not know just what the provisions were. There were special restrictions on women whose children died just after or else before birth: they must not get water from fresh or salt source, they must not eat outdoors, and when fishing with a hook must never take off their mittens while near the fishing place. [. . .]

JULY 27 [. . .] Marriage. Marriage at Kittegaryumiut is not countenanced between adopted brother and sister. A man may have two sisters for wives, either simultaneously or successively. A half-sister or an adopted sister are considered exactly as near relatives as full sisters.

JULY 28 Dug in a house just west of the whalers graveyard but found nothing. [. . .]

Smell. The smell of a white man, say of his hand after he has thoroughly washed it, is considered to be different from that of an Eskimo and those not used to it are said to dislike it very much. There was much talk of this a few years ago but there is little now, for one used to the smell does not dislike it (Mamayauk). Some Eskimo of both sexes are known as having a disagreeable smell. [. . .]

JULY 30 I am disposed and doing nothing. [. . .]

JULY 31 Terms of relationship (Kittegaryumiut). Brother and sister older than he, "atkalualuik," brother and sister younger than he, "naiyagik"; two brothers or two sisters, "nukarik" [. . .]. A brother will address an older sister often as "agaraluñ" and she may be spoken of as "agaralua." "Aniñaraluñ" is used by older sister to brother; "aniñ" by younger sister to brother (e.g. Noashak to Palaiyak). [. . .]

AUGUST 3 Skin dressing. Skins are never scraped by men at Kittegaryumiut. Never heard of kayak skins being chewed (cf. Boas). They are rotted and sewn while wet. In fly time they are protected from blue bottles by being encased in a sealskin "pok." Men who had no wives sometimes scraped deer legs for boots, etc. M. thinks therefore scraping skins was not aglernaktok but the men were merely lazy.

Cannibalism. Cannibalism heard of by M. only in case of a man who had killed an Indian and who was told by a shaman to eat a piece of the dead Indian. M. does not know the reason, but is sure that there was no scarcity of food at the time. [. . .]

Importance of early ethnological work. Five years ago (1906) Memoranna (Roxy) pretended to give me minutely the difference in the Mackenzie system of counting used "long ago" from that used today. The differences were trifling. Today for the first time I happened to note the numerals in Petitot's "Monographie." They show an excellent system of counting and wholly different from that given by Roxy. I have no doubt Petitot is substantially right. Thus, in a few years, has been lost from people's memory an interesting and significant fact. Some of the people who accompanied Petitot to Good Hope were of Roxy's own family, uncles or aunts, I forget which.

Taboos. Mam. told today that her people (Kittegaryumiut, etc.) are gratetul to the missionaries for letting them know that Sunday is aglernaktok (taboo). The idea underlying this gratitude seems to be that they suppose many of their past ills to be due to violation of this taboo, the existence of which they did not know; now they know the taboo, can avoid breaking it, and hope thereby to escape many ills.

AUGUST 4 Cardinal points. In reading today Thalbitzer's "Skraelingerne: Markland, etc.," p. 207, where he says the Labrador people thought the "Karaler" dwelt on the same side of Davis St. as they did, i.e., in the north, whereas they really dwelt to the east, in South Greenland, I am reminded of an interesting thing told me by Ilavinirk several weeks ago: At Kotzebue Sound the old men used to say and all the people believed it, that the seacoast was as a whole straight and that bends in it (e.g., Pt. Hope) were only local like kinks in a fairly tightly stretched line. This fits in with their absolute (as I believe) lack of comprehension even today of our cardinal points. An Eskimo who started north along the Labrador coast and finally got to South Greenland by way of Smith Sound would think of himself as going east, north, or whatever the original direction was, the whole time he would no more be conscious of changing direction than we would if we traveled around the earth on a meridian. To begin with, Kavuñamun, etc., does not mean "to the north," "to the south," "to the east," or anything else in terms of our points of the compass, it means "up the coast" or "down the coast " as nearly as it can be translated into our speech. [. . .]

AUGUST 9 Still "under the weather." Writing an article on certain Eskimos which I consider to throw a light on the direction of their ancient migratory movement—find it difficult to keep my mind on the subject in hand. Palaiyak hunting on top net—not home yet (9 A.M.) [. . .]

AUGUST 9 *Correct date.* This is the same day as is entered under the head of August 10 above—I find I have become day ahead of right date in my reckoning. [. . .]

AUGUST 19 [. . .] The spirit of the fire [. . .] was fed with a little blubber, tallow, akutok, or other fat by Kittegaryumiut after fire was built [. . .]. "Iliat oktjoviaktorlit," was said by people in boats as they passed any grave except a recent one; as they said this some sort of fat was thrown into the water, or on the beach if the boat was so near shore that it could be done. "Iliat aviutjaktarlit" was the universal expression that covered such an offering not only of fat but of any sort of food; "aviutjak" was any sort of food intended for spirits. Water was similarly given the spirit of the grave by being poured out anywhere while the giver was in sight of the grave.

AUGUST 20 [. . .] Names. Names at Kittegaryumiut were never given by persons themselves or even by bystanders. If a stranger wanted to know a person's name he would wait till that person was out of hearing and then ask someone. A person would not tell his parents' names, the name of wife (or husband) any more readily than his own. They would readily, however, tell the names of their brothers and sisters, and of their own children.

AUGUST 21 Brought home meat killed yesterday. Tannaumirk accompanied me there and hunted beyond—not home at 8 P.M. Pal hunted NE and saw 9 and 2 deer in the river far off. [. . .]

Beliefs: When the new moon is first seen a person should spill a cup of water saying that it is for the "tatkimima" to drink (Kit-Mamayauk). The water should be spilled on the ground in the direction of the moon. [. . .]

AUGUST 23 Boys returned 10 P.M. last night had been to Isuqluk but had seen no big game. Tannaumirk had been sick most of the day [. . .] and was barely able to get home.

Whistling (Tannaumirk says and my observation confirms it, though I never thought to enquire) is not practised by the Copper Eskimo. They used to succeed in whistling, however, on seeing him do it; they kept continually asking him to whistle more. At Kittegaryumiut whistling was probably "always" known he thinks. It was practised especially in hunting white whales [. . .].

AUGUST 24 [. . .] The stars. The stars must be living things because their excreta are often seen dropping to the ground. Those who have examined these say it is plain they feed on seals (Tannaumirk and Mam.).

AUGUST 26 Sent Pal. and Tannaumirk to Langton Bay partly at their own will and partly to leave letter for Anderson saying we shall make to the head of Coal Creek to look for deer, when they become more numerous around here [. . .].

Beliefs. Shadows and reflections were made objects of fear to children at Kittegaryumiut though Mam. never knew just what the fearsome thing was. She thinks people may have been "playing" somewhat as white people do who scare children with imaginary creatures. Children were especially told not to bend over the seal oil dish in eating, for they might see their reflection if they did. She was frequently told "get your face away from that oil dish; your reflection (tarran) may smile at you." Some people used to say there was no danger in seeing your reflection in anything except oil, i.e., it was well enough to look for your reflection in a river or pond.

AUGUST 27 White whale hunting customs. On the afternoon of each day a shout was raised by someone who had climbed to the roof of one of the two Kittegaryumiut kajigis. This was a sign for the kayakers to gather on the roof of the kajigi to talk of who should be the head kayaker [. . .] for tomorrow. Generally, there was a new head each day, though a man who was considered "better" than the rest might serve several days. While a man was leader, it was incumbent on his wife to be careful her fire should never quite go out, and during the pursuit of whales she must not go outdoors from her tent until the last whale had been killed or had escaped. When a whale had been killed, a single straw that had grown upon a grave was stuck into the wound and withdrawn. If several wounds, all were treated with the same straw, M. thinks, but is not sure. She thinks the straw was then thrown away. [. . .] A similar custom was observed with regard to caribou. A man who had killed a white whale (or caribou, or other large game animal) usually had his earholes pierced, and must not eat blubber till the holes had healed. It was kept from closing by the use of a small peg. No one who had lost a relative by death must eat within the following year any part of a whale uncooked. If they did the man who had killed that whale would never get another whale. [. . .]

SEPTEMBER 2 Tan. brought home meat remaining in the field of bear killed Aug. 23. [. . .]

Campsites of Eskimo are numerous around here. There are two "tent rings" of stones at a creek mouth half a mile west of sled route river (seen by the natives only). I found in various places scattered rotten sticks and broken bones, indications that someone had camped (either Eskimo or Indian) between here and Isugluk, and about halfway to Isugluk probably half a dozen tent sites, with stone fireplaces, pieces of kayak slats, etc., clearly showing they were of Eskimo origin. There are no deer swimming places near, so either the parties were en route somewhere, or they used kayaks to set nets. Found also campsite of ship's natives a mile southwest of Isugluk, plenty broken boxes, canned meat tins, etc. A half dozen long sticks of firewood I raised up in tipee frame style, thinking someone may need them sometimes for wood. These are in a hollow, at the north end of a small lake.

SEPTEMBER 3 [. . .] Customs. "Show me your tongue" [. . .] is said at Kittegaryumiut (especially to children, but also to older persons in jest) if one thinks the speaker may be telling fibs. They do not know why people speak so, they never heard of the tongues of fibbers looking otherwise than of those who tell the truth. Icelandic children are told, however, that if they fib, a black spot appears on the tongue, and "show me your tongue" is frequently said to them. [. . .]

SEPTEMBER 5 Left behind meat on drying rocks and moved camp south, intending to go to my meat kill of yesterday. [. . .]

Beliefs. Tannaumirk was frequently told when small, not to eat standing up as it would make his feet weak and liable to swell up. Mam. was told not to sing when eating but she never knew the penalty. [. . .]

SEPTEMBER 12 [. . .] Found a very old Indian brush lodge on the N. front of Coal Creek. [. . .]

Taboos. At Kittegaryumiut during the beluga season all were forbidden to "work earth," i.e., holes or pits must not be dug, macu roots must not be gathered, etc. Berries might be gathered, however. Children at play were reprimanded whenever found breaking this taboo. The beluga skins were cut usually or always around the throat and the waist, i.e. the piece of skin between throat and waist was dried for bootsoles, canoe covers, lines, etc. The skin of the head and tail was eaten as maktak. When being dried this piece of skin was pegged on the ground as sealskins are. It was strictly required that the headward part of the skin should be towards inland, the tailward towards the sea. It was said if a skin were dried in the reverse position the beluga would cease visiting that part of the coast. During the beluga season no new deerskin garments must be made but old ones were mended; new sealskin clothes were made, however. New caribou clothes or clothes of muskrat (perhap other skins too) must not be made while the sun was absent. No one attempted hooking or otherwise catching fish during the dark days. Mam. never heard that there was a prohibition, but it was said none could be caught.

Eskimo tent sites (two tents) seen Monday just east of the treeline about eight miles southeast of camp, stone fireplace and a few small sticks of firewood on top of a stoneless woodless hill.

SEPTEMBER 13 Boys back to our camp of August 31 (the brush lodge) to get tobacco, tea the bearskins etc. Soon after they left rain started, which kept me in camp all day. [. . .]

Beliefs. Growing girls were told that when they wake up in the morning they must not linger in bed but must go outdoors at once, if but for a moment. Some were not even allowed to dress, but were made to go outdoors naked or partly clad. They were told that doing this would make child delivery easy, while if they lingered in bed while young they would have slow and painful delivery when they came to have children. Growing boys were also made to go outdoors similarly but Mam. does not know what they were told would happen if they did not (Kittegaryumiut). [. . .]

SEPTEMBER 18 *News:* The police stationed at Herschel Island died to the last man the past winter. [. . .] Five men froze and starved to death between Dawson and McPherson and Inspector Fitzgerald, ex-policeman, Carter serving as guide, private Kimney and two men whose names did not reach us. [. . .]

Though we lack the details, the case is plain enough. Sickness—and other reasons which may be learnt from Fitzgerald's diary which he kept to the last—delayed them so long, they either made no effort to get game or failed in doing so, starved or got weak [. . .]. This is a trip which I made alone in autumn and Darrell made done in winter. It was considered by the police an easy trip [. . .]. There are roadhouses and Indians part of the way. Most of the route is through a good game country, well wooded. Possibly they lost their way and wandered about [. . .].

The news struck me like a blow. It kept me from sleep far into the night, and long before day I wake from dreaming of it to think about it [. . .]. I knew inspector Fitzgerald well and could almost say as much of Carter, both were true fellows. Kimney I had seen several times. Fitzgerald and

Carter were both experienced men. Anderson heard that Fitzgerald's diary did blame Carter. Knowing about these men and liking both I should say that charge is probably founded in past, bitterness of starvation. [. . .]

There is no particular lesson for us in this tragedy for our methods are not those which an abundance of reasons makes flexible for the police. We start journey and continue it to its end under ever present consciouness of the danger of running out of food; for that reason we are comparatively safe. [. . .]

Sgt. Selig. a friend more especially of Anderson than of mine though I liked him so far as I knew him, died at Herschel Island after the leaving for Dawson of the party whose fate is mentioned above. [. . .]

The outside world: news is told as follows: Successful revolution in Mexico, Diaz dead on way to Europe: Portugal a Republic, World Fair in Frizco to celebrate Panama Canal in 1915 when canal is supposed to be finished. [. . .]

SEPTEMBER 20 [. . .] *Natkusiak,* the only man one has who is of any account for long journey, is lost to us through getting married at Baillie Islands in August. He now has to follow his father-in-law Kutukak who went west towards Mackenzie River. So far as I see this kills my chances of sledding around the north east of Victoria Island next spring for Anderson is led to his blind calling—as I suppose I should be towards my archaeological work though that would be both archaeological interest and ethnological in the north-Victoria Island trips. [. . .]

SEPTEMBER 22 [. . .] Originality. Mam., Tannaumirk, and Pal. say that people commonly say that the Kiglavait refused to enter the ark when Noah invited them in, preferring to hide from the flood underground. This is a case of grafting on to the new Christian mythology a bit of their own folklore, which was merely to the effect that the Kiglavait lived underground like moles. Some seem to have believed they all became extinct anciently; others that they still live underground mole fashion; are very rare animals, though not extinct, and come out only at night. All our Eskimo believe that the refusal of the mammoth to enter the ark is recorded in the Bible. They have no notion it is an Eskimo emulation of the Jewish account.

SEPTEMBER 30 Beliefs. A woman who has a child she wants to grow tall should sew the side seams of its coat with sinew from the neck of a swan (Kittegaryumiut-Mam.). Sinew from the wing (breast) muscles of ptarmigan Mamayauk has known to be used, braided. One man she knows put a pair of soles in his boots with ptarmigan sinew.

OCTOBER 1 [. . .] Rattles. Children at Kittegaryumiut used to play with rattles made of ptarmigan crops blown up. The rattle was produced with berries found in the crop. Children were reprimanded for making such playthings out of snared birds. Mam. thinks that this taboo applied only in the winter and spring, but is not sure. [. . .]

OCTOBER 5 Mamyauk severely ill last evening after 5 P.M. till about midnight—internal pains which made her so weak that by midnight she could not turn over or hold a cup for drink. Gave a ½ gr. morphine pill to lose pain and got badly scared soon after by noting that her heart at time beat slowly [. . .]. No particular pain after midnight, but so weak today that she can hardly move around. She thought that she was going to die, which may have had some effect in weakening her. Today she keps repeating as if determined it shall prove true: "If I get sick this way again, I *will* die."[. . .]

OCTOBER 26 Ilavinirk, Pal. and Noashak brougt home on a sled some fish cached before and 34 caught today—about ⅔ Piguktul and other trout. Dr. Anderson skinned 2 fish for specimens. Wrote some Eskimo, finished calculating the cephalic indices of the Copper Eskimo measured thus far—212 individuals. Plotted comparison of the Prince Albert Land and Pt. Willams Eskimos as compared with the rest of the Copper Eskimo. The curve shows a considerable variation from the rest which corresponds with the blond couples out of these groups—decided less dolichocephalic than the others. [. . .]

OCTOBER 30 *Missionary yarns:* The story is of a missionary at Pt. Hope "fat, and with a hawbeak nose" who was replaced by Dr. Driggs—his name had been forgotten by Ilavinirk. He had been labouring for some time without much success. One evening however he made a decent impression. His address was something as follows: "I have told much about God, but you will not believe. Now I will tell about this nevertheless" (here follows his account of the natures, purpose and works of the revolver). "Now, do you believe what I say? If you don't just let me shoot at you and see if it works as I said. Who wants to be shot at? Then truly don't you want me to? You believe what I have told you about the revolver—then why don't you belive what I have told you about God?" The argument made a decided impression, and from that time men began to believe in God. Ilavinirk was present. [. . .]

OCTOBER 31 *Missionary yarns:* Ilavinirk says Mr. Whittaker has told the Eskimos that Jesus gave us (white man) our alphabet [. . .]

NOVEMBER 2 Missonary yarns. Influence of missionaries. Ilavinirk and Tannaumirk say all the missionaries have told them never to forget Jesus. If they do, he will not take them into heaven. Therefore neither of the two informants ever ceases to think about Jesus when awake, nor does any converted Eskimo even when angry, when hunting caribou, when dancing, singing etc. [. . .]

NOVEMBER 22 [. . .] Roger left behind because apparently sick. I followed the sled an hour later, after a talk with Anderson in the seldom privacy of the crowd's absence. Caught up with the sled near mouth of Jimmy's River. [. . .]

NOVEMBER 23 [. . .] Customs. All here are horrified at my telling of the Puiplirmiut that they pick frozen deer droppings off the snow, keep them in pails, and eat them like berries. Ilavinirk says that while this practice is repulsive the Puiplirmiut deer droppings are really a fine thing when boiled and used to thicken blood soup. This is much practised in Western Alaska.

NOVEMBER 24 [. . .] Langton Bay. Langton Bay inhabitants. From notes taken, August 10, 1911 at the Baillie Islands by Ilavinirk from Panigyuk, the oldest woman there. Langton Bay harbor sandspit is called Nuvuayuk. Its people lived on whale, seal, caribou, and fish at different seasons. There were no fish nets while she was at Langton Bay (till about 1845) nor even at Baillie Islands till later. Fish were hooked and speared. Another settlement was where we dug house ruins in July, 1911. There the people also had a "mine" of clay for pots. [. . .] Most people had only clay pots, but a few had stone ones. All stone pots and all lamps came from the east. A settlement north towards Parry was Annigak [. . .]. It is marked by remains of platform caches. There were also people at Booth Islands and, she heard, everywhere east along the coast to the Nogatokmiut. There were two years (not successive) where many people died (Ilavinirk did not know if of hunger or sickness); after the second all people left the vicinity of Langton Bay (about 1845, a little before Richardson's visit whom P. saw at Baillie), some went to Baillie, others east; nothing ever heard of those that went east. People used to hunt and fish southeast on top hill. How far they sometimes penetrated is not clear, I have seen camps about eight miles southeast of our house in Coal Creek. The most frequented lakes she knew of were Omatilik (about six miles southeast of Nuvuayuk, a lake with a "heart shaped" island) and Amituaryuk, about five miles southeast of Monayuk.

The sandspit settlement at Baillie was called Iglulualuit and Iglu was near the Smoking Mountains. Tutipkirk was the V-shaped river valley right by Capt. Wolki's house. [. . .]

DECEMBER 5 [. . .] Man. cheeks have the "Heating flesh" that often accompanies consumption: Hav. complexion too dark to show this, probably. [. . .]

DECEMBER 10 Severe headache and threatening look of weather kept us from starting to river today.

Beliefs. An añatkok in Uñulivik on the shores of Immaruk, on the edge of the Mallemiut territory was Ilavinirk's father's "arnakata" (really katta, i.e., their fathers had exchanged wives). Out of his mind with drink he had shot his wife, of whom he was really very fond. There were three of her relatives present. They spread a skin over the murdered woman where she had fallen on the ground; then one of them wanted to kill the murderer at once, but the other two said this was no real murder, for the man was as if asleep and dreaming. They therefore deprived the bloodthirsty man of all weapons and kept him away. The añatkok, Axañak, was told of the tragedy when he recovered from his drunk. When he knew what he had done he sent for the relatives of his wife and asked them to kill him at once, to place his body under the same skin with his wife and to bury them together. To this the bloodthirsty one at once agreed, the others protested, but the añatkok's will and the desires of the one relative overcame the objections of the other two, and they killed Axañak with a spear. They then cut off his head, and his arms at the shoulders. They put the head into a bag which Ilavinirk thinks was the man's own stomach, slit open his thorax along the sternum (one side of it) and put the head in. Then they left the body in a clump of willows. The cutting up, etc., was "for fear of the dead man's nappata." Ilavinirk's father later gave the body the customary burial and took the head out of the chest. The three men "as was the custom with mankillers" drank some of the dead man's blood, to appease or confuse his soul (?). The bloodthirsty of the three brothers soon died of starvation apparently, though he always ate with a good appetite. He grew thin without being sick, and died. Another got sores which broke out on one part of his body when they healed on another, and he too soon died. The third lived a long time but was unlucky in most things he did, especially in that no animals were ever caught in his traps and he had great difficulty and rarely was successful in approaching any game animals. Ilavinirk never heard of eating the dead man's heart or of taking out his eyes. [. . .]

DECEMBER 11 [. . .] Taboos. Ilavinirk tells that (about 1885 or 1888) the use of any but antler ice picks was taboo for the making of holes through which it was intended to hook for fish on the "Lagoon" (Imarruk) in Kotzebue Sound at the mouth of Kuwuk and Selawik Rivers. [. . .]

DECEMBER 16 [. . .] The Coronation Gulf Eskimo, uniformly told us that white whales (beluga) did not come into the Gulf. They did not even know the name (so my Eskimo say) [. . .]. Live bowheads are not seen but a dead one carrying a brass "whaling iron" was stranded on an island not far off shore from the mouth of the Kuguryuak and I saw a harpoon foreshaft made of the brass "iron." Several sleds there are shed with whalebone (lower maxillary). Walrus are known by hearsay from the east. [. . .]

DECEMBER 23 Cleanliness. Pannigabluk tells: The people of the Neriktoglirmiut (Yukon flats) are so lousy that even the dry fish they sell others is full of lice. Lice crawl all over their faces while they are eating and they lick them into their mouths when they come too near the lips. A dog sleeping on the house floor was killed in one night. These people wear clothes of fish and bird skins and of grass plaits. They call lice neriktit, hence their tribal name. [. . .]

For the last two days (since Friday morning) I have had a headache of varying severity and with symptoms which I take to be those of some kidney trouble—apparently chiefly the right kidney. Dr. Anderson had rubbed me energetically several times, applying counter irritant (capsoline) of which we have little left having used the greater part on our natives [. . .]. My pulse varies from 57 to 56 while lying down and sitting up. The lowest I have known before is 60. The beat is fairly regular but not strong. [. . .]

DECEMBER 26 Still unwell. Dr. Anderson getting ready for trip to Baillie Islands. [. . .]

DECEMBER 27 Dr. Anderson started for Baillie Islands at ca. 9 A.M.—took two sleds, thirteen dogs, but very little meat as we fear hunger before he comes back in case I keep sick. Dr. Anderson took Palaiyuk, Tannaumirk and Pannigabluk—the last to leave us permanently. [. . .]

DECEMBER 27 Beliefs. In Kotzebue Sound and elsewhere each fish net used to have its own añroak, usually the skin of some bird of prey. A feather of each particular net's patron bird was tied to the net when it was used in fishing. The better the charm, the more the net would catch (Ilavinirk). [. . .]

DECEMBER 28 Feeling somewhat better today. For a while the evening of the 26th (before Anderson left) and for most of yesterday, my pulse was 45 when lying quietly on my back, and 50 or 51 when sitting up. Today the pulse has never been under 52 and about 60 when sitting up. [. . .]

DECEMBER 29 [. . .] Feeling better, but not well. They tell me my eyes are badly sunken and I seem to have lost lot of flesh—through not eating much. Ate almost normal meal today. By mistake Dr. A took away with him the nethylin blue pills which I was using "for want of anything else."

A linguistic theory: Halbitzer (Phonetical Study, p. 115) [. . .]. The theory suggested is: If a people was to move from warm to cold district any labial sounds would tend to be eliminated through the difficulty of forming them outdoors in winter—the forms which the stiffness of the lip imposed on the people when outdoors in winter would gradually emerge and finally eliminate previous forms. [. . .]

DECEMBER 31 [. . .] Sign language. Among the Kittegaryumiut a raising of the eyebrows means "Yes"; a raising of the upper lip that produces vertical wrinkles along the nose as well as a wrinkling of the nose itself, means "No." Sidestepping with arms raised above the head: caribou or other big game in sight. Standing with arms horizontal: come here. A motion with both hands as if to put something on the ground: stop, don't come closer. Among Copper Eskimo, running sidewise from the trail and back across it: strangers are coming. Hands above the head: we are unarmed (a sign of peace).

1912

JANUARY 1 *The fishing* is suddenly falling off. As against 20 to 30 fish every other day two weeks ago we now get 5 to 7, though there has been put down a fine new net to replace the old torn one. The fish must evidently either all of a sudden have ceased swimming about much, or else they have gone to deeper parts of the lake. [. . .]

The name: Today we had a curious example of the final grasping of an idea which one would think should have come years ago. I have a thousand times at least heard Mamayauk address her daughter Noashak as *amañ* or *amamañ*, and I have long known that *ama* and *amama* = his (her) mother. I have, however, in this case either let the word pass uninterpreted through my ears or else have (when occasionally I have conjectured a meaning) considered it analogous to a married man with us addressing his wife as "mother" (copying the children's use of that word). Today I heard Noashak speak of Memoranna's (Jimmy's) wife Sanikpiak as panniga (= my daughter) and asked the explanation. I learnt then that S. speaks of Noashak as mother, the reason being that the name "Noashak" is that of Sanikpiak's dead mother—the little girl Noashak is by S. identified with her dead mother (Sanikpiak's). Noashak also bears the name Panigyuk which is that of Mamayauk's mother. This makes Noashak her own mother's "mother" and "Mamayauk" her own daughter's daughter (though Noashak never makes use of the word "daughter" to Mamayauk but only to Sanikpiak). This may be characterized as a sort of *reincarnation* theory, where Noashak is looked upon as *being* rather than representing two dead individuals.

Note: Compare this with "uvaña kait kain" (ante) used on sneezing (= I myself, come here). If a mother uses this formula for her infant child she says: "*Noashak* (e.g.) kait kain" where the *Noashak* being addressed is not the child *Noashak* but the dead person of that name, or the soul of that dead person. Later when Noashak has learnt to speak and can use the formula for herself, uvaña = *not* what it would with us, but = the dead *Noashak,* or her soul. The *atka* (= name, soul) of the dead person is therefore *I myself,* somewhat as our ancestors used to speak of *my mind* and *my body,* as if the mind and body *were not I,* but merely the possessions of *I,*—the *I* in our case being the hypothetical *immortal soul.* [. . .]

JANUARY 8 For a part of last night severe pains in the region of the heart—weak and tired after. The uncomfortable feeling about the pain of my right kidney has never quite stopped and is now a little worse than the last five days. [. . .]

JANUARY 12 *The sun* was seen by Ilavinirk from 11: A. to 1:30 P. by our time. It never quite reached the horizon. (I am in some doubt, however, as to his making a mistake in the time—11: to 12:30 seem more reasonable.) From his account it must have been up yesterday, but hidden by the drifting snow—he said last night that it looked as if the sun was up.

Indians used to hunt to the head of Harroby Bay in summer when the caribou skins were thin. For that reason a place at the head of the bay was (and is) called Satoksiarvik (a cutbank Ilavinirk thinks). The Eskimo did not for that reason hunt there and even today many Baillie Islands people have never been to the head of Harroby Bay. [. . .]

Mr. Whittaker at Herschel told that when Noah invited the Kiligavuk (mammoth) to enter the ark he refused on the ground that the ark was too crowded, and that his legs were anyway long enough to keep his head above the water. The mammoth were therefore all exterminated by the flood, and their bones only remain.

Baptism was explained by Mr. W. as making a man's head and it's surroundings shine so it could be seen in the dark like the light of a window. Ilavinirk saw one baptised man (Añusinnaaux) last summer, but the halo did not show because it was not dark, but he has no doubt it can be seen now that it is winter with dark nights.

Gifts or anything else handed by one man to another must be passed with the right hand (this is a religious commandment for which Mr. W. is authority). *Usuayak,* Oniak's father, is said to be the only Eskimo who has remained unconverted. For that reason his son makes him live in tent by himself and eat with food utensils (plate, etc.) which no one else touches (Ilavinirk tells). [. . .]

(Ilavinirk tells). Anaktak's mother Kajak refused to accept the faith. Mr. Whittaker then told them that they should test her with fire—if it burnt her she was to take the faith, if not she would have some ground for her pretensions to know more than other people as to what should be or should not be believed. She would not submit to the test so her son put some burning coals (or a burning stick) on her head while she slept. It burnt her and the pain woke her up, but so stubborn was she that even after that—and up to the present—she was only partly converted.

Unconverted at Kit are Oyangiuna, Kalakutak, and Kudualuk is only partly converted. At Baillie is only one man Lyituanyuk. Also near Mackenzie Usuayak (properly Uhuayak) a Killirmiut (?) and (in part) the woman Kajak [. . .].

Child adoption at Kit. was always accompanied by a present—"any little thing"—to the child's mother "to keep the child from becoming ill." There were usually presents in Kotz both at adoption and "now and then" after—if the real and adopted parents lived far apart, there were small presents to the real parents whenever they chanced to meet the adopters.

Burials (Ilavinirk tells) often took place among Nogatogmiut before man was dead. Ilavinirk saw one man hauled out who sat up in the sled on the way, and there were said to be frequent cases of bundled up men (corpse fashion) who kept hungry dogs at bay for a while by saying "goh" to them. [. . .]

Beliefs. A man, Pallañazlurak, [. . .] told in Ilavinirk's hearing that a "fire" once found him one forenoon when he was far from houses and pursued him all day till near dark when he got home and escaped into a house. A "fire" [. . .] is a "falling star" or meteor. They are considered living things and some at least are añatkok on a spirit flight. They pursue people who are not protected by the proper charms. [. . .]

JANUARY 18 *"Pains."* Analogous to the "pains" of the Indians are sokotak. They enter the body and cause sickness. Our people have heard about them often but never heard them described, so they don't know what they are like. "Innum sokotaktlugu anniaktita" was frequently heard at Kit. so it is to be inferred they were either made magically and sent to make people sick, or that they were already in existence and the añatkok merely gained power and then sent them. "Sokerktok"= he is sick (account of having a sokotak). This method of making people sick may be called the converse of the other one (described ant.) of stealing a man's soul (nappan). If a man fell and hurt himself or suffered some accident, his illness was not due to a sokotak—also wounds, frostbites etc. Most other things were magically originated illnesses.

Fake shamanistic performance: At Pt. Hope were several clubhouses (3 in recent years) 4 was the number before. They are Karimaktok, Uñasiksikat, Kañilirkpait. The men of Karimaktok were especially given to shamanism. When they were performing in the evening men who wanted to go out used to see a frightful tupilak (meaning of word unknown to Ilavinirk—not used by his people) in the hallway and fled back to the interior. A young man from curiosity hid himself on a platform cache and watched. Shortly after the performance began a man came out of an isolated house near Karimaktok, and went in. Towards morning only he came out of the clubhouse and went home. This was repeated 3 nights. On the third night the watcher peeped into the hallway and saw the man whom he had been watching squatted in the half-lit hallway. Next day the young man told. It came out the tupilak had been a man dressed in a bird skin coat, wearing a wooden mask and with hands stained red with ochre. No one's faith in shamanism was impaired by this incident.

Añatkok beliefs. Both at Kittegaryumiut and Kotzebue certain dogs are añatkok. They do not fly or perform many of the shamanistic tricks, but they drive away spirits just as human añatkok do. Like humans, dogs differ greatly in their añatkok powers. Almost any dog can be made an añatkok by feeding him certain charms (añroak) and by performing certain spells over him when a pup. He will then have special powers of seeing spirits and frightening them away and will protect his master and his house from them. Whenever a dog barks "at the air" or howls, it is that he sees spirits.

JANUARY 19 [. . .] *Beliefs* (at Kit.). Male children were prevented from walking on the house floor in their stocking feet or barefooted in the morning just after they got up. Some mothers only took care to have their boots well on, but others, even after the boots were on would carry them from the bed platform and set them down through the trap door into the alley way, so the first thing their feet touched was the alley way floor. After they had once been out of the house, they might the rest of the day walk about the floor barefooted or another way they pleased. (This custom is unknown at Kotz except that male children were carried or sent out of doors the first thing in the morning. They were often undressed all day.) At Kit. the prohibition against walking on the floor without boots did not apply if the child was carried out of doors first—whether naked or half-clad. (At Kotz taking children outdoors early prevented laziness in later life and made them good food providers). Mam. does not know the reason or penalties at Kit. Children (males only?) were also prevented from drinking the water of the first spring thaws—this prohibition lasted for several days (perhaps weeks?). The reason and penalty are unknown to Mam. (Unknown at Kotz) Ap. story of "Ulutina" written today from Mamayauk's dictation. This tale unknown in Alaska, so far as Ilavinirk knows. [. . .]

JANUARY 23 [. . .] *Añatkok beliefs:* I asked Ilavinirk about the occurrence of the belief that persons can see through solid walls (as in Iceland, "*í gegnum holt og hæðir*"). I have always understood that in Iceland this meant that the walls or hills were transparent. The belief in the transparency of opaque objects seems wanting everywhere between Parry and the Yukon. Añatkok only can see through walls, and that is because the walls lift up—so they really don't see through the walls, but under them. Añatkok, without sending their spirit or body off on a spirit flight can see things at any distance, and whether present, past or future. Sometimes they have this farsight in simple ecstasy, [. . .] in others they employ certain paraphernalia. The common method in Alaska, so far as Ilavinirk knows, was to take the drum baton (or other stick if baton was wanting?) and bore with it a hole in the floor equal to rather more than half the length of the baton. Looking down into this, the añatkok could see distant places—a birds-eye view—as if they were only a little way below him. He could thus see past and future things. Cf. Prince Albert Sound belief as shown by their taking my field glasses as an appliance for seeing caribou that would come tomorrow; they too asked me to turn them on the village to see inside which house our primus stove "needle" was hid (cf. the Icelandic "*Skuggsjá*"). These "far sight" beliefs were the same at Kit., so far as Mam. knows. They were experts there, Ilavinirk tells, in recent years in detecting small hidden articles. His stories mostly concern whisky. In one case a man with a small (¼ pt.) bottle hidden inside his coat came into a house where Ovayuak and Alualuk were dancing—a semi-conjuring event—and no sooner had he entered than Alualuk proposed a treat to himself and Ovayuak "from the bottle which I see hidden inside your coat." Another story concerns Ilav's buying 8 bottles when no one but himself and the whaling captain were there, he went home and saw no one on the way, put 6 bottles where they could be seen and 2 he hid. Then he invited others in and they drank up the six bottles. When they were emptied, Alualuk told him to bring out the other two "which you have hidden in that box." [. . .]

JANUARY 25 About 2 inches snow last night and one more inch today, with a snowless spell in morning and no snow after 2 P.M. [. . .] Today was a good day and I wrote about 400 words—it is hard to keep at it long continuously, for Mam. becomes tired easily, and when not sick she will not average over 300 words for day. I am not paying much attention to meanings except so far as is needed to identify the words with the Greenland ones—I am not yet competent anyway to make a dictionary, even had I the time and paper—the phonetics (sound changes are the main thing) I aim at [. . .].

JANUARY 27 *Knowledge of physiology:* Mamayauk (who had had a bad cough some time) told me today that what is coughed up is not from the lungs (as I thought) but from the stomach and comes up through the gullet and not the windpipe. She does not remember ever having been told this, but just "thinks so herself." So while they are excellent anatomist's they appear to be but poor physiologists. [. . .]

JANUARY 30 Dr. Anderson, Palaiyuk and Natkusiak arrived at ca. 11 A.M.—Natkusiak's wife is dead, Palaiyuk's mother, old Kunasluk and several others. Jannovsmirk remained behind at Baillie Islands. No foxes are being caught on the coast and people feeling blue—apparently an epidemic has taken the foxes off. Dr. Anderson had a good trip in most ways. [. . .]

FEBRUARY 1 Ilavinirk etc. fixing broken sled. Wrote a letter and ca. 120 words of Port Clarence (Kaviaragmiut) dialect.

Letter from the American Museum received as follows: one dated May 12, 1910, duplicates of which were received in December, 1910, and two letters (duplicates) dated December 28th, 1910—these were received by me January 30th, 1910. There were also two personal letters and one from the

Alumni Bureau of Iowa—this was my whole mail. The rest must have been sent *via* Barrow; the ones received came down the Mackenzie. [. . .]

Beliefs: If the first person who goes out of a morning comes back in with the report of "fine weather" (sila asi) someone in the house should say: tatkani (out there, out-doors). This will have the effect of keeping the weather good for that day. Another expression almost as effective may replace "tatkani"—"akana taima." (If there is a folk-tale behind this, it is at least not known to Mamayauk). [. . .]

FEBRUARY 7 *Vegetable foods:* All Eskimo known to me eat contents of stomachs and intestines of hares, rabbits, squirrels, ptarmigan, and stomachs of caribou. Sheep stomachs are eaten only in time of scarcity, as "they do not taste good." Berries, etc. found in blackbear stomachs were eaten by Kotz people. Ilavinirk never knew of the roots from an aklak stomach being eaten. [. . .]

FEBRUARY 10 Dr. Anderson—who has nothing to occupy him and therefore soon gets tired of being in camp—accompanied Pal. back to the hunting camp near Isugluk (Isugluk = the head of a marrowbone). They will probably move camp down to the woods at the bend of Horton River, and will go back home in a few days. Dr. Anderson is anxious we go "to Parry or somewhere" but I am lucky to have the good house where we are comfortable and I am accomplishing every day—Parry promises nothing now but a problematic polar bear skin—and caribou are more valuable scientifically, I feel than bearskins (polar). Dr. Anderson shows little enthusiasm for more caribou—is pretty homesick it seems, and wants to be on the move always to "kill time." Today I started Kittegaryumiut report section on the working of skins questioning Mam. at every term and embodying many points which are not to be found in my diary. By writing here where someone is always at hand to answer questions as they arise and settle most doubts I can get more satisfactory results than if I put the matter off till New York. In formulating an account aiming at completeness questions occur to me which I should never come to think of asking. [. . .]

FEBRUARY 12 Mam. says that the old Kittegaryumiut women used to tell her that when they boiled pounded caribou bones for grease, they found they always got less fat off the first potful than from the succeeding ones. M. says she did not use to believe this, but she has found it by experience to be true. This certainly seemed to work out today, there being more tallow from the second and third pots than from the first. [. . .]

FEBRUARY 14 [. . .] *Blindness:* Since about 20 years ago there has been but one case of blindness among the Kit.—an old woman named Pannimirianna. She became blind when old, but not very old. She was the grandmother of Nanyak (Nanyañk), a boy who seemed to be about 10 years old when he lived at Tuktuyaktok 1906–07. [. . .]

FEBRUARY 15 *A review:* The entries for the past month or two do not perhaps give a picture of the daily routine—that is not needed for me, for it cannot be forgotten. The present paragraph is written for others: My own constant effort has been acquiring a knowledge of the language—rather its nature than of its vocabulary, for I have decided that a pretentious dictionary is not worth attempting. My ear is continually giving me new ideas of the natives of the sounds that compare the Kit. dialect, and my alphabet is therefore even yet a very unstable thing. The natives soon get tired of monotonous questioning, especially if a difficult point comes up—of course they don't appreciate that anything of importance can be involved. Their answers become careless and almost misleading—they try to make me think I understand things which I don't understand (e.g. by declaring verbs to be synonymous which are really not so, this to get me to quit asking questions). Ilavinirk has tended traps almost every day but to little purpose [. . .]

Food. Marrow (Ilavinirk says) was not eaten directly to any great extent by Nogatogmiut. The bones were pounded and boiled, the marrow was then mixed with the tallow. This sort of mess would get high in summer. This high taste some liked and some did not. Among Copper Eskimo it is considered a great delicacy when high. [. . .]

Names from vegetable kingdom are rare at Mackenzie. Gavlaluk (Man) a black berry larger than pauñrak grows on grass stem. Kittegaryumiut, dead over twenty years ago. Oyarak (stone) and all such names are wanting. [. . .]

Names from birthplaces are rather common in many parts of Alaska. Auksarkerk, from a mountain near the Nogatogmiut—a Noga. man whose given name was Kuinirk (Tartar pipe). [. . .]

FEBRUARY 20 Started 9:50 A.; made tea by Dr. Anderson's cache of yesterday (with wood left there last winter) and got to Langton Bay house ca. 7 P.M. Found Aliñnak and wife there. They had just come from Cape Perry and the Barth Islands—saw 4 old beartracks and no foxtracks at all. [. . .]

FEBRUARY 25 Relations with Indians. Guninana tells that her father [. . .] had two tattoo lines (tunnerit, pl. only) on each side of his face. These ran from near the top of his nose just back of the alae to a point a little front of and below the ear. This was because he was an Indian killer, but G. does not know if he killed more than one, she thinks two for the lines were probably "awarded" on the same basis as whaling lines, one for each whale killed. This killing was on the Anderson (Mcfarlane) River; G. also knows of the killing told of by Roxy and recorded by me (about as G. tells it) in 1906.

A woman named Arnapluk [. . .] the younger sister of Panigyuk (the old woman still living who was about fourteen in 1846 when Richardson passed) was carried off by Indians, violently, G. thinks. They heard she had become the second wife of a powerful Indian chief.

A young girl named Atañana was sold to some Indians by her dead mother's brother Karrayaluk for a new rifle. She was about six or eight years old at the time. It was said the buying was by the orders and for a white man at "the big houses" (Fort Good Hope). It is said that Mrs. McDonald of McPherson told later that this girl had been married to a white man "Umialik" and had been taken by him far away. [. . .]

FEBRUARY 27 Wrote from Guninana's dictation "The Man who Made Mock of Dead Animals" and "The Man Befriended by Bears." [. . .]

Names. Macfarlane was known by two names at Baillie and Nuvuayuk (Pt. Atkinson). The one that was most favored and which has now become the only one used is Misipalla. On one of his trips Macfarlane was accompanied back to the Fort by two Baillie Islands men. One was Mamayauk who died probably at Kittegaryumiut in the last epidemic about eight years ago, the other may have been Sokaluk, dead some twenty-five or thirty years ago. Mamayauk always spoke of Misimikpala. This was considered by others to be a wrong pronunciation and was not followed. Nuvuayuk was inhabited permanently until the epidemic referred to (Guninana). [. . .]

FEBRUARY 29 Dr. Anderson, Ilavinirk and Pal. came home at ca. 3:30 P.—started from their camp near the SE. corner of the main body of Langton Bay about noon. Distance from harbor to SE. corner of bay therefore about 10 miles. [. . .]

This diary probably contains about 155000 words. One sparsely scribbled page contains 608 words (there are but few so scribbled); a closely written page gave 1428 words on an estimate based on a count of 10 lines, ca. 1000 words to the page is therefore probably a conservative estimate. [. . .]

MARCH 1 Dr. Anderson skinning out "scientific skin" of young bull caribou; I wrote story of "The Poor Couple Aided by Plovers" from Guninana's dictation. Ilavinirk back to the deer hunting camp with one sled—Pal. and Anderson will follow tomorrow. [. . .]

MARCH 3 *Beliefs:* The "vapor" (puyora) of a new-born child is likely to make people sick. For that reason immediately after the delivery of the child a hole is pierced in the window to let out the "vapor," a ceremonial act, for the hole is usually very small and the open ventilator of the house carries off far more warm air than this hole does. Some people are not afraid of the "vapors" of a childbirth provided the windows are pierced promptly; others will go outdoors and not come in till the child is delivered. There is no belief to the effect that these "vapors" make a hunter unsuccessful, they merely may cause illness.

When a woman is with child, she must keep all her food utensils very clean, else her child will be filthy, lousy, and prone to slovenly habits, she must not be lazy, for if she is, the child delivery will be slow and difficult. For this reason she is especially instructed to run out-of-doors when visitors come or when sounds or other signs indicate that someone out-doors needs assistance, in hitching or unhitching dogs or for any other work (Mam. and Guninana).

Alaskan Eskimo generally, e.g. Nogatomiut, believe that if a woman has difficult labor it is because she has had sexual relations with someone and failed to tell about it. For that reason a woman in labor will rehearse all her relations with men from her youth up, but especially any that have occurred during pregnancy. This custom was unknown at the Mackenzie so far as Gun. and Mam. know till after the ships began bringing western women. In general, among the Mackenzie Eskimo there was about the same subterfuge and secrecy about "illicit" sexual relations that there is among Europeans. Women, after marriage, would often, however, tell such things to other married women; things that had happened before marriage chiefly. This was looked upon as a "confidence"; the story often went far, however; but the husband was never informed by anyone. In general men did not keep so much secrecy, though they were not supposed to tell, and many never did. As a matter of fact women were, however, much better informed of the acts of their husbands than these were of the infidelity of their wives (Gun. and Mam.)

Alaskan Eskimo considered it a duty of both parties to tell at once; otherwise serious misfortunes would follow. "Illicit" sexual relations were seldom, if ever, kept secret among them. Among the Copper Eskimo there is a semblance of secrecy in some cases; in March, 1911, off the mouth of the

Kogluktualuk, Ivarlualuk in the presence of the women her husband and many others rehearsed the pre-matrimonial adventure of Anaktak, wife of Niakoptak. Ameraun's (Akuliakattak) relations with Komirk were an "open secret." A.'s husband was jealous and used to beat her, but showed no ill will to Komirk. [. . .]

Trade relations. White whale skin for bootsoles and boat covers were bought by the Nuvorugmiut from the Kittegaryumiut, as well as tobacco, beads, and latterly matches and other "Fort" goods. They bought these with caribou skins (two fawn skins were equal to one white whale skin), sealskins of various kinds, and latterly fox skins. Wolverines were also occasionally bought from the Kittegaryumiut.

Hunting. It was rare any Nuvorugmiut people joined the Kittegaryumiut for the summer beluga hunt. They went in winter to buy skins only. In summer, they devoted their main energies to the caribou hunt, chiefly to the east of Nuvorugmiut as far as Innuksuit. There were many caribou, especially on the islands between Nuvorugmiut and the river that runs out of the Eskimo lakes for that was part of the hunting ground of the Inuktuyut formerly and later of the Kittegaryumiut. Some who intended to winter on the Kuralak to hunt foxes, etc., also hunted caribou there. There were several caribou spearing places, yet much hunting was with bows. Meat was thrown away and only the skins taken, when animals were killed far from camp. Large quantities of dried meat were made; umiaks used to return deep loaded with dry meat, fat, and skins from the hunt in the fall. Seal oil was the main fat source in winter. Only those of the Kittegaryumiut who neglected the white whale hunt, and they were few, got any considerable number of deer during the season of suitability for clothing; hence, their need to buy skins. [. . .]

Siberian reindeer skins in small numbers came as far east as Baillie Islands, at least before the whaling ships first came. They were considered much more "stylish" than caribou because of their rarity and cost much more (Guninana). [. . .]

MARCH 4 Computed face indices of Kanghiryuarmiut (av. 97 [. . .]). [. . .]

Taboos. At Kittegaryumiut caribou meat must not be cooked in the kitchen (igak), but by a fire outdoors; at Nuvuayuk caribou might be cooked in the kitchen, but the fire for it was built a trifle to one side from the fireplace used for seals; at both Kittegaryumiut and Nuvuayuk birds were cooked over a fire built a trifle one side of that used for other food. Fish and seal cooked over fire built in same place. [. . .]

MARCH 6 [. . .] Beliefs. Few of the mysterious beings and processes in which the Eskimo believe are very clear or definite in their minds [. . .]. Thus, though both Mam. and Gun. talk freely of tatkok, they cannot when pressed give a coherent or consistent account of their attributes [. . .]. Mam. tells (probably from Alaskan sources) that in the case of wolves and arluk (killer whale?) at least each has during lifetime its double, i.e. every wolf on land has a tatkok at sea that is an arluk. If the wolf has trouble in finding food on land he goes to sea and seeks his double, the arluk. Here Mam.'s knowledge becomes vague. This much she has heard, but she does not know if the wolf remains at sea as a wolf, if it merges with its double and they become one, or if it becomes an arluk so that there now are two arlut, the one that always was at sea and the other driven there by hunger. Guninana says the above must be information from western sources. She knows too that arlut are the tatkoks of wolves; she always supposed that it was only on the death of a wolf that its tatkok went to sea and became an arluk. Still "come to think of it" she has heard that arlut hunt caribou too, so evidently they are part of the time in wolf shape. She refers to her own story of the woman who lived with the arlut as the source of some of her information. She never heard of a wolf voluntarily going to sea to become an arluk because of hunger. She thinks that if an arluk were to die that would be the end of him, but she never heard of one dying. Both M. and G. have heard that bowhead whales are the tatkok of musk-oxen. [. . .]

MARCH 7 [. . .] Cure of disease. Certain persons of both sexes are endowed with the power of curing disease by blowing their breath on the sick person or paining part of the body. This power is inborn, not acquired [. . .]. Such a person is supillgoyok or anerillgoyok. One who has this gift discovers it by trying his breath some time on a sick person; if the person gets well, he knows the curative power is his; if the invalid fails to get better it is because the person who blew on him hasn't the power. Of course, after a man learns he has the power he may now and then fail to effect a cure through one of the myriad counteracting accidents and influences against which the shamans too must contend. A man does not need this power to blow away false spirits in foot lifting [. . .]

Saunirk and Atka. The atka of a person is the soul (nappan) of some dead person who has been summoned to a child to remain by it and be its companion, protector, or "guardian angel." The atka will, if the child be not scolded so as to offend the atka who takes to himself any words or acts towards the child, protect the child from illness, assist it, e.g., to learn to walk, protect it from accidents, etc. The older the person gets the less the atka seems to help him, and people differ as to whether a boy's atka will help him in his first caribou hunt, i.e. the more able a child becomes to think or act for himself the less will the atka trouble about his welfare. The atka is sometimes in a child, sometimes near it, sometimes it goes quite away. When a child's atka gets farther from it than a fathom or so the child will begin to cry and will not cease till the atka returns. Sometimes a shamanistic performance is resorted to, to get the atka to return. There seem to be no charms for this purpose which the mother or relatives can use; a shaman must always be called in. As the child attains age it becomes less and less unsafe to scold or reprimand it, for the atka gets less sensitive and less apt to take hard words, etc., as a personal affront.

Besides the above and other "practical" reasons for naming a child, there is also the further practical reason that a man whose father was A will consider the child A^1 as an embodiment of his father and will treat it accordingly, will make it gifts and do for it other things prompted by his filial feelings as well as by the dictates of custom. He will address the child as "father" instead of by such terms as "nephew," etc., used by other relatives.

There are too, reasons of love for the naming. A woman will name her daughter after her mother not only because she wants to provide for her mother's soul's welfare but because, as Mamayauk says, she wants "to have her mother near her because she is so fond of her." While the soul of a dead person is the child's atka, the child is that soul's saunñra. So far as the Mackenzie people are concerned there seems to have been no other idea of a pleasant abode for the soul. The character of this abode depended in no way on the dead person's merits in life, but only on the accident of how the child, his saunñra, was treated. It was a duty to relatives to provide them with saunirks. People of the Mackenzie, therefore named their children after relatives usually, but not always, of the sex of the child, and worried if there were no children to speedily provide the dead with homes pleasanter than their graves. Some persons had more prejudice than others against having the atka of a different sex from the child. Some would let their fathers go unprovided with saunirks rather than name a girl baby after them; but this was merely depriving the dead of one alternative refuge, as there was sure to be someone else's boy named for one's father. An añatkok was also saunirk to his familiar spirit [. . .].

The soul. Mamayauk's story that the child is born with a soul which is its own, as opposed to the souls of others which merely live near the child, is partly discredited by the fact that when her daughter Noashak sneezes she (N.) says: "Uvaña kaitkaitkain" while M. when N. was small used to say when N. sneezed: "Noashak kaitkaitkain," i.e. she seems to have identified the name (atka) Noashak with her daughter. Questioning her on this point yields no result, for her thinking is very confused. It seems likely, too, that because she has always called her daughter Noashak, she has long now begun to think of this as we would, i.e. as the name for the entity which is her daughter. As noted elsewhere, she speaks to her daughter habitually as "my mother" in which case she seems to identify her with Panigyuk instead of Noashak.

The name among the Mackenzie people while as yet little influenced by the westerners, was dropped by men and women at the birth of their first child as our women drop theirs at marriage. They would thereafter be known by the name of their eldest child, even after that child died, provided it had lived long enough to establish the impression of its individuality upon the community, according to M. and G., about ten years. If a child lived to be almost grown, its parents would be always called after it (A's father, A's mother) even though a child a year younger only were to survive it indefinitely. If an only child died before the age of eight or ten, the parents would cease being known as his father and his mother and would go back to their original names. The sex of the child was immaterial; the parents would be designated always by the name of a daughter who was a year older than their oldest son, no matter how prominent a man he became. This even held for twins; if a girl is born the earlier of the twins, her parents are known by her name if she lives, though her twin brother may stay with his parents and she be adopted even by people of another village. The names of some people were therefore completely unknown to a large part of the community in some cases where they attained great age. [. . .]

A man or woman is never spoken of when dead as so-and-so's parent, but always by the name he or she used to be called by before the birth of their first child. [. . .] The custom has grown into disuse the last twenty years under the combined influence of Alaskans and whites in the Mackenzie.

Names and terms of relationship are used in many parts of Alaska by all children in addressing any person at all. Among the Mackenzie people terms of relationship are used only for real relatives or for those whose relationship to the family is such as to make them seem like relatives. The people one addressed by terms of relationship are "ones to be ashamed before." A sister must never look her brother in the face squarely, to do so would be "a thing to be ashamed of" (kañonaktok); nor should she do so with any male relative who is an adult. Some women do, however, and are said to be "shameless." It is a far greater offense to look a man in the eye, even though he be not a relative, than it would be to have illicit sexual relations with him; yet looking an unrelated man in the eye is less offensive than doing so with her own brother. A woman should not tell, even if asked, the name of any relative if that relative be present; nor the name of parent, brother, sister, or husband whether they be present or absent. She should look away modestly and appeal to a bystander to give the information. Such necessity arises only with whites, however; natives, Mackenzie Eskimo at least, would never make such enquiries, i.e. they would never ask "who is your husband" though they might stumble on forbidden things by such a question as "Who was the lame man I saw walking this morning?" Men have somewhat greater liberties in telling names of relatives, but they differ according to their "sense of modesty." Some will and some will not tell the names of their wives. A man will hospitably offer his wife for loan or exchange, but will be prevented by modesty from telling her name. It seems that the feeling is the same as that which we call modesty. No man should ask anyone the name of anyone present, [. . .] but should wait till the subject of inquiry is out of sight and hearing. In general the "modesty" prohibitions on a woman are stronger with those relatives older than she than with those younger. Some women [. . .] will speak of younger brothers by name. This applies really only to the rare cases where a woman has so many younger brothers that it would be difficult to differentiate them by terms of relationship. [. . .]

MARCH 10 Dr. Anderson, Ilavinirk and Alinnok came home ca. 2 P.M. Had shot 11 deer and seen several small bands. [. . .]

To become a shaman. A man may buy one of his spirits from a shaman who has many. Some men who do not themselves suspect it are particularly fitted for shamanism, their insides are very white. Spirits are eager to serve them, if they should call the spirits they would come at once, while others have to call for them for weeks, months, and even years before there is any answer, according to the varying darkness of these men's insides.

This doctrine makes the missionary's phrase: black heart, black soul, a readily assimilable thing. In some cases the spirits come to these men without being called; in fact, the man or woman receives a call in this way: He puts aside in some place where it could not possibly be lost some article, e.g. he lays his pipe under his pillow on going to sleep; sticks his snow knife into the snowbank he is cutting and looks away for a moment. When he wants it, the pipe, knife, or other article, is gone. A spirit has taken it to notify him that it wants him for a saunirk. There are some men who do not care to become shamans and who do not heed even several calls of this sort. Gun. never heard of the refusal to become a shaman causing the spirits anger. If the man wants to heed the call, which is usually the case, he begins at once observing the general prohibitions, e.g. refrains from pounding, and soon will have a dream vision [. . .]. A man who cannot get spirits to serve him in the regular way will sometimes buy one from a shaman who has it to spare. Before a sale, the shaman must ask his spirit if he is willing to be transferred; the answer is usually, if not always, affirmative, but it occasionally happens that the purchaser displeases the spirit and it returns to its original master without ever having manifested itself to the buyer. Interpreted from our point of view this means that certain men are honest enough to admit that they have seen no spirits nor become aware of the manifestations of any. These men are more or less looked down upon by the community. They are deficient in one of the essentials of a prominent man, and it takes a great deal of ability of another sort to make up for this weakness. [. . .]

Names of spirits. Spirits do not usually bear the same names as men, but in case a woman is barren, or in case she wants more children than she already has, she or her husband may pay an añatkok to perform a ceremony making her fruitful. This is merely an ordinary conjuring performance, such as he would perform to cure disease, bring good weather, or make the hunting season successful. When it appears that the woman is with child, the añatkok may bring her a message from the spirit through whose agency she became fruitful saying he has made the child to grow within her and wants as part of his pay that the child be named for the spirit or by some name he has selected which may be the name of some dead human being, or a name from the spirit world. Gun. does not know any person named after a spirit but has often heard the above explained. [. . .]

MARCH 12 Visitors from Baillie Islands arrived about sundown: Komman, his wife Ituyuk their daughter Siksigak, and Alinnok's father, Ijituaryuk. They came from Nororvik (where the people are). [. . .] Got two seals in cracks in the ice west of Horton River, but were out of food, had about half a breakfast. They tell that Tuyak's wife, Inonñranna, who was in a sort of half-witted stupor when Dr. Anderson left Baillie in January, is now so insane that she no longer recognizes food or drink as such when set before her: sings, weeps, laughs, or talks, constantly. Komman, named also Katpak, aged about forty-five, at Kittegaryumiut, is also reported dead at Nororvik, apparently blood poison from an abscess on the leg, died February 28th. Few foxes are being caught and no bears. Tulugak's elder girl, Anayu, is said to have been near death with "dry throat" (palirktuak) which is their name for any disease in which the throat swells more or less, feels dry, and the throat and tongue are in some cases coated white. Natkusiak's wife [. . .] is considered to have died of "dry throat," but the white men considered it pneumonia.

Theory of disease. Our people tell in concert that whitening of the tonsils is sure to be fatal; some die in three or four days, some live for years and are periodically half-cured till at last they die of "palirktuak." There have been in Nogashak's throat for a week or so two lozenge-shaped white spots about the size of an ordinary black bean. They have their long diameter at right angles to the axis of the mouth passage and are about even with the uvula. When they get white there is considered to be an open wound, "which sometimes bleeds, sometimes not." The wound will not heal unless the white is scraped off with the point of a sharp knife. This is a painful operation, but healing sometimes follows it. This healing is seldom or never permanent.

MARCH 13 Nothing much done today account of crowded house. [. . .]

The name. Frequently a person before dying will give special instruction as to the bestowal of his soul as the atka of a child. These instructions consist usually, however, in specifying which he prefers, to be named after the first child born, whatever its sex, or after the first male child or first female child, in all cases, children of relatives. In case no instructions are left, only male children are named for male dead; an old man occasionally specifies he wants to have his soul become the name of a woman; women also occasionally prefer to become the name of males. In this relation children of families that have exchanged wives are relatives. [. . .]

MARCH 14 [. . .] *Religion (modern):* Ilavinirk said to Dr. Anderson that he had heard Christ intended to come to all lands and teach all peoples: it was therefore a great pity he should have been killed so soon: had he been allowed to live he would no doubt have come to the Eskimo long ago. As it is they must now be content with second-hand information abut him.

Mode of thought. *With a command of language sufficient for the purpose of clearness* I have often tried to explain to Ilavinirk why it is that people in our country and *I myself* think that they would have been better off if whites had never come, i.e. now they are dying off, etc., through imported diseases, vices, houses, and food. He, however, refuses to believe that we can object to ships coming here on any other ground than that we grudge the poor Eskimo the large quantity of flour, cloth, etc., that the ships carry up here. He thinks I fear scarcity of flour for the white people because whalers bring flour up here. [. . .]

MARCH 16 [. . .] People preceding Eskimo such as are told of by most Eastern Eskimo and as far west as Banks Islands (called by Kan. turñnrat) are unknown under any name here so far as I can find out. *Kommana—and many others I have asked—answer negatively only.*

MARCH 17 [. . .] *Mankilling custom.* A man killer, whatever the circumstances, must do no work for five days, and must refrain from certain food for a year; insides of all animals and heads. In general, the taboos connected with man killing were the same as with whale killing. The taboos in whale killing affect only the man who struck the whale and the one who steered the boat, held the steering paddle. In man or whale killing the killer, but not the steerer, was entitled to a tattoo line across the face; the man killer, at least in case of Indians, had a line from nose to each ear, the whale killer from corners of mouth to ear. The boat steerer had whale badges, one line tattooed on each shoulder. [. . .]

Man killing. Before Komman's birth (is about forty-five) a man [. . .] was killed by three men, Apsirmirk (the father of Guninana), Tutigak, and Napigak. Soon after this the latter two were killed [. . .]. Apsirmirk, however, lived a long time and finally died of disease probably between 1885 and 1890. In 1911 (summer) K. took a knife off Apsirmirk's grave and gave it to me today. [. . .]

MARCH 18 Decided today to go west along the coast towards Cape Smythe for a review of the ground and so as to get "outside" sooner than otherwise, chiefly in the hope of getting back to work in the Arctic again as soon as possible. Especially I want to get a good cranial collection near Pt. Barrow to supplement my extensive cephalic data—skulls in any number cannot be got elsewhere. [. . .]

MARCH 19 Alinnokis and Komman's families left for Okato. Packing stuff for the trip. Clear, SW 10 or 15, not cold. [. . .]

MARCH 24 Started ca. 7:15 A. At about 12: noon came to 5 or 6 house winter camp at Nonnarvik ca. 8 miles E. of Baillie. Cooked lunch here and got to Baillie ca. 4: P.M. White men all well but many natives (about half) sick—several with (probably) syphilitic sores. Slept at Capt. B's house and Dr. Anderson at "Old John's" tent. [. . .]

MARCH 28 [. . .] Illness. Nanyavuk says that before the ships (whalers) came there were some epidemics, but between times few were ever sick; no prevalence of swellings and running sores as now and colds were less frequent and less severe at any rate. He thinks there "were no colds."

This corresponds pretty well with our present observations of the Eastern Eskimo.

Whaling. (Nanyavuk). The small iñutok whales were preferred to the larger because they were easier to handle and the meat was more tender and tasted better.

MARCH 29 [. . .] Settlement with natives: We owe Ilavinirk $600^{oo}. He asks me to take $400^{oo} of this to New York and send him up $200^{oo} worth of goods in 1913 and $200^{oo} in 1914. In 1913 he wants 1000 35 cal. winchester cartridges (for box magazine heavy rifle) 1000 30–30 cal. cartridge, about $10^{oo} netting twine (linen gilling), some cod lines, three or four aluminum pots, 20-gauge single barrel shot gun, two [. . .] primus stoves, large (10 × 16 or so) wall tent, silk or linen, 100 yards fairly heavy drilling or light duck, some kakhi, 50 lbs. Golden Gate (or similar) English breakfast tea, and such small articles as I know they would like, up to value of $200^{oo}. I am to arrange for credit with Cottle for $200^{oo} to be used by Ilavinirk. We owe Tannaumirk $200^{oo}: Dr. Anderson will give him some things and charge them, and I will try to get credit with Cottle for the balance. We owe Pannigabluk about $250^{oo} but she is drawing a monthly allowance from the "Rosie H." for which we pay in fox skins at ca. $5^{oo} for skin: Anderson will get her account whenever she shall leave Baillie for the Mackenzie and I am to try arrange credit for her with Cottle. We owe Billy about $350^{oo} but he is going with me to Cape Smythe and must be settled with there. [. . .]

MARCH 31 [. . .] Nanyavuk says no fights with Indians took place in his time, but he saw many who had taken part. Panigyuk's mother was Nogatogmiut, father probably from near Langton Bay. All tunirktut lamps and few pots from E., lamps were made also of stone from lowland towards foothills west of Mackenzie near Pokeik's place. [. . .]

APRIL 8 Helped Frye vaccinate people. Heard that Navalluk wife of Añusinnaaux, knew Nerrivik story.

APRIL 9 Went ten miles S.E. to where Memoranna's and Añusinnaaux's families are camped to get from Navalluk the story of Nerrivik. It turns out to be not the Sedna myth I hoped for, but an Eskimoized European tale. [. . .]

APRIL 10 Pal. had a severe cold and headache today, we overslept, and it was a mild SW blizzard—the combination kept us from travel. Day spent in talks with Eskimo chiefly in hopes of linguistic information. [. . .]

APRIL 13 [. . .] *Linguistic theory:* My theory (noted last winter somewhere in my diary) of Eskimo lip-sounds being few on account of the cold climate has been advanced for the language of Tibet by Col. Waddell—see Hazell's Annual, 1906 p. 533 [. . .].

APRIL 18 Crazy. Kunasak, a woman, Kittegaryumiut, was crazy for about a year but is now all right. Kalurak's wife.

Large men. An Indian named Sasuk was shot by Sipatualum because he had carried off Sipatualum's wife. The Indian was so large that a man could dodge between his legs. Roxy and Ovayuak saw his grave. Uprights which were set up at head and feet were the length of two men apart. [. . .]

APRIL 21 Staying to gather various information. Boys writing folklore for me. People live from hand to mouth, they can get rabbits when they want them. Yesterday they were too interested in us to hunt, and today we are all a little hungry for no one dares to shoot or fish (they hook connies here) on Sunday. [. . .]

APRIL 23 Started 12:30 P.M. cooked and stopped several times. After four and a half hours' travel came at about 7:30 P.M. to camp of Keruk and Itkitk (with I.'s wife and girl child about six years old. They are en route from up river to trade at ship. Camped near there. K. spent last winter near Nome—*says almost everyone he saw kept asking about me—so there must be some interest taken in us "outside."* [. . .]

The Eskimo language, Keruk says, has already been forgotten, or, rather, was never learned by a number of the younger generation at Nome.

In travelling from Point Hope to bottom of Kotzebue he said, uanmuktuami. In talking about this later, Annaktok explained that uanmun was used no matter what direction as to the sun one had to curve in following the coast one way, and kivannun for the opposite way. He is the first Eskimo I ever saw who seems alive to the real difference between our points of the compass and their "up the coast," etc.

Prices, distances, etc.: Keruk had to pay $\$2.^{00}$ per day for his dogfeed and $\$1.^{00}$ for meal for himself and $\$1.^{00}$ for bed whenever he went among whites. Among Eskimo he did not pay.

MAY 2 [. . .] Language. In talking with Artumirksinna I find his accent and vocabulary resemble Cape Smythe dialect; in fact his accent is closer to Cape Smythe than to Kittegaryumiut. He is said to preserve the Herschel idiom (tuyormiat) correctly. This goes to show their closer relation with the west than I have suspected from their known Barter Island summer trading. [. . .]

MAY 5 Custom. A crazy woman (perhaps only out of her head from illness) named Kagrok, was abandoned in winter at Nunaluk. She froze to death. This was B.'s first year at Herschel, when Comiskey was captain of the "Narwhal." Her relatives, those who abandoned her, including her brother who was older than she, are now dead. Woman was young, perhaps not full grown. At our camp tonight (two or four miles W. of Nunaluk) is the grave of an old man Kisun (called Jags by whites) who was abandoned (the winter 1904–5?) to freeze in a tent. He had been alone between one and two weeks when he was found by Billy and Tapkaruk who were hauling meat for the "Narwhal" (Captain Leavitt). He was then past speech and both legs were frozen to the knees or below. They camped by him. He died on third day and they put his body on a high rack. He was later buried by Cockney (white-footless) of Narwhal. He was abandoned by Saglu, Kurugak (now Rampart House) and Kipkina, Mackenzie Delta. All these are inland Eskimo, probably Colville or Nogatogmiut. Saglu some sort of relative. [. . .]

MAY 16 [. . .] *Beliefs:* Inyukuk's wife abstains from white men's food because she is with child. After delivery of child she may eat it. If no meat is obtainable she may eat a little bread, but no other "civilized" food. (She is of Kuwuk and Nogatogmiut parentage, brought up on Colville till two years ago.) [. . .]

MAY 28 [. . .] One reason for keeping one's emotions out of this journal is that anyone with imagination can guess what they are. They need only set before them a dreamer thrown among the harshest realities of our earth, one who longs for sympathy placed among people not unsympathetic but as incapable of seeing the things he sees as we are of seeing ultra-violet light. Only one more thing can be added to a pathetic and in a way tragic picture—the uncertainty that the game will be considered worth even a cheap candle by those who know of the game at all—the small circle of scientific men who are not always sympathetic or generous—who are not even always scientific. [. . .]. To my unfortunate mind nothing seems worthwhile—no success as seen by others, no success though I myself should have to admit it complete in every other respect, would be to me worthwhile. I can not picture myself a heaven and no one has pictured a heaven for me, that holds out its promise: "this will satisfy you." One heaven may be better than another and all may be better than hell, but none can satisfy. The best thing I can hope for is work. Work will drown sorrow better than any other thing I have tried—as yet I have not tried drink, and I shall probably never try it, for others have tested it for me and found its promises unfulfilled. The best to be hoped is congenial work [. . .] and I am fit for nothing else by now. I have the education that colleges and banks give, I have the education that experience gives, I know the land and I am learning the language and the people—and that learning is my work, together with telling what I learn. For twenty years yet I am likely to have the strength to fight the climate and to find food for myself and my companions as I have found it the past years. If I am to follow Peary (as I started out to do a few moments ago) what I want to confide to any reader of my journal is that the one thing I want is the interest (shown by the giving of money and the lending of willing ears) that shall keep me at work here for twenty years. When one gets old, it is said, one begins to long for simple rest, and to find in the hope of rest a satisfying goal.

Supplementary to the above [. . .] is the desire to be able to keep abreast of my time. [. . .] I am being left behind in dark ages of my own creating. To be narrow in knowledge is bad; to be narrowed in sympathies is worse. [. . .] I am hoping that if scientific bodies can be found to pay my expenses while I work, my own "popular" writing can pay for my play time. Wherever, in Europe or America, there are men who are shaping the thought of our time, there I want to be (if they will tolerate me for the share I am trying to do) to spend my play hours with them. [. . .]

MAY 30 [. . .] *Psychological:* I seem to be a different person nowadays from what I have been for four years. There is an insatiable hunger for other men's ideas. Leffingwell gave me a number of old magazines and I can't go to sleep for six or eight hours evenings (after camping) for the desire to read or to write—letters to friends. Hence we are in camp about 24 hrs. each time we stop. Nothing is really lost by this, as my work is all behind me, and the sooner I get to Barrow the longer will be the wait there for ships. The fact that my work is behind me obsesses me too at times—I feel as if I were going to a court-martial for cowardice. Fear of money complications (shared by Dr. Anderson—on whose advice I acted, which is of comfort), a momentary "tiredness" of a hard, grinding task, and a fear that ships might fail to get east beyond Barrow [. . .]. Of course I must get out sometime to record my results and find out what others are thinking and doing, before I proceed with the work up here. [. . .]

JUNE 3 In camp, writing. [. . .] *Hardships:* Someone about two years ago sent Dr. Anderson a Sunday paper clipping giving a page of our "hardships" and the writer's reflections thereon. What he told of were such things as going a few days without meals. In itself the experience of starvation is not nearly so trying as one might infer from multiplying mentally the acute hunger sensations one has whose circumstances keep him from his regular dinner hour. Our real hardships up here are subjective—mental. On the present homegoing trip, with my work ended but not finished, with unappraised achievements behind and unknown conditions ahead, I am in a mental condition more trying than any physical hardship of the four years has been. [. . .] Perhaps the wisest man I know—George Foot Moore at Harvard—said to us once apropos of the gloomy philosopher and religious: "Pessimism and despair are luxuries of the upper classes—the poor and hungry have no time for such things." I have tried this out and found it so. Hunger keeps all your thoughts on the dread of hunger, makes all your hopes and fears cluster about the acquisition of food, and when you have secured it (as you inevitably will, you are soon freed of all worries). [. . .]

JUNE 5 [. . .] The world has evidently been moving the last four years. One of the old magazines Leffingwell gave me speaks of eugenics without explaining what the term means—four years ago that could not have been done. An American School of Archaeology seems to be at work in the South West—and the "Outlook," by implication, gives the credit to Norton, though I heard him in 1904 make an impassioned, almost tearful, plea at the annual convention of the Arch. Inst. of Am. that an organization founded for the study of Greek civilization should not be powered into growling in American savagery.

This work in the southwest makes me wish (a highly original wish) that I were wealthy. I have no ambition to make all knowledge my province—except so far as to allow an intelligent interest in all progress; I do not want even to make all ethnology my province, but the archaeology and ethnology of all America is probably thoroughly woven into one whole, and it would be a fine thing to have. The money that would enable me to give the necessary time to the study of the results others gain in every part of our continent—then might I be able to see the bearing of my own work, the meaning in relation to the whole of phenomena which now stand isolated. Not only could I then profit by the work of others, but others would be more likely to profit by my work. [. . .]

JUNE 9 Snowing heavily—large flakes and so thick, visibility is only a mile. [. . .]

Introspective: I can appreciate now the feelings of men who after being long under a monotonous ship's routine at sea long to get into port to go on an unrestrained drunk—that particular extreme suggests itself to them, being of all extremes the now most antipodal to the life they have been enduring. The antipodal extremes we seek vary somewhat with our inherited and acquired tastes, but in general the one who has been busy seeks rest, the one who has suffered nervous strain wants freedom from worry, one who has starved dreams of banquets, or at least of food—and I who have for four years been moving slowly, plodding from place to place, hunger for swift motion without effort, for rushing from place to place on extra-fare trains and five-day liners. More than all, I who have so long associated with people who believe in witchcraft, dream of being with men who doubt the nebular hypothesis. After the tent on the silent barrens I want, Broadway by arc light and the Strand at five o'clock; after the iglu I want the Century Club and the Criterion; after the *kajigi* monologues on the forefathers' wisdom I want scientific conventions where we learn things which the wisest over a year ago had been unable to find out. [. . .]

JUNE 13 Started ca. noon and ca. 2 P.M. got to Tom Gordon's. Found all well, though Tom had been pretty sick last winter—perhaps scurvy? [. . .] All my old friends seem glad to see me. Brower gave me letters from Bridgman and the Museum [. . .]. Cutter had left with him, and I got five letters at the post office—several had been "returned to writer" because they all supposed I was out of the country by way of the Mackenzie. [. . .]

My mail is very satisfactory, what there is of it. There is no word from the Survey. The Museum writes, bear the signature of "I. A. Lucas, Director" that they congratulate us on accomplishing "the primary object of the expedition, namely the study of the Eskimo tribes of Coronation Gulf and vicinity," seem to have voted on "an additional appropriation of $1.000 toward meeting the expenses of your expedition." Further on they say: "In addition"—"the Museum stands ready to defray your travelling expenses and Dr. Anderson's back to New York when you return." That they no longer insist on a date of return is implied in "We infer from your last letter it is your intention to return to New York in 1912." This letter is dated November 21th, 1911. [. . .]

The tone of the letter is most satisfactory, and is seems that it and Mr. Adams' (Am. Geog. Soc.) letter corroborate each other in indicating that people outside are favourably impressed with our work. In a way I think we deserve it. We have fulfilled most of our promises, and if in some cases the measure is slack, in others it is heaped—and it has taken considerable hard work—and a little willpower at times to keep at the work, especially under the cloud of the Museum's ultimatum that we must be home in 1910 or shift for ourselves. Had it not been for that letter (the one received December 4th, 1910) we should have accomplished more than we have done [. . .]. Besides, one cannot be at his best working at trying tasks when encouragement is wanting. [. . .]

JUNE 21 Settlement with Billy was finished today as follows: His time is computed at roughly 3½ years (a reference to my diary would show the exact number of days) between July, 1908, and June 13, 1912, deducting the months from late July to late December, 1911. The wages agreed on in advance were $100 per year and ½ fox and other furs caught by him. He has as a matter of fact been allowed far less time for trapping them than my other Eskimos and has therefore generally been allowed to keep all his skins. [. . .] All other things received by him from me are to be considered as presents made in consideration of the especially valuable nature of his services. These include the five-dog team we drove up here, the rifle he is using, our primus, old pyramid silk tent, cooking utensils, etc. and a new Waltham watch ($20) and chains ($75) purchased of Mr. Brower. [. . .]

JUNE 30 In cases of death at childbirth the foetus was removed from the dead woman. Mr. Brower saw one case at Point Hope. Two days after the woman's body had been placed in the graveyard two women went out and uncovered the body. One of them then made a cut well up on the abdomen, reached in with a hook and pulled the foetus out. The other woman fainted at the sight. The knife used was flint, the hook, he thinks, was ordinary blubber hook used for "pokes." Navel string also at childbirth were always cut with flint. [. . .]

JULY 4 Alahik calls her son Gusirk, "Apa" (I cannot hear it Apañ). Mr. Brower says that he has noticed, though he never tried to explain to himself, that almost every person calls some younger one "father" or "mother," irrespective of the sex of child. [. . .]

When Mr. Brower first lived at Cape Smythe, wolf pups were often raised by hand. When their fur became good they were killed with flint-pointed arrows made for the purpose. The bow was then out of use for hunting generally, i.e. except by boys or for ptarmigan in an emergency.

Sea animals were given a drink by both Cape Smythe inlanders who hunted on sea and Point Hope people (symposium of both tribes and several others agreed to this today). Cape Smythe people only ones who gave drink also to caribou. Behind the lamp in the house was a stand (sort of a crane)—called paugusirk from which hung suspended by a strip of whalebone a small bucket of wood or whalebone called pirktaligaurak. This always had water in it. The water was poured into a seal's mouth. When a whale was killed the bucket was fetched from the umialik's (killer's, owner of first boat to strike) house and poured on the whale's nose (not into his mouth or blowhole). At Cape Smythe (and probably in most other coast communities), blubber was rubbed on caribou's hoofs and small pieces or a few drops of oil were put into their ears. [. . .]

JULY 6 Marking property. Nallikam nalluñaiyutaña, the mark of Nal., adopted father of Paniulak (both Killirmiut) appears on the handle of a titalirk hook bought today. There are three diagonal marks called kipuak and one titirak. [. . .]

JULY 7 The wind finally left the NE the night before yesterday, and yesterday morning it was blowing SE 10. Yesterday was the first comfortably warm day this summer—warm enough to be comfortable outdoors in woollen clothes, without windbreak. [. . .]

Commerce. Kivianna, husband of Kittegaryumiut woman Paniulak (yak), says that when in winter or summer the Utqiaguigmiut went to Point Hope they usually had tobacco-getting in view chiefly. They sold skins of wolf, wolverine, red fox, caribou, never white foxes as these were used for clothes at home occasionally. They bought tobacco, copper articles, and brass articles (e.g. copper thimbles, hooks, and bracelets (tallirak), iron knives, copper and brass pots, etc. [. . .] If a boat came to Cape Smythe or went to Point Hope it would winter. Sleds would make a round trip; sleds seldom came to Cape Smythe. It was want of tobacco sent Cape Smythe people west. (Double-edged iron knives came from west also.) [. . .]

JULY 13 The NE wind still continues to vary between 15 and 25 miles. The floe is almost as wide as a week ago here off Birnirk [. . .]. On this ice Pt. Barrow sled and 4 or 5 people going to C.S., were carried adrift Friday night (when it broke off) but were picked up by two natives [. . .].

Mr. Brower and the rest of the party (his family, Ikpik's, and Mr. Clark) moved a ¾ mile E across to Brand Point [. . .] Friday and I am left alone (of our party) here [. . .]. There are 4 Eskimo tents—people waiting for the expected flight of ducks. [. . .]

JULY 23 Snowhouse model. Bought a model of a snowhouse with a takusiun so dogs cannot get the lowest of the suspended things. There were on the string feathers of eagle, hawk, raven, etc. according to owner of house. There were also gifts. The tatkoa of the caribou used the feathers for charms and made more materialistic use of the other gifts which are in order from top of pole down: akluna (common seal), nelluakartuñaksrak, kitkoerksak, artuñaksrok, oxsrogon [. . .].

Arrows at Cape Smythe and among Oturkarmiut (and elsewhere probably inland) were of the length of the head plus the distance the sternum to the second thumb joint of the left hand held in the position of shooting horizontally. [. . .]

JULY 26 [. . .] *Regarding "Billy":* Last spring I promised Billy that if I took him out to Cape Smythe I would send him back by whaler. July 24 the *Elvira,* Capt. Pedersen [. . .] passed us without dropping anchor. She reported [. . .] that no ships are coming to go east beyond here. I was therefore in a fix with Billy. Found that Mr. Brower would sell him a whaleboat if I endorsed the note formally and so I arranged to buy it. Had to buy him, besides, ropes and tackle; and provisions and ammunition for the trip—all of which will appear in my expense account pending the Museum's approval. Billy has agreed to hold himself in readiness to join me both summer 1913 and summer 1914 [. . .]. Sent with him some presents for people who told me folklore stories last winter. [. . .]

JULY 28 *Record of packing cases; Archaeological and Ethnological Collection;* The shipping directions are: American Museum Natural History, New York (abbreviated in some cases). The boxes are further marked: Stefansson Expedition.

Packed July 28

No 1. Rifle case full of lamps—ca. 250 or 300 lbs.
2. Lamps and model of deer drier
3. Models of traps, etc.
4. Ptarmigan ruts and C.S. archaeology
5. Archaeology Miscellaneous

6. Trap models
7. C.S.—Pt. B. archaeology, bow, horn, etc.
8. Miscellaneous Archaeology (chiefly bow + horn) [. . .]
9. Miscellaneous Archaeology from C.S. and Binirk—unpack compartment separately
10. Trap models
11. Small box [. . .]
12. Archaeology miscellaneous chiefly stone
13. Traps etc. and archaeology miscellaneous unpack compartment separately
14. Wooden ikpiairuk and miscellaneous archaeology
    Song box; seal harpoon and traps [. . .]
15. And 17 butter barrels filled with lamps, mammoth teeth, etc. [. . .]

JULY 28 Taboos. Mr. Brower says for a long time after 1884 no Eskimo would scrape deerskins for clothes before first snow fell. After sun came back no one would scrape them who intended to have anything to do with whaling next season. [. . .]

Customs and beliefs: A Noatogmiut man, Negrun, got a yaukukalirk (-guga-), a large knife, shaped like a Wilson skinning knife, of soft iron. Because the knife was a large one, better than other peoples' knives, a knife to be proud of, he always carried it in his hand. For this he was nicknamed Savikpallik. This soon became the only name he was called. About the time he died the present Savikpallik (a Noatogmiut man at Cape Smythe, over forty years old, perhaps sixty) was born. He was named Negrun by his mother and was so called while she lived, but on her death people began to call him Savikpallik (*why (I can't learn) did this follow upon his mother's death?*). [. . .]

AUGUST 8 Day before yesterday afternoon and all day yesterday it blew rather unusually hard—NE ca. 30 or 35. A few cakes of ice came around Pt. B. and then followed the coast around, some going within 200 yards off the beach at Gordon's [. . .]. Today no ice in sight.

The Revenue Cutter's not coming is beginning to worry us. She is expected here in ice-free seasons about the last of July or first of August. Backland is said to have been here on the sixth of August last year. [. . .]

AUGUST 12 Currents: The wind, though about 3 points off the land, has been so strong the last three days (Friday to Sunday) that Capt. Slade has been unable to come ashore for the breakers at Gordon's—NE 35 or more. [. . .]

The massive okumailuta of a walrus spear was always made of the jawbone of a walrus and the line that held the harpoon point was passed through a nerve hold in the okumailuta. This of course does not apply to the pigleriak but only to the unarkpuk. [. . .]

U.S. Revenue Cutter "Bear." August 18th, 1912. [. . .]

Sent wireless as follows:

(1) W. Museology, New York, Left Parry March 22, arrived Barrow June 13. Winter linguistics, summer archaeological fifty thousand (specimens). Anderson and eastern collections due Frisco November whaler. Write Seattle.

(2) Geological Survey. Ottawa: All well; coming via Seattle. Shall I cable details?

Notes

Introduction (pages 3–6)

1. See Vilhjalmur Stefansson, *Discovery: The Autobiography of Vilhjalmur Stefansson* (New York: McGraw Hill Company, 1964).

2. See, for instance, D. M. LeBourdais, *Stefansson, Ambassador of the North* (Montreal: Harvest House, 1963); Richard J. Diubaldo, *Stefansson and the Canadian Arctic* (Montreal: McGill-Queen's University Press, 1978); and William R. Hunt, *Stef: A Biography of Vilhjalmur Stefansson, Canadian Arctic Explorer* (Vancouver: University of British Columbia Press, 1986).

3. Henry B. Collins, "Stefansson as an Anthropologist," *Polar Notes* 4 (1962): 8.

4. V. Stefansson, *Discovery,* 45.

5. Paul T. W. Baxter, "From Anthropological Texts to Popular Writings," *Bulletin of the John Rylands Library,* 73, no. 3 (1991): 123.

Stefansson's Expeditions (pages 7–21)

1. V. Stefansson, *Discovery,* 55.

2. Ibid.

3. V. Stefansson, "The Icelandic Colony in Greenland," *American Anthropologist* 8, no. 2 (1906): 262–70.

4. Diubaldo, *Stefansson and the Canadian Arctic,* 21.

5. V. Stefansson, "The Eskimo Trade Jargon of Hershel Island," *American Anthropologist* 11 (1909): 217–32.

6. From V. Stefansson's diaries, 22 December 1906.

7. See Maurice Bloch, *Marxism and Anthropology* (Oxford: Oxford University Press, 1983).

8. The diaries, 12 December 1908.

9. Beau Riffenburg, *The Myth of the Explorer: The Press, Sensationalism, and Geographical Inquiry* (London: Belhaven Press and Scott Polar Research Institute, 1993).

10. Letter to V. Stefansson from the American Museum of Natural History, 13 April 1908.

11. Hunt, *Stef,* 54.

12. See Diubaldo, *Stefansson and the Canadian Arctic,* 42.

13. Letter to Clark Wissler, American Museum of Natural History, from V. Stefansson, 5 December 1910.

14. V. Stefansson, "Stefansson-Anderson Expedition," *Anthropological Papers of the American Museum of Natural History,* vol. 14 (New York: AMS Press, 1914).

15. Quoted in Diubaldo, *Stefansson and the Canadian Arctic,* 48.

16. Ernest S. Burch, Jr., *The Iñupiaq Eskimo Nations of Northwest Alaska* (Fairbanks: University of Alaska Press, 1998), 60, 81.

17. The diaries, 10 January 1907.

18. The diaries, 13 May 1910.

19. See, for instance, Edward L. Schieffelin and Robert Crittenden, eds., *Like People You See in a Dream: First Contact in Six Papuan Societies* (Stanford: Stanford University Press, 1991), on first contact in some Papuan societies.

20. Malcolm Crick, *Explorations in Language and Meaning: Towards a Semantic Anthropology* (New York: John Wiley, 1976), 164.

21. See, for instance, Gísli Pálsson, ed., *Beyond Boundaries: Understanding, Translation and Anthropological Discourse* (Oxford: Berg Publishers, 1993).

22. V. Stefansson, "The Icelandic Colony in Greenland; V. Stefansson, *The Three Voyages of Martin Frobisher,* vols. 1 and 2 (London: The Argonaut Press, 1938).

23. Letter to Clark Wissler from V. Stefansson, 5 December 1910.

24. Philip Goldring, "Scientist and Showman," *The Beaver* (April–May 1987): 59–61; Burch, *The Iñupiaq Eskimo Nations;* see also V. Stefansson, *Great Adventures and Explorations* (New York: Dial Press, 1945).

25. Diubaldo, *Stefansson and the Canadian Arctic,* 61.

26. Marcel Mauss, with Henri Beuchat, *Seasonal Variations of the Eskimo: A Study in Social Morphology* (1906; reprint, London: Routledge, 1979).

27. Quoted in Diubaldo, *Stefansson and the Canadian Arctic,* 68.

28. V. Stefansson, *The Friendly Arctic* (New York: Macmillan, 1921), 687.

29. See, for example, Hunt, *Stef.* See also V. Stefansson, *The Adventure of Wrangel Island* (London: Jonathan Cape Ltd., 1925).

30. See Mauss, *Seasonal Variations,* 15.

31. The diaries, 10 September 1914.

32. Bernard Saladin d'Anglure, "Arctic," in *Encyclopedia of Social and Cultural Anthropology,* ed. Alan Bernard and Jonathan Spencer (London: Routledge, 1996), 52. On the latter, see Knud Rasmussen, *Intellectual Culture of the Copper Eskimos* (Copenhagen: Gyldendalske boghandel, 1932).

33. Gerald Sullivan, ed., *Margaret Mead, Gregory Bateson, and Highland Bali: Fieldwork Photographs of Bayung Gedé, 1936–1939* (Chicago: University of Chicago Press, 1999), 1.

34. Kessler E. Woodward, "Persuasive Images," in *Imaging the Arctic,* ed. J. C. H. King and H. Lidchi (Seattle: University of Washington Press, 1998).

Reflections of Fieldwork (pages 22–25)

1. See, for instance, Nigel Rapport, "Surely Everything Has Already Been Said About Malinowski's Diary!" *Anthropology Today* 6, no. 1 (1990).

2. For early examples, see Paul Rabinow, *Reflections of Fieldwork in Morocco* (Berkeley and Los Angeles: University of California Press, 1977); James A. Boon, *Other Tribes, Other Scribes: Symbolic Anthropology in the Comparative Study of Cultures, Histories, Religions, and Texts* (Cambridge: Cambridge University Press, 1982); and George W. Stocking, Jr., ed., *Observers Observed: Essays on Ethnographic Fieldwork* (Madison: University of Wisconsin Press, 1983).

3. V. Stefansson, "Stefansson-Anderson Arctic Expedition."

4. Raymond Firth, "Second Introduction," in *A Diary in the Strict Sense of the Term,* by Bronislaw Malinowski (New York: Harcourt, Brace and World, 1989).

5. Ibid., xxxi.

6. James Clifford and George E. Marcus, eds., *Writing Culture: The Poetics and Politics of Ethnography* (Berkeley: University of California Press, 1986).

7. James Allison, Jenny Hockey, and Andrew Dawson, eds., *After Writing Culture; Epistemology and Praxis in Contemporary Anthropology* (London and New York: Routledge, 1997).

8. Roger M. Keesing, "Exotic Readings of Cultural Texts," *Current Anthropology* 30, no. 4 (1989): 459–79; Roger Sanjek, ed., *Fieldnotes: The Makings of Anthropology* (Ithaca and London: Cornell University Press, 1990); Han F. Vermeulan and Arturo Alvarez Roldán, eds., *Fieldwork and Footnotes: Studies in the History of European Anthropology* (London and New York: Routledge, 1995); G. E. Marcus, *Ethnography through Thick and Thin* (Princeton: Princeton University Press, 1998); Judith Okely, "Anthropology and Autobiography: Participatory Experience and Embodied Knowledge," in *Anthropology and Autobiography,* ed. J. Okely and H. Callaway (London and New York: Routledge, 1992); and Gísli Pálsson, *The Textual Life of Savants: Ethnography, Iceland, and the Linguistic Turn* (Chur, Switzerland: Harwood Academic Publishers, 1995).

9. See Ludger Müller-Wille, *Franz Boas Among the Inuit of Baffin Island 1883–1884* (Toronto: University of Toronto Press, 1998), 11; on Boas and his Inuit diaries, see also Douglas Cole, "'The Value of a Person Lies in His *Herzensbildung*': Franz Boas' Baffin Island Letter-Diary, 1883–1884," in *Observers Observed.*

10. V. Stefansson, *Discovery,* 130–31.

11. Robert L. Welsch, *An American Anthropologist in Melanesia: A. B. Lewis and the Joseph N. Field South Pacific Expedition, 1909–1913* (Honolulu: University of Hawaii Press, 1998).

12. Ibid., 564.

13. Stuart E. Jenness, ed., *Arctic Odyssey: The Diary of Diamond Jenness 1913–1916* (Hull, Quebec: Canadian Museum of Civilization, 1991).

14. See Bronislaw Malinowski, *A Diary in the Strict Sense of the Term* (1967; reprint, New York: Harcourt, Brace and World, 1989), ix.

15. Firth, "Second Introduction," xxi, xxii.

16. Cited in Rapport, "Surely Everything," 9.

17. Xerox University Microfilms, Ann Arbor, Michigan.

18. Arjun Appadurai, "Introduction: Place and Voice in Anthropological Theory," *Cultural Anthropology* 3, no. 1 (1988): 20.

19. Robert Paine, ed., *The White Arctic: Anthropological Essays onTutelage and Ethnicity* (Toronto: Institute of Social and Economic Research, Memorial

University of Newfoundland, 1977); Cornelius H. W. Remie, "Changing Contexts, Persistent Relations: Inuit-White Encounters in Northern Canada, 1576–1992," *Native American Studies* 7, no. 2 (1993): 5–11; Talal Asad, ed., *Anthropology and the Colonial Encounter* (London: Ithaca Press, 1973); and Edward Said, "Representing the Colonized: Anthropology's Interlocutors," *Critical Inquiry* 15: 205–25.

The Expedition Diaries and the Present Edition (pages 26–33)

1. The diaries, 23 March 1909.
2. The diaries, 17 September 1910.
3. The diaries, 19 May 1910.
4. The diaries, 22 September 1906. All translations from the Icelandic are by the editor, Gísli Pálsson.
5. Malinowski, *A Diary*.
6. The diaries, entry for 26 August 1909.
7. Letter from D. M. LeBourdais, 24 January 1963.
8. LeBourdais, *Stefansson, Ambassador of the North*.
9. Letter to D. M. LeBourdais from Richard Finnie, 31 January 1963. See also Richard S. Finnie, "Stefansson's Myth," *North* (Nov./Dec. 1978): 2–7.
10. Quoted in Jeanette Mirsky, *To the Arctic! The Story of Northern Exploration from Earliest Times* (Chicago: The University of Chicago Press, 1970, xvi; emphasis added.
11. Diamond Jenness, *Dawn in Arctic Alaska* (Minneapolis: University of Minnesota Press, 1957): 9.
12. See Diubaldo, *Stefansson and the Canadian Arctic,* 201.
13. The diaries, 4 October 1909.
14. The diaries, 29 September 1910.
15. The diaries, 15 February 1912.
16. The diaries, 12 May 1912.
17. The diaries, 10 August 1909.
18. The diaries, 3 November 1909.
19. The diaries, 11 November 1909.
20. The diaries, 23 November 1910.
21. The diaries, 30 May 1912.
22. The diaries, 3 June 1912.
23. The diaries, 9 June 1912.
24. See V. Stefansson, "Stefansson-Anderson Expedition," 151.
25. V. Stefansson, *My Life with the Eskimo* (New York: Macmillan, 1913): 213.
26. LeBourdais, *Stefansson, Ambassador of the North;* V. Stefansson, *Discovery;* Diubaldo, *Stefansson and the Canadian Arctic;* and Hunt, *Stef.*
27. Welsch, *An American Anthropologist in Melanesia*.
28. Müller-Wille, *Franz Boas Among the Inuit*.
29. See Malinowski, *A Diary,* viii.
30. S. Jenness, *Arctic Odyssey*.

Relations with the Inuit (pages 34–37)

1. See Diubaldo, *Stefansson and the Canadian Arctic,* 28.
2. V. Stefansson, *My Life with the Eskimo,* 2.
3. Ernest S. Burch, Jr., "The History of Arctic Ethnography—As Seen from the Conodoguinet," Paper presented at the twenty-second annual meeting of the Alaska Anthropological Association, 24 March 1995, 15.
4. See Mick Conefrey and Tim Jordan, *Icemen: A History of the Arctic and Its Explorers* (London: Boxtree, 1998), 12.
5. V. Stefansson, *The Friendly Arctic,* 20.
6. The diaries, 26 November 1910.
7. Henry F. Srebrnik, "The Radical 'Second Life' of Vilhjalmur Stefansson," *Arctic* 51, no. 1 (1998): 60.
8. Carl C. Seltzer, "The Anthropometry of the Western and Copper Eskimos, Based on the Data of Vilhjalmur Stefansson," *Human Biology* 5, no. 3 (1933): 313–18; Collins, "Stefansson as an Anthropologist."
9. See, for instance, Björg Evjen, "Measuring Heads: Physical Anthropological Research in North Norway," *Ethnos* 2 (1997): 3–30, on anthropological studies of the Norwegian "Lapps."
10. See, for instance, Hunt, *Stef.*
11. The diaries, 3 March 1910.
12. The diaries, 15 February 1912.
13. The diaries, 22 January 1911.
14. The diaries, 9 January 1911.
15. The diaries, 20 April 1910.
16. The diaries, 21 January 1911.

Stefansson's Inuit Family (pages 41–50)

1. V. Stefansson, *My Life with the Eskimos* and *Discovery*.
2. V. Stefansson, *My Life with the Eskimos,* 117.
3. Ibid., 126, 158.
4. V. Stefansson, *Discovery,* 105.
5. Ibid., 110.
6. Georgina Stefansson, "My Grandfather, Dr. Stefansson," *North* 4 (1961): 25.
7. *The Traditional Land Use Inventory for the Mid-Beaufort Sea,* vol. 1 (North Slope Borough on History and Culture, n.d.), emphasis added.
8. See, for example, June Helm, "Long-term Research among the Dogrib and other Dene," in *Long-term Field Research in Social Anthropology,* ed. G. M. Foster, T. Scudder, E. Colson, and R. V. Kemper (New York: Academic Press, 1973); Helm, *The People of Denendeh: Ethno-history of the Indians of Canada's Northwest Territories* (Iowa City: University of Iowa Press, 2000); June Helm, personal communication, 16 March 1998.
9. Letter from Kenneth Chipman, 30 April 1914; see Hunt, *Stef,* 120.

10. Hunt, *Stef,* n. 15, p. 279.

11. June Helm, personal communication, 16 March 1998.

12. S. Allen Counter, *North Pole Legacy: Black, White and Eskimo* (Amherst: University of Massachusetts Press, 1991).

13. Evelyn Stefansson Nef, personal communication, 9 March 1998.

14. The diaries, 27 November 1910; 3 December 1910.

15. Letter to E. M. Weyer from Richard Finnie, 4 December 1973. See also Finnie, "Stefansson's Myth."

16. Rosie Albert Stefansson, personal communication.

17. A. Wang, quoted in D. M. LeBourdais's letter to Richard Finnie, 24 January 1963.

18. Harold Noice, *With Stefansson in the Arctic* (New York: Dodd, Mead, 1924).

19. S. Jenness, *Arctic Odyssey,* 190, 254. The editor comments (n. 2, p. 754): "Some members of the C.A.E.'s Southern Party were aware of and commented on the relationship, notably Chipman . . . , but neither the author nor Dr. Anderson mentioned it".

20. Murielle Ida Nagy, *Aulavik Oral History Project on Banks Island, NWT: Final Report* (Inuvik, NWT: Inuvialuit Social Development Program, 1999), 40.

21. George H. Wilkins, journals. Wilkins notes in his journals, one may note: "I was at liberty at any time to demand facilities to take any picture I wanted, but on the other hand was to take any picture the leader thought necessary" ("From a hundred above to fifty below," p. 6).

22. Letter to D. M. LeBourdais from Richard Finnie, 31 January 1963.

23. Letter to Erika S. Parmi, Darmouth College Library, from Richard Finnie, 29 October 1973.

24. Letter to Richard Finnie from Edward M. Weyer, 4 December 1973.

25. Letter to Edward M. Weyer from Richard Finnie, 10 December 1973.

26. Finnie, "Stefansson's Myth," 2.

27. June Helm, personal communication, 16 March 1998.

The Intimate Arctic (pages 51–55)

1. The diaries, 3 April 1909.
2. The diaries, 4 October 1909.
3. The diaries, 17 March 1911.
4. The diaries, 20 May 1910.
5. The diaries, 23 June 1909.
6. The diaries, 2 September 1909.
7. The diaries, 6 September 1909.
8. The diaries, 24 January 1911.
9. The diaries, 4 October 1909.
10. The diaries, 9 December, 1909.
11. Hunt, *Stef,* 45.
12. The diaries, 19 December 1909.
13. The diaries, 16 March 1910.
14. The diaries, 1 May 1910.

15. The diaries, 29 January 1911.
16. The diaries, 27 February 1911.

Race, Gender, and Ethnicity (pages 56–70)

1. Louise Pratt, *Imperial Eyes: Travel Writing and Transculturation* (London and New York, Routledge, 1992).
2. Donna Haraway, *Primate Visions: Gender, Race, and Nature in the World of Modern Science* (London and New York: Routledge, 1989).
3. Clive Holland, ed., *Farthest North: A History of North Polar Exploration in Eye-Witness Accounts* (London: Robinson Publishing, 1994).
4. Lisa Bloom, *Gender on Ice: The American Ideologies of Polar Expeditions* (Minneapolis: University of Minnesota Press, 1993), 3.
5. Richard G. Condon, "Natkusiak (ca. 1885–1947)," *Arctic* 45, no.1 (1992): 92; See also Nagy, *Aulavik Oral History Project*, 44–48.
6. Rosie Albert Stefansson, personal communication, July 2000.
7. Bloom, *Gender on Ice,* 128.
8. Edwin Ardener, "Belief and the Problem of Women," in *Perceiving Women,* ed. Shirley Ardener (London: J. M. Dent and Sons, 1975).
9. See Bloom, *Gender on Ice,* 105.
10. Quoted in Ibid., 104.
11. On the immigrant tension in the writings of Icelandic Canadians, see Daisy Neijmann, *The Icelandic Voice in Canadian Letters* (Carleton: Carleton University Press, 1997).
12. Pálsson, *The Textual Life of Savants,* 77.
13. V. Stefansson, *Discovery,* 19.
14. Ibid., 69.
15. The diaries, 10 April 1911.
16. See Guttormur J. Guttormsson, "Tveir þættir: I. Indíáninn John Ramsey," *Andvari* (Reykjavík) (1975): 75–83.
17. Anne Brydon, "Memory and Forgetting as Modernity's Malaise: Icelandic-Canadian Identity and the Ambiguities of History," In *The Icelandic Presence in Canada: A Story of Immigration,* ed. D. Neijmann (Winnipeg: University of Manitoba Press, n.d.).
18. Guttormsson, *Kvæði, úrval* (1920; reprint, Reykjavík: Bókaútgáfa Menningarsjóðs og þjóðvinafélagsins, 1976) 35.
19. Haraldur Bessason, *Bréf til Brands* (Reykjavík: Ormstunga, 1999), 65.
20. Paul Shankman, "Sex, Lies, and Anthropologists: Margaret Mead, Derek Freeman, and Samoa," in *Research Frontiers in Anthropology,* ed. M. Ember, C. Ember, and D. Levinson (Englewood Cliffs, N.J.: Prentice Hall, 1994).
21. Bronislaw Malinowski, *The Sexual Life of Savages in North-Western Melanesia* (New York: Eugenics Publishing Company, 1929); Donald Tuzin, "The Forgotten Passion: Sexuality and Anthropology in the Ages of Victoria and Bronislaw," *Journal of the History of the Behavioral Sciences* 3 (1994): 114–37; Susan Seizer, "Playing the Field: The Sexual Life of Anthropologists," *Transition* 72 (1997): 100–13.
22. Margaret Willson, "Play the Dance, Dancing the Game: Race, Sex and Stereotype in Anthropological Fieldwork," *Ethnos* 62, no. 3–4 (1997): 25.

23. G. Stefansson, "My Grandfather, Dr. Stefansson."
24. Burch, *The Iñupiaq Eskimo Nations,* 8.
25. The diaries, 3 March 1912.
26. The diaries, 13 May 1910.
27. The diaries, 23 September 1906.
28. See Burch, *The Iñupiaq Eskimo Nations,* 18.
29. The diaries, 27 December 1911.
30. The diaries, 23 December 1911.
31. V. Stefansson, *My Life with the Eskimo,* 359.
32. Evelyn Stefansson Nef, personal communication, 9 March 1998.
33. The diaries, 29 March 1912.
34. See Diubaldo, *Stefansson and the Canadian Arctic.*
35. See Hunt, *Stef,* 117; see also Srebrnik, "The Radical 'Second Life'."
36. Stephen Gudeman and Alberto Rivera, *Conversations in Colombia: The Domestic Economy in Life and Text* (Cambridge: Cambridge University Press, 1990), 190.
37. G. E. Marcus, *Ethnography through Thick and Thin* (Princeton: Princeton University Press, 1998), 118.
38. Ibid., 122.
39. Pálsson, *The Textual Life of Savants,* 171.
40. See, for instance, Bernadette Bucher, "Le Journal de Stendhal: Discours sur le sexe et écriture ethnographie," *L'Homme* 39, nos. 3–4 (1989); Gary Alan Fine, "Ten Lies of Ethnography: Moral Dilemmas of Field Research," *Journal of Contemporary Ethnography* 22, no. 3 (1993): 267–94; Peter Wade, "Sexuality and Masculinity in Fieldwork among Colombian Blacks," in *Gendered Fields: Women, Men and Ethnography,* ed. Diane Bell, Pat Caplan, and Wazir Jahan Karim (London and New York: Routledge, 1993).
41. See Don Kulick and Margaret Willson, eds., *Taboo: Sex, Identity and Erotic Subjectivity in Anthropological Fieldwork* (London and New York: Routledge, 1995).
42. Seizer, "Playing the Field," 110.
43. F. Markowitz and M. Ashkenazi, eds., *Sex, Sexuality, and the Anthropologist* (Urbana and Chicago: University of Illinois Press, 1999), 20.
44. The diaries, 9 December 1909; emphasis added.
45. Charlotte Aull Davies, *Reflexive Ethnography: A Guide to Researching Selves and Others* (London: Routledge, 1999).
46. Clifford and Marcus, *Writing Culture.*

Arcticality (pages 71–78)

1. See Bloom, *Gender on Ice;* Holland, *Farthest North;* David Arnold, *The Problem of Nature: Environment, Culture and European Expansion* (Oxford: Blackwell, 1996).
2. Barry Lopez, *Arctic Dreams: Imagination and Desire in a Northern Landscape* (Toronto: Bantam Books, 1986); J. C. H. King and H. Lidchi, eds., *Imaging the Arctic* (Seattle: University of Washington Press, 1998).
3. Mauss, *Seasonal Variations of the Eskimo.*
4. Ibid., 75.
5. Ibid., 76.

6. Ibid., 52.
7. Ibid., 79.
8. Roy Ellen, *Environment, Subsistence and System* (Cambridge: Cambridge University Press, 1982), 24.
9. See Gísli Pálsson, *Coastal Economies, Cultural Accounts: Human Ecology and Icelandic Discourse* (Manchester: Manchester University Press, 1991).
10. The diaries, 8 October 1906.
11. Letter to R. R. Marrett from V. Stefansson, 12 November 1914.
12. The diaries, 9 November 1908.
13. Kessler E. Woodward, "Persuasive Images: Photographs of Vilhjalmur Stefansson in the Stefansson Collection on Polar Exploration at Dartmouth College," In *Imaging the Arctic,* 179.
14. Ibid., 175.
15. The diaries, 13 November 1909.
16. Vilhjalmur Stefansson, *The Northward Course of Empire* (London, George G. Harrap and Col. Ltd., 1922).
17. Arnold, *The Problem of Nature.*
18. Ibid., 142.
19. V. Stefansson, *The Three Voyages of Martin Frobisher.*
20. Welsch, *An American Anthropologist in Melanesia,* 567.
21. The diaries, 9 April 1911.
22. C. Shore and S. Wright, "Introduction" in *Anthropology and Policy: Critical Perspectives on Governance and Power,* ed. C. Shore and S. Wright (London: Routledge, 1997), 13.
23. Wendel H. Oswalt, *Eskimo Explorers* (Lincoln and London: University of Nebraska Press, 1999), 284; see, for instance, Robert F. Spencer, *The North Alaskan Eskimo: A Study in Ecology and Society* (Washington: Smithsonian Institution Bureau of American Ethnology Bulletin 171, 1959); James F. Vanstone, *Point Hope: An Eskimo Village in Transition* (Seattle: University of Washington Press, 1962); Hugh Brody, *Living Arctic: Hunters of the Canadian North* (Seattle: University of Washington Press, 1987); Norman A. Chance, *The Iñupiaq and Arctic Alaska* (Fort Worth: Holt, Rinehart, Winston, 1990); Igor Krupnik, *Arctic Adaptations: Native Whalers and Reindeer Hunters of Northern Eurasia* (Hanover, N.H.: University Press of New England, 1993); Murielle Ida Nagy, *Yukon North Slope Inuvialuit Oral History,* Occasional Papers in Yukon History No. 1, Yukon Heritage Branch, 1994; Richard G. Condon, *The Northern Copper Inuit* (Toronto: University of Toronto Press, 1996; Burch, *The Iñupiaq Eskimo Nations;* Julie Cruikshank, *The Social Life of Stories: Narrative and Knowledge in the Yukon Territory* (Lincoln and London: University of Nebraska Press, 1998); Mark Nuttall, *Protecting the Arctic: Indigenous Peoples and Cultural Survival* (Amsterdam: Harwood Academic Publishers, 1998); Pamela R. Stern, "Learning to Be Smart: An Exploration of the Culture of Intelligence in a Canadian Inuit Community," *American Anthropologist* 101, no. 3 (1999): 502–14; Helm, *The People of Denendeh.*
24. Burch, "The History of Arctic Ethnography," 15.
25. Mark Nuttall, personal communication, May 2000.
26. The diaries, 10 April 1911.

Glossary

The following list shows most of the Inuit and non-English terms used in the diaries and the Introduction. For some Inuit terms Stefansson supplied meanings in his diaries, sometimes on the basis of brief acquaintance and limited understanding of the language, particularly in the early stages of his fieldwork. Most of these have been reproduced here, occasionally in slightly modified form. For other terms the meanings have been deduced from his diary text and other sources. For some of the Inuit terms, translation is more of a guess; this is indicated by "*." A few terms in Stefansson's text have been omitted as no meaningful translation seemed possible.

aglernaktok — taboo.
aipani — to kill.
aklak — land bear.
akluna — common seal.
akpek — Arctic raspberry (low bush).
akuttok — dish made of melted deer and minced meat.
akuvilli — let him lie down.
akuvittin — you lie down.
alianaituaraluit — they are good.
ama (amama) — mother.
amaox — trick with a string.
amarak (amaruk) — wolf.
amihuaryuit — many.
añatkok — shaman.
añayura — my older brother.
anerillgoyok — person endowed with healing abilities.
anmark — stone knives.
anñroak — about-to-be-excreted excrement of a moose.
anñroat — around the neck.
annirut — lice.
añroak — charms.
arluk — killer whale (plural, arlut).
arnakata — female cousin, female companion.
artuñaksrok — material for a thong/rope (e.g. bearded-seal skin).*
atka — name, spirit.

atkittok (atkittuat) — children who never cry.
avariksut — chips of the same block, alike.
Blond Eskimo — Copper Inuit.
Danish Tongue — Old Norse.
Eiríks saga — one of the Icelandic family sagas.
ekaluakpuk — large fish, shark.
ellopa — are you cold?
Erstlingsreise — initiation trip (German).
gox — what a song says.
igak — kitchen.
iglu — snow house.
iglum kivata — interior of a house, away from the door.
iglum uata — the door-ward part of the interior of a house.
ignirkariaktuat — things to make a fire with, flints.
iglupauraks — something like a large house.
ikpuksak — a few days ago.
ilhut — you.
ilialuk — man who has neither umiak nor kayak.
ilyiranaitturu(t) — something scary.*
innukcuit — deer stockade.
innum uatane — navel.
Inuktitut — Inuit language.
Inuvialuktun — Inuit language.
itigaaittok — footless.
itjaliganrak — tent.
iyarrl — so be it.
kablunak — white man.
kagmane — in the east.
kajigi — communal (men's) house.
kaksrauk — black-throated and red-throated loon.
kallrovik — tent.
kañonaktok — a thing to be ashamed of.
katatje — trading representative.
katitarigik — child betrothal (a betrothed couple, dual).
katluk — thunder.*
kattigak — ribs.
kavane — in the east.
kavuñamun — by the coast.*
kayak — skin boat (small).
keyukokat — spirits of the shamans.
ki, ki, kilamik — come, hurry up!
kikak — voice box in a deer.
kilalua — white whale, beluga.
kiligavuk — mammoth.*
kimmek — trick with a string.
kina atka — what's his name.
kingmuk — dog.

kipuak—trade, swap.*
kirktjak—type of meat.
kivalina (kivalinirk)—place for a messenger.*
kivrarniaktuña—herald.
kiyirk—blue jay.
kjeata—forepart of an animal.
kodlik—seal oil lamp.
koonie—wife (actually means "kiss").
kublua—(the) thumb, his/her thumb.
malliktallirk—time/place to be followed, place to be hit by waves.
maktak—black seal skin.
mashu(k)—edible root.*
mɪsu maluk—torso, very wet.*
mitiravik—great bird, greater eider duck.
nagomiut—excellent people.
nagosok—good (something that pleases).
nagoyurut tamapta—all of us are grateful.*
nallikam nalluñaiyutaña—sign/symbol of love (or groin, genitals).
namnakturut—things to be carried on the back, backpack.
napoktok—tent, similar to an Indian tipi.
napaktulik—forest, place with upright trees.
nappan—soul.
naunaitturut—we reveal ourselves, make visible.*
nelluakartuñakskrak—material for white (winter) boot soles.*
neriktik—lice (or food, edibles).
nerkiksran parkittutin—you have found something meant for you to eat.
nigirk—easterly wind.
nitte—mist.*
niuyakti—man who steers a boat.
Nolouganmiut—McKinley Bay.
nukkara—my younger brother.
nunaluk—old ground.
nutirn—always.
o-bloomy—today.
okpek—Arctic owl.
oktjuk—whale meat.
okumailuta—very heavy.
oma atka—the one from whom a child is named.
ovayuaraluk—a great swimmer (fish).*
oxsrogon—with animal fat.*
palirktuak—dry throat.
panapkak—white man's style wall tent.
panniga—my daughter.
pauñrak—berry (and berry bush).
pigleriak—something that bounces.*
pingok—permafrost heave or hill.
piptje—dried fish.

Portagee — Portuguese sailor (dark-skinned).
pubraktuak — to swim.
puyora — vapor.
saunirk — bone, person with same name.
saunñra — my bone, person with my name.
sivullivut — forebears.
skrælingi — native (Icelandic).
skrælingjakona — native woman (Icelandic).
sulupaurak — eel, tube.
supillgoyok — person endowed with healing abilities.
taksipuk — it is foggy, getting dark.
takusiun — thing to see with, telescope.
tarningit — their souls.
tarnik — soul (one of three).
tatkoa — those things, there, spirits.
tatkok — spirit, it is dark, fog, kidney.*
tautuk — see.
titalirk — fish.
titirak — personal mark.
Tjiglik — Eskimo (or MacKenzie Delta).
tjuna pishunktu — what do you want?
tsila — outside.
tuktu — trick with a string.
tuktwok — moose.
tulurak — raven.
tummitok — he/she/it makes footprints (in snow).
tunnirk — tatoo.
tunnerit — tattoo lines.
tupergruk — house.
tuperk — house or tent.
turnmaktuak — to wade in deep water.
turñnrat — ancestors of Inuit, ghosts, spirits.
tusaryuk — understand.
tusaryuk ilhut — do you understand me?
tutak — stone.
tuyormiat — Herschel idiom.
ualinermiut — the name often used for people to the west.
ualinirk — east of.
ualinirk — the part of the interior of a house nearest the front door.
uata — hind part of an animal.
uatani — people to the west of another people.
ugrug — bearded, square flipper seal.
ula-hula — dance.
ulitcuilat — never gets full, never reaches a tide.
ulu — (iron) women's semilunar knife (may be made of iron).
umiak — large open skin-boat.
umialik — the man who steers an umiak.

unikpak — folklore, story.
unnalik — owner.
uvaña kaitkaitkain — I'm spinning around.*
uyoriun — fight him.
Xian — Christian (not Eskimo).
yaukukalirk — a large knife.

Bibliography

Allison, James, Jenny Hockey, and Andrew Dawson, eds. 1997. *After Writing Culture: Epistemology and Praxis in Contemporary Anthropology*. London and New York: Routledge.

Appadurai, Arjun. 1988. Introduction: place and voice in anthropological theory. *Cultural Anthropology* 3 (1): 16–20.

Ardener, Edwin. 1975. Belief and the problem of women. In *Perceiving Women*, edited by Shirley Ardener. London: J. M. Dent and Sons Ltd.

Arnold, David. 1996. *The Problem of Nature: Environment, Culture and European Expansion*. Oxford: Blackwell.

Asad, Talal, ed. 1973. *Anthropology and the Colonial Encounter*. London: Ithaca Press.

Baxter, Paul T. W. 1991. From anthropological texts to popular writings. *Bulletin of the John Rylands Library* 73 (3): 105–24.

Bessason, Haraldur. 1999. *Bréf til Brands*. Reykjavik: Ormstunga.

Bloch, Maurice. 1983. *Marxism and Anthropology*. Oxford: Oxford University Press.

Bloom, Lisa. 1993. *Gender on Ice: American Ideologies of Polar Expeditions*. Minneapolis: University of Minnesota Press.

Boon, James A. 1982. *Other Tribes, Other Scribes: Symbolic Anthropology in the Comparative Study of Cultures, Histories, Religions, and Texts*. Cambridge: Cambridge University Press.

Brody, Hugh. 1987. *Living Arctic: Hunters of the Canadian North*. Seattle: University of Washington Press.

Brydon, Anne. n.d. Memory and forgetting as modernity's malaise: Icelandic-Canadian identity and the ambiguities of history. In *The Icelandic Presence in Canada: A Story of Integration*, edited by D. Neijmann. Winnipeg: University of Manitoba Press.

Bucher, Bernadette. 1989. Le Journal de Stendhal: Discours sur le sexe et écriture ethnographique. *L'Homme* 29 (3–4): 179–93.

Burch, Ernest S., Jr. 1994. North Alaskan Eskimos: A changing way of life. In *Portraits of Culture*, edited by M. Ember, C. Ember, and D. Levinson. Englewood Cliffs, N.J.: Prentice Hall.

——1995. The history of Arctic ethnography—as seen from the Conodoguinet. Paper presented at the twenty-second annual meeting of the Alaska Anthropological Association, 24 March.

—— 1998. *The Iñupiaq Eskimo Nations of Northwest Alaska*. Fairbanks, Alaska: University of Alaska Press.

Chance, Norman A. 1990. *The Iñupiat and Arctic Alaska*. Fort Worth: Holt, Rinehart, Winston.

Clifford, James, and George E. Marcus, eds. 1986. *Writing Culture: The Poetics and Politics of Ethnography*. Berkeley: University of California Press.

Cole, Douglas. 1983. "The value of a person lies in his *Herzensbildung*": Franz Boas' Baffin Island letter-diary, 1883–1884. In *Observers Observed: Essays on Ethnographic Fieldwork,* edited by George W. Stocking, Jr. Madison: University of Wisconsin.

Collins, Henry B. 1962. Stefansson as an anthropologist. *Polar Notes* 4: 8–13.

Condon, Richard G. 1992. Natkusiak (*ca.* 1885–1947). *Arctic* 45 (1): 90–92.

—— 1996. *The Northern Copper Inuit*. Toronto: University of Toronto Press.

Conefrey, Mick, and Tim Jordan. 1998. *Icemen: A History of the Arctic and Its Explorers*. London: Boxtree.

Counter, S. Allen. 1991. *North Pole Legacy: Black, White and Eskimo*. Amherst: The University of Massachusetts Press.

Crick, Malcolm. 1976. *Explorations in Language and Meaning: Towards a Semantic Anthropology*. New York: John Wiley.

Cruikshank, Julie. 1998. *The Social Life of Stories: Narrative and Knowledge in the Yukon Territory*. Lincoln and London: University of Nebraska Press.

Davies, Charlotte Aull. 1999. *Reflexive Ethnography: A Guide to Researching Selves and Others*. London: Routledge.

Diubaldo, Richard J. 1978. *Stefansson and the Canadian Arctic*. Montreal: McGill-Queen's University Press.

Ellen, Roy. 1982. *Environment, Subsistence and System*. Cambridge: Cambridge University Press.

Evjen, Björg. 1997. Measuring heads: Physical anthropological research in North Norway. *Ethnos* 2: 3–30.

Fine, Gary Alan. 1993. Ten lies of ethnography: Moral dilemmas of field research. *Journal of Contemporary Ethnography* 22 (3): 267–94.

Finnie, Richard S. 1978. Stefansson's mystery. *North* (Nov./Dec.): 2–7.

Firth, Raymond. 1989. Second introduction 1988. In *A Diary in the Strict Sense of the Term,* by Bronislaw Malinowski: New York: Harcourt, Brace and World.

Goldring, Philip. 1987. Scientist and showman. *The Beaver* (April–May): 59–61.

Gudeman, Stephen, and Alberto Rivera. 1990. *Conversations in Colombia: The Domestic Economy in Life and Text*. Cambridge: Cambridge University Press.

Guttormsson, Guttormur J. 1975. Tveir þættir: I. Indiáninn John Ramsey. *Andvari* (Reykjavík): 75–83.

—— 1976. *Kvæði, úrval*. Reykjavik: Bókaútgáfa Menningarsjóðs og Þjóðvinafélagsins.

Haraway, Donna. 1989. *Primate Visions: Gender, Race, and Nature in the World of Modern Science*. London and New York: Routledge.

Helm, June. 1973. Long-term research among the Dogrib and other Dene. *In Long-Term Field Research in Social Anthropology,* edited by G. M. Foster, T. Scudder, E. Colson, and R. V. Kemper. New York: Academic Press.

—— 2000. *The People of Denendeh: Ethnohistory of the Indians of Canada's Northwest Territories*. Iowa City: University of Iowa Press.

Holland, Clive, ed. 1994. *Farthest North: A History of North Polar Exploration in Eye-Witness Accounts*. London: Robinson Publishing.
Hunt, William R. 1986. *Stef: A Biography of Vilhjalmur Stefansson, Canadian Arctic Explorer*. Vancouver: University of British Columbia Press.
James, Allison, Jenny Hockey, and Andrew Dawson. 1997. The road from Santa Fe. In *After Writing Culture: Epistemology and Praxis in Contemporary Anthropology*, edited by Allison James, Jenny Hockey, and Andrew Dawson. Routledge: London and New York.
Jenness, Diamond. 1957. *Dawn in Arctic Alaska*. Minneapolis: University of Minnesota Press.
Jenness, Stuart E., ed. 1991. *Arctic Odyssey: The Diary of Diamond Jenness 1913–1916*. Hull, Quebec: Canadian Museum of Civilization.
Keesing, Roger M. 1989. Exotic readings of cultural texts. *Current Anthropology* 30 (4): 459–79.
King, J. C. H. and H. Lidchi, eds. 1998. *Imaging the Arctic*. Seattle: University of Washington Press.
Krupnik, Igor. 1993. *Arctic Adaptations: Native Whalers and Reindeer Herders of Northern Eurasia*. Hanover, N.H.: University Press of New England.
Kulick, Don, and Margaret Willson, eds. 1995. *Taboo: Sex, Identity and Erotic Subjectivity in Anthropological Fieldwork*. London and New York: Routledge.
LeBourdais, D. M. 1963. *Stefansson, Ambassador of the North*. Montreal: Harvest House.
Lopez, Barry. 1986. *Arctic Dreams: Imagination and Desire in a Northern Landscape*. Toronto: Bantam Books.
Malinowski, Bronislaw. 1929. *The Sexual Life of Savages in North-Western Melanesia*. New York: Eugenics Publishing Company.
——— 1989 [1967]. *A Diary in the Strict Sense of the Term*. With a new introduction by Raymond Firth. New York: Harcourt, Brace and World.
Marcus, G. E. 1998. *Ethnography through Thick and Thin*. Princeton University Press: Princeton.
Markowitz, F., and M. Ashkenazi, eds. 1999. *Sex, Sexuality, and the Anthropologist*. Urbana and Chicago: University of Illinois Press.
Mauss, Marcel. 1979 [1906]. *Seasonal Variations of the Eskimo: A Study in Social Morphology*. In collaboration with Henri Beuchat. Translated with a foreword by J. A. Fox. London: Routledge.
Mirsky, Jeanette. 1970 [1934]. *To the Arctic! The Story of Northern Exploration from Earliest Times*. Chicago: The University of Chicago Press.
Müller-Wille, Ludger, ed. 1998. *Franz Boas Among the Inuit of Baffin Island 1883–1884*. Toronto: University of Toronto Press.
Nagy, Murielle Ida. 1994. *Yukon North Slope Inuvialuit Oral History*. Occasional Papers in Yukon History No. 1. Yukon Heritage Branch.
——— 1999. *Aulavik Oral History Project on Banks Island, NWT: Final Report*. Inuvik, NWT: Inuvialuit Social Development Program.
Neijmann, Daisy. 1997. *The Icelandic Voice in Canadian Letters*. Carleton: Carleton University Press.
Noice, Harold. 1924. *With Stefansson in the Arctic*. New York: Dodd, Mead.
Nuttall, Mark. 1998. *Protecting the Arctic: Indigenous Peoples and Cultural Survival*. Amsterdam: Harwood Academic Publishers.

Okely, Judith. 1992. Anthropology and autobiography: Participatory experience and embodied knowledge. In *Anthropology and Autobiography,* edited by J. Okely and H. Callaway. London and New York: Routledge.

Oswalt, Wendel H. 1999. *Eskimo Explorers*. Second edition. Lincoln and London: University of Nebraska Press.

Pálsson, Gísli. 1991. *Coastal Economies, Cultural Accounts: Human Ecology and Icelandic Discourse*. Manchester: Manchester University Press.

—— ed. 1993. *Beyond Boundaries: Understanding, Translation and Anthropological Discourse*. Oxford: Berg Publishers.

—— 1995. *The Textual Life of Savants: Ethnography, Iceland, and the Linguistic Turn*. Chur, Switzerland: Harwood Academic Publishers.

—— 1998. The intimate Arctic: An early anthropologist's diary in the strict sense of the term. *Ethnos* 63 (3): 413–40.

Paine, Robert, ed. 1977. *The White Arctic: Anthropological Essays on Tutelage and Ethnicity*. Toronto: Institute of Social and Economic Research, Memorial University of Newfoundland.

Pratt, Louise. 1992. *Imperial Eyes: Travel Writing and Transculturation*. London and New York: Routledge.

Rabinow, Paul. 1977. *Reflections of Fieldwork in Morocco*. Berkeley and Los Angeles: University of California Press.

Rapport, Nigel. 1990. "Surely everything has already been said about Malinowski's diary!" *Anthropology Today* 6 (1): 5–9.

Rasmussen, Knud. 1932. *Intellectual Culture of the Copper Eskimos*. Report of the Fifth Thule Expedition 1921–24, vol. 9. Copenhagen: Gyldendalske boghandel.

Remie, Cornelius H. W. 1993. Changing contexts, persistent relations: Inuit-white encounters in Northern Canada, 1576–1992. *Native American Studies* 7 (2): 5–11.

Riffenburgh, Beau. 1993. *The Myth of the Explorer: The Press, Sensationalism, and Geographical Inquiry*. London: Belhaven Press and Scott Polar Research Institute.

Said, Edward. 1989. Representing the colonized: Anthropology's interlocutors. *Critical Inquiry* 15: 205–25.

Saladin d'Anglure, Bernard. 1996. Arctic. In *Encyclopedia of Social and Cultural Anthropology,* edited by Alan Barnard and Jonathan Spencer, 51–57. London: Routledge.

Sanjek, Roger, ed. 1990. *Fieldnotes: The Makings of Anthropology*. Ithaca and London: Cornell University Press.

Schieffelin, Edward L., and Robert Crittenden, eds. 1991. *Like People You See in a Dream: First Contact in Six Papuan Societies*. Stanford: Stanford University Press.

Seizer, Susan. 1997. Playing the field: The sexual life of anthropologists. *Transition* 72: 100–13.

Seltzer, Carl C. 1933. The Anthropometry of the Western and Copper Eskimos, based on data of Vilhjalmur Stefansson. *Human Biology* 5 (3): 313–18.

Shankman, Paul. 1994. Sex, lies, and anthropologists: Margaret Mead, Derek Freeman, and Samoa. In *Research Frontiers in Anthropology,* edited by M. Ember, C. Ember, and D. Levinson. Englewood Cliffs, N.J.: Prentice-Hall.

Shore, C., and S. Wright. 1997. Introduction. In *Anthropology and Policy: Critical Perspectives on Governance and Power,* ed. C. Shore and S. Wright. London: Routledge.

Spencer, Robert F. 1959. *The North Alaskan Eskimo: A Study in Ecology and Society*. Washington: Smithsonian Institution Bureau of American Ethnology Bulletin 171.

Srebrnik, Henry F. 1998. The radical "second life" of Vilhjalmur Stefansson. *Arctic* 51 (1): 58–60.

Stefansson, Georgina. 1961. My grandfather, Dr. Stefansson. *North* 4: 25.

Stefansson, Vilhjalmur. Correspondence and diaries. Special Collection, Dartmouth College Library, Hanover.

—— 1906. The Icelandic colony in Greenland. *American Anthropologist* 8 (2): 262–70.

—— 1909. The Eskimo trade jargon of Herschel Island. *American Anthropologist* 11: 217–32.

—— 1913. *My Life with the Eskimo*. New York: Macmillan.

—— 1914. Stefansson-Anderson Arctic expedition. *Anthropological Papers of the American Museum of Natural History*, vol. 14, edited by Clark Wissler. New York: AMS Press.

—— 1921. *The Friendly Arctic*. New York: Macmillan.

——1922. *The Northward Course of Empire*. London: George G. Harrap and Co. Ltd.

—— 1925. *The Adventure of Wrangel Island*. London: Jonathan Cape Ltd.

—— 1938. *The Three Voyages of Martin Frobisher*, vols 1 and 2. London: The Argonaut Press.

—— 1945. *Great Adventures and Explorations, from the Earliest Times to the Present, as told by the Explorers Themselves*. New York: The Dial Press.

—— 1964. *Discovery: The Autobiography of Vilhjalmur Stefansson*. New York: McGraw-Hill Company.

Stern, Pamela R. 1999. Learning to be smart: An exploration of the culture of intelligence in a Canadian Inuit community. *American Anthropologist* 101 (3): 502–14.

Stocking, George W., Jr., ed. 1983. *Observers Observed: Essays on Ethnographic Fieldwork*. Madison: University of Wisconsin.

Sullivan, Gerald, ed. 1999. *Margaret Mead, Gregory Bateson, and Highland Bali: Fieldwork Photographs of Bayung Gedé, 1936–1939*. Chicago: University of Chicago Press.

The Traditional Land Use Inventory for the Mid-Beaufort Sea, vol. 1. N.d. . North Slope Borough on History and Culture.

Tuzin, Donald. 1994. The forgotten passion: Sexuality and anthropology in the ages of Victoria and Bronislaw. *Journal of the History of the Behavioral Sciences* 3: 114–37.

Vanstone, James W. 1962. *Point Hope: An Eskimo Village in Transition*. Seattle: University of Washington Press.

Vermeulen, Han F., and Arturo Alvarez Roldán, eds. 1995. *Fieldwork and Footnotes: Studies in the History of European Anthropology*. London and New York: Routledge.

Wade, Peter. 1993. Sexuality and masculinity in fieldwork among Colombian blacks. In *Gendered Fields: Women, Men and Ethnography*, edited by Diane Bell, Pat Caplan, and Wazir Jahan Karim. London and New York: Routledge.

Welsch, Robert L., ed. 1998. *An American Anthropologist in Melanesia: A. B. Lewis and the Joseph N. Field South Pacific Expedition, 1909–1913*. Honolulu: University of Hawaii Press.

Wilkins, George H. Journals. Dartmouth College Library, Hanover. Msc 62 I 11.

Willson, Margaret. 1997. Playing the dance, dancing the game: Race, sex and stereotype in anthropological fieldwork. *Ethnos* 62 (3–4): 24–48.

Woodward, Kesler E. 1998. Persuasive images: Photographs of Vilhjalmur Stefansson in the Stefansson Collection on polar exploration at Dartmouth College. In *Imaging the Arctic*, edited by J. C. H. King and H. Lidchi. Seattle: University of Washington Press.

Index

Library of Congress Cataloging-in-Publication Data

Stefansson, Vilhjalmur, 1879–1962.
Writing on ice : the ethnographic notebooks of Vilhjalmur Stefansson / edited and introduced by Gísli Pálsson.
p. cm.
Includes bibliographical references and index.
ISBN 1–58465–119–9 (alk. paper)
1. Inuit—Social life and customs. 2. Stefansson, Vilhjalmur, 1879–1962. 3. Ethnology—Field work. I. Gísli Pálsson, 1949– . II. Title.
E99.E7 S822 2001
306'.089'9712—dc21 2001001365